"55 YEARS • 55 HEROES"

A Celebration of Minnesota Sports

by
Ross Bernstein

Nodin Press

"55 YEARS • 55 HEROES: A Celebration of Minnesota Sports"
by Ross Bernstein

(WWW.BERNSTEINBOOKS.COM)

ISBN# 0931714-98-2

Published by Nodin Press • 530 North Third Street • Minneapolis, MN 55401 • (612) 333-6300

Printed in Minnesota by Printing Enterprises, New Brighton (651) 636-9336

Edited by Joel Rippel

Cover Photo by Tony Martin Photography: (612) 305-0992

PHOTO CREDITS
University of Minnesota: 13, 15, 20-24, 26, 27, 30, 31, 36-40, 42, 64, 65, 67, 70, 71, 83-85, 88-89, 93, 96-99,
102, 103, 106-109, 117, 123-126,134, 135, 137, 138, 140, 141
Pioneer Press: 8, 11, 25, 32, 53, 56-59, 62, 72-74, 82, 86, 87, 100, 101, 104, 105, 110-113, 119, 120
Minnesota Twins: 5, 30, 33, 46-51, 60, 61, 76, 77, 116, 142
Minnesota Vikings: 7, 41, 63, 68, 69, 75, 92, 126
Dick Jonckowski Collection: 2, 9, 10, 12, 35, 43, 52, 127
Minnesota Historical Society: 16, 17, 28, 34, 73
U.S. Hockey Hall of Fame: 14, 19, 54, 78, 90
Northeast Minnesota Historical Center: 115
University of Minnesota Duluth: 94, 95
St. John's University: 44, 114
Augsburg College: 66
Bruce Kluckhohn: 132, 133
Vince Muzik: 128-131
Tim Cortes: 136
Eric Miller: 121
Sandy Thompson: 122
Rick A. Kolodziej: 118, 139
Janet Karvonen: 80, 81
Patty Berg: 29
Canturbury Park: 42
John Beargrease Sled Dog Race: 55
Ann Bancroft: 54
Babe Winkelman: 91
Jill Trenary: 91
Leroy Nieman: 79
Charles Schulz: 79

A SPECIAL THANKS TO DICK JONCKOWSKI!

One of the funniest human beings on the planet, Dick Jonckowski has spent a life-time making others laugh. He is also one Minnesota's biggest sports fanatics. In fact, the basement of his Shakopee home is a venerable fire hazard, because it is crammed so full of wonderful pieces of sports memorabilia. Full of signed pictures, programs and random treasures, it is a collection like no other, and truly shows the passion he has towards the world of sports. So, thanks Dick for letting me showcase some of your great "stuff" on the cover of my book!

With a lifetime of sports radio broadcasting, and color commentating experience, "Joncko" is a walking encyclopedia of sports information. (He puts Cliff Claven to shame!) This "Polish Eagle" has also become one of the Midwest's top after-dinner speakers, emceeing roasts and banquets from Des Moines to Duluth along the way. In addition, he has gained much notoriety as the voice of Gopher baseball, football and basketball, serving as the teams' long-time public address announcer. He has also hosted a radio program called "The Coaches Round Table" for some 35 years as well. A true living legend, (hey, just ask him…), Dick is a true Minnesota Sacred Cow!

"Sports and laughter are the center of my universe," says Dick. "Ever since I was a kid, sports were the only thing I cared about. Laughter is so important, I just love to see people happy."

For Sara and Campbell, the two loves of my life...

TABLE OF CONTENTS

In memory of Paul Giel — a great athlete, a great person and a great friend.

1932 - 2002

Welcome to "55 Years • 55 Heroes: A Celebration of Minnesota Sports," the new, expanded and updated version of the 1997 Best-Seller, "50 Years • 50 Heroes." The amazing popularity of that book led me to redo it five years later and I am proud to say that it is now better than ever. Here is how the book is set up: Each year, going back 55 years, features one of the greatest moments in the world of Minnesota sports. That event is then tied into an interview and biography of a hometown or homegrown hero who played a key role in that particular event.

I also wanted to not only update all the biographies in the book, but I also added a ton of new information with regards to the "Minnesota Sports Sidebar" pages as well, which appear every five chapters. These "Cliff Claven" fun-facts, if you will, are just random samplings of some of the other great sports figures and events which have also been a part of our sports landscape. It is important to note, however, that this book is not a list of the 55 greatest heroes in Minnesota sports. Rather, it is a fun way to celebrate 55 great events, tied into 55 great men and women. In fact, it was oftentimes really tough to decide which events warranted real-estate in certain chapters as well. For instance, in 1976 the Vikings went to the Super Bowl, the Gopher Hockey team won the national championship and the Kicks made it to the Soccer Bowl. As a result, it was difficult to choose just one event.

While some chapters feature detailed accounts, extensive quotes and game summaries, others focus on different aspects of that particular event or person. No two chapters are alike, and hopefully that will add to the uniqueness of the book. I also tried to put as many little tid-bits of other pertinent information in the bottom time-line as well, showing you what else happened in those particular years. Basically, I tried to have fun with it and pick interesting people and events to feature. Many times it was like trying to fit a square peg into a round hole, but overall I would like to think that it all worked out. There are hundreds of individuals who have either been born and raised in Minnesota, or have played here on either a professional or collegiate team that definitely could've been featured in this book. Obviously I couldn't accommodate all of those people, so I chose to celebrate a sampling of men and women who have made a difference in the world of Minnesota sports. For those left out, I am truly sorry.

Overall, this book is about celebrating the wonderful sports achievements that have made our great state what it is today. Time and again you'll hear Minnesota's native sons in the national media talking about how they are willing to take a lesser salary in order for them to come home again. The common denominator in almost all of those instances seems to be our amazing quality of life that we have here. I think that as Minnesotans we are proud of our own, and equally as proud of those who represent our entire state on the playing field. Something that I have always liked is the fact that Minnesota's pro sports teams are all named after the state, and not after a particular city — like most other teams are. I think we all enjoy when our teams do well, and we all whine when they don't. But win or lose, sports is an integral part of the fabric of our lives here.

I think it is also important to note that the word hero is a very subjective word, and can mean a lot of different things to a lot of different people. Particularly after the tragic events of September 11th, when the word hero took on a meaning that shouldn't even be mentioned in the same collective breath with anything that has to do with sports. In my opinion, sports heroes are people that we looked up to when we were kids. These relationships are fostered early on in life and grow from there. As a kid growing up, my heroes were guys like Fran Tarkenton, Neal Broten and Kirby Puckett. But, I think that at a certain age, people become painfully aware of the fact that sports is a business, and at that point they no longer view athletes as heroes, but as businessmen. Let's face it. Some of these guys are jerks, and that is about as good as you can sugar-coat it. But, I have chosen to take the high-road in this book and try to celebrate the achievements that these heroes have accomplished. Translation: Yeah, Randy Moss is in here, and despite what he may or may not have done in his past, he is still a hero to a lot of little kids who dream of catching touchdowns the way that only he can. Enough said.

With that, I would hope that the readers of this book will be able to reflect back, reminisce, and remember a team, a player or even a special day at the ballpark that he or she might have spent a long time ago just hanging out with someone special. Sports are constantly changing today and I think it is important that we not only look to the future with optimism, but remember and celebrate our past, which is full of great history and wonderful memories.

With hundreds of photos, "55 Years • 55 Heroes" is both entertaining as well as insightful. Featured in it are hundreds of this past century's greatest professional, minor league, amateur, collegiate and high school teams, along with countless biographies and stories of their star players. While some of those players' accounts are inspirational, others are simply hilarious. Hundreds of wonderful stories, along with countless personal memories from the stars themselves dot the canvas of this epic tale. So jump in, relax and reminisce. I tried to capture the pure essence of just what sports means to so many of us here in the Land of 10,000 Lakes, and pay homage to the countless men and women who have made the game what it is today. Enjoy!

FOREWORD BY BUD GRANT

Without question, Bud Grant is one of the greatest athletes and sports icons to ever play and coach in Minnesota. From his days as a three-sport star at the University of Minnesota — where he lettered in football, basketball and baseball; to his two NBA championship seasons with the Minneapolis Lakers; to becoming an All-Pro NFL and CFL wide receiver; to coaching the Winnipeg Blue Bombers to four Grey Cup titles; to his 18 incredible years and four Super Bowls behind the bench with the Vikings. The NFL & CFL Hall of Famer even beat out Gopher Football legends Bronko Nagurski and Bruce Smith to be voted the top Minnesota athlete of the first half century way back in 1950. Modest as ever, Bud is a part of our fabric of life here and would have to be considered as the grand patriarch of sports in our state. In fact, I would have to say that he is the quintessential All-American hero, and represents everything that is good about sports and athletic competition. And just because he is retired, don't think for a second that he is slowing down. Nope. When he is not consulting for his beloved Vikings, he is either out in a duck blind, deer stand or watering hole — reeling in a lunker. So, with a resume like that, could there be anyone better suited to represent the past 55 years of Minnesota sports than Bud Grant? I didn't think so!

"When Ross Bernstein first called to interview me for a book he was writing about the history and heroes of Minnesota sports, I was skeptical 'How could someone possibly do justice to so many people and events?' I wondered. But he has done a fine job. Anyone who is interested in Minnesota sports will undoubtedly relate to someone or something in it.

I am proud to have played a part in contributing to the wonderful history of Minnesota sports. Having been a member of the Gophers, Lakers, and Vikings, I have a unique perspective on sports in Minnesota. Sports has come a long way in this state. I remember always playing in front of capacity crowds at Williams Arena and Memorial Stadium at the University of Minnesota. But, today there is more competition for people's interests, especially with sports.

Like myself, people enjoy the outdoors here. Whether it's boating, fishing, hunting, camping, golfing, or anything else, outdoor activities are precious to Minnesotans. These people like to participate in sporting activities, but they still find time to watch them as well. Sports fans here are knowledgeable and they appreciate good competition as well as good sportsmanship.

Fans in places like New York, Philadelphia, and Chicago are fanatics about their local teams, but it's a narrow band of people. Our state has a broader group of fans. Sports in Minnesota encompass more of the mainstream, from casual observers to the die-hards, who will check to see how the Twins, Vikings, Timberwolves, or Gophers did, even if they didn't watch or listen to the game. It doesn't matter if they're from International Falls or Pipestone: people love and follow our teams here because they're interested, and they genuinely care.

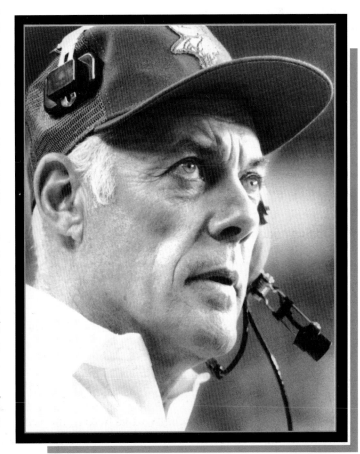

Traveling throughout Minnesota over the years, it has always amazed me at just how insightful our fans are and how closely they follow Minnesota's athletes and teams. And, they are proud of their accomplishments and exploits.

In addition to following what's happening in Minnesota sports, it's nice to sit back and reflect on what's happened — to reminisce about our past and allow it to conjure up fond memories. This book will help sports fans do just that. There's something for everyone in it. If you enjoy reading about sports, history, biographies and funny stories, then you'll love this book because it's all in there. This is history, and it's significant that it has finally been captured on paper for all to see.

We have a wonderful sports heritage to be proud of here in Minnesota, and it's all brought to life in the book."

In 1947 a group of Twin Cities businessmen which included the likes of Ben Berger, Morris Chalfen and a young newspaper reporter by the name of Sid Hartman, decided to bring major league professional basketball to Minneapolis. After a year of research the group went ahead and acquired the financially-strapped Detroit Gems of the National Basketball League (NBL) for the whopping sum of $15,000, and moved them to Minnesota, where they would be renamed as the Minneapolis Lakers. They then hired John Kundla, who was coaching at St. Thomas, to be their coach, and former fight manager and restauranteur Max Winter to serve as their general manager.

The Lakers opened the first four games of their inaugural 1947-48 season with Jim Pollard at center. Pollard was an All-American at Stanford, but was a forward playing in the pivot. With that, the club knew it needed a true center, and had a plan on just how to get one. You see, the Lakers, by virtue of having the worst league record from the season before as the Gems, were now entitled to the first pick of a league-wide dispersal draft. (The Gems had posted a horrible 4-40 record that season — the worst in modern history! But Hartman and Co. knew that the league was about to go belly-up all along, and that is why they bought the team.) So, it came as no surprise to anyone when they selected the star of the NBL champion Chicago Gears, Center George Mikan — the game's greatest player.

Although the Lakers held Mikan's draft rights, they still had to sign him to a contract. So, Winter flew the young center to Minneapolis with the hopes of wining and dining him. George came to the Twin Cities but wasn't sure if he wanted to be a Laker. The two sides were unable to come to terms on a deal, so George decided to go home to Chicago. That's when Sid Hartman, who handled the teams wheelings and dealings, saved the day by mysteriously getting lost while driving big George to the airport. As a result, Mikan missed his flight and was forced to stay one more night. That next day, George sat down with Winter again, this time inking a deal. It would be the beginning of a beautiful relationship.

In addition to Mikan and Pollard, Tony Jaros and Don "Swede" Carlson, both of whom had previously starred at the U of M as well as at Minneapolis Edison High School, were also added to the roster.

With that, the Lakers came out and dominated under their new big man. Mikan was awesome. At six-foot-ten he was a giant that teams simply couldn't stop. The Lakers then went on to win the Western Division title that year by 13 games over runner-up Tri-Cities.

It was now off to the playoffs for the upstart Lakers. There, they breezed through the quarterfinals against Oshkosh, three games to one, and then swept Tri-Cities in the semifinals to advance to the NBL Finals against the Eastern Conference champion Rochester Royals. Before the Finals though, the Lakers accepted an invitation to play in the annual World Professional Tournament in Chicago. (Believe it or not, at that time winning the WPT was considered a bigger deal than an NBL title.) There, the Lakers rolled over the Wilkes-Barre Barons, 98-48, in the opening round, and then knocked off the Anderson Packers by three points in the semifinals. They then took on the defending champion New York Rens, an all-black barnstorming team, in the title game, and led by Mikan, who set a tournament record with 40 points, the Lakers beat the Rens, 75-71, to win the World Pro Crown.

Minneapolis now had just one day of rest before taking on Rochester in their best-of-five series at the Minneapolis Armory. (Their usual arena, the Minneapolis Auditorium, was full of campers and fishing boats for the annual Sportsman's Show, so they incredibly had to find another locale!) The Royals, led by a pair of guards from Seton Hall, Bob Davies and Bobby Wanzer, were a finesse squad. The Lakers meanwhile, had garnered a reputation as a bunch of bruisers. The big news for Rochester though, was the fact that their six-foot-nine All-Star Center, Arnie Risen, had suffered a broken jaw and would miss the entire championship series — a real break for Minneapolis.

The series opened to a jam-packed Armory with the Lakers taking Games One and Two. It then shifted to New York for the remaining games, as the Royals came back to take Game Three, 74-60, despite Mikan's 32-point performance. Then, in Game Four, the Lakers came out and dominated. They led from the opening buzzer and thanks to 27 points from Mikan and another 19 from Pollard, the Lakers cruised to an impressive 75-65 win — taking the NBL Crown in just their first year in the league.

For the season Mikan finished with a record 1,195 points, (nearly doubling the league's old mark), while averaging 21.3 points per game and leading the NBL in virtually every offensive category. For his efforts he was named as the league's MVP. In addition, he and Pollard were both named to the NBL's All-Star team. The worst-to-first Lakers were now kings of the court, and quietly, a new sports dynasty was born.

"We were being judged on whether or not we could make it in the world of professional basketball," said Mikan, "and the excitement of winning that first Laker championship was just fantastic. It put us on the map, because at the time, big cities looked at Minneapolis as a tiny hick town. Well, we 'hicked' them all-right — we became league champions."

From the Windy City to the City of Lakes
George Lawrence Mikan Jr. was born in 1924, in Joliet, Illinois. He went on to enroll at DePaul University, where he learned the game under legendary Coach Ray Meyer. Meyer worked his prized pupil mercilessly, putting him on a regimen which greatly improved his agility, quickness and coordination, with drills that included skipping rope, throwing the medicine ball, shadowboxing and even ballet dancing. He would even tell George to try and dance with the shortest and smallest girls he could find at school dances, forcing him to either improve his footwork, or never get a date! Then, at the end of each practice, he would make him take 250 right-handed hooks followed by another 250 with the left — a grueling repetition which would later become known simply as the "Mikan Drill" in basketball "how-to" manuals everywhere. Mikan went on to become the nation's biggest college star,

leading the Demons to the 1945 NIT title along the way.

Following his playing days at DePaul, George entered the then uncertain world of professional basketball, first with his home-town Chicago American Gears of the National Basketball League, and then with the Minneapolis Lakers, where he would lead his team to six world championships. Mikan revolutionized the game. Whereas in the past, guards and occasionally forwards had been the games' stars, Mikan redefined the center position. While most teams used them only to rebound and set picks, because most big men were considered too awkward to actually shoot the ball, George quickly changed all the rules. With his wide shoulders and firm elbows, he began to dominate the game like no other before him.

In a very "Jordanesque" way, George was the big draw for the new league. Fans came from all over the Upper Midwest to see the gentle giant. One time, in 1951, the Lakers were playing New York at Madison Square Garden, and the marquee in front of the Garden advertising that night's game read: "GEO. MIKAN vs. KNICKS." As game time neared, Mikan found himself to be the only player dressed for the game in the locker room. So, finally he said to his teammates, "Come on, gentlemen, we have a ballgame to play." His teammates then jokingly replied back: "No, George. You have a ballgame to play, and we can't wait to see how you do against the Knicks!"

Opposing teams soon found out that the best way to beat the Lakers was to simply try to keep the ball away from Mikan. In 1950, the Fort Wayne Pistons refused to shoot the ball and dared not give up their possession, ultimately just sitting there and stalling out an unbelievable 19-18 victory. (That was the lowest scoring game in NBA history and ultimately resulted in the creation of the 24-second clock.)

And that wasn't the only rule change in basketball that was a direct result of Mikan. You see, George did most of his damage down in the lane, which, at the time, was only six feet wide. This allowed him to set up in the low post right next to the basket, making him virtually impossible to stop. So, in 1951, the league doubled the width of the foul lane to 12 feet. This move was aimed at big men in general, but Mikan in particular. (The league, in an attempt to level the playing field, even tried raising the basket to 12 feet. Luckily though, that experiment lasted for just one game before cooler heads prevailed.)

On September 24, 1954, Mikan, who by now had received his law degree from the U of M, announced his plans to open his own law practice and retire as an active NBA player. Financially, he was set, and as the game's first bigger-than-life star, he had a bunch of endorsement deals lined up for everything from sneakers to beer to chewing gum. Regularly featured on magazine covers and on television, George was famous and wanted to settle down to raise his family. So Winter, wanting to focus his attention on landing an NFL franchise for Minnesota (ultimately the Vikings), then sold his stock to Mikan, announcing that the big fella would succeed him as the team's general manager. George attempted a comeback in 1956, but struggled, eventually becoming the Laker's coach in 1957-58. But with a 9-30 record, Coach Mikan once again left the game he loved.

A Laker from 1948-54, and again in 1955-56, his statistics were incredible. Mikan became the first player in history to score 10,000 points, ultimately finishing with 11,764. (At the time of his retirement the next closest player, Joe Fulks, was more than 3,700 points behind him.) A perennial seven-time all-star, four times he led the league in scoring. And, amazingly, George missed only two games in his career with Minneapolis. He was the Lakers leading scorer 348 out of the possible 458 regular-season games that he played in, finishing with career averages of 22.9 points and 13.4 rebounds per game.

He returned to pro basketball again in 1967 though, this time as the first ever commissioner of the upstart American Basketball Association. With their trademark red, white, and blue ball, the new

rebel league distinguished itself from the mighty, yet conservative, NBA. There, Mikan was influential in creating many of the innovations that are commonplace in the game today, such as the three-point shot as well as non-basketball halftime and on-court entertainment for fans. When the ABA moved its headquarters to New York City in 1969, Mikan resigned.

And, although Wilt Chamberlain, Bill Russell, Kareem Abdul-Jabbar and Shaquille O'Neal would follow, Mikan was the NBA's first truly dominant center and the first big man capable of carrying his entire team. In 1950, Mikan was named as the "Greatest Basketball Player for the First Half of the 20th Century" by the Associated Press, and 46 years later, as part of the NBA's 50th Anniversary Celebration, George was named as one of the "50 Best Players" in league history. In 1959, he was inducted as a charter member of the Pro Basketball Hall of Fame.

After basketball, Mikan, who ran a very successful law firm in the Twin Cities, also got into real-estate as well as the travel business. He later resurfaced onto the hardwood once again in the mid-1980s as the head of a task force which ultimately brought professional basketball back to Minneapolis — in the form of the expansion Minnesota Timberwolves. A tremendous family man, George and his wife Pat raised six children and presently reside in Scottsdale, Ariz. (One of George's sons, Larry, a former Gopher, also played pro ball with Cleveland in the early 1970s.)

But for George, who recently had his right leg amputated just below the knee due to complications from diabetes, his greatest honor might have come at the Minneapolis Target Center on April 8th, 2001, when he was honored in a "Celebration at Center Court" during the halftime of a game between the Los Angeles Lakers and Timberwolves. There, in front of dozens of his former teammates, George was presented with a life-size bronze sculpture — which will stand forever in the arena's lobby. Fittingly, it depicted the 6-foot-10 legend with his back-to-the-basket and his arm extended into the pose of a hook-shot — George's signature move, as he was about to score the game-winning basket. It was a larger-than-life tribute to a larger-than-life man who has certainly made us all very proud. A true gentleman, George Mikan's contributions to the sport and his impact on the NBA still loom as large as his enormous frame. The cornerstone of the league's first dynasty, George was simply the best.

"He was the greatest competitor and a team player I ever had," recalled former Coach John Kundla of his star player. "He made the Minneapolis Lakers, and made this town a major-league city. I remember Wilt Chamberlain and Bill Russell telling George that he was their idol growing up, and the two said that he was partially responsible for much of their success in the NBA. He brought big league basketball to Minneapolis, and did so much for Minnesota. He is 'Mr. Basketball,' and I owe all my success to him. He is the greatest."

Laker Tombstone: "Well, I guess I would want to be remembered as 'Mr. Basketball,' I earned that honor."

Gopher tackle Leo Nomellini is named to the All-American football team	Gopher center Jim McIntyre is named to the All-American Basketball team	Gopher track star Fortune Gordien wins a bronze medal for the discuss toss in the 1948 Olympics

JIM POLLARD
THE LAKERS GO BACK-TO-BACK

The Lakers went ahead and made a major decision during that off-season when they, along with the Rochester Royals, Fort Wayne Pistons and Indianapolis Jets, opted to jump ship and defect from the struggling NBL to Maurice Podoloff's upstart rival Basketball Association of America — which had just completed its second year of operation. The BAA was already an eight-team circuit that featured franchises in several major markets including: New York, Philadelphia, Boston, Baltimore, St. Louis and Chicago. Now, the four new NBL teams, which took up residence in the BAA's Western Division, along with Chicago and St. Louis, would make up a perfectly balanced 12-team league. The addition of the four clubs really bolstered the BAA's reputation as well. It already had the marquis arenas in the major markets, but this gave it the big-name players it needed. The biggest of those names, of course, was George Mikan — who was very excited to now get the chance to showcase his talents in big venues such as New York's Madison Square Garden.

Minneapolis opened the 1948-49 season in Baltimore against the defending BAA-champion Bullets with Laker Forward Herm Schaefer's 23 points leading the way to a 84-72 victory. There were several new faces on the roster that season, including Johnny Jorgensen, a former teammate of Mikan's at DePaul, Mike Bloom, a former All-American forward at Temple and Guard Earl Gardner from Depaw. (During the season the Lakers would also add University of Utah Forward Arnie Ferrin, as well as NYU's Don Forman and DePaul's Whitey Kachan.)

On November 24, the Lakers set a single-game BAA scoring record when they dumped the Providence Steamrollers, 117-89. Mikan then made history a few weeks later when he unloaded for 48 points to set another new league mark. Mikan topped the 40-point plateau on seven different occasions that season while twice surpassing 50, ultimately fending off Philadelphia's Joe Fulks to win the league scoring crown with 28.3 points per game.

Minneapolis also played the Harlem Globetrotters that season as well, splitting the home-and-home battle with the legendary club. Both Jim Pollard and Swede Carlson sat out the away game in Chicago,

but returned to lead the Lakers past the Trotters, 68-53, in front of a record 10,122 fans at the Auditorium. In the game, Laker Guard Don Forman decided to perform some crowd-pleasing antics of his own, including a dazzling dribbling exhibition that brought the crowd to its feet.

The Lakers wound up finishing the regular season with a 44-16 record, good for second in the Western Division, one game behind their old nemesis, the Rochester Royals. The play-offs opened that March with the Lakers sweeping the Chicago Stags on Mikan's two-game, 75-point effort.

From there Minnie took on Rochester in another best-of-three series in the Western Division Finals. And, while Royals Center Arnie Risen had been absent in the '48 Finals, he was rarin' to go this time around. The series opened in New York with the Lakers watching a 17-point lead wither away behind an amazing rally which gave the Royals a two-point advantage with just under a minute to go in the game. That's when Tony Jaros nailed what proved to be the game-winning basket with just 18 ticks on the clock as the Lakers hung on for a dramatic 80-79 win. Back at the St. Paul Auditorium for Game Two, the Lakers went on to outscore the Royals 18-3 in the fourth quarter as they cruised to a 67-55 victory and a berth in the BAA Finals.

Next up for Minneapolis were the Eastern Division champs from Washington. The Capitols, who were guided by legendary Coach Red Auerbach, were led by six-foot-nine Center Bones McKinney, Forwards Bob Feerick and Kleggie Hermsen, and Guards Freddie Scolari and Sonny Hertzburg. The best-of-seven series opened at the Minneapolis Auditorium and behind Mikan's 42-point performance, as well as a pair of last-second free-throws by Carlson, the Lakers hung on to take Game One, 88-84. Auerbach's strategy of isolating his defense to blanket Mikan in Game Two worked out though as they held the big-man to just 10 points. But the rest of the Lakers lit it up with Carlson and Schaeffer each tallying 16 and 13 points, respectively — as Minneapolis took a 2-0 lead with a 76-62 win. The series then shifted to Washington's tiny Uline Arena for Game Three, where Mikan poured in 35 points to lead the Lakers to a 94-74 win and a 3-0 lead.

The Caps came out strong in Game Four though, beating Minneapolis by the final of 83-71. Bones McKinney played Mikan tough throughout the game, but George hung in there to score 27 points — despite chipping a bone in his wrist early in the game on a flagrant foul by Kleggie Hermsen that knocked him into the first row of seats.

Mikan recalled the play in Roland Lazenby's 1996 book, "The NBA Finals: A 50 Year Celebration:" "Red told them to drag me off the court and get the game going. Hermsen made sure he fouled out quick after that. There's such a thing as retribution in sport. You didn't necessarily have to get back at someone because your teammates would." (Hermsen, a former Gopher and native Minnesotan, feared that if the series shifted back to Minneapolis, the hometown crowd might want to lynch him for his tackle of Big George!)

So tough was Mikan that he scored 22 points in Game Five with a huge cast on his right wrist. He played on though, despite being hacked at by the Caps throughout the game.

"I can remember playing with my broken arm held up in the air during that game," said Mikan, "and on one play in particular, the Washington players were going for my arm and not the ball — which was on my other hand!"

The Caps were too much in the end and won the game, 74-66, to bring the series to three games to two. And, despite the obvious attempts by the Caps to hack at his injured wrist, Big George kind of liked having the cast as part of his artillery. His opponents were already fearful of his powerful drop step and this just added to the fun.

"That cast was hard as a brick; it fit right in with his elbows," Bones McKinney would later recall. "It would kill you. And it didn't bother his shooting a bit."

The Lakers got serious in Game Six (now back at the St. Paul Auditorium because of the annual sportsman's show), however, as Mikan scored 29 points to lead the Lakers to a 77-56 victory. The more

St. Paul's Marcenia Toni Stone Alberga signs a contract with the Indianapolis Clowns of the Negro Leagues, thus becoming the first woman to every play professional baseball for a men's team.	Colin Connel, a Gopher, wins the NCAA's 165 lbs. Boxing Championship	The Hamline Pipers, under legendary coach Joe Hutton, beat Regis College of Colorado to win the National Association of Intercollegiate Athletics (NAIA) championship	Gopher center Jim McIntyre is named to the All-American basketball team	Gopher tackle Leo Nomellini is named to the All-American football team	Gopher center Clayton Tonnemaker is named to the All-American football team	The Saint Paul Saints, the Triple-A baseball farm-team of the Brooklyn Dodgers, win their 9th and final American Association pennant.

than 10,000 screaming fans loved every minute of it as the defending NBL champs were now the BAA champs as well.

While Mikan averaged a league-best 28.3 points per game, Pollard, who was often left wide open thanks to George's double and triple-teaming, also averaged 15 points. In addition, Guard Herm Schaefer averaged 10.4 points and Swede Carlson chipped in 9.5 as well. By now the team was selling tickets like crazy and was operating in the black. A big part of that success came from the team's booster club, the "Laker Clubhouse" (one of the first organized booster organization's in pro sports), which was a group of civic leaders who helped to promote and sell season tickets.

The Kangaroo Kid

Jim Pollard will always be remembered for the spring in his legs and his amazing jumping ability, hence the nickname: "The Kangaroo Kid." In fact, he had such leaping ability that he became the first bona fide "dunker" in pro basketball, although his acrobatic dunks were done mostly in practice — because dunking during a game in those days was thought to be ungentlemanly! They didn't measure the players' vertical leaping ability back then, but if they would have, Pollard's would've certainly been astonishing, even by today's standards. He was truly the Michael Jordan of his day.

Born on July 9th, 1922, Jim Pollard's roots were formed in Oakland Calif., where he starred on the Oakland Technical High School basketball team. Full of promise and potential, Pollard took his talents to Stanford University, where as an All-American he led the Indians to the 1942 NCAA championship. From there he joined the U.S. Coast Guard and played on several service teams over the next couple of years, followed by a few semi-pro AAU squads as well.

The story of how Pollard became a Laker is as interesting as the man himself. Just before the Lakers first season in 1947-48, Team Executive Sid Hartman was assembling the pieces to put together a winning team. Specifically, they were trying hard to land a young six-foot-five jumping jack out of the California Industrial league named Jim Pollard, who was playing for the local AAU Oakland "Bittners." (On the East Coast, pro basketball was all the rage, but on the West Coast, there were only the AAU leagues, and they were every bit as good as the eastern pros. In fact, a lot of pro teams had previously tried and failed to sign Pollard, who had been training for a spot on the coveted 1948 Olympic team.)

But somehow, someway, Sid was able to persuade the young star to forego his Olympic dreams and move to the tundra. The news spread quickly that somebody had finally talked him into signing. Oakland Mayor Joe Smith even called Pollard and pleaded with him not to go. But Jim liked the tenacious Hartman and agreed to sign a Laker contract. There was one catch though. In addition to his $12,000 annual salary, plus his $3,000 signing bonus, Pollard made Sid agree to bring along three of his Bittner teammates. He reluctantly agreed, and went on to become one of the game's all-time great ones. The rest, they say, is basketball history.

"We used to know when Pollard had been in the building," recalled Washington Capitols star, Horace "Bones" McKinney, in Roland Lazenby's 1993 book, "The Lakers: A Basketball Journey," "because the tops of the backboards would be clean where he raked them. Pollard was fast, too. You couldn't press him either. He was too good moving with the ball. He'd get by you in a cat lick."

In 1955, Jim Pollard announced his retirement from the Lakers to accept the head coaching position at LaSalle College in Philadelphia, where he would ultimately post a modest 48-28 record. Then on January 2, 1960, after a three-year stint in Philly, Pollard rejoined his beloved Lakers, this time as their coach, taking over the reigns in mid-season from John Castellani. He would have his work

cut out for him though. The Lakers were 11-25 at that point, and things were not looking good. Minneapolis would finish the season at 25-50, and, while they did upset Detroit in the first round of the playoffs, they ultimately lost to the St. Louis Hawks in the Division Finals. That season would be Pollard's last, as well as the last for the Lakers in Minneapolis. (He would later go on to coach the Chicago Packers, an NBA expansion team run by Sid Hartman in 1961-62, the ABA's Minnesota Muskies in 1967-68, as well as the Miami Floridians from 1968-70 — when the Muskies franchise was relocated from the Twin Cities to Florida.)

Pollard, the team's first captain, was the last of the original Lakers. A fabulous rebounder and all-around team player, he would finish his illustrious eight-year career with 6,522 points — good for a 13.1 points per game scoring average. He also grabbed 2,487 (5.0 rpg) rebounds from 1950-55 as well. (Rebounds were not tracked until the 1950 season so there were plenty more that went unrecorded.)

Along with George Mikan, he was the only Laker to be a member of all six championship teams. And, while Big George had been named the "Best Basketball Player of the First Half Century" by the Associated Press, two years later, all of the players who had been in the league since its inception were given another poll as to who they thought was the greatest player ever. This time they chose Jim Pollard. The four-time NBA All-Star, who was the high scorer of the 1954 All-Star Game in Madison Square Garden with 23 points, was inducted into the Basketball Hall of Fame in 1977. Sadly, he died in 1993 at the age of 71.

TRIBUTES

"We were very close friends and roommates for several years," said Vern Mikkelsen. "He was probably the best athlete that I have ever played with or against. He was a very moody player, but on the floor, he played way above his head. He was just a marvelous athlete and a great friend. I miss him."

"Jim Pollard was probably the most graceful ballplayer that I ever had," said John Kundla. "He could do everything: run, pass, shoot, jump or whatever. He was the creator of the jump-shot. He was so graceful and smooth with everything. He could be playing today. When they put the press on, Jim would bring the ball down the court and nobody could guard him. We didn't keep track of assists back then, but he had a ton of them — most of them going to George! He was just an excellent all-around ballplayer with and without the ball."

"The Kangaroo Kid, he was one fabulous ballplayer," said George Mikan. "He was just an extraordinarily fine basketball player who could do it all. He could run like a deer, and had a great ability to pass the ball. His pin-point passes were just amazing. What can I say, he was just a tremendous leaper, a great ballplayer and a fine person."

"He was one of those guys that could do everything," added Bud Grant. "Just like Julius Erving, he could take off at the top of the circle and glide into the basket and lay it in. He could hang in the air and shoot with different hands. He was special."

By the 1949-50 season the BAA had severely crippled the NBL financially, and a truce of sorts was called when the two rival leagues decided to merge. The result was the newly created National Basketball Association, or NBA. The league's 17 charter members included the BAA's: Minneapolis Lakers, Baltimore Bullets, Boston Celtics, Fort Wayne Pistons, Washington Capitols, Rochester Royals, Philadelphia Warriors, Chicago Stags, New York Knickerbockers and St. Louis Bombers. The NBL then provided the: Anderson Packers, Syracuse Nationals, Indianapolis Olympians, Tri-Cities Blackhawks, Denver Nuggets, Waterloo Hawks and Sheboygan Redskins.

It was a wild time for pro basketball at this juncture with many of the clubs joining the upstart circuit literally teetering on the verge of bankruptcy. Trying to arrange the travel logistics and coordinate the scheduling all of those games was a huge headache as teams were suddenly scrambling just to find local gyms and arenas to play their games in. The Lakers, now playing in their third league in just three seasons, were placed in the Central Division along with Chicago St. Louis, Rochester and Fort Wayne. The others were then divided into both the Eastern and Western Divisions.

The Lakers played well and went on to finish the regular season on top of the NBA's Central Division with a 51-17 won-loss record. They then won six straight playoff games, sweeping Chicago, Fort Wayne, and Anderson, to gain yet another shot at their third straight league title. Now, in the The NBA Finals, the Lakers would face-off against the Syracuse Nationals, who were led by their fiery Player/Coach, Al Cervi, and star, Forward Dolph Schayes. Syracuse, winners of the Eastern Division championship, came into the series with a regular season record of 51-13. Both teams, however, had lost only one game apiece at home during the course of the regular season.

The best-of-seven series kicked off at Syracuse's State Fair Coliseum. In Game One, behind George Mikan's 37 points, the Lakers pushed the Nationals into overtime. Behind 66-64, with about a minute to go, Coach Johnny Kundla called for a double pick with Jim Pollard taking the final shot. The ball swung around as designed, but when Pollard got the ball, instead of shooting, he threw it to Bud Grant.

Said Grant: "I was the most surprised guy in the place, but I took a long shot and it went in to tie the game." Then in overtime, Bobby Harrison drained a 40-footer at the buzzer to win the thriller, 68-66.

The Nats then went on to win Game Two, evening the series at one game apiece. The Finals now headed back to the Twin Cities, but with the annual Sportmen's Show occupying the Minneapolis Auditorium, the Lakers suddenly found themselves homeless. They tried to book the Minneapolis Armory, but that, too, was booked, so they looked to the University of Minnesota and the Gophers' home, Williams Arena. Nervous about the basketball competition though, U of M Athletic Director Frank McCormick had already pushed through a Big Ten rule that prohibited pro teams from playing in conference facilities. Ultimately, the Lakers wound up at the St. Paul Auditorium. The unfamiliar surroundings didn't seem to bother them though, as they took Games Three and Four.

From there it was back to New York for Game Five. There, Syracuse rebounded to defeat Minneapolis, narrowing their series lead to three games to two. Back in Minnesota they had finally cleared out the fishing boats and campers from the Minneapolis Auditorium just in time for Game Six. Feeling right at home, the Lakers battled the Nats in a wild one that would ultimately go down as one of the most memorable in Lakers history.

Epitomizing the style of play which was commonplace of the era, the Lakers took it right to the Nats. Fights broke out all over the place as Pollard squared off with Paul Seymour, and Slater Martin and Swede Carlson both went at it with Billy Gabor before the police rushed in to break it up. To make it even more exciting, the volatile Cervi got tossed in the third quarter and four Lakers fouled out in the fourth. When it was all said and done, Mikan had poured in 40 and Pollard added 16 of his own in a 110-75 blow-out. The team celebrated at half-court and the crowd went nuts. The Lakers were now officially a dynasty.

"We had won a championship in all three different leagues at that point," said Kundla. "That was really a wild series. I remember Harrison sinking that 40-footer to win the first game at the fairgrounds. Then in the final game, I remember Seymour was guarding Mikan, and he was pinching George every time he got the ball. Finally George got so upset that when he went up for a shot, he gave him an elbow right to his forehead, giving Seymour a giant knot right on the noggin. George blew his top and I had to take him out of the game, but he did make the shot and the ref even called a foul on Seymour. Cervi, the player-coach, was really a mean competitor, and his teams would fight anybody. That series was a real brawl and at the time it was even more meaningful because our teams didn't like each other very much. It was a great series, and it is always special winning a championship, particularly that one, because it was our first NBA title."

The Original "Coach K"

John Kundla was born on July 3, 1916, in Star Junction, Pa., and grew up in Minneapolis, where he attended Central High School. After a great prep career, he went on to play basketball under coach Dave MacMillan at the University of Minnesota. John also played baseball at Minnesota, but his main sport was hoops. In basketball, he earned three varsity letters and led the Gophers to the Big Ten co-championship in 1937. He captained the Gophers in 1939 and also earned All-Big Ten Conference honors that year as well.

Following graduation, he played one season of professional baseball with Paducah in the Class C Kitty League. Kundla also stayed active as a player as well during this time, even leading his semi-pro Rock Spring Sparklers, of Shakopee, to the 1943 World Pro Tournament in Chicago.

Kundla then returned to Minnesota and served as a basketball assistant to MacMillan before accepting the head coaching job at DeLaSalle High School in downtown Minneapolis. There, he coached the Islanders to a pair of Minnesota State Catholic Championships in

TIMELINE

| Gopher guard Whitey Skoog is named to the All-American basketball team | Legendary Gopher Football coach Bernie Bierman retires | Millers third baseman Ray Dandridge is named the league's MVP | The Minneapolis Millers finish first in the American Association | Minneapolis Miller's pitcher Dixie Howell throws a no hitter in a 6-0 win over Columbus | St. Paul's Francis "Moose" Goheen is named the Outstanding Midwestern Hockey Player of the first 50 years of the 20th century. The two-time Olympian starred for the St. Paul Saints and led them to two McNaughton Trophy's in 1916-17. He is one of only a handful of Americans to be enshrined in both the Hockey Hall of Fames in Toronto and Eveleth, Minn. |

12

the mid-1940s. Following a two-year stint in the Navy in World War II, Johnny then decided to get back into coaching, this time at St. Thomas, where he coached the Tommies to a modest 11-11 record in 1947.

By this time, the Minneapolis Lakers had come to town. Originally, they had offered the head coaching position to coaching legend Joe Hutton, who had been Hamline's skipper since 1931 and had built the Pipers into a national small college power. But, when Hutton politely declined, the Lakers decided to hire the 31-year-old Kundla as their first coach. He then left the security of St. Thomas and signed a three-year deal with Minnesota's upstart professional basketball franchise for a whopping $3,000 per year.

In 11-plus years as the Laker head coach, Kundla compiled an impressive record of 466-319. At the time of his retirement, only the great Red Auerbach of the Boston Celtics had more professional coaching wins. Johnny also won 70 playoff games while losing just 35, a record that translated into an amazing six world championships for the state of Minnesota. In addition to coaching four NBA All-Star Games (1951-54), he also became one of only three coaches in NBA history to have guided teams to three consecutive world titles.

"I've seen a lot of great teams, at least on paper, that won nothing," said the legendary Auerbach. "Sure, Kundla had a great team, but he did great things with them."

In 1958-59, tired of the stress and travel demands, Kundla stepped down as coach of the Lakers, and became the teams' general manager. (By now the team was under new ownership.) In his first move as G.M., he hired George Mikan to be his coaching predecessor. It was a short-lived move though, as Kundla found himself back on the bench shortly thereafter. He would stick it out for one more year before finally calling it quits. Then, the day after the Lakers lost to the Celtics in the NBA Finals that next season, he announced his resignation.

Coach K would now return to his alma matter as head basketball coach of the Gophers. He would guide the Maroon and Gold for nine seasons, from 1959 to 1968, earning 110 career wins against 105 losses along the way. He also guided the U.S National Team into competition in 1964-65, and also served on the NCAA Rules Committee. In 1968, University of North Dakota Coach Bill Fitch took over for the Gophers, and Kundla went over to the U's St. Paul campus, where he became the school's Physical Education Director.

In1995 Coach Kundla was inducted into the Pro Basketball Hall of Fame alongside his star pupil, Vern Mikkelsen, making it the first time a coach and player were enshrined with one another.

"I can still remember Ray Meyer walking me down the aisle in Springfield, at the Hall of Fame, it was such a thrill," Kundla recalled. "My family was all there, and I don't think I will ever experience anything any better than that."

Kundla, a humble and quiet man, always kept an even demeanor on the court. Even as a young coach, he displayed sound judgement and always stuck to his beliefs that defense and discipline were the keys to success. A tremendous tactician, his greatest asset as a coach might have been in recognizing the strengths of his players, and then utilizing them. He somehow managed to keep three superstars: Mikan, Mikkelsen and Pollard, all happy and content — a feat nearly impossible by today's standards. He was a "players coach" and for that his men loved him. He will forever be remembered as one of the game's greatest.

"I was very lucky to be a Laker, and there is no greater thrill than winning a world championship," said Kundla. "The national recognition we got for the state of Minnesota was such a thrill for me to see. I was very proud of our Laker teams and I owe it all to my players. I'm grateful to Mikan, Mikkelsen, Martin, Pollard, Skoog, Grant, and all the others. We had players with such character, team spirit, and

a will to win. I was just very lucky to be their head coach."

"Sid Hartman actually talked me into becoming the Laker coach," added Kundla. "They paid me twice as much as I was making at St. Thomas. How lucky could I get? I mean the first player we got was Pollard, then we got Mikan, and then Mikkelson two years later! I didn't even have to coach them. They were so good that they did it all themselves. Those guys were just great players with great talent and so much character.

Johnny and his wife Marie later settled down in Minneapolis where they had six kids and many grandkids. He remains active in the Twin Cities to this day and still follows the game. In 2002 Kundla, along with several other former Minneapolis Laker greats, were honored by the Los Angeles Lakers for their achievements. It was a fitting tribute for the Hall of Famers that was long overdue.

What did it mean for you to be a Gopher?

"It meant a lot to me. It was such a thrill just to play for the University of Minnesota. I can still remember winning the Big Ten co-championship in 1937. Playing with guys like Gordy Addington, Gordy Spears, Paul Maki, Martin Rolick, and Butch Nash was just great. Then, to be able to come back and coach my alma mater was something very special to me. It was a great honor to be a Gopher player and later their coach."

Laker and Gopher Tombstones:

"As an active player with the Gophers, I was just happy to make the team. Professionally, I was very proud of our Laker teams and I owe it all to my players. I'm grateful to Mikan, Mikkelson, Martin, Pollard, Whitey Skoog, Bud Grant, and all the others. We had players with such character, team spirit, and a will to win. I was very lucky to be their head coach."

TRIBUTES

"John Kundla is one of the greatest coaches of all time," said Vern Mikkelsen. "He's never been given the proper credit simply because everyone said that anyone could've coached our championship teams. I sort of look at John similarly today as I did with the Chicago Bulls head coach, Phil Jackson. Like Jackson, John was wonderful at coaching each of us at our own individual levels, and that really motivated us to play for him and win. I am just very grateful for the fact that he gave me the opportunity to play with the Lakers."

"John is just an excellent guy," said George Mikan. "He had a great way about him, and he could keep the players focused on the game. He also had the ability to help you when things weren't going your way. He could critique your game and correct any problems that you had to get you back out there. He was also great at analyzing team defenses and he was a master at setting up plays that would help us excel. He is a wonderful person and a great coach."

"John Kundla just got better and better, until he was one of the greatest coaches in basketball," said Bud Grant.

In 1951 the boys from Eveleth came down to the State High School Hockey Tournament at the St. Paul Auditorium with the title of "three-time defending champion" in front of their names. These Iron Rangers were somewhat of an enigma with the Twin Citians, who by now had heard of them much like they had heard about Paul Bunyan and Superman — with a sort of mythical God-like connotation. The team was led by one of Minnesota's greatest all-time coaches, the legendary Cliff Thompson, who coached the Golden Bears from 1920 to 1958, finishing with an astounding 534-26-9 record.

Led by All-Staters John Mayasich, Ron Castellano and Dan Voce, the Bears came in to the state tourney riding an amazing 66-game winning streak. And, they were fresh off of yet another undefeated 16-0 season in which they scored 179 goals, while yielding only 30.

The Bears began their title defense by taking on Williams in the quarterfinals. There, in a replay of the 1951 title game, the Bears came out smoking. John Mayasich scored just 57 seconds into the game and didn't stop until he had scored three more in that first period alone. This one got ugly early as Eveleth went on to hammer the Wolves, 12-0, and advance onto the semifinals.

In the semis Mayasich showed why he was the greatest ever, scoring an unbelievable tournament record seven goals against Minneapolis Southwest. After a quick goal by Eveleth winger Dan Voce, Mayasich tallied three quick ones in the first period to get warmed up. Southwest then rallied back to make it interesting behind three goals from the Meredith brothers. That was just the wake up call Mayasich would need though, as he scored again in the second, and added another hat trick in the third. The Castellano's each added one as well for the Bears, as they cruised to an 11-5 victory.

That put the Golden Bears into the title match against St. Paul Johnson, who had beaten Thief River Falls in the other semifinal contest by the score of 6-2, thanks to a pair of goals each from Bob Youngquist and Ray Youngberg.

So, on Saturday, February 24th, 1951, in front of 7,163 Auditorium fans, Eveleth hit the ice to try and make it four-straight crowns. Johnson's own legendary coach, Rube Gustafson, knew that he would have to get a near perfect performance from his boys if they were going to have a chance. There was speculation before the game as to what kind of defense the Governors were going to throw at the Bears. Some teams had achieved a marginal level of success against them that season by running a "1-5" defense, in which one skater stayed at the blue line and the other four hung around the goalie. Or, perhaps he would just have the other four hang around Mayasich? Deciding to play it straight and take their chances, Johnson came out strong and held the Bears

scoreless through the first on tough goaltending by Johnson keeper Warren Strelow. But, just a minute into the second, who else but John Mayasich beat Strelow to go up 1-0. Ten minutes later he scored again, and decided to add two more in the third just for good measure. His fourth and final goal of the game was a beauty, beating Strelow on a 20-foot blast from the point. Johnson's Bob Schmidt added a meaningless goal late, but to no avail, as Eveleth and Mayasich prevailed, 4-1.

For Mayasich, who finished with 15 goals and three assists for 18 points, which is still a tournament record, it was as sweet as it gets. He would finish his storied prep career with four consecutive tourney titles and an unbelievable all-time record of 69-0.

"I remember that St. Paul Johnson game was a tough one," recalled Mayasich, "and there was a lot of pressure on us to keep the winning streak going through that fourth year. As far as the streak went, every year we were expected to play better than the one before, so I looked at it that way and played that way myself. When it was all over we couldn't believe what we had done, it was very special."

"When we were growing up, we didn't think about college hockey or the Olympics or the pros," he added. "We thought about making the high school team and getting to the state tournament. Eveleth had won the first state tournament in 1945, when I was in sixth grade, and that gave us something to strive for. In Eveleth you were expected to win and it was just assumed you would. As a result, we didn't take any time for sightseeing when we came down to St. Paul. All we did was watch and play hockey."

Minnesota's Best Ever

John Mayasich has long been regarded as one of the finest amateur hockey players ever produced in the United States, and is without question the greatest to ever lace em' up in Minnesota.

Mayasich grew up playing hockey in Eveleth. "We got our start learning hockey on the ponds and outdoor rinks in the city," recalled Mayasich. "The older kids would pick sides and the younger kids would learn from them. It went on from generation to generation. When the ice melted, we played street hockey and broomball. We had a lot of fun and we learned a lot playing those sports as well."

Eveleth has often been referred to as the birthplace of American hockey because of its wonderful puck traditions and roots that can be traced back to the sport's American beginnings. That's why the U.S. Hockey Hall of Fame is situated in this relatively small town on the Mesabi Iron Range, an hour's drive north of Duluth. Many

MAYASICH'S STATE TOURNEY RECORDS

Most All Time Total Points:	46	(1948-1951)
Most All Time Total Goals:	36	(1948-1951)
Most Consec. Games Scoring:	12	(1948-1951)
Most All Time Hat-Tricks:	7	(1948-1951)
Most Points One Tournament:	18	(1951)
Most Goals One Tournament:	15	(1951)
Most Points One Game:	8	(1951)
Most Goals One Game:	7	(1951)
Most Points One Period:	5	(1951)
Most Goals One Period:	4	(1951)

Gopher fullback & tackle Bronko Nagurski is inducted into the College Football Hall of Fame	Gopher Neil Oftshun, wins the 125 lb. NCAA Boxing Championship	Hall of Famer Willie Mays plays 35 games for the Millers. He hit .477 with 8 homers and 30 RBI's.	Jimmie Foxx, a Minneapolis Miller coach in 1958, is inducted into the Baseball Hall of Fame	Gopher center Gordon Watters is named to the All-American hockey team	The Hamline Pipers win the National Association of Intercollegiate Athletics championship.	The NCAA Championship Basketball Tournament is played at Williams Arena as Kentucky beat Kansas State to win the title	Gopher goalie Larry Ross is named to the All-American hockey team	Gopher guard Whitey Skoog is named to the All-American basketball team

hockey greats came from this hockey Mecca, names that ooze with tradition: Mariucci, Brimsek, Karakas, LoPresti, Matchefts, Ikola, Finnegan, Dahlstrom, and Palazzari, among others.

After high school Mayasich headed to the University of Minnesota, where he would join up with another Eveleth hockey legend, Gopher Coach John Mariucci. There, John led the Gophers to a couple of NCAA Final Fours and took college hockey by storm.

In 1953, his sophomore year at the U of M, the Gophers won the Midwest Conference championship and went all the way to the NCAA Finals in Colorado Springs. In the semifinal game they knocked off R.P.I., 3-2, in a nail-biter to make it to the championship game, where they lost a heartbreaker to Michigan. That next season, they made it to the Finals once again, this time crushing Boston College, 14-1, in the semis, only to lose to their old nemesis, R.P.I., in a 5-4 overtime nail-biter for the title.

"It's a loss that sticks with me still today," said Mayasich on the loss to R.P.I.. "To lose in overtime was bitter. It's not the ones you won that you remember, it's the ones you lost. To me, that was probably my biggest individual disappointment in all my years of hockey."

Before his career was over, the perennial All-American had tallied Gopher records of 298 career points and 144 goals. His totals worked out to an incredible 1.4 goals per game average with nearly three points per game. (To put it into perspective, Pat Micheletti, the next Gopher player on the career goal-scoring list, had 24 fewer goals despite playing in 51 more games. In other words, in his 162 games, Micheletti would have had to amass 435 points just to match Mayasich's per-game average. That's an additional 166 more than his career total!) Mayasich also holds the records for most goals and most points in a single game. In his senior year, he had an incredible six-goal game against Winnipeg and also tallied eight points against Michigan that same season.

At the end of his playing career with the Gophers, Mayasich fulfilled his military obligations and then went on to play with eight U.S. Olympic and National Teams. He was also a member of the 1956 silver medal-winning U.S. Olympic hockey team in Cortina, Italy. The highlight of that tournament came against perennial power Canada, which had won seven of the eight Olympic gold medals since the Games had begun. There, John played an incredible game, scoring a hat trick, en route to defeating the mighty Canucks. The Americans played tough but wound up taking home a Silver medal for their efforts.

The most celebrated of his Olympic events, however, was the first "Miracle on Ice," the 1960 U.S. Olympic team, which won the gold in Squaw Valley, Idaho. The U.S. team beat the mighty Russians for the first time that year, and, in the process, put hockey on the map.

"At the time we were thinking it would be a great accomplishment if we could win a bronze, we had no idea we would win a gold," said Mayasich. "Beating the Russians was amazing and very similar to the 1980 team victory as well. I think for both teams, playing at home, in America, was a big factor, because it's nice having the fans there to support you. This was probably one of the biggest thrills of my life."

John Mayasich was a "velvety-smooth skater," with a keen, sixth sense into the psyche of the goalie's every move. He is credited as being the first college hockey player to develop the slap shot, a new weapon that instilled fear into an already perplexed group of goaltenders who tried to stop him. John was an artist with his stick and his stick-handling skills were legendary. On opponent's power-plays, he could kill penalties by toying with opposing defenses. He used to take the puck and simply weave around the rink without ever passing to a teammate until the penalty had been killed. With amazing ability like that, it's hard to believe that he was often criticized for passing too much.

"The camaraderie was the best, those friendships go back 40 years now," recalled Mayasich on his playing days at the U of M. "Playing with the players who I had played against throughout my high school career was really exciting. We had great Gopher players like Dick Meredith, Dick Dougherty, Gene Campbell, Ken Yackel, Wendy Anderson, and Stan Hubbard. I got to see the world through hockey, and the purity of the game is the bond that keeps these friendships together today. It was quite a time to be involved with the Gopher program as it was just taking off back then. It made me proud of the fact that I was there when all of this was happening. Now, to see what the program has grown into today, and to think that maybe, in a small way that I had something to do with it, is incredible. My time at the U of M was great."

Declining professional hockey opportunities in the then six-team NHL, Mayasich devoted his remaining pro hockey career to the minor league Green Bay Bobcats. After his hockey career John went into business with his old Gopher teammate Stan Hubbard, where he worked as an executive for KSTP Radio for many, many years.

Mayasich received numerous honors during his hockey days, including being the first Minnesotan to be voted into the National High School Athletic Hall of Fame. In 1976 he had a homecoming of sorts, being inducted into the U.S. Hockey Hall of Fame in his native Eveleth, and in 1998 John received the coveted Lester Patrick Award, for his outstanding contributions to American hockey. In addition, in 1998 John became the only Gopher ever to have his number retired when his No. 8 was hung into the Mariucci Arena rafters forever.

Things have changed in the world of hockey since Eveleth's incredible run. While the attendance for the entire 1951 high school tournament was 18,582, the attendance in the new millennium approaches 120,000. However, in all those years, no one has come close to topping Mayasich's records, nor his legend. He was the best hockey player ever to wear a sweater in the Gopher State, and is a real living legend. But as great an athlete as he was, so is his humility. Often in the limelight, he was always quick to share the credit and the glory with his teammates and coaches.

Gopher Tombstone:
"I was blessed with the opportunity of playing with and against some great players. I was at the right place at the right time with the right people, and I made a contribution through a lot of hard work & effort."

TRIBUTES
"John Mayasich brought college hockey to a new plateau," said John Mariucci. "He was the Wayne Gretzky of his time, and if he were playing pro hockey today, he would simply be a bigger, stronger, backchecking Gretzky. The words to describe him haven't been invented. When I say he's the best, that's totally inadequate."

"John was a quiet fox," added former Gopher Coach Doug Woog. "He was the best player I ever saw play in Minnesota. Hockey made his life. What can I say, he is just such a wonderful guy."

The 1952 Lakers added some depth when they signed Rochester's six-foot-two, two-handed set-shot sniper, Pep Saul. In addition, the Lakers also added a couple of local homers in former Gopher star Whitey Skoog, and a pair of Hamline stars: Joe Hutton Jr. and Howie Schultz.

The Lakers got off to a good start that season, eventually finishing in second place in the West with a record of 40-26, one game back from rival Rochester. There were some highlights along the way too, including Mikan's 61-point performance in a double-overtime win over those very Royals. He also set an NBA record by hauling in 36 rebounds in one game, beating Syracuse's Dolph Schayes' old mark of 35. The Laker's big three of Mikan, Pollard and Mikkelsen each topped the 1,000 point mark that year, giving the team its most balanced scoring attack ever. So dominant were the trio that famed Basketball commentator John Devaney noted that "standing shoulder to shoulder, Mikan, Mikkelsen and Pollard looked like a ragged row of alpine mountains…"

By the end of the season Skoog was sidelined with a bum knee, something the team would have to work around. In the playoffs Minneapolis breezed past Indianapolis in the opening round, then headed to Rochester for the start of a best-of-five semifinal series against the defending champion Royals.

There, the Lakers lost Game One by 10, despite Mikan's 47-point effort, but came back to take Game Two. Minneapolis then took Game Three back home, and thanks to Pollard's last-second game-winning stuff-in, was able to also take the deciding Game Four, 82-80, to win the series. From there the Lakers prepared to do battle with the New York Knicks, who, under Coach Joe Lapchick, were making their second consecutive trip to the NBA Finals. Led by such stars as Max Zaslofsky, Sweetwater Clifton, Al & "Tricky Dick" McGuire, Connie Simmons, Ernie Vandeweghe, Harry Gallatin and Vince Boryla, the Knicks would be a formidable opponent.

The Finals opened at the St. Paul Auditorium, where Jim Pollard led the way with 34 points in a 83-79 win. The game wasn't without controversy though, as Al McGuire had a basket go in that wasn't counted. Amazingly, the refs, who gave him two foul shots on the play, didn't see the ball go in, and despite protests, refused to count it. The 10,000 fans there that night saw it go in, but didn't complain too hard when the overtime game ended with their Lakers victorious. The Knicks rebounded to take game two, 80-72, only to see Minneapolis steal Game Three, 82-73. The game was played in New York's 69th Regiment Armory because Madison Square Garden was being occupied by the circus. Game Four was another overtime thriller with the Knicks, who held big No. 99 to just 11 points, etching out a 90-89 win. Pollard, who had

injured his back in the game, was replaced by Bob Harrison. Game Five, which saw Mikan and Pollard each tally 32, was all Minneapolis, 102-89. Game Six, however, went to the Knicks, 76-68, setting up a decisive Game Seven back in the Minneapolis Armory — a place the Knicks had never won a game in. There, thanks to Mikan's 22 points and Pollard's 10 down the stretch, the Lakers blew out New York, 82-65, to capture their fourth championship in five years. And, for their efforts, the players received a whopping $7,500 bonus.

The Askov Iron Man

At six-foot-seven and 230 pounds, Vern Mikkelsen cleaned the boards and scored down low in the paint with such a reckless abandon that he was considered by many to be pro basketball's first real power forward. A rock-solid defender, "Big Mik" was also beloved by his teammates for his relentless work ethic. The ultimate team-player, he became a fixture on one of the game's greatest all-time front-lines alongside the likes of fellow Laker Hall of Famer's George Mikan and Jim Pollard. A gentleman in every sense of the word, Vern Mikkelsen is truly a Minnesota basketball legend.

The original "Great Dane," Arild Verner Agerskov Mikkelsen was raised in the tiny town of Askov, a small Danish community of just 300 souls, nestled halfway between Minneapolis and Duluth in northeastern Minnesota. The son of a Lutheran minister, Mikkelsen went on to lead his Askov High School team to the District Finals during his senior year of 1945, only to lose to rival Pine City.

Vern, who also participated in baseball and track, went on to graduate that Spring. "I was ranked No. 4 in my graduating class, but still finished out of the upper third," he said jokingly of his eight other classmates. By now though the three-time All-Conference Center had grown to six-foot-five and had inklings of playing college ball. He thought about giving the University of Minnesota a shot, but reconsidered when he found out that All-State Center Jim McIntyre, who had just led Minneapolis Henry to two straight state high school titles, had also signed up to play for Coach Dave MacMillan's Gophers.

Then something happened that forever changed Vern's life. That summer, Al Holst, a Hamline professor who used to travel the rural Minnesota countryside to check out basketball recruits for Coach Joe Hutton, was on his way up to the Iron Range to check out a hot prospect. As luck would have it, on his way up north he got a flat tire in Askov. So he pulled into the local Chevy dealership where Elmer Morgansen, who just happened to be a Mikkelsen family friend, got to visiting with him while he was fixing his flat. When Al explained to him that he was a basketball recruiter, Elmer said that as long as he was there he might as well check out Askov's star player. Al obliged and with that, set out to find Vern, who was working that afternoon in his neighbor Chris Hendricksen's rutabaga field.

"I can still remember seeing him pull up in his 1936 Buick," recalled Vern. "We all knew that he had to be someone important because nobody in our town had a car like that."

Sure enough Al found his way there and before he knew it, wound up coming back to the Mikkelsen's home for dinner. There, he was able to sign up the Piper's next prized recruit.

"Back in those days my parents didn't have a lot of money," said Vern. "So, my Lutheran father, himself an accomplished gymnast back in his native Denmark, quickly overlooked the fact that Hamline was a Methodist school. It was an opportunity of a lifetime and something that seemed too good to be true. It was as if I had hit the lottery!"

With that, at just 16, Vern enrolled at Hamline University, where he was about to play basketball under legendary coach Joe Hutton. Now, although Hamline was considered a small college (back then there were no Division I, II or III classifications), the school played a big-time national schedule against many colleges and universities which would be considered D-I powers by today's standards.

Also a Piper track and field standout, Vern would go on to become one of college basketball's finest players, leading his Pipers to three straight MIAC conference titles as well as the 1949 NAIA National Championship. By his senior year Vern, who was averaging better than 17 points per game, had grown to be six-foot-seven and weighed in at 235 pounds. He quickly became one of the most coveted NBA recruits in the nation.

With his Physical Education degree nearly in hand, Vern, who would graduate with honors, was now ready to take that next step into the world of pro hoops. And as luck would have it, his hometown Minneapolis Lakers wanted him badly. By this time the Lakers, who had already won the 1948 NBL and 1949 BAA crowns, were a basketball dynasty. They were on a roll, and saw Vern as the perfect compliment to their star center, George Mikan. With that, the Lakers then used their "territorial draft choice" (which allowed teams to select a local player from within its own 50-mile area in the first round by substituting their regular draft position) to select Vern.

Mikkelsen started out his pro career by seeing very little playing time, instead serving as an understudy to big George. Then something happened that truly changed the game of basketball. In a game against Fort Wayne, Laker coach John Kundla decided to play both of his big men at the same time. Calling his creation the "double pivot offense," Coach Kundla stationed both Mikan and Mikkelsen as a pair of centers — with Mik playing high and George down in the low post. The new "twin tower" lineup was good, but ultimately clogged up the narrow six-foot lane. So Kundla went back to the drawing board, this time putting Mikkelsen out on the perimeter and facing him towards the basket. In so doing, the coach had inadvertently created the NBA's first true power forward. Mikkelsen's new role was not to score, but primarily to rebound, set picks, and pick up Mikan and Pollard's missed shots. Although he would develop a great two-handed overhead set-shot, Vern's new position was not an easy transition for him. The center spot had been the only position he had ever known, and now, as a professional, he was being asked to change everything.

Teams were so intimidated by Mikan and Mikkelsen's brute strength, size and technique that they would use stalling tactics to simply keep the ball away from them for minutes at a time. As a last resort, the league finally evened the playing field by widening the lane from six to 12 feet and later instituted the 24-second shot clock, thus giving the other teams a fighting chance. (Both rules were credited as "Mikan Rules" because Big George truly changed the game.)

Known as the Lakers' "Iron Man," Mikkelsen went on to play in 699 games out of a possible 704 — a stretch which included an amazing run of 642 consecutive games played. For 10 glorious seasons, which included four NBA championships and a pair of runner-up spots, the "Great Dane" was a Laker fixture. He played on six NBA All-Star teams, was named All-Pro four times and served as the team's captain for five years, ultimately finishing with 10,063 career points (14.4 ppg) and 5,940 rebounds (8.5 rpg). (Vern was only the sixth player in NBA history to reach the prestigious 10,000 point club.) He also added 1,141 points (13.4 ppg) in 85 playoff games as well.

His amazing achievements still rank him among the all-time leaders in nearly a dozen Lakers statistical categories, right alongside fellow Hall of Famers Wilt Chamberlain, Jerry West, Kareem Abdul-Jabbar, Magic Johnson and Shaquille O'Neal. (Just how tough was Big

Mik? He even still holds the NBA record for most game disqualifications, with 127!)

Vern ultimately decided to hang up the sneakers after the 1959 season, one year before the team was sold to a group in Los Angeles. He clearly had the ability to keep playing (just two months before he retired he hit for a career high 43 points against Cincinnati), but wanted to leave the game on his own terms.

Laker Owner Bob Short tried to convince him to stay on as a player/coach, even offering him a whopping $25,000 salary and a 25% ownership in the franchise. Vern passed on the offer though because he wanted to devote more time to his family and his aspiring insurance business. Five years later Mikkelsen can still remember coming down to breakfast and having his wife Jean show him the newspaper headline revealing the news that Short had sold the Lakers to Jack Kent Cooke for a whopping $5 million. Said Vern jokingly, "She knew exactly what 25% of five million dollars was!"

Following his NBA retirement, Mikkelsen, who later got his masters degree in Educational Psychology from both the Universities of Minnesota and Oslo, in Norway, built a very successful insurance business. But, in 1967, he got that basketball itch one more time and accepted the offer to become the GM of the upstart Minnesota Muskies of the American Basketball Association. The team got into some financial problems later that season though and wound up moving to Florida. That following summer, George Mikan, who was the commissioner of the league, called Vern to tell him that the defending ABA champion Pittsburgh Pipers, with their star Connie Hawkins, were in financial trouble and were moving to Minnesota. They needed a GM, and once again Vern reluctantly agreed. But, like the Muskies, the team lasted just one season and wound up moving back to Pittsburgh.

And, other than a brief stint as Breck High School's basketball coach, Vern's affiliation with the game has evolved into a purely fun one. He still continues to do fundraising work for his beloved Hamline University, and also does some public speaking. The ultimate honor for Vern finally came on May 15, 1995, when he became the first Minnesota player ever to be enshrined into the Naismith Memorial Basketball Hall of Fame. Escorted down the red carpet by fellow Hall of Famer and friend, Bob Pettit, of the St. Louis Hawks, Mik would later say of his former rival: "That was the longest time I ever spent with Bob without having him score a point against me!"

Vern's most recent achievement was to help coordinate the 2001 George Mikan Gala at the Target Center which included the presentation of a life-size bronze statue and tribute honoring his long-time friend and teammate. Proud grandparents, Vern and his wife Jean have two sons, Tom and John, and currently reside in Wayzata.

TRIBUTE

"He was the first power forward," said George Mikan. "He was a fantastic guy and a fierce competitor on the court. He was a great rebounder and he learned to shoot from the outside. He was a good friend and a very important part of our team."

Minneapolis' Clarence "Biggie" Munn, a former All-American guard on the Gopher Football team, wins his second consecutive national championship as the head coach of the Michigan State Spartans. With a 54-9-2 career record in East Lansing, Munn is a member of the College Football Hall of Fame.

MINNESOTA'S "BREAKFAST OF CHAMPIONS"

You know that you've it made as a star athlete if your face appears on a Wheaties box. It's even better than being on the cover of Sports Illustrated because it happens only occasionally, and is reserved for extremely special athletic achievements. That orange backdrop is some of the most coveted real estate in all of sports!

The story of Wheaties actually goes back to 1921, when a health-conscious Minneapolis man accidentally spilled bran gruel on a hot stove. The result was a crispy flake that not only tasted great but was nutritious to boot. The man then contacted the Washburn-Crosby Milling Company, the forerunner of General Mills. In 1924, the creation was made into Gold Medal Wheat Flakes, and later the name became Wheaties. The breakfast cereal became an instant hit, and two years later a popular radio jingle that asked, "Have You Tried Wheaties?" made the product a household name.

Then, in 1933, its association with sports came to life when General Mills agreed to sponsor Minneapolis Millers baseball games on WCCO Radio broadcasts. As part of the promotion, a Minneapolis ad agency coined the phrase, "Wheaties, The Breakfast of Champions," for a giant bill-board that was erected at the ballpark. They soon began doing national baseball broadcasts and became one of the first big-time sports marketers in the country.

It has even been said that if it weren't for those Wheaties baseball broadcasts, Ronald Reagan would never have been President of the United States. When "Dutch" Reagan, who was a baseball play-by-play broadcaster for the Chicago Cubs, was voted as the most popular Wheaties radio announcer, he won both a free trip to the Cubs' California training camp, and a Warner Brothers acting screen test. The rest, they say, is history.

The cereal became readily associated with athletic success, and before long Babe Ruth became one of the first big-time athletes to endorse it. In 1939, Wheaties even sponsored the first televised sports broadcast. From 1956-1970, gold medal pole-vaulting champion Bob Richards directed the Wheaties Sports Federation and also served as its spokesperson. Decathlon gold medalist Bruce Jenner took over the role in 1977 and began promoting physical fitness. In the mid-1980s, gold medal gymnast Mary Lou Retton became the first woman ever to appear on the Wheaties box. In 1985, when Pete Rose broke Ty Cobb's all-time hits record, he became the first major league baseball player to make the cover. Walter Payton, Chris Evert, Michael Jordan and Emmitt Smith are among the others who have graced its cover. And in 1987 our Cinderella Twins were immortalized forever when they made the trademark orange box.

MINNESOTA FATS

Perhaps the most recognizable figure in the history of pool is Rudolph Wanderone, better known as "Minnesota Fats." Although he never actually won a designated "world championship," Wanderone, the game's leading comic, orator and publicity generator, probably did more for the game in terms of sheer exposure than any other player. Initially nicknamed "Brooklyn Fats," and "New York Fats," Wanderone dubbed himself as "Minnesota Fats" after the film version of "The Hustler" hit movie screens around the country in the early 1960s. Yeah, that's right. This guy wasn't even from Minnesota!

Since that time he went on to become known around the world as pool's foremost side show. "Fats" went on to host a national television show, "Celebrity Billiards," during the 1960s and did quite a bit to promote the game around the world. Rudolf Wanderone was inducted into the Billiards Hall of Fame in 1994 and died on January 18, 1996, at the age of 83.

MINNESOTA: THE SNOWMOBILE CAPITAL OF THE WORLD

In 1954 three entrepreneurs from Roseau decided to go into business for themselves, constructing farm machinery. Edgar and Allan Heteen and David Johnson created a company named after the North Star, called Polaris Industries, Inc. One day, Allan and Dave, tired of having to ski across the rough and snowy terrain whenever they wanted to get around to their favorite winter spots, decided to scrounge together various parts that were lying around and build a snow contraption. The new machine would move them across the snow much quicker and a lot more efficiently than skiing. Edgar, upset at Allan and Dave for wasting their time and resources, sold the odd-looking machine to a local businessman in order to meet their payroll. Allan, unfazed by Edgar, went ahead and built a new one, which he affectionately called "No. 2." This time, after Edgar sold it, they thought that they might be on to something. So, they started to build more, which they renamed as "Iron Dogs." In their first year, they sold a grand total of six "Iron Dogs" to the locals, who found them to be quite useful in getting around up in the north woods.

Nearly a half century later, the Polaris plant in Roseau continues to mass-produce the finest snowmobiles in the world. Today it is one of the largest companies of its kind, and the publicly traded company's headquarters are located in Plymouth. Not only do they manufacture snowmobiles, they also make watercraft, all-terrain vehicles, and motorcycles. They went from a tiny farming operation of just three workers to a major multinational company which employs nearly 3,500 people world-wide, with annual sales of more than $1.5 billion.

Interestingly, in the mid 1960s, Edgar left Polaris and his brother behind to start his own snowmobile company, called Polar Manufacturing. That company evolved into Arctic Enterprises, or Arctic Cat Snowmobiles. He has since left that company and it has new ownership under the name of Arctic Cat, Inc. Based in Thief River Falls, Arctic Cat is one of the world's largest manufacturers of snowmobiles, Tiger Shark personal watercrafts and all-terrain vehicles. With some 2,000 employees, the company's annual sales are upwards of $500 million.

CHRISTIAN BROTHERS HOCKEY STICKS

Billy and Roger Christian grew up as most kids did on Warroad's south side, playing hockey on the river. Today the pair make up the "brothers" part of Christian Brothers, Inc., one of the world's largest manufacturers of hockey sticks and equipment.

The brothers' success only helps add to the mystique of the tiny town of Warroad, otherwise known as "Hockey Town, USA." The tiny town, which lies on the shores of Lake of the Woods on the Canadian border, has a rich hockey tradition.

Billy and Roger led Warroad the 1953 State High School Hockey Tournament, where they finished runner-up to the St. Paul Johnson Governors. Both graduated from high school in 1956, and both played for Warroad's amateur team, the Lakers. That team was coached by the legendary Cal Marvin, who guided the club for more than a half a century.

They then earned spots on the US National team, also coached by Marvin. That team was the first to play behind the Iron Curtain, playing both in Moscow and Prague, ultimately finishing fifth in the World Tournament, in Oslo. After that, the brothers returned to Warroad to work with their father as carpenters. The next year, Roger skated for the Warroad Lakers, while Bill played on the University of Minnesota's freshman squad.

Both brothers later went on to star on the 1960 team that won a gold medal at the Winter Olympics in Squaw Valley, Calif. In that fabled event, Billy scored the tying and winning goals in the 3-2 pivotal win over the Russians. Roger and Duluth's Tommy Williams were his linemates. Roger also had a four-goal game against the Czech's, in what may have been the most memorable contest of the games. With the U.S. down 4-3 going into the third, Roger scored a hat-trick in the final period to ice the game. The two brothers continued to play on U.S. National teams and again made the 1964 Olympic squad in Innsbruck, Austria. That next year the boys led their hometown Lakers to a Hardy Cup, the championship of intermediate amateur hockey in Canada.

With the family's construction business prospering, Roger's brother-in-law, Hal Bakke (they're married to twin sisters), came up with a business proposition for the two brothers — manufacturing hockey sticks. The idea sounded good, so they dove right in. The three of them started their company at the old creamery in Warroad. With no money, they scraped and scrapped to get by, all the time working like dogs to get the company off the ground. Then, in the 1965 World Tournament in Finland, which was coached by former Gopher Ken Yackel, and managed by Cal Marvin, the brothers got to show-off their custom-made sticks to their teammates. They got a lot of great feedback, reinforcing the idea that their idea was a good one.

Back in Hockey Town, USA, they continued to work nights and weekends, with little or no pay for several years, hoping to catch a break. Then, in 1969, after deciding to raise capital by selling stock in their company, they constructed a new manufacturing facility along Highway 11 that would allow them to ramp-up and become a profitable corporation. When the company started in 1964, Northland Hockey Sticks represented their main US competitor. CCM in Canada, who also made sticks, got out of the stick business shortly thereafter. "We were basically copying the Northland Stick," said Bakke. "We even toured their plant, and I think they were sorry they ever allowed us to do that."

Today, with more than 60 loyal employees, and international and domestic sales of sticks and equipment reaching nearly $10 million annually, the company is on a roll. (They are still a distant second in annual revenues to the Marvin's though, who own Marvin Windows!) Not only are they one of the nation's top hockey equipment producers, they are also one of the most respected with regards to quality and innovation. There are more than 150 NHL players who use Christian Brothers hockey sticks and that number is only growing. The brothers still get a chuckle out of the fact that former UMD and NHL star, Brett Hull, who endorses Easton Hockey Sticks, has refused to use it with anything other than a Christian Brothers replacement blade.

Billy and Roger, along with Cal Marvin, have all been inducted into the US Hockey Hall of Fame in Eveleth. The Christan's are synonymous with hockey in Minnesota, and there are already second and third generations that have come along to carry the torch. For example, Bill's son Dave, who skated two years at UND, played on the gold medal winning 1980 US Olympic Hockey team, and played for than 14 years in the NHL with the Jets, Capitals, Bruins, Blues and Blackhawks, before joining the IHL's Minnesota Moose in 1995, has the most goals of any Minnesotan in the NHL.

With their trademarked Diamond Design stick blades, Christian Brothers sticks are among the best in the world. And, more importantly, they are made right here in Minnesota.

JOHN MADDEN

Did you know that John Madden is one of us? That's right, Madden was born on April 10, 1936 in Austin. He moved from Spamville as a kid though and was raised in Daly City, Calif.

Before becoming one of the most famous football broadcasters on the planet, Madden first made his mark as the coach of the Oakland Raiders. In fact, his Raiders even beat our Vikings in Super Bowl XI, in Pasadena. In fact, his winning percentage of .750 is the best of any head coach in NFL history.

Through the years he has become synonymous with NFL football and has endeared himself to millions of fans nationwide for his ability to explain the game's finer points with a unique sense of humor. After more than two decades as a game analyst for CBS and Fox, this legendary broadcaster presently serves as an expert analyst on Monday Night Football. His video games and television endorsement deals have made him a household name and a very wealthy man. From his "Madden Cruiser" bus, to his numerous books, to his six-legged turkey award on Thanksgiving day — this 15-time Emmy Award nominee wreaks of football... and that is why we love him.

Paul Giel was one of Minnesota's greatest ever athletes and could seemingly do it all. On the football field he lined up all over the place and forced opposing coaches to account for his every move. While Giel's storied gridiron career consisted of three fabulous seasons, 1953 stands alone. The football gods blessed Paul during his senior campaign. And why not, it was the greatest individual season any Gopher has ever had in Gold Country.

Optimism was running high in the Land of 10,000 Lakes in 1953, as the Gophers looked poised to finally make a run for the roses. Minnesota, under Head Coach Wes Fesler got off to a very slow start that year, and after losses to USC, Michigan State and Northwestern, was just 1-3 heading into the big Michigan game. The game was significant because it was the Silver Anniversary of the Little Brown Jug, the team's vaunted traveling trophy. Many of the stars from 1903, including Sig Harris and Ed Rogers, were even on hand for the festivities and the atmosphere was electric. Fesler knew it was a big game, and came down hard on his players that week. He knew that if they were to win though, it would come down to the play of one player — Paul Giel.

Giel, who had the power to call his own plays and audible at the line whenever he felt necessary, was ready to make history, and turn the season's misfortunes around that Saturday. And boy did he ever. In what many have called the greatest-ever single performance in Gopher history, Giel single-handedly crushed the Wolverines.

The game got exciting early when Gordy Holz recovered a Michigan fumble on the Gopher 29-yard line. Just four plays later Giel called his own number, and after deking out several Wolverines, found himself standing in the end-zone with his squad up 7-0. He would repeat that feat yet again in the first quarter, leading a 62-yard drive which was capped by another run around the end to make it 14-0.

Giel provided more heroics in the third when he returned a punt 41 yards, down to the Michigan 34-yard line. From there, after nice runs by McNamara and Holme, Giel hit Bob Rutford in the end-zone to make it 20-0. The Gophers added a late safety to make the final score 22-0, and regain the precious Jug that had eluded them for a decade.

Giel set a Big Ten record that day by handling the ball on 53 of 63 offensive plays, of which he ran for 112 yards. He also completed 13 of 18 passes for another 169 yards, returned one kickoff for 24-yards and had four punts for 59-yards too. Oh yeah, on defense the cornerback also intercepted a pair of Michigan passes to end a couple of key drives. Not bad! It was an unbelievable performance from an unbelievable player.

"They had kicked us around pretty good in those previous years and I really wanted to beat them badly," Giel later said. "From a per-

sonal standpoint, I would have to say that it was my best all-around game ever."

The Gophers went on to beat Pittsburgh, 35-14, behind Giel's three touchdowns, and Indiana, 28-20, before getting shut out by Iowa, 21-0. They ended the season by tying Wisconsin, 21-21, this time fumbling on the Badger two-yard line with just a minute to go, to finish with a 4-4-1 record — far short of preseason expectations.

Giel averaged more than 100 yards per game that year though, and for his efforts was again named as a unanimous All-American. In addition to being awarded the prestigious Big Ten Medal of Honor, he was the first-ever two-time Big Ten MVP. He was also given the Walter Camp Award for "Back of the Year," and was chosen as UPI's "Player of the Year" as well. The highlight, however, was his runner-up finish to Notre Dame Halfback Johnny Lattner in the Heisman Trophy race. It was so tight that it remains the closest balloting ever recorded. Many felt he would've won the nation's top honor had he been on a better team. It didn't matter. Minnesotans knew that he was simply the greatest.

The Winona Phantom

As a young boy, Paul Giel grew up playing football and baseball on the sandlots of Winona during the Great Depression. There, he would often try to emulate the smooth moves of his childhood hero, Heisman winning Gopher Halfback Bruce Smith. Paul's imagination was refueled every Saturday morning, when he religiously listened to his beloved Gophers on the radio. Soon he grew into an incredible prep athlete in his own right, starring in football, baseball and basketball at Winona High School. By 1950, not only was he one of the most celebrated prep football prospects in Minnesota history, he also had an opportunity to sign on with several major league baseball teams right out of high school as well. The kid was a natural, and luckily for us, he had decided long ago that he too was going to wear the maroon and gold.

"Coming out of high school in Winona, I was really steeped in the tradition of the Gophers, and because of guys like Bruce Smith, I wanted to be a Gopher," said Giel. "Also, because I could play both football and baseball there, it was even better. It meant everything for me to be a Gopher."

Giel came in and literally took the Gopher sports world by storm. By the time he had finished his illustrious career in Minnesota, he had shattered most of Bruce Smith's records, while single-handedly rewriting the record books. All in all, he rushed for 2,188 yards, caught 281 passes for 279 yards, and posted 417 return yards on both punts and kicks, for a total of 3,165 career all-purpose yards. He also had 22 touchdowns — a number that still ranks eighth all-time as of the new millennium.

He was a throwback. Not only was he an unbelievable halfback, but he was also an tremendous quarterback, defensive back, punter, punt returner, kick returner and kicker. It is a wonder how he ever had time to come off the field to catch his breath!

Giel's offensive regime is often credited for developing what was then called the "spread formation," which by today's NFL standards is called the "shotgun." It was that set-up that defenses feared most. Here Giel lined up five yards back from center. This is where he could do the most damage. Having the advantage of not having to take a seven-step drop to get set to throw, he could see the defense from

TIMELINE

Ken Bartlett, a Gopher Gymnast, wins both the NCAA Still Rings and Rope Climb National Championships	The Gopher Hockey team loses to Michigan, 7-3, in the NCAA Finals	Gopher Wrestler Dick Mueller wins the 123 lb. National Championship	Brainerd's Charles Albert (Chief) Bender, a Chippewa Indian, is inducted into the Major League Baseball Hall of Fame. Called by legendary owner Connie Mack as "the man I would pick to pitch the one game I had to win," the Chief won 210 games and threw a no-hitter in 1910. The first player ever to win six World Series games, he played for 16 years, mostly with Philadelphia, in the big-leagues and retired in 1925 with a 2.45 ERA.	The Lakers win the NBA Championship	Minneapolis native and Gopher track star Fortune Gordien sets the world record in the discuss with a throw of 194 feet, six inches.

20

the pocket, giving him valuable time to raise holy hell in the backfield. Often he would pass, lighting up the secondary. Other times he would follow his fullback up the middle or his halfback around the end. He could hand-off the ball to Gopher All-American Bob McNamara or split wide in the single wing formation to run the option. Sometimes he would line up at the running back position behind either quarterback Geno Cappelletti or Don Swanson in the power-T formation and blast full speed ahead. Occasionally he would fool the defense and pull a quick kick or even punt the ball. Whenever he got into trouble, he would scramble — and boy could he scramble! On the other side of the ball Giel played cornerback, constantly making spectacular tackles. And with a quarterback's instincts, he could anticipate pass patterns to force timely interceptions. He was unstoppable.

In addition to all of that, he also starred on the baseball diamond, where, as a pitcher on Coach Dick Siebert's Gopher Baseball teams, he was simply amazing. In fact, Siebert said "Pitching Paulie" Giel was the hardest-throwing pitcher he had ever coached. From 1952-54 he was named to the All-American and All-Big Ten teams. On the mound, he earned 21 wins, and had the same number of complete games. He still holds the Gopher record for the most career strikeouts with 243, and remains fourth all-time for the most single season strike-outs, with 92. He finished his brilliant career with a 2.16 ERA.

So, with a resume like that, what was Paul to do after graduation? "I knew in my heart that I wanted to play baseball over football, and I was trying to be realistic about myself," said Giel. "I wondered where in the heck I would play in pro football. I mean I wasn't fast enough to be a halfback in the pros, and I couldn't have made it as a pure drop-back quarterback. So, I thought I still had a shot to make it in baseball."

His tenure as "Mr. Everything" at the U of M, however, was just a springboard for bigger and better things to come in the world of Minnesota sports. He is truly a home-grown hero in more ways than one. Despite being drafted by the NFL's Chicago Bears, Giel opted to instead try his hand at professional baseball with the New York Giants. He would make his big-league debut for legendary Manager Leo Durocher on June 29, 1954, striking out the side in the 9th inning of a 10-7 loss at home to the Pirates. It would be the beginning of a steady six-year major league career, interrupted only by a two-year stint to serve his country in the military. From New York he went to San Francisco, and then to Pittsburgh for two seasons before finishing up his pitching career with his hometown Twins in 1961. He would hang up the spikes for good that same year. He would finish his career with an overall record of 11-9, and a modest ERA of 5.39.

From there Giel simply did it all, working first for the Vikings doing public relations and game management; followed by an eight year career as Sports Director of WCCO Radio — broadcasting prep, college and pro sports throughout Minnesota. In 1972 he was asked to return to his alma mater and serve as the University's Athletic Director, a position he would gladly accept and perform masterfully for more than 17 years. When that was up he even became a Vice President with the North Stars. Having seemingly covered every sport possible in the Land of 10,000 Lakes, in 1990 Paul settled down and took over as the Vice President of the Minneapolis Heart Institute Foundation, where he raised millions for heart health research and education. It was only fitting that a man with a heart as big as Paul's round out his illustrious career at such an appropriate place.

Tragically, Paul died in the Summer of 2002, leaving behind a legacy that will never be equaled. His legacy is that of a legend at the University of Minnesota. He was one of those players that comes around once in a millennium. He played the game like no one will again, and did it with an unpretentious demeanor, earning the respect of his teammates and his opponents alike. It has been more than four

decades now since he first lived out his dream of playing football and baseball for the Golden Gophers. The old brick stadium is gone and so is that old baseball diamond, but memories of Paul Giel will live on forever.

On Prep Football in the New Millennium:

"I'm glad to see that many of our kids today are getting the opportunity to play and learn at major Division I schools, because that's what it's really all about. Sure, it's not the same as the old glory days back in the 1930s and '40s, when the University's rosters were lined with all Minnesota kids, but as a state, we are contributing more and more onto the national scene. Coach Mason is doing a great job of recruiting, landing and developing more and more of the local and national blue-chippers, which is imperative to our program's success."

"In addition, I really like the fact that we have so many Division II and III schools here for kids to play at as well. We have a lot of pretty dog-gone good football players in this state and it's great to see so many kids who maybe don't have a shot at playing D-I, striving to go on and play at the next level after high school. The MIAC is a wonderful conference, and our D-II schools: Mankato, Duluth and St. Cloud, have great programs too. I remember going to a St. John's vs. St. Thomas game up in Collegeville, and I have to tell you, that is some darn good football! In addition to being entertaining, it was great to see those kids playing for the love of the game, knowing that none of them are receiving any scholarships."

"All in all though, with the exception of the youth game, football today is big business. And frankly, I don't miss the pressure of it all. But I can tell you this. Being a Gopher meant so very much to me that it is really hard to put it into words. It had been a dream of mine since I was a kid and it was without question the wisest decision I ever made in my entire life. The opportunities that it afforded me both academically and athletically were immeasurable. It truly made me who I am today. To play for my home-state school, in front of so many wonderful fans who supported me so much through all those years was an honor I can't even begin to describe. Sometimes I have to pinch myself because it seems like a dream-come-true."

Perhaps Big Ten Commissioner Kenneth "Tug" Wilson said it best when he described Giel as being a great ambassador for collegiate athletics: "He was not only an inspiration to his teammates, he was an inspiration to anyone who was privileged to watch him play. A modest unassuming individual off the field, once on the gridiron, Giel seemed to be inspired."

Gopher Tombstone:

"I owe everything I have to the University of Minnesota. It gave me a chance academically, athletically, and because of my visibility as a Gopher, it got me a chance to work with the Vikings and later WCCO where my name meant something. I might have been angry with a few individuals at the time I left the position of athletic director, but not the University itself, and certainly not the Athletic Department. It was a great experience for me."

John Mariucci is the godfather of American amateur hockey and the patriarch of the puck sport in our state. In fact, what John did for the sport was immeasurable. With his passion for competing, teaching, and spreading the gospel about the sport he loved, Mariucci went on to become the country's most important figure in the development of amateur hockey. After a storied career in the NHL, Maroosh came home to his alma mater to coach the Gophers. Although he never won the NCAA championship during his 14-year tenure at the U of M, he came pretty darn close in 1954 with the best line ever to play college hockey. Here is the story of a true Minnesota legend.

When the 1953-54 collegiate hockey season started, the U of M was on a mission to avenge their NCAA Finals loss to Michigan the season before. After losing the first two games of the new season, the Gophers got back on track and lost only one of the next dozen games. After splitting with Michigan, Minnesota then swept Michigan State twice, Michigan Tech, North Dakota, and Denver, only to get beat twice by Michigan at season's end. The Gophers finished the year with a 24-6-1 record, the best in the nation, and won their second straight WIHL Conference crown.

Hockey fans were anticipating a rematch in the NCAA Finals in Colorado Springs between Minnesota and Michigan. But the maroon and gold had to first get by Boston College in the semifinals. Minnesota pummeled an outmanned BC club, 14-1, behind an amazing effort from the best line in college hockey: John Mayasich scored three goals and added four assists, Dick Dougherty scored four goals and added two assists, while Gene Campbell added three goals and two assists. Then, to the Gophers' disappointment, they found out that the Michigan Wolverines had been knocked off by unheralded Rennselaer Polytechnic Institute (RPI) in the semifinals.

Minnesota was clearly favored to win it all, (by five goals) in most spreads. Colorado Springs' Broadmoor Arena was packed with puck fanatics as the game got underway with the Engineers striking first at 17:07 of the first, on an Abbey Moore back-hander that beat Gopher Goalie Jim Mattson. Then RPI scored a shorty on a Gopher power-play to make it two-zip. At 2:45 of the second, the Fighting Engineers threatened to run away with it when they scored again to make it 3-0. The Gophers were stunned, but, 24 seconds later, Minnesota got on the board with a Kenny Yackel blast, followed by a Dougherty one-timer from Campbell that made it 3-2. Then, after peppering the Engineer goalie, Mayasich put in a back-hander to even it up at three-apiece in the third. Four minutes later Mayasich set up Dougherty on a pretty "five-hole" goal to finally take the lead. But, at 16:10 the men from Troy, N.Y., evened things up one more time, as Moore scored again to send

the game into overtime.

At 1:54 of the extra session, after a mix-up out in front of the net, RPI's Gordie Peterson, grabbed a loose puck on the doorstep and promptly drilled it home to win the game by the final of 5-4. It was a devastating defeat and a big blow to Mariucci, who wanted so badly to win the big one for Minnesota. After the game, the players huddled around their coach to shield him from the press and their cameras. It was the first and only time Minnesota hockey players would ever see this giant of a man shed a tear. Despite the loss, Yackel, Mattson, Dougherty, and Mayasich were all named to the All-American team.

Growing up in Hockey Central

John Mariucci was born the son of Italian immigrants on May 8, 1916, on the great Mesabi Iron Range in Eveleth — the birthplace of hockey in the United States. He grew up on Hay Street, also referred to by locals as "Incubator Street" because it was said that there were so many nationalities living there, and every house had eight or nine kids inside. Many of the kids of the immigrants would play hockey to stay out of trouble. Some kids didn't even have skates, so they wore overshoes, while others used tree branches for sticks. John found his first pair of skates in a garbage can and, because he didn't have money to buy equipment, wrapped old magazines around his shins for pads.

Even though it was a mid-sized Minnesota Iron Range town, Eveleth was as sophisticated as New York City when it came to hockey. Eveleth even had a team, the "Reds" which played big-time pro hockey against cities such as Toronto, Philadelphia and Chicago. Eveleth kids would try to emulate the many Canadians who were imported to the city to play hockey as one of the forms of entertainment provided for the iron-ore miners. John learned the game from legendary hall of fame coach Cliff Thompson, whose tenure as the Eveleth High School hockey coach lasted nearly 40 years.

In 1936, Maroosh left the Range and headed south to the University of Minnesota. There he starred as a defenseman for Larry Armstrong's Gopher hockey team and also played offensive and defensive end alongside of Butch Nash under legendary football coach Bernie Bierman. In 1940, led by Goalie Bud Wilkinson, the future football coaching legend at the University of Oklahoma, Mariucci captained the National AAU Championship team. (At the time that was the only championship available in college hockey.) After the season, Maroosh, who was named as an All-American, was offered the head coaching position at the U of M, but turned it down to play in the pros.

After a brief stint with Providence in the American Hockey League, Maroosh joined the Chicago Blackhawks to finish out the 1940 season. At that time the NHL employed few Americans and not many college-bred players. (To put this into perspective, by 1968, only six Americans and five collegians had ever played in the NHL!) Johnny played there until 1942, when he was summoned to join the U.S. Coast Guard in New York. There, he played for the Coast Guard team in the Eastern Amateur League during the second world war. After turning down another offer to coach at the U of M, he returned to the Hawks for the 1945 season. Then, in 1947, Maroosh became the first American-developed player ever to captain an NHL team.

The rugged Maroosh was one of the biggest celebrities in Chicago during his playing days there. He became famous among Windy City hockey fans for his brawls. One in particular, with Detroit's Black Jack Stewart, remains the NHL's longest ever — last-

Gopher defenseman Ken Yackel, Sr. is named to the All-American hockey team	Gopher halfback Bob McNamara is named to the All-American football team	Gopher goalie Jim Mattson is named to the All-American hockey team	Gopher end Bert Baston is inducted into the College Football Hall of Fame	Gopher fullback Herb Joesting is inducted into the College Football Hall of Fame	Gopher coach Fritz Crisler is inducted into the College Football Hall of Fame	Gopher tackle Ed Widseth is inducted into the College Football Hall of Fame	Gopher tackle Dick Wildung is inducted into the College Football Hall of Fame	Gopher winger Dick Dougherty is named to the All-American hockey team

ing more than 20 minutes. In 1948, Maroosh left the Hawks. For his career in the NHL he scored 11 goals and 34 assists for 45 points over 223 games. He also played in two Stanley Cup playoffs. More importantly though, he led the team in penalty minutes, racking up more than 300 over his career. A goal-scorer he wasn't. This guy was a role-playing hatchet-man who protected and defended his teammates. That's why they loved and appreciated him.

Mariucci went on to play for St. Louis of the American League, St. Paul and Minneapolis of the U.S. League, and again with a Coast Guard team before hanging up his skates for good as an active player in 1951. He then turned to coaching, when he was named the head coach of Minneapolis Millers hockey team of the A.A.L.

After a year with the Millers, Maroosh finally elected to coach the Gophers, replacing former Blackhawk and Gopher, Doc Romnes. It was only a part-time job for him though, as he continued to also work as a salesman for the Martin Falk Paper Company as well. In his first season in Gold Country he was awarded Coach of the Year honors. It would be his first of many.

He got Minneapolis residents excited about college hockey, and they responded by coming out in droves to see his Gophers. The U even had to add an upper tier of seats to the Williams Arena rink to accommodate them all. Always a kidder, Maroosh was always trying new things to keep the fans interested and was always looking for new recruits. One time while watching the giant Bill Simonovich, from Gilbert, Minn., play with the varsity basketball team, John said: "Man, what a goalie he'd make! Give him a couple of mattresses and a pair of skis and nobody would ever score on him."

In a sport dominated by Canadians, Maroosh championed the Americans and in particular, Minnesotans. After watching an NCAA Final one time, he said: "It's asinine that the only two Americans on the ice for the NCAA championship game were the referees." Maroosh was a visionary and saw the potential growth of the sport.

"College could be a developmental program for our own country, for the Olympics and for the pros," he said. "College hockey is a state institution and should be represented by Minnesota boys. If they're not quite as good as some Canadians, we'll just have to work a little harder, that's all."

It became political for him as he battled to stop the importation of the older Canadians and give the American kids an equal playing field. In the late 1950s, the U's Athletic Director, Marsh Ryman, refused to play Denver's Canadian-filled teams. This ultimately led to the end of the WIHL and the creation of the WCHA in 1959.

"What I was against was the junior player who played in Canada until he was 21, then, if the pros didn't sign him, he would come to this country to play college hockey as a 22-year-old freshman against our 18-year-olds," said Mariucci. "It wasn't fair to our kids, who were finishing college at the same age Canadians were freshmen."

The Noble Roman left the University in 1966 with a record of 207-142-15, including conference championships in 1953 and 1954, as well as three NCAA playoff appearances (including another Final Four appearance in 1961). Included in his tenure was an Italian homecoming of sorts, when he was led the Americans to a silver medal in the 1956 Olympics in Cortina. There were 11 Minnesota natives on the team that stunned heavily favored Canada before falling to the Soviet Union. Mariucci's successor at the U of M was Glen Sonmor, a former teammate with the Minneapolis Millers.

In 1966, another chapter of Mariucci's storied life unfolded as he became chief scout and special assistant to Wren Blair, GM of the NHL's expansion North Stars. There, Maroosh applied his vast knowledge of recruiting, coaching, and scouting. In 1977 Mariucci coached the U.S. National team and a year later he rejoined the North Stars, this time as the Assistant G.M. under his former player, Lou Nanne.

"One word of advice to all you coaches," said Maroosh. "Be good to your players — you never know which one might someday be your boss..."

John's accomplishments and honors are far too great to list here. Some of his more notable ones, however, include: Being inducted as a charter member of the U.S. Hockey Hall of Fame in his hometown of Eveleth; being inducted into the NHL Hockey Hall of Fame in Toronto; and receiving the NHL's coveted Lester Patrick Award for his contributions to U.S. hockey. He also made a difference by giving to others. In fact, he devoted much of his life to Brainerd's Camp Confidence, for the mentally-retarded, a cause he dearly loved.

On March 2, 1985, in an emotional ceremony to give thanks and immortalize the man forever, the U of M renamed the hockey half of Williams Arena as Mariucci Arena, in his honor. It was also declared as "John Mariucci Day" in Minnesota by Governor Perpich. During the ceremony, long-time friend Robert Ridder said: "During the 1980 Olympics, a U.S. Destroyer passed a Russian ship and signaled to it: 'U.S.A. 4, Russia 3.' Probably nobody on that boat ever heard of John Mariucci, but it wouldn't have been possible without John Mariucci."

In 1987 Maroosh died at the age of 70 after a long bout with cancer. He had seven children and several grandchildren.

This gentleman brawler was a legend, on and off the ice. Although he was tough as nails, his wit, intelligence, and personality were one-of-a-kind. John was one of the toughest Italians who ever lived. His face has often been referred to as a "blocked punt," because it was so beat up. But what separated him from the goons was that he wouldn't just knock his opponents down, he'd pick them up and then make them laugh.

Perhaps Herb Brooks said it best: "In all social causes to better an institution, there's always got to be a rallying force, a catalyst, a glue, and a magnet, and that's what John was, for American hockey. The rest of us just filled in after him."

Full of wit, he was described as a newspaperman's dream-come-true. From his famous brawls, which included once breaking thumb-wrestling champion Murray Warmath's thumb, Mariucci gained a lot of mileage. Local reporters found themselves having a lot of dinners that turned into breakfasts while listening to his endless stories. The sports community was in awe of him, and he made journalists who hated the sport of hockey want to start covering it.

He was also the pioneer in the development of hockey in Minnesota. Because of that, his legacy will live on forever. Every kid that laces up his or her skates needs to give thanks to the man that started it all. He started grassroots youth programs, put on coaching clinics, attended new arena openings in countless cities across the state, helped former players find coaching positions, and even encouraged hockey moms to write to city councils to build rinks and develop recreation programs. Because of him, hockey in Minnesota carries the same pedigree as basketball in Indiana or football in Texas. Described best by his friends and players as "father-like, magical, and even super-human," he was simply the greatest. *Thanks Maroosh.*

The Lakers win the NBA Championship

Gopher tackle Leo Nomellini is inducted into the College Football Hall of Fame

Chuck Mencel could flat-out shoot, and that's why he was one of the greatest guards ever to play for the University of Minnesota basketball Gophers. Mencel had poise, court-savvy, tremendous ball-handling skills, and was extremely accurate from the field as well as from the line. He worked hard at the fundamentals and optimized the cliché, "lead by example." In 1955, Chuck was honored as the first Minnesota player ever to be named as the Big Ten MVP. But, he would have traded it all to knock off the powerful Iowa Hawkeyes that year for the conference title.

Minnesota was coming off a respectable third place finish in the Big Ten in 1953-54, with a 10-4 conference mark. The outlook was cautiously optimistic for the 1954-55 season. Although the Gophers were young, they had returning All-Big Ten players Chuck Mencel and Dick Garmaker, both of whom were named as the upcoming seasons' co-captains. The other three Gopher starters were Forward David Tucker, Center Bill Simonovich, and Guard Gerald "Buck" Lindsley.

The season opened in the Windy City, where Ray Meyers' DePaul Blue Demons knocked off the Gophers, 94-93, in an overtime thriller. Minnesota rebounded a week later when the Blue Demons came to Minneapolis as part of a home-and-home series to kick off the season, and this time the Gophers prevailed, 94-84. From there the Gophs were beaten by Oklahoma A&M, but rallied to win their next four games. The first two victories came at Williams Arena against SMU and Notre Dame. The Maroon and Gold then flew south to play in the Dixie Classic in Raleigh, N.C. There, they defeated Wake Forest and Duke, but lost to North Carolina State for the championship.

It was back to Chicago for the U, as they took on Northwestern to open the Big Ten Conference schedule. In a heartbreaker, the Wildcats beat the Gophers, 72-74. Next stop, Iowa, where the Gophers beat the arch-rival Hawkeyes, 81-80. That would prove to be a pivotal game for the squad as they sent a clear message to the Big Ten that they meant business. The U of M went on to win its next two over Indiana and Purdue before losing to Michigan State, 75-87. From there the team rattled off seven straight wins, including triumphs over Northwestern, Purdue, Ohio State, Illinois, Indiana, Michigan, and Wisconsin.

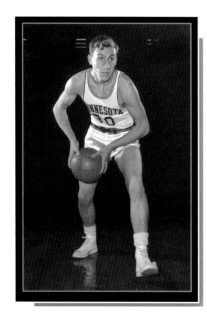

In the game against the Badgers, Mencel poured in 23, while Garmaker had 28 to lead the way. Wisconsin, led by Dick Miller, who scored 31 in the game, rallied to go up by seven at the half. In the second, Hibbing's Garmaker took over, scoring 12 points in first five minutes to get the score to 49-48. The Badgers held the lead until Garmaker's tip-in made it 63-63. It then went back and forth with less then two minutes to go as Mencel stripped the ball from Miller. He quickly passed it up to Garmaker, who then put it in to make it 69-apiece. Now,

with only 15 seconds to go, Mencel took the ball upcourt and got fouled. With only six ticks left on the clock, Mencel nailed both free throws to ice the game, 71-69.

The stage was now set for the Big Ten title game as hated Iowa came to town for the much-anticipated rematch of the titans. A record crowd, of 20,176 fans, showed up at Williams Arena that day in anticipation of the dynamic duo of Mencel and Garmaker bringing down the vaunted Hawkeyes. Williams Arena had never held so many spectators for a basketball game, and it will never again as fire codes now prevent such an occurrence. The contest went back and forth early on as Minnesota shot 43 percent in the first half to take a 35-33 halftime lead.

The Hawks were led by their big man, Bill Logan, who had 15 of his 25 points in the first half. In the second half, the battle continued as both teams sparred like heavyweight champions. With just over four minutes to play, Mencel scored six straight of his team-high 27 points to give the Gophers a 70-67 lead. But at 2:23, Iowa's guard play brought the Hawks back on top, 71-70. With two minutes to go, Mencel missed a key shot, followed by Buck Lindsley, who had a chance to get the Gophers back into it but missed a free throw at the end of the game. It was Iowa's night as they shot an incredible 67 percent in the second and held on to beat the Gophers, 72-70.

It was an incredibly crushing loss for Minnesota and somewhat ironic in that Iowa, the league's worst from the charity stripe, won the game on the line, beating Minnesota — the league's best free throw shooting team.

The last game of the year featured a rematch with the Badgers. The Gophers not only needed to win the game, but also had to have some help from Lady Luck to have any chance to win the conference title. This would ultimately be the great Mencel's farewell to Williams Arena. And, appropriately enough, his last game was against his home-state Badgers. Minnesota, its backs to the wall, hung it all out on the line that night. Coach Ozzie Cowles' boys held the lead at the half, 32-31, after Mencel popped a deuce from the post.

Then, the Badgers went ahead, but the Gophers rallied with 12 minutes to go, narrowing the gap to 50-48 off a pair from Lindsley, who had 17 points. At the four-minute mark, the Gophers were still in it at 72-67, but that would be as close as they would come in the season finale. Cowles removed Mencel and Garmaker with a minute left and the crowd responded with a thunderous roar of appreciation for all their hard work over the years. Minnesota lost by the final of 78-72, and as a result, Iowa was now off to the NCAA Tournament.

How good was Iowa that year? Led by Logan, Carl Cain, and Sharm Scheuerman, the Hawkeyes waltzed past Penn State and Marquette before losing to All-American sensation Tom Gola and LaSalle in the NCAA Final Four by the tally of 76-73.

"It was a letdown for me at the time, but it also became the springboard to a much more expanded view of opportunity, both in an athletic and business sense," Mencel would later recall. "I'm not going to say we should have won the Iowa game, but we could have easily won it. I've got a video tape of the game, and I still bring it out and watch it every now and then. It was a great, great game — a disappointment — but definitely my most memorable as a Gopher. The thing that stands out for me most, was that it was probably my best game as a Gopher, but we still lost. And then losing to Wisconsin in the next game was a tough way for me to bow out."

TIMELINE						
Gopher forward Dick Garmaker is named to the All-American basketball team	"The Buffalo Rodeo" is started. Today, 43 years later, it is the state's oldest and largest continuous rodeo event.	The state's largest lake trout is caught by G.H. Nelson on Lake Superior, near Hovland: 43 lbs., 8 oz.	Gopher coach Bernie Bierman is inducted into the College Football Hall of Fame	The Minneapolis Millers host the American Association's All-Star Game	The Millers beat the Rochester Red Wings for the Junior World Series Championship	The Hibbing Curling Club host's its first annual "Last Chance Bonspiel." Today, 42 years later, the invitational affair features 128 men's teams from both the US and Canada, which compete in five events over a five day period. A total of 13 sheets of ice are put into place at the Hibbing Memorial Arena for the event, therefore making it the largest bonspiel of its kind under one roof. The Hibbing Curling Club, rich in tradition, has won an amazing 14 National Championships since its inception in 1913.

The Gophers led the Big Ten in defense that season, and finished the year with a 10-4 record in the Big Ten and 15-7 overall. But because of the Wisconsin disappointment on the last day of the season, they wound up as the conference bridesmaids. Mencel was named as the team's MVP that year and was also named to the All-Big Ten and All-American squads. For his efforts he was also awarded the Silver Basketball Award, signifying the Big Ten's most valuable player.

The Golden Touch

Chuck Mencel was born in Phillips, Wis., the oldest of three children. He grew up spending much of his time shooting hoops at the YMCA.

"When my parents got divorced while I was in the seventh grade, the basketball gymnasium became my safe haven," said Mencel.

He went on to play basketball at Eau Claire High School, becoming the only non-senior to make the squad. His team made it all the way to the Wisconsin State High School Tourney Finals, but lost in the championship game to St. Croix Falls. During that season, he broke his school's single-game and season scoring records. Then, after his senior year, he was selected to the national high school All-American team. After a stellar prep career, Mencel accepted a scholarship to attend Bradley University in Peoria, Ill. But when allegations of a basketball betting scandal broke out that summer, Mencel elected to transfer to Minnesota instead.

"The scandal was a big red flag for me, so I immediately decided to attend the U of M," said Mencel.

Because of the Korean War, freshmen were now allowed to participate in intercollegiate sports, and Mencel took every advantage of his playing time. Interestingly, while at the U, Chuck wound up living in possibly the most athletic dorm room of all time. That's because his roommate was Gopher Hockey star John Mayasich.

Averaging 16 points per game, Mencel held five Gopher scoring records during his tenure at the U, and he still ranks among the best in career scoring, with 1,391 points. He would hold the school's scoring record for nearly a quarter of a century, until Mychal Thompson came along and broke it in the late 1970s. He also set the record for the most field goals attempted, with 1,635. In addition, during his sophomore, junior, and senior seasons in the Big Ten, he scored 766 points, then a school record. An outstanding student, he graduated that same year with a bachelor's degree in Business Administration. What's even more impressive is that he did it all while taking care of his family. You see, Chuck married his high school sweet-heart when he was a sophomore at the U, and before he graduated, he had two children.

Mencel's partner in crime during the mid-50s was fellow All-American Dick Garmaker, a transfer student from Hibbing Junior College. Garmaker was a tremendous rebounder, defender, free-throw shooter and could do a lot of damage with his jump shot. Over his career at Minnesota, Garmaker would set eight scoring records. Later, he and Mencel even went on to play together for a couple of years with the Minneapolis Lakers as well. Garmaker ultimately went on to finish his NBA career with the New York Knicks.

"Dick Garmaker and I were the two seniors on an otherwise underclass team," said Chuck. "We had a great time playing together for the Gophers and, later, the Lakers. He was certainly my closest friend on the team and he was a great player. We're still close today."

Chuck had the golden shooting touch and was acknowledged as one of Minnesota's greatest team players. He was widely regarded as the premier pure shooter of his day and, because of his quickness and shooting ability, revolutionized many aspects of the game. There's no telling just how good Mencel would have been if he had played in the NBA after the dawn of the three-point line. Although he didn't bring home the hardware for Minnesota in 1955, he made Minnesota proud of the U's basketball program and got people all over the state

excited about college hoops again.

After his illustrious career at Minnesota, Mencel was drafted by the Minneapolis Lakers. But, that summer before his first season, he was invited to play on the traveling team that played the Harlem Globetrotters. It was a 24-city tour and he was paid $100 per game. By the way, this was a real team Mencel played for, and not the stooge teams like the Washington Nationals that we see today. They played it straight.

After that Chuck then went on to start as the point guard for the Lakers. He averaged seven points per game and led the team in assists with three per game as well. His career was cut short after only two years in the NBA though, due to the fact that he was required to fulfill his military obligation, which he had deferred out of college. So he joined the Army as a second lieutenant in the Transportation Corps and was stationed in Fort Eustis, Va. After that, Chuck decided to abandon the NBA altogether and enter the world of business, where he applied that same zealous attitude of hard work and success that he had on the court. Following his playing days Chuck went on to become the President and CEO of Caterpillar Paving Products, in Brooklyn Park.

What did it mean for you to be a Gopher?

"In hindsight, it really set the table for a lifestyle that was unparalleled in my expectations as a young person. To have played and been successful at a major institution like the U of M, and in a conference such as the Big Ten, was just incredible. As an athlete, it was wonderful stepping stone to the business world that gave me the ability to raise my family and live a standard of life that I never dreamed would be possible. If I had not come to Minnesota —who knows? I can't imagine that it would have been any better for me anywhere else. It was a wonderful experience."

Gopher Tombstone:

"I see myself as a very fierce competitor, never giving up hope of a victory. I hope that I demonstrated that during my playing time. I felt like I always expected victory, but I was never discouraged by defeat."

TRIBUTES

"Chuck was such a good, sound ballplayer," said John Kundla. "He was solid with the fundamentals and, not only that, he had such a great shot. He had that jumpshot of his down pat! He was a super guy and a great player. He had a great career at the University and he was a great addition to our Laker teams."

"He had a nice career here with both the Gophers and the Lakers and was just a real good player," said George Mikan.

"I met Chuck as a freshman in Pioneer Hall, and we became roommates and best friends," said John Mayasich. "I really admired him as an individual. He had such a wonderful personality. We were like brothers. We helped each other socially, athletically and academically. He was a great athlete, student, and friend. He exhibits the same traits today, and we're still the best of friends."

There were plenty of reasons for optimism as the University of Minnesota baseball team headed into the 1956 season under Coach Dick Siebert. The Gophers were coming off a respectable 19-9 campaign that previous Spring and had all the necessary confidence to make a legitimate run for the Big Ten title.

The maroon and gold finished the regular season that year with an incredible 33-9 overall record, as well an 11-2 conference mark. They captured the Big Ten title, but didn't stop there. They went on and become the first Golden Gopher baseball team to win the NCAA championship at the College World Series in Omaha.

It was a storybook year that saw the club breeze through its competition and coast into the Mideast Region Semifinals, which were held in Minneapolis. There, the Gophs edged Notre Dame, 4-3, in Game One. They could only manage a 5-5 tie in Game Two, but they rebounded in a big way in Game Three to crush the Irish, 10-1, and take the series. Minnesota kept it going that next week in the Mideast Regional Finals in Athens, Ohio, though, where they swept Ohio, 5-0 and 6-2, to advance to the College World Series.

Gopher Pitchers Jerry Thomas, Rod Oistad and Ron Craven all made big contributions in leading Minnesota to its first national championship. Thomas, an All-American, would appear in three games during the World Series, going 1-1 with two complete games, while Oistad and Craven, meanwhile, would each earn a complete-game victory as well. So, on June 9th, the Gophers opened up the big dance by downing the University of Wyoming, 4-0. In Game Two the Gophs, behind Pitcher Jerry Thomas' three-hit gem, topped Arizona, 3-1. Then, in Game Three, they beat up on Mississippi, 13-5. On the fourth day of tournament play Minnesota just kept on rolling, beating Bradley, 8-3. But then, in the first game of the Finals, the Gophers finally got beat, losing to Arizona, 10-4, in the double-elimination tournament. They rebounded in that next game though, thoroughly pounding the Wildcats, 12-1, to claim their first ever NCAA championship.

The Gophers jumped out to a quick 1-0 lead in that championship game when Bill Horning led off the first inning with a single, stole second, and then scored on a Doug Lindblom double. Minnesota never relinquished the lead after that. Doug Gillen followed with another double and, before you knew it, coach Siebert's boys were up by 3-0. It became 4-0 in the fourth after two walks, plus another Horning single, and 10-0 after a six-run fifth inning where the Gopher bats really came alive. With the score 10-1 in the seventh, Horning belted his second homer of the game to put the final nail in the Wildcat coffin. Along with Horning's four hits, other Gophers who played big in the game included Gillen, McNeeley and David Lindblom, who each had a pair of hits, while

Jack McCartan, Jerry Kindall, R. Anderson and Gene Martin, each added one apiece as well.

Gopher Pitcher Jerry Thomas pitched masterfully, giving up only five hits en route to mowing down four Wildcats, and walking only one. Amazingly, Thomas retired the side 1-2-3 in six of the nine innings and, at the plate, even added two hits for the cause. It was only after an error and a questionable wild pitch that Arizona even got on the board. For his efforts, Thomas, who earlier had also beaten Arizona, 3-1, was selected as the MVP of the Series. After the final out, Siebert rushed out to the mound to give his star pitcher a hero's ride on his shoulders back to the dugout. With the convincing final score of 12-1, the Gophers had won their first ever NCAA baseball championship.

In 1956, Minnesota featured a superb blend of intimidating hitting, dominating pitching, and smooth fielding. Led on the mound by All-American and Tournament MVP Jerry Thomas, who won 12 games that season while going 5-0 in conference games, the Gophers started a string of what would be 11 Big Ten championships and three NCAA titles over coach Siebert's brilliant 31-year career. Leading the way offensively was slugger Jack McCartan, who was not only an All-American third baseman on the baseball team, but was also an All-American goalie on the John Mariucci's Gopher Hockey team. Another key member of that squad was Shorty Cochran, who stole 22 bases that year as well.

The Gophers hit .320 as a team that year while posting an amazing .976 fielding percentage. The conference title ended an 18-year drought for the Gophers, who were typically at an arctic disadvantage geographically against the southern schools, which had the luxury of having longer and more temperate practicing weather.

"You're always prejudiced about your own kids, but I think this was the greatest team that ever played in the College World Series. This was my greatest thrill, barring none," said Coach Siebert on winning his first NCAA crown.

Two weeks later All-American Gopher Shortstop Jerry Kindall, who hit a record 18 home runs that year in Gold Country — a single-season record that would stand for 40 years, turned pro by signing with the Chicago Cubs. (It is interesting to note that Kindall, who would later play with the Twins, would make history some 20 years later when, as head coach of those same Arizona Wildcats, he led his teams to three national titles. In the process, he became the only person ever to play on and coach a College World Series champion.)

The Chief

A native of Fall River, Mass., Dick Siebert began his baseball days at St. Paul Concordia High School and went on to attend Concordia Junior College. From there he moved to the Concordia Seminary in St. Louis with full intentions of becoming a Lutheran minister. But the lure of baseball was too much for the calling of the pulpit, so Dick started his pro baseball career in 1932. Originally a pitcher, Siebert switched over to first base when he developed some arm problems.

He went on to play for Ohio, Pennsylvania, and New York minor league teams, and, in 1935, he joined Buffalo in the International League. Siebert then became a member of the Brooklyn Dodgers system, and later the Chicago Cubs and St. Louis Cardinals systems until 1938, when he became a regular first baseman for the Philadelphia Athletics under the legendary Connie Mack.

Siebert played for the A's through 1945 and even appeared in

TIMELINE

Freeborn County's Burdette Haldorson wins a gold medal on the Olympic Basketball team	South Bend's Dick Meredith wins a Silver medal on the Olympic Hockey team	Minneapolis' Gene Campbell wins a Silver medal on the Olympic Hockey team	Eveleth's John Matchefts wins a Silver medal on the Olympic Hockey team	Eveleth's John Mayasich wins a Silver medal on the Olympic Hockey team	St. Paul's Wendell Anderson wins a Silver medal on the Olympic Hockey team	Eveleth's Willard Ikola coaches the US Olympic Hockey team to a silver medal	The Gopher Baseball team beats the University of Arizona, 12-1, for the NCAA National Championship	First baseman Orlando Cepeda wins the Northern League's Triple Crown with the Class-C St. Cloud Rox

26

the 1942 All Star game. He was chosen as an all-star again in 1945 only to see the game canceled due to wartime restrictions. Siebert later recalled his greatest day in the big leagues was when he broke up a no-hit attempt by Cleveland great Bob Feller. Siebert played in 1,035 games over his big league career and finished with a very respectable .282 lifetime batting average.

Siebert's pro career came to an abrupt end in 1946 due to some unfortunate contract problems with management. He simply traded in his first-baseman's mitt for a microphone when he accepted the position of sportscaster with WTCN radio in Minneapolis. But, only one year later, Siebert would get the baseball itch one more time. This time it was to take over as head coach of the Golden Gophers. (Later he would do radio and television work with WCCO as well.)

Dick took the reigns as the University of Minnesota head coach in 1947 from then-head coach David MacMillan. No one in the school's athletic department could've known it at the time, but they were creating a living legend when they hired him as head baseball coach. The "Chief" would go on to become one of the greatest coaches in college baseball history.

Siebert helped develop baseball at all levels in Minnesota. He was a pioneer and was also credited with introducing the aluminum bat and designated hitter to college baseball as well. As a coach, he emulated many of the mannerisms of his long-time mentor, Connie Mack.

And, while he served as the president of the American College Baseball Coaches Association, twice was named as college baseball's Coach of the Year, and won three NCAA titles, Siebert considered the trouncing of Arizona in the 1956 College World Series and the amazing come-from-behind win over USC in the 1960 Series as his most memorable moments in baseball. He compiled one of the most incredible records in college baseball history. Until 2002, when John Anderson broke his record, Siebert was the winningest coach in Gopher history with a 754-361 record, and a .676 winning percentage.

He is one of only a few coaches at major universities to have coached a team to more than 700 wins. He sent five different teams to the College World Series and, of course, he brought home three titles. His teams also captured 11 Big Ten titles as well. Amazingly, he endured only three losing seasons. He is a member of the College Baseball Hall of Fame and was a recipient of college baseball's highest award, the Lefty Gomez Trophy, which recognizes the individual who has given the most outstanding contribution and service to the development of college baseball.

Siebert coached 31 seasons in Gold Country, and his last season was 1978. Sadly, on December 9, of that same year, the Chief died, succumbing to numerous respiratory and cardiac illnesses. Dick was survived by his wife Marie and their children: Marilyn, Beverly, Richard, and Paul — who went on to play ball in the major leagues with the Mets and Cardinals.

In his last year of life, Siebert was quoted as saying: "I actually expected my coaching job at the U to last a few years and then I would go into business. No one in the world could have convinced me then I would still be here 31 years later. But I loved it, working with great young men and staying active in the best form of baseball I knew, the college game."

On Saturday, April 21, 1979, the University of Minnesota Baseball Stadium was officially renamed "Siebert Field," in honor of their great coach and friend. The entire baseball world mourned his passing, and tributes to the coach poured in from every corner of the baseball world.

For more than three decades, the Chief brought honor and respect to the University of Minnesota baseball program. Dick was a true ballplayer and a real throwback to another era. A tireless worker, his life was consumed with Gopher baseball. The cold weather was no

match for the Chief, because he worked at his craft all-year long. Whether it was from his old Cooke Hall office, or from the fieldhouse, he was always trying to improve and help his teams to win.

He was a man who learned virtually every aspect of the game of baseball throughout his life and chose to teach others what he had to learn mostly on his own. He was a teacher, a coach, a mentor and a friend. We appreciate coach Siebert for all these things, but also, and maybe especially, for the fact that he did so much of it with local home-grown talent. He will be forever thought of as the standard to which all other coaches will be measured against and will go down as one of the best. He was, in every sense, the Chief.

TRIBUTES

"He was a tremendous teacher," said Paul Molitor. "I think baseball at the University of Minnesota was successful under him because of the fact that he knew how to teach college players to be fundamentally sound. He taught us how to execute and gave us a chance to be competitive with any college team in the nation. When you played for the Chief, you were playing for a man with a national reputation. He felt he never had to go out of the state to get his players, and he competed on a national scale. The Chief put a lot of pride in that Minnesota uniform for us."

"Dick Siebert was a great coach, and I really enjoyed my playing days at the University of Minnesota working with him, said Dave Winfield. "I felt that I was as good a hitter as I was a pitcher in college, but they wouldn't let me hit, insisting instead that I become specialized. My friends would come to the games and yell at him, 'Put in Winfield and let him hit, because he's the best hitter you've got!' But it didn't matter how good or bad you were, you had to get out there and work when you played for the Chief. You could be a star on his team, but he played no favorites and treated everyone alike. I learned a lot playing for him."

"Dick Siebert was just a heck of an all-around guy," said Paul Giel. "He was a very fine coach, and I had so much respect for him as a man. He knew the fundamentals of the game so well, but he had a sense of humor and made it fun for you. I learned the game from Dick, and even while I was in the majors, I still felt like he was better than most of the managers that I had. Every person on the team respected him and he got a lot out of his kids."

"When you think about Dick, you don't just think about his record at Minnesota, which is distinction enough in itself," said Jerry Kindall. "But I don't think people realize what he did for college baseball in general. Dick was one of the leaders in restoring good relations with major league baseball. There was a time when there was an antagonistic, very tense, relationship between the colleges and the pros. He overcame that. And he was the biggest expert of all college baseball coaches on the rules of the game too. He served on virtually every committee that college baseball has instituted. I think it's safe to say — and I don't think I'm stretching it at all — that Dick was the most highly respected and honored coach in collegiate baseball."

| Gopher tackle Bob Hobert is named to the All-American football team | Gopher shortstop Jerry Kindall is named to the All-American baseball team | Gopher pitcher Jerry Thomas is named to the All-American baseball team | The St. Paul Saints beat the Minneapolis Millers 4-0 in the last ever game played at Lexington Park Stadium | Duluth's Walter Hoover, considered one of the great oarsmen of his time, coaches the Olympic Rowing team to five medals. | Gopher track & field star, Ron Backes, wins the NCAA National Indoor shot-put Championship | Metropolitan Stadium is completed in a Bloomington cornfield, and the Millers are its first tenant | Gopher track star Fortune Gordien wins a silver medal for the discuss toss in the 1956 Olympics |

TIMELINE

The greatest woman golfer ever to hail from Minnesota has to be Patty Berg. Born in Minneapolis in 1918, Berg's storied career as a golfer began in 1933, when, at the age of 15, she entered her first tournament. It wasn't exactly an auspicious beginning, but since she has accomplished more than any other woman in the history of the game. She is today without question the matriarch of women's golf, as witness to the fact that she was a founder of the LPGA (Ladies Professional Golf Association) in 1949 and having served as its first president.

Berg's career resume is a Who's Who and What's What of women's golf; her list of tournament victories, lifetime achievement awards, honors, and tributes rendered her by organizations within and without the sports world, borders on the incredible. She is indeed a living legend.

In 1940, having won 28 amateur titles, and having decided she wanted to make a career in golf, Berg turned professional. Apart from whatever else her decision may have resulted in, from 1941 through 1962 she won 57 professional tournaments, 15 of which were deemed majors. In all, throughout her career as both an amateur and a professional, she won 85 tournaments.

A standout year for Berg was 1957. Named Woman Athlete of the Year by the Associated Press, she won five tournaments, two of them majors — the Titleholders Championship and the Western Open. Her other victories included the World Championship, the All-America Open, and the Havana Open. With earnings of $16,272, she was that years leading LPGA money-winner. (By way of contrast, today's LPGA leading money-winner earns upwards of several million.) (Interestingly, another Minnesotan, Bev Vanstrum, won a couple of major tournaments on the links that year as well.)

Early on Berg showed signs of being a natural athlete. She played baseball, took part in track and field events, and as a member of the Minneapolis Powderhorn Club even won several national medals as a speed skater. She even played quarterback on her neighborhood football team, called the "50th Street Tigers." Patty was the quarterback because, as she puts it "I was the only one who could remember the plays!" Another famous Minnesota athlete, Bud Wilkinson, was a tackle on that team. Wilkinson, of course, went on to the University of Minnesota where he became an All-American football and hockey player for the Gophers. According to Patty, it was only after Wilkinson suggested she "was too short and too slow, and that there was no future in football for me that I gave it up." Furthermore, her parents wanted her to specialize in a less violent sport, one that didn't tear her clothes. So the freckled-faced tomboy swapped her sneakers for golf shoes.

Patty's father came home one day in 1931 only to find his daughter digging up the back yard with one of his golf clubs. So, Herman Berg, a successful grain merchant, took his 13-year-old daughter to play at the prestigious Interlachen Country Club. It wasn't too long before she was outplaying her father. The kid was just a natural.

Ready to test her new-found skills, patty entered her first ever tournament — the 1933 Minneapolis City Ladies Championship. "I qualified for the last flight with a 122," she recalled. "Then the woman I played in the first round beat me like a drum!"

A self-proclaimed perfectionist, Berg vowed to learn from that experience by going home and practicing for an entire year. "I said I'm going to work, and I'm going to work, and I'm going to see if I can't do better," she said. "And I worked. I concentrated and took my lessons, and finally, a year later, I came back and I won that same Minneapolis City Ladies Championship!"

It was this relentless determination and pride that made her the premier player she was to become.

Patty won the Minnesota state title in 1935, then finished as runner-up to one of her golfing idols, Glenna Collett Vare (the woman for whom the LPGA's low annual scoring average honor is named) in the U.S. Women's Amateur, which was played at Interlachen. Three years later, and in between stints at the University of Minnesota, Patty won the U.S. Women's Amateur title and was also named as the Associated Press' Woman Athlete of the Year.

Patty's father had a big influence on her as she grew up. In many ways her persona as a gallery favorite was shaped by him as he encouraged her both as a player as well as an entertainer.

"I had played nine years of amateur golf, and during that time, when I wasn't in a tournament, my father had me play in a clinic and exhibition every weekend around the state of Minnesota to promote golf," said Patty. "I'd take a popular football player or amateur golfer with me. The local club pro would put it (a clinic) on and we'd hit shots. Dad said that I had to do something for the game, and he felt this was a great idea." On train rides between exhibitions, Patty recalled reciting her favorite poems, particularly "Casey at the Bat," to keep herself busy.

In 1940, after winning 28 amateur titles, including three Titleholders Championships, which were then considered majors, Patty signed a contract with the Wilson Sporting Goods Company. Wilson took advantage of her outstanding communication skills as a motivator and educator by having her give clinics and exhibitions at colleges and universities throughout the country. An already famous woman and only in her early 20s, her name now appeared on several different lines of Wilson golf clubs for women.

In 1941, after winning the Western Open, the Asheville Open, and the Lake Champlain Invitational, Patty was involved in an automobile accident that seriously injured her knee. As a result, she was sidelined for a year and a half. Then in 1943, with the nation at war, Patty enlisted in the Marine Corps, serving as a first lieutenant and doing what she did best — recruiting, public relations, and promotions.

Over the next six years Patty won 15 tournaments including the first-ever Women's National Open Golf Championship, two Westerns, and one Titleholders Championships — all considered major wins. As the first half-century ended, women's golf was gaining momentum, and there were new LPGA tour stops being created across the nation with the prize money increasing annually.

TIMELINE

Gopher goalie Jack McCartan is named to the All-American hockey team	The state's largest Muskellunge is caught by Bena's Art Lyons on Lake Winnibigosh 54 lbs.	The St. Paul Saints historic Stadium, Lexington Park, is demolished	Midway Stadium opens in St. Paul, and the Saints are its first tennent	St. Paul's Thomas Milton is named as the greatest race-car driver of all time by the National Race Board. The first two-time winner of the Indianapolis 500 (1921-22) at one point held 50 racing titles. A winner of 23 national championships in 104 starts, he finished in the top three, 82 times. In 1920 he set a land-speed record of 155 mph that stood for six years.	The Lakers finish tied for first place in the Western Division

Golf's Grande Dame

Throughout the ensuing years Patty was a vital, driving force behind the growing and struggling women's professional golf tour. From 1950 to 1962 she won 41 tournaments, seven of them majors, including four Western and three Titleholder Championships. She also received her third AP Woman Athlete of the Year award in 1955. In 1959 at the U.S. Women's Open at Churchill Valley Country Club in Pittsburgh, she made a hole-in-one, becoming the first woman ever to do so in the event. Her 57 tour victories rank third all-time for women, only behind Kathy Whitworth's 88 and Mickey Wright's 82. A true legend, her amazing stats will stand the test of time.

It must be remembered that Patty Berg once literally dominated women's golf. Accordingly, she has received nearly every major golf award known to the sport. Other accomplishments included setting a world record for a par 72 golf course by shooting a 64 (which stood for 12 years); becoming the LPGA top money winner in 1954, 1955, and 1957; and winning the Vare Trophy (emblematic for the lowest tour scoring average) three times. As an amateur, she also was a two-time member of the U.S. Curtis Cup Team which competed internationally.

Along with being inducted into the LPGA, American, Minnesota, Florida, and PGA Halls of Fame, Patty was formally inducted into the World Golf Hall of Fame at Pinehurst, N.C., in 1974. Her fellow inductees included such legends as Jack Nicklaus, Ben Hogan, Arnold Palmer, Sam Snead, Gary Player, Byron Nelson and Gene Sarazen.

The LPGA even later named one of its top awards after Patty in recognition of attributes that include sportsmanship, diplomacy, goodwill, and overall contributions to the game. Then, in 1995, Patty became the first woman ever to receive the PGA's coveted Distinguished Service Award. It placed her in some fast company alongside such dignitaries as Gerald Ford, Gene Sarazen, Byron Nelson, Arnold Palmer, and Bob Hope.

Patty has won nearly every major award for sports achievement and humanitarianism. What she did for, and gave to, golf is immeasurable. In great demand throughout the U.S. as a speaker, she once was described as having the delivery of "Winston Churchill and FDR rolled into one." And she was sure to give everybody goosebumps at the end of her talks when she said, "God be with you and God Bless America!"

One of Patty's former golf students, fellow LPGA Hall of Famer Kathy Whitworth, recalled, "We all accused Patty of being a frustrated actress. Her clinic was really a staged production. It ran like clockwork. Even though we all knew each line of Patty's, we'd still laugh and get tickled every time we heard her."

In a business relationship that has stretched nearly six decades, the Wilson company eventually rewarded Patty with a lifetime contract. What started as a speaking job for the company evolved into the clinic and exhibition routine she now calls her "golf show." It has been estimated that she alone has entertained several million golfers worldwide at her humorous yet informative instructional clinics and exhibitions. "She has done more to promote golf than any person in the history of the game," said LPGA great Betsy Rawls.

Known for her shot-making ability as well as her showmanship, she will be remembered as one of the game's all-time best. Much of her marvelous iron play and pin-point accuracy can be traced back to the teachings of former University of Minnesota golf coach, Les Bolstad, who advised her for more than 40 years.

"I learned so much from Les over the years," said Patty. "He always told me that I had to learn the golf swing so that I could always teach myself how to conquer my flaws. He also taught me that all the clubs were equal, and one was no more important than another."

"Patty was a colorful performer and drew big crowds," said Bolstad. "She had it right from the start. Champions are a breed apart. They have a little extra stamina, talent, and coordination, plus a will to win. They can do things ordinary mortals can't do. They just stand out. Patty Berg was one of them, and she was a scrapper. She made clutch putt after clutch putt from above the hole to win tournaments."

A Goodwill Ambassador

Patty's name is synonymous with golf in that she has transcended gender and age to become one of the game's great goodwill ambassadors. Undoubtedly she's the best female promoter golf has ever had. And she truly made a difference in the world. One of its most admired and highly respected women, she is a sports role model kids can truly look up to. She was a pioneer, a good friend to all who knew her, and she devoted her entire life to the game she loves. And there's a generous and humanitarian side to her as well, as she continues to give of herself — evidenced by her name on the cancer wing of the Southwest Medical Center in Fort Myers, Florida.

Golf Tombstone:

"I always tried to do the very best that I could, and that way if I ever lost I could always go home and put my head on my pillow still feeling satisfied. I remembered my mistakes and I learned from them. I always kept a journal of my mistakes so that in the off-season I could practice on my flaws. That was part of my will to win — practicing the things that I needed to work on to improve my game every year."

On giving back to the game:

"Golf has been so wonderful to me. In return, I enjoy doing something for it. If I can help somebody play a little better it makes me happy. If I feel that through showing them different shots, and making them laugh a little bit, and putting a few smiles on peoples' faces, well, that makes me happy, too."

What would you change?

"I wouldn't change anything, I couldn't be this lucky twice."

Where are they now?

Today, Patty is just "12-over-par" at the tender age of 84. She is still as active as ever and keeps her game sharp by regularly hitting balls at the practice range. As enthusiastic as ever, she continues to be involved wherever there's a need. She makes speeches, meets with groups of her devoted fans, receives new awards and honors annually, and continues to give her time to junior programs to youngsters who seek her guidance and wisdom. She also lends her name and support to two annual charity tournaments — one for women, the other for men — that raise funds for the American Cancer Society. In addition, Patty is active in the staging of an annual tournament known as the Nolan Henke/Patty Berg Junior Masters. An unofficial junior event, it's played on her home course (Cypress Lake Country Club in Fort Myers) and is entered by 18-and-under boys and girls from around the world.

HALSEY HALL

Halsey Hall was a Minnesota sports institution. With his now trademark line, "Holy Cow!", Halsey became synonymous with the sport of baseball. Hall wasn't just a beloved sports broadcaster though, he was also an accomplished journalist whose first newspaper byline appeared in the Minneapolis Tribune way back in 1919.

And, when Halsey wasn't calling games or writing about them, he was out on the speaking circuit doing sports banquets, where he became a world-class storyteller. Always a sucker for a good cigar and an "occasional" glass of scotch, Halsey was as colorful a character as there was. From his fear of flying to his love of soap operas, he was a classic.

Hall's storied career on the diamond first got going in 1933, when he broadcast his first Minneapolis Millers game at Nicollet Park on WCCO Radio. He would also do play-by-play announcing for Gopher Football games during this era, where he later coined the nickname of "Golden Gophers." In 1961 Hall became a member of the original Minnesota Twins broadcast team, along with Herb Carneal and Ray Scott. He would stay there until 1972, until retiring to focus on public speaking and promotional work. He still was able to do the pre-game ceremonies at Met Stadium though, as he attended every game he could.

Sadly, Halsey died of a heart attack at his home in St. Louis Park on December 30, 1977, at the age of 79. Perhaps his close friend and colleague, Dick Cullum, said it best at his funeral: "Halsey Hall laughed his way through life, and he kept the rest of us laughing, too."

RAY CHRISTENSEN

One name that has become synonymous with Gopher sports is broadcaster Ray Christensen, who, after more than 50 years behind the microphone, decided to finally hang it up in 2001. Christensen's signature voice is synonymous with Golden Gopher basketball and football broadcasts and he is a truly a part of the fabric of life in the state of Minnesota.

Ray called more than 1,300 basketball games and 510 football games for the Maroon and Gold, entertaining and informing us all along the way. With his wonderful play-by-play and color-commentary, Ray became an icon both with WCCO Radio, as well as with the thousands of adoring fans who listened to his broadcasts for more than a half-century.

It was only fitting that in his last year of service with the Gophers that he finally get to witness the Gopher Football team beat Ohio State, in Columbus. It was the first time that the team had beaten the Buckeyes on the road in over half a century, and for Ray it was worth the wait.

Upon retiring in 2001, Ray authored a book about his golden memories entitled appropriately enough, "Gopher Tales." Ray is a real Gopher legend and an all-around great guy.

HERB CARNEAL

As the long-time voice of the Twins, Herb Carneal, has simply become synonymous with Minnesota baseball. After learning the broadcast trade as a young man in Richmond and Syracuse, Herb received his big break in the biz back in 1954, when he got the coveted radio play-by-play gig for both the Philadelphia Athletics and Phillies baseball games. Then, in 1957, Carneal teamed up with his mentor, Ernie Harwell, to do Baltimore Orioles broadcasts. Five years later Herb found himself in sunny Minnesota, and believe it or not, he has been here ever since.

Herb Carneal is one of the most respected sports journalists in the business today and has entertained literally millions of fans over the past four decades. From his strong professional approach to the game, to his wonderful sense of humor, he has simply become an institution throughout the entire Upper Midwest — where countless fans have grown up listening to him. Whether they are out mowing the lawn with a pocket radio or up at the cabin in the boat, when the fans listen to their Twins, it has always been Herb taking them through it pitch by pitch. Through the good times and the bad, Herb has been there for it all. We have let him into our homes and into our hearts, and in return he has entertained us and informed us like no other along the way. In 1996 Herb was given the highest honor a broadcaster can get, when he was awarded the coveted Ford C. Frick Award, for outstanding broadcast journalism. Simply put, Herb Carneal is a true class act and a real gentleman.

THE HOBEY BAKER AWARD: A MINNESOTA HOCKEY TRADITION

Each April the nation's best collegiate hockey player receives the Hobey Baker award, college hockey's equivalent to the Heisman Trophy. The recipient is the player who best exemplifies the qualities that Hobey Baker himself demonstrated as an athlete at Princeton University in the early 1900s. Baker was considered to be the ultimate sportsman who despised foul play, picking up only two penalties in his entire college hockey career. With his speed and superior stick handling, Baker opened up the game of hockey and set new standards for the way the game was meant to be played. A true gentleman, his habit of insisting upon visiting each opponent's locker room after every game to shake their hands became a model for today's players. A hero, Baker gave his life as an American pilot in World War I.

In 1981 Bloomington's Decathlon Club founded the Hobey Baker Memorial Award and each year presents the coveted honor to the nation's top skater. Fittingly, the nation's top hockey state hosts the top hockey player finalists from around the country for the gala event. The club also commissioned a Twin Cities sculptor, Bill Mack, to create their signature trophy. Since the award's inception back in 1981, four University of Minnesota Golden Gopher players and three University of Minnesota Duluth Bulldog players have won it. All were first team All-Americans and all have gone on to play in the NHL.

Year	Player
1981	Neal Broten, Gopher Center
1984	Tom Kurvers, Bulldog Center
1985	Bill Watson, Bulldog Defenseman
1989	Robb Stauber, Gopher Goalie
1994	Chris Marinucci, Bulldog Center
1996	Brian Bonin, Gopher Center
2002	Jordan Leopold, Gopher Defenseman

THE ROETHLISBERGERS: A GYMNASTICS FAMILY DYNASTY

If you want to talk about the history of gymnastics in Minnesota, then you will undoubtedly spend a great deal of time discussing the Roethlisbergers. This family has completely rewritten the record books when it comes to the sport that they love. Father Fred, daughter Marie, and son John are all former Olympians, and each has made giant contributions to the sport. Each was also a tremendous athlete, scholar, and competitor.

John

John is without question the greatest gymnast ever to hail from Minnesota. At the end of his four-year reign at the University of Minnesota, he shattered most every record and took no prisoners along the way. The four-time Big Ten athlete of the year is a five-time NCAA champion, 10-time conference champion, and 15-time All-American. He won three NCAA titles in the all-around competition, one on the parallel bars and another on the pommel horse. The first gymnast in Big Ten history to win four all-around championships, he is also a two-time All-Academic All-American.

In 1993, his senior year, he won the prestigious Nissen Award, presented to the nation's most outstanding senior gymnast based on athletic and academic achievement. A three-time Olympian, he also competed in the 1992 Summer Olympics in Barcelona, the 1996 Summer Games in Atlanta and the 2000 Summer Games in Sydney.

Marie

Marie is arguably the most decorated female athlete in Minnesota history. She became the first female University of Minnesota gymnast ever to win an NCAA championship as well as the first to earn a spot on the US Olympic team. Incredibly, the four-time All-American did it all despite having to overcome a partial hearing loss she suffered as a young girl caused by spinal meningitis. In 1990, her senior year at gold country, she won the uneven bars title at the NCAA championships. The same year Marie earned the NCAA's highest accolade when she became the first Minnesota athlete to be named as an NCAA Top Six recipient, awarded to the country's top six athletes.

Marie was named as the Big Ten gymnast of the year from 1987 to 1989, earned All-Big Ten All-Academic honors for three straight years, and also received the Big Ten Medal of Honor. In 1984 she earned a spot the US Olympic team set to compete in Los Angeles, but unfortunately an injury prevented her from competing. She did, however, compete on the 1985 US World Championship team. She graduated in 1990 and went on to become a physician.

Fred

Fred is the modern patriarch of men's gymnastics in Minnesota. For more than a quarter century, the head coach has been responsible for much of the success of the University of Minnesota men's gymnastics program. A former star at the University of Wisconsin, Fred went on to win the school's Athlete of the Year Award in 1966. He earned his bachelor's degree that same year and his master's in 1970. At the 1968 Olympic Games in Mexico City, Fred was the second-highest scorer on the U.S. team. He also captained the 1967 Pan American team in Winnipeg, where he won gold medals in the all-around, horizontal bar and parallel bars.

During his coaching tenure, which has spanned more than a quarter century, the Gophers have won 11 Big Ten team titles. In addition, his teams have placed in the Top 10 in the nation a total of 16 times, finishing second, by a mere tenth of a point in 1990. He is a four-time Big Ten Coach of the Year, five-time Mideast Region Coach of the Year, and four-time U.S. Gymnastics Federation Coach of the Year. An assistant on the 1992 U.S. Olympic team, he also coached the 1994 World Gymnastics Championship Team that competed in Germany. In 1990, he was inducted into the U.S. Gymnastics Hall of Fame as a gymnast, coach, and contributor.

The remarkable baseball history of the minor league Minneapolis Millers goes way back to the good old days at Athletic Park in the late 1880s, then over to Nicollet Park in the early half of the century, and finally ends at Metropolitan Stadium in the 1960. The late '50s were the golden years for the Millers, highlighted by two Junior World Series titles in 1955 and 1958, as well as a legendary runner-up finish against Fidel Castro and the Havana Sugar Kings in the series of 1959.

No good story would be complete without a rival, and the Millers' cross-town counterparts were the St. Paul Saints, who were the Brooklyn Dodgers' triple-A farm club. The Millers-Saints rivalry was a legendary one that often featured weekend double-headers at each stadium. Fans would take the trolley between the games from Nicollet Park in Minneapolis to Lexington Park in St. Paul, cheering all the way. A lot of Hall of Fame players played for the Millers over the years on their way to the big leagues, including the likes of Willie Mays, Carl Yastrzemski, and the great "Teddy Ballgame," Ted Williams.

In 1955, the Minneapolis Millers celebrated their ninth American Association pennant en route to winning their first ever Junior World Series title against the International League champion, Rochester Red Wings. They were led by the Association's MVP, Shortstop Rance Pless, and wins leader, Pitcher Al Worthington. The 1955 Junior World Series saw the last game ever played at old Nicollet Park near Lake Street and Nicollet Avenue, however, as the Millers moved outside the city to the newly constructed Metropolitan Stadium in Bloomington that next season.

Two years later, when the Giants moved to San Francisco, the Millers were moved to Phoenix, Arizona, where they became the "Phoenix Giants." To fill the vacancy though, the San Francisco Seals (a Boston Red Sox farm team) were moved to Minneapolis to fill the void. The "new" Millers then hit the field with a feisty player/manager by the name of Gene Mauch and a first base coach by the name of Jimmie Foxx — a future Hall of Famer. In addition, the Millers were blessed with a 19-year-old rookie by the name of Orlando Cepada that year, who would go on to become a Hall of Famer as well.

Gene Mauch, who was the team's manager and second baseman in 1958, led his ballclub to a third place finish in the American Association with a record of 82-71. Even so, things looked promising for the young club as they steamrollered into the playoffs, where they knocked off Wichita right out of the gates.

From there they proceeded to upset Denver in the next round, and with that they found themselves right back in the Junior World Series. Their opponent this time would be the mighty Montreal Royals, who were led by a young pitcher named Tommy Lasorda. The Millers took Games One and Two, 6-2 and 7-2, followed by Game Three, 3-2. Then, in Game Four, the Millers completed the sweep by downing the Royals in their own backyard, 7-1, to claim their second Junior Series Championship in just three years. It was a truly amazing season for the new ballclub.

"I remember sweeping Montreal four in a row and winning it all in 1958," said Mauch years later. "I was still playing and managing at that point, and it was a pretty special championship for me. That year was great, and I even still have the pennant from when we won that series."

Now, while the Millers were kings of the world in 1958, the 1959 squad is an even better story. That year the Millers finished second in their division with an impressive 95-57 record. They then opened the playoffs against Omaha, where the series went back and forth until both teams had split two games apiece. Then, back home at the Met for the fifth game of the series, the Millers newest recruit, who had just been activated before the game, scored the game-winning run in the bottom of the tenth inning. His name was Carl Yastrzemski. (Like Ted Williams had done 22-years earlier, "Yaz" spent a season in Minneapolis playing triple-A ball, before heading to Boston, where, ironically, the Hall of Famer would succeed the great Ted Williams in the outfield.)

The game was officially protested by Omaha, who challenged Yaz's series eligibility. The Omaha officials were proved to be right, and with that, the league president ordered the game replayed. So, even without the services of Yaz, the Millers went out and still won the next game, to take the series. Led by their feisty manager, Gene Mauch, they went on to beat the Fort Worth Cats for the league title, earning a trip to the Junior World Series against the Havana Sugar Kings. (Incidentally, Fort Worth was led by a couple of Minnesotans in former Gopher Jerry Kindall and former Mankato State star Bob Will.)

This Junior World Series would prove to be one of the most amazing spectacles in sports history. The first two games were played at Metropolitan Stadium, but because of freezing weather and even some snow, Game Three was moved to sunny Havana. During the first two games of the series, the Sugar Kings, not quite used to Minnesota's balmy climate, could be seen in their dugout guzzling hot coffee and huddling around a fire they had lit in a trash can to stay warm. An early highlight was a two-run-homer hit by Mauch's brother-in-law, Roy Smalley, Sr., in a 6-5 Game Two victory. (Smalley's son, Roy Jr., would subsequently go on to play a key role in Twins' history.)

Now, Cuba in 1959 was no longer a tropical paradise. The Cuban Missile Crisis and Bay of Pigs were just around the corner, and this area of the world was practically a military state. They loved their baseball though and the five games played in Havana drew more than 100,000 fans, not counting the thousands of Castro's gun-toting soldiers, who were stationed throughout the stadium. Down three games to one, the Millers rallied in the series and won Games Five and Six.

With the series tied at three games apiece, the stage was now set for the much anticipated Game Seven. (Stew Thornley captured the scene best in his book "On to Nicollet") As Fidel, a former pitcher himself, made his entrance to the game, he walked by the Millers' bullpen with his hand on his revolver and said to the Minneapolis pitchers, "Tonight we win..." It was looking great for the Millers as they built a two-run lead going into the eighth, but Havana came back. They evened it up in the eighth, and then in the bottom of the ninth, Havana's Don Morejon ripped a liner into center field. Raul Sanchez,

TIMELINE

| Williams Arena hosts the first NCAA Hockey Championship ever played outside of Colorado Springs | Gopher goalie Jack McCartan is named to the All-American hockey team | Gopher third baseman Jack McCartan is named to the All-American baseball team | Gopher center Mike Pearson is named to the All-American hockey team | Gopher winger Dick Burg is named to the All-American hockey team | Gopher halfback Francis "Pug" Lund is inducted into the College Football Hall of Fame | St. Paul's Michael Gibbons, known as the Phantom, is inducted into the Boxing Hall of Fame. The uncrowned king of the welter weights and middleweights, was named the greatest Minnesota boxer for the first 50 years of the 20th century. |

32

who was on second, then rounded third and slid home ahead of Umphlett's throw to score what proved to be the winning run. The crowd erupted as the Sugar Kings had won the Junior World Series crown. The Millers came home dejected, but happy to be alive!

"I imagine it was about as gripping a time as I had ever experienced," said Mauch, who first met Castro when the two played together in the Cuban winter league in 1951 and knows him personally to this day. "It was standing room only every night," he added. "Fifteen minutes before game time, Castro would come walking in through center field with his entourage. Every fan rose and waved a white handkerchief and yelled 'Fidel,' 'Fidel!' Then he would come sit down behind home-plate. No baseball player in history was ever greeted the way he was greeted down there. About half of my players were afraid to win the title game because there were Cuban soldiers on the bench with loaded rifles and bayonets. In fact you couldn't get from the batters box to the dugout without wading through 50 to 100 soldiers. A lot of my players were fearful, and wanted to get the hell out of there, I know that. The whole thing was quite an experience."

On October 27, 1960, it was announced that Calvin Griffith was moving his Washington Senators to Minnesota. As a result, major league baseball would mean the end of the Millers and Saints. One golden era of baseball was over, but the Twins would start another.

A Managerial Icon

Gene Mauch was born in Salina Kan., on November 18, 1925. At the age of 13, his family moved to Los Angeles. Gene grew up playing sports and in high school played football, baseball and basketball. He had the opportunity to attend USC or Stanford on football and baseball scholarships, but instead went into the service where he became an air cadet. After the service, he went back to his true love, baseball.

From there he would go on to play a total 16 seasons in the major leagues. He first started out playing ball in Durham, in 1943, and from there the list of cities is long: Montreal, Brooklyn, St. Paul, Pittsburgh, Indianapolis, Chicago (AL & NL), Boston (AL & NL), St. Louis, Milwaukee, Atlanta, Los Angeles, and finally the Minneapolis Millers, where he retired as an active player. He had a career .239 batting average, nothing to write home about, but solid nonetheless.

Gene started managing at the age of 27 with the Atlanta Crackers in the Southern Association. He continued to manage with the Millers and got his big break in 1960 when he took over for the Phillies. He stayed in Philadelphia until 1968, when he left to guide the expansion Montreal Expos.

Mauch then managed the Twins from 1976-80, posting a career record of 378-394. From there he went on to guide the Angels, until finally hanging it up for good in 1987. He is among a select fraternity of big-league skippers on the all-time seniority list, having managed for more than three decades. He also holds the dubious distinction of managing the most years (26) without winning a pennant.

Mauch was an intense competitor, and a great ambassador of baseball. He played when it was still a game and was a true throw-back to another era. He will be forever remembered as an integral thread in the fabric of Minnesota's baseball history.

On the Twins:

"It was a wonderful experience. I worked with some great, great people: Calvin Griffith, Rod Carew, Tony Oliva, Larry Hisle, Lyman Bostock, Butch Wynegar, and my nephew, Roy Smalley. I mean being able to have the opportunity to manage guys like Rod Carew and Tony Oliva, I felt like my time in Minnesota wasn't a job, it was a privilege."

Any Regrets?

"Originally, when I came to Minneapolis, I thought that I would even-

tually go on to become the manager of the Red Sox, because we were their triple-A farm club. One of the biggest disappointments of my life came in 1959, when Boston didn't name me to be their manager. Bucky Harris, the Red Sox G.M., said I was too young and didn't think that I would be able to handle guys like Ted Williams, who, at the time, was older than I was. Not being able to manage some of those kids like Carl Yastrzemski, who played for me up in Minneapolis, with the Millers, was a real disappointment."

On the Fans of Minnesota

"I loved the people up there, they were just outstanding, super people, and were just wonderful to me. Hell, they even gave me a new car! I was just so intrigued by Minnesota and was really thinking of moving there. I still maintain close relationships with a lot of people from that area."

Millers and Twins Tombstones:

"There were guys in baseball, such as Casey Stengel and Joe Cronin, whom I thought so much of and had so much respect for. But now when you mention their names, no one even knows who the hell you're talking about. So it seems like kind of a superfluous thought. Why should you even worry about being remembered?"

TRIBUTES

"We went through some tough times together in 1977 and 1978, when the fans were on us about nepotism," said his nephew, Roy Smalley, Jr. "It was a difficult situation, but it was also a great situation to be in, at the same time, because we were able to be together. I learned that being successful takes care of everything, and once I realized that, everything took care of itself. We have a lot of love and respect for each other. He was one of my heroes growing up. I've played for 15 managers throughout my career, and there was nobody that could hold a candle to him. He was just the best. I learned more baseball in my time with him than with all the rest combined. He was the best prepared, best tactical, and best teaching manager I've ever been around. I can't imagine a better manager in the game, ever."

"Gene was one of the best managers that I ever played for," said Rod Carew. "He could really get the best out of his players and teach them the correct way to play the game. We both had tremendous respect for each other, even to this day. I knew that if I ever had any problems on or off the field, I felt comfortable enough that I could always go in and talk with him, and he would always help me through it. He was a great person."

"He managed a long, long time, and he was a great manager," said Tony Oliva. "He was very serious about his job, and he wanted to win no matter what. He knew a lot about the game and was just a great person to be around."

"I liked Gene very much," added Harmon Killebrew. "I thought he was a very good manager and certainly an intense guy. When he was managing the Twins, he asked me to come back to the club to help out as a hitting instructor, and I was grateful for that."

The only good thing that came from the Lakers finishing in the cellar, in 1957 was that they would now get the first pick in the college draft. They needed a miracle, and, incredibly, that's just what they got. Their savior, was none other than Elgin Baylor, a flashy young six-foot-five rookie small forward out of the University of Seattle, who, as the nation's leading rebounder, had just taken his Seattle Chieftains to the NCAA Finals, where they eventually lost to Kentucky. Blessed with the ability to somehow hang in mid-air, he would become known as the league's first sky-walker, long before the likes of Dr. J. and Air Jordan.

It was not going to be easy to sign the kid though. Baylor had publicly stated his intention to complete his senior year at Seattle and not enter the NBA draft. But with draft day nearing, and the Minneapolis franchise's future in doubt, team owner Bob Short opted to gamble and drafted Baylor with his first pick, eventually signing him after month of negotiating. Short was later quoted as saying that if Baylor had turned him down, the club would have "gone out of business and declared bankruptcy." The NBA had put the Lakers on financial probation and specified that if the club didn't average at least $6,600 in gate receipts for home games, the league would have the power to take over the team. All that changed, however, as the fans poured into the Minneapolis Auditorium to see their new phenom.

Baylor, who started opposite Forward Vern Mikkelsen, was joined by Center Larry Foust and Guards Dick Garmaker and "Hot Rod" Hundley — giving Johnny Kundla's Lakers a solid starting five. Baylor was also joined by new teammates Alex "Boo" Ellis, and the six-foot-eight Steve Hamilton, who would later go on pitch for the New York Yankees as their ace-lefty out of the bullpen. The Lakers came together late in the season to post a marginal 33-39 record — good enough for second place in the West and a trip to the post-season.

Baylor wasted little time in making his presence known in the NBA by becoming the first rookie ever to garner MVP honors at the All-Star Game. Another highlight from the regular season came near the tail end, when the Lakers played Boston in a real barn-burner. By the time the dust had settled in this one, the Celtics had beaten Minneapolis by the final score of 173-139 — which was good for a new NBA record in total points.

From there they beat Detroit, two games to one, in the first round of the playoffs. Now, the 1959 NBA Finals were supposed to feature the two best teams in the NBA that year, Boston and St. Louis, in what would've been their third-straight meeting for the championship. However, in the West, the Baylor-led Lakers knocked off the defending world champs from St. Louis in the conference finals. The Hawks had won two of three to start the series against the Lakers, but Minneapolis won the final three by the scores

of: 108-98, 98-97 (in overtime at St. Louis), and 106-104, back in Minneapolis, to set the stage for the mighty Celtics. It wouldn't be easy though, as the team had lost 18 straight against the Beantowners, and, to make matters worse, Elgin was nursing a badly bruised knee.

The rejuvenated Lakers quickly realized that Red Auerbach's squad, which featured Bill Russell, Bob Cousy, Tommy Heinsohn, Bill Sharman and Frank Ramsey, was going to be a handful. Owner Bob Short even tried to motivate his players by offering them presents such as new sets of tires and sport coats if they won the championship. While that might have spared Johnny Kundla from any Knute Rockne-like motivational speeches that he had to deliver to get his players ready to play the mighty Celtics, it certainly didn't help much.

With that, the Celtics came out and sent a message to Minneapolis right out of the gates, spanking them in Games One and Two, 118-115 and 128-108, respectively. By the time the series had returned back to Minneapolis, it was all but over. The Celtics were dominant and took no prisoners. After a Celtics' victory in Game Three back in Minnie, 123-110, the Lakers decided to make Game Four interesting. Two nights later, on April 9th, Baylor and Bob Leonard combined to give the Lakers a brief 95-93 lead early in the fourth quarter, but Boston clinched the series with a 118-113 victory thanks to Bill Sharman's phenomenal outside shooting. Baylor had 30 points, while Leonard finished with 21, but it was too little too late. Even though they kept the margins of victory to within less than five points for three of the games, the Celtics were able to sweep the Championship Series four games to none. It was the first time ever that an NBA Finals would end in a sweep, and for the Celtics, it was their first of eight straight world titles.

For the season Mikkelsen averaged 13.8 points and 7.9 rebounds while Foust contributed 13.7 points and 8.7 rebounds, but Baylor was the real star, leading the team in nearly every offensive category en route to averaging 25 points, 15 rebounds and four assists per game. For his amazing efforts he was named as the NBA's Rookie of the Year, earned All-Star Game MVP honors, and was named as a first team All-Pro. He also finished third, behind Bill Russell and Bob Pettit, in the Player of the Year voting as well.

"My rookie year with the Lakers was a great one for me," said Baylor. "Being the number one player chosen in the draft, playing on the NBA All-Star team, and just to be playing in the NBA was wonderful. The reception by my teammates in Minneapolis was great, and I was accepted and treated like one of them right away. The year before the team had finished in last place, so it was a thrill because no one thought we would get close to the Finals. We beat the defending world champion St. Louis Hawks to win the West, and we were all very proud of our accomplishments that season. Minneapolis had a good year, made a great run, and a lot of wonderful things happened that season, but the Celtics had a better team, and they beat us."

The Original Sky-Walker

Born in Washington D.C., Elgin Baylor went on to star at Washington's Springarn High School. From there he then opted to first attend the College of Idaho in 1954 on a football scholarship. There, after being noticed by the school's basketball coach, he joined the squad and led the team to a 23-4 record while averaging 31 points and 20 rebounds per game. The following season Elgin transferred to Seattle University and, after sitting out the year because of the NCAA

TIMELINE

Zack Wheat, a Minneapolis Miller in 1928, is inducted into the Baseball Hall of Fame

The Millers host the American Association All-Star Game

Gopher winger, Murray Williamson is named to the All-American hockey team

St. Paul's Jeanne Arth, a St. Thomas University graduate, wins the doubles tennis championship at Wimbledon. She was also a two-time U.S. doubles champion, and seven-time Minnesota State Open champion.

Two NFL Cardinals games are played at the Met. The purpose was to see if the Minnesota fans were excited about the possibility of pro football coming to town.

Former Gopher Francis "Pug" Lund is named to Sports Illustrated's Silver Anniversary team. The All-America halfback, who ran, passed and kicked, was the Big Ten's MVP in 1934 and led the Gophers to their first national championship that same year. Bernie Bierman called him "the best player he ever coached."

34

transfer rule, led Seattle to a 22-3 record. Elgin, who pulled down 508 rebounds and averaged 30 points per game that year, went on to average 32.5 points and 559 rebounds per game that next year.

Although the top-rated senior in college basketball was Indiana's Archie Dees, Seattle University's Elgin Baylor was the player every team wanted. Elgin, who led the nation in rebounding in 1957, had taken his Seattle Chieftains to the 1958 NCAA Finals before eventually losing to Kentucky.

The All-American had publicly stated his intention to complete his senior year at Seattle and not enter the NBA draft. But the Lakers rolled the dice and drafted him anyways. He was later signed and proved to be the savior of the franchise. His popularity was amazing and he wound up becoming one of the team's biggest fan-favorites.

So good was Baylor that the next season, when he got called to fulfill his military commitment in the Army Reserve Medical Corps training program in San Antonio, the team moved its entire training camp to Texas so that he wouldn't miss a beat! The team even hired John Castellani, who had been Baylor's coach at Seattle University, that next year to replace the retired Johnny Kundla.

And, ironically, while Baylor may have saved the Minneapolis Laker franchise from going out of business in 1959 by leading his club back to the NBA Finals, in the process he also helped the team become good enough to become marketable. With the team on the rise, Lakers Owner Bob Short moved the franchise to Los Angeles in 1960. Minnesota wouldn't see NBA action again for another 29 years, until the Timberwolves came to life.

Baylor was more than the first of the great skywalkers, he was an explosive scorer whose career scoring average is exceeded only by Wilt Chamberlain and Michael Jordan. Baylor used his body control and unbelievable creativity like no other before him. His Laker career stats from 1958-1972 included averaging: 27.4 PPG, 13.5 RPG, 4.3 APG, and he was a 10-time All-NBA first teamer. Baylor also appeared in 11 All-Star games and was named the league's MVP in 1959. He even still holds the NBA All-Star game record for most career free throws attempted (98) and made (78). Baylor was named to the NBA's 35th Anniversary All-Time Team in 1980 and was enshrined in the Basketball Hall of Fame in 1976.

He is also considered among the greatest rebounders for his size the NBA has ever known, posting-up any big man. He could pass and dribble with the best guards in the league, and his speed made him a stellar defender. Baylor, who teamed with Jerry West to form one of the most feared scoring duos in NBA history, retired early in the 1971-72 season due to nagging knee injuries. Ironically, the Lakers won the NBA championship that year, an achievement that somehow eluded him over his amazing career. He was undoubtedly the greatest NBA player never to win a title. His Los Angeles teams lost in the Finals seven times in 11 years and three of them were decided in seventh games with the Celtics, which the Lakers lost by a combined total of seven points.

"It was really exciting for me to be a Minneapolis Laker," said Baylor. "In college I never thought about playing professionally. The only thing I thought about was being able to go to college. Growing up, I knew my family could not afford to send me to college, so I really hoped that I could just get a scholarship either in football or basketball. Then, to be able to play for Minneapolis was very special to me. The honor, the pride, and the glory of just being a pro in the sport of basketball was great. Playing with and against the best players in the world was tremendous. All the traveling, meeting people, and making friends was all very special to me. I loved Minneapolis. It still is a great city and the people there were great to me."

Baylor may be best remembered most for his unbelievable driving, twisting, lay-ups which featured spectacular mid-air antics.

The terms "hang time" and "body control" became synonymous with him. He was also known for following his own shot, and it has been said that if that statistic would have been kept, he may very well hold the NBA record for scoring the most points off of his own put-backs. Often, during the course of a tight game, when the Lakers really needed him, he would switch from the forward to guard or even center, whatever the situation warranted. And, when the opposition was engaged in a full-court press, Baylor was the only one trusted to bring the ball upcourt.

Elgin has even been called the father of the modern aerodynamic game. Boston Celtic great Bob Cousy remembers: "Elgin was the first one who would go up for the jump shot, hang up there for 15 seconds, have some lunch and a cup of coffee, and [then] decide to shoot the thing. Elgin was that spectacular. He was the first guy who literally couldn't be stopped."

After basketball Baylor went on to become the Head Coach of the Utah Jazz before settling down as the long-time General Manager of the Los Angeles Clippers. Elgin and his wife Elaine have two daughters and a son and reside in the Los Angeles area.

Laker Tombstone:
"A person who cared about other people and cared about his profession. I felt like I gave it all that I had and I played as hard as I could."

TRIBUTES

"I can't say enough about Elgin," said John Kundla. "He could play an entire game without getting tired because he had more stamina than any player I ever saw. He was a tremendous all-around ballplayer. He could just hang up in the air and he could do it all — passing, shooting, dribbling, jumping and defending. He was just great. His first year with us was so terrific and right away I knew he was one of the best all-around athletes I ever saw play the game of basketball. One time, he scored 50 points in a game off of only two field goals he shot from the outside. His other points came off of rebounds and put-backs. He was a truly special player."

"My last year with the Minneapolis Lakers was Elgin's first, and we were kind of a rag-tag bunch when he came in as a rookie," said Vern Mikkelsen. "Coach Kundla wanted me, as team captain, to teach Elgin about how to play the pro game. He didn't need any teaching. Elgin had a pocket full of press clippings, and he was the best there was to came out of college at that time. I could tell he was in a class by himself. He had all the ability in the world and became such a fabulous player. But, at first, he was also kind of a loner, and we couldn't really get him into being a part of our bunch. Later he joined the poker-playing group of players called the 'dead-enders,' which consisted of Dick Garmaker, Hot Rod Hundley, Slick Leonard and I. Garmaker used to say that he would pick Elgin up at his house and bring him to the airport for the road games because he didn't want any chance of him missing the plane. Dick even said that he made more money off Elgin in poker than he made in salary! He had a wonderful career with the Lakers, both in Minneapolis and LA, and he is a great person."

The Gophers opened the 1960 season by beating the No. 2 ranked Nebraska Cornhuskers, 26-14, in Lincoln. Quarterback Sandy Stephens led the charge in this one, running three yards for one touchdown while passing for another. That following week Minnesota spanked Indiana, 42-0, and the Gophers won their third straight over Northwestern that next Saturday, 7-0. Tom Brown led the defensive surge to shut-out the Wildcats, while Stephens' lone four-yard touchdown run was enough to give Minnesota the victory. Next up were the Illini, a team Minnesota would hang on to beat, 21-10, on a fourth quarter rally as Stephens came in to cap a 66-yard game-winning scoring drive with a nine-yard touchdown — his third on the day.

At 4-0, Minnesota was starting to gain some respect in gridiron circles. They would make some more believers that next week, when they blanked a very good Michigan team, 10-0, at Ann Arbor, to reclaim the Little Brown Jug. The Gophers forced five fumbles that day and held the Wolverines to just 76 yards rushing and 68 yards passing. Jim Rogers finally capped a 44-yard scoring drive when he ran in what would prove to be the game-winner from the two yard line.

Kansas State then fell to the Gophers, 48-7, setting up an epic showdown between the suddenly No. 2 ranked Gophers and the No. 1 ranked Iowa Hawkeyes. Forest Evashevski's Hawks had owned the Gophers over the last five years, surrendering just 21 points over that time period. More than 65,000 Gopher fans somehow jammed into 53,000-seat Memorial Stadium on that November 5th to see history as the Gophers beat the Hawks, 27-10. The hero of the game was Outland Trophy winner Tom Brown, who played like an animal. "Brownie" had been stuffing the Hawkeye linemen all day and was just dominating both sides of the line. On one particular third-down play, with the ball on the Gopher five-yard line, Brown fired through the line just as the ball was snapped and knocked the center into the quarterback, who then flew back into the fullback — pancaking all three of them on their butts for a five-yard loss. After that game Brown proudly hoisted the Floyd of Rosedale trophy over his head for all to see.

With the big win, Minnesota found itself as the No. 1 team in the land. That's when last-place Purdue came to town and wrecked everything, upsetting the Gophers, 28-14. Down, but not out, the Gophers traveled to Wisconsin for the final game of the regular season with a Big Ten title and possible Rose Bowl berth laying in the balance. Minnesota "rose" to occasion that afternoon though, scoring a pair early and a pair late, as their top-rated defense shut down the Badgers to secure a 26-7 victory.

By now the Gophers found themselves at the top of both the AP and UPI final polls, declaring them as consensus national champions for the first time in two decades. And, although they had a better record, the Gophers had to share the Big Ten title with Iowa. This was due to the fact that their early rout of Indiana, who was on probation for recruiting violations, did not count in the final standings. Fittingly, Murray Warmath was named as Coach of the Year.

With their Big Ten title, their first in two decades, the Gophers would now have to sit back and wait to find out if, and where, they would be spending New Year's Day. You see, at the time, the Big Ten-Pacific Coast Rose Bowl pact was not in effect, which therefore allowed the PAC-10 champion, Washington, to choose its opponent. Luckily, they chose Minnesota, and the Gophers were off to Pasadena to face the Huskies in their first-ever Rose Bowl.

Once there, the Gophers were showered by well-wishers who simply couldn't get enough of this Cinderella story. When the game got going though, it became a different tale. Washington, unlike the star-struck Gophers, had been there before, crushing Wisconsin just the year before by the final of 44-8.

Nearly 100,000 fans were on hand to watch what would later be considered to be a tale of two halves. The game got underway with the Huskies scoring early on a 34-yard field goal by George Fleming. From there they went on to score a pair of touchdowns in the second quarter, thanks in large part to the efforts of Husky Quarterback Bob Schloredt, who threw for one and ran in the other from 31-yards out to give his squad a 17-0 half-time lead.

The Gophers, meanwhile, could muster just two first downs the entire half, while Stephens' interception didn't help much either. It was a different story in the second though, as the Gophers came out and rallied behind a Bob Deegan fumble recovery which set up an 18-yard touchdown pitch from Stephens to Munsey. Minnesota threatened to get back in the game by driving to the Washington six-yard line midway through the fourth, but were held when Stephens was blitzed for a 13-yard loss. The Gophers then tried a little razzle-dazzle by going for a fake field-goal on fourth-down, but came up short when Stephens, the holder, pulled up and threw an interception on a pass intended for Tom Hall at the Husky one yard line. The Gophers got the ball back late, but were unable to get past the 35-yard line. Washington added a field goal to ice it, and the Gophers, who ended the game with 60 more total yards than did the Huskies, came up on the short side of a 17-7 game.

"We didn't play as well as we could, and on that day we played one of the best football teams I've seen in 18 years at Minnesota," Coach Warmath would later say. "But as the game wore on, we started coming on fast and they were fading. Another 15 minutes and we maybe would have won."

"We made some stupid mistakes in that Rose Bowl game, but we knew we had a good team," said Stephens. "After the game, I recall that I had never felt so bad after losing. However, it was a fantastic experience for me. The Rose Bowl was everything I thought it would be and more. The whole first half we were sort of awe struck, but the second half we were ready to play. I think they only got one first down in the entire second half, and that was off a long quarterback sneak. We just couldn't get any offensive momentum going at that point, and we couldn't overcome Washington. I don't want to take anything away from the Huskies, they were a fine team. But they were just a better football team on that day. We lost the game, but were still national champions, and they can't take that away from us."

Despite losing the Rose Bowl, the Gophers still remained as National Champs, due to the fact that the voting was done prior to the

Zack Wheat, a Minneapolis Miller in 1928, is inducted into the Baseball Hall of Fame	The Millers host the American Association All-Star Game	Gopher winger, Murray Williamson is named to the All-American hockey team	St. Paul's Jeanne Arth, a St. Thomas University graduate, wins the doubles tennis championship at Wimbledon. She was also a two-time U.S. doubles champion, and seven-time Minnesota State Open champion.	Two NFL Cardinals games are played at the Met. The purpose was to see if the Minnesota fans were excited about the possibility of pro football coming to town.	Former Gopher Francis "Pug" Lund is named to Sports Illustrated's Silver Anniversary team. The All-America halfback, who ran, passed and kicked, was the Big Ten's MVP in 1934 and led the Gophers to their first national championship that same year. Bernie Bierman called him "the best player he ever coached."

post-season. That wasn't the only award the team would win either as Bobby Bell and Tom Brown each earned All-American honors. Brown, who also received the Outland Trophy, as the best interior lineman in the nation, went on to be named as the Big Ten MVP, and even finished as the runner-up in the Heisman Trophy voting — a first for a lineman.

A True Trailblazer

Sandy Stephens grew up in Uniontown, Pa., where his parents encouraged him in his academic and athletic endeavors. Upon high school graduation, more than 50 colleges and universities, eight from the Big Ten alone, recruited him. Sandy felt pretty strong about his football roots: "We always felt that those of us who lived in Western Pennsylvania had the best high school football in the country, bar none — including Ohio and Texas too!"

Stephens was a tremendously gifted all-around athlete, earning nine letters in football, basketball and track. He garnered high school All-American honors in football, was an All-State basketball player, and, although he never played high school baseball, was a good enough pitcher and centerfielder to be romanced by several major league baseball teams — including his home state Philadelphia Phillies, who drafted him out of high school.

With assurances that he would be given a shot at quarterback, as well as the opportunity to play baseball, Stephens enrolled at the University of Minnesota in the fall of 1958. So did an old friend and high school rival from Clairton, Pa., who would be his roommate for the next four years, Running Back Judge Dickson. In so doing, the two became pioneers for all young African American men who wanted to play college athletics in the predominantly white northern schools.

Still considered by many to be one of the top five all-time greatest players ever to wear the Maroon and Gold, Sandy is a football legend in Gold Country. From 1959-1961, he threw for nearly 1,500 yards. For his career he still remains fifth on the all-time career rushing touchdowns list with 20, and twice he led the team in punting. In 1961, Sandy led the Gophers to their second consecutive Rose Bowl and defeated UCLA by the score of 21-3. He also led the team in rushing that year with 534 yards while throwing for nine touchdown passes as well. For his efforts in leading the conference with 1,151 yards of total offense that year, he was named the Big Ten MVP, an All-American (first-ever black man ever to be so honored), College Back of the Year and the Los Angeles Times Back of the Year. He also finished fourth in the balloting for the Heisman Trophy as well.

After college, Sandy was drafted in the first round by the New York Titans of the American Football League. "At the time," Sandy said, "the Titans didn't want a black man playing quarterback. Cleveland had my NFL rights, but the NFL still wasn't ready for a black quarterback. So, I was forced to play in Canada." With the promise that he would be given a chance to play quarterback, Sandy then went north of the border to the Montreal Alouettes. Montreal had finished last in the Canadian Football League the year before, but their rookie quarterback Stephens led the Als to the CFL Finals.

After three years in Canada, Sandy's life was abruptly changed when he was involved in a nearly fatal car accident. The doctors said that he wasn't supposed to ever walk again, but Sandy was determined. In 1964, Sandy's old teammate and friend, Bobby Bell, asked his Chiefs coach, Hank Stram, to give his old friend a shot at a comeback. Sandy overcame the odds and went on to play with Kansas City for two seasons, both as a defensive halfback as well as a quarterback. He retired from the game in 1970.

In 1997, Sandy was inducted into the Rose Bowl Hall of Fame. "Getting this honor now, after all these years, is thrilling and definitely a high point in my life," said Stephens. In addition, Sandy's No. 15 jersey was retired at half-time of the 2000 Minnesota vs. Iowa

game which celebrated the 40th anniversary of the 1960 national championship. Sandy was the greatest quarterback to ever wear the maroon and gold. He blessed the University of Minnesota football program with his talents and leadership like no other, before or since.

Before his tragic death in June of 2000, Sandy had been recognized as a major influence in the breakthrough of African American athletes in collegiate athletics. He was a real pioneer both on and off the field and a was a true trailblazer in life.

Gopher Tombstone:
"I hope that they'll remember the championship teams that we had. That's my biggest thing. I have always been a team player. The only reason that you achieve accolades is because of the teammates that you have, and I had great teammates all the way through. We were all champions."

TRIBUTES
"Sandy was a great quarterback," said Bobby Bell. "If they would've given Sandy the opportunity to have played in the NFL, he would have been the first black quarterback in league; that's how good he was. He was a player that just wanted to win. He had the quickness, the speed, the arm and the agility. Defenses couldn't pin him down and contain him because he was so fast and so smart. He could beat you in a lot of ways, but especially one-on-one. He was so versatile; he would punt, pass, run, and do just about anything for the team. He hated to lose. I don't care if you were playing ping-pong, he wanted to beat you. He drove us to win and to be national champions. He was an all-around fun guy to play with and a tremendous competitor."

"He was a great leader and commanded a lot of respect from everybody," said Tom Brown. "His teammates really liked him and always played hard for him."

"He was the field general, in the truest sense of the word," said Carl Eller. "He was in command out on the field, and there was no question about it. We had total confidence in him and we knew that he could get it done. He would tell us in the huddle that we were going to either run over my side or over Bobby Bell's side, and we would do it. He had a lot of confidence in us. He was just a fabulous player."

"I grew up only a block away from Sandy, and we grew up together playing sports," said Bill Munsey. "After my senior year, I had received 58 full scholarship offers, but I chose to go to Minnesota because my best friend Sandy was there. I saw those big Swedes and Norwegians on the line and thought about the possibility of playing with Sandy in the backfield. He was stubborn, and there is probably no cockier person in the world than Sandy, but to play quarterback you have to have those ingredients. He had so much ability and was just a great natural athlete."

"He was a hell of a great football player, but he was never given the publicity and acclaim he deserved," said Murray Warmath. "He was one of the greatest football players I ever saw. He was a great running back, a good passer and an excellent defensive player. He could do everything and do it well."

1961

BOBBY BELL
THE GOPHERS SMELL THE ROSES

The defending national champs from Minnesota weren't going to sneak up on anyone in 1961 like they had done the year before. The Gophers, who lost a few key players to graduation, including Tom Brown and Joe Salem, still had a nucleus of stars in Bobby Bell, Sandy Stephens, Bill Munsey, Judge Dickson, and a new sophomore Tackle by the name of Carl Eller, who stood six-foot-five and weighed in at 240 pounds. Eller and Bell, a pair of outstanding tandem bookend Tackles from North Carolina, would anchor the Gopher defense and eventually led the squad back to Pasadena.

The team's season opener against Missouri attracted a lot of national interest because the Tigers were the team that Minnesota had climbed over to earn the No. 1 ranking in the polls after the last week of the 1960 season. The playing conditions that day were less than desirable, to say the least. "It was the worst game in terms of weather conditions that I ever played in," said Stephens. "It was just awful, and it was so cold that I couldn't feel the ball when it was centered." Amidst constant rain and wind, the Tigers hung tough and upset the Gophers by the score of 6-0.

Minnesota won six in a row after the sorry Missouri opener though, starting with Oregon, who they rallied to beat, 14-7. Stephens scored both Minnesota touchdowns in this one, with the speedster from Fairmont, Jimmy Cairns, adding a two-pointer for good measure. Then, against Northwestern, Stephens tallied on a one-yarder, while Judge Dickson added a 31-yard field goal of his own to give the Gophers a 10-3 victory. In Champaign, Stephens beat the Fighting Illini all by himself, passing for four touchdowns and scoring a fifth on a short run.

In the 23-20 win over Michigan, Stephens (who was married just two days prior), played one of his best games ever, racking up over 300 all-purpose yards in another come-from-behind victory. Then there was the 13-0 shutout over the then top-ranked Michigan State Spartans at Memorial Stadium, where Munsey, who had recovered from an injury that sidelined him from the Wolverine game the week before, scored both touchdowns for the Gophers.

Next up was Iowa. After giving up an early safety, Tom Loechler's field goal early in the second gave Minnesota a 3-2 lead. Then, in the third, Stephens tallied on a 39-yarder, followed by a touchdown on a blocked punt by Dick Enga, which was recovered in the end zone by John Campbell to give the Gophers a 16-9 victory.

Purdue was next, as an all-time record crowd of 67,081 crammed into Memorial Stadium to watch the Gophers beat the Boilers, 10-7. Minnesota went ahead 10-0 on Tom Loechler's 25-yard field goal, followed by Stephens' four-yard score. The Boilermakers rallied back to score, but the Gopher defense, which yielded just 27 yards of rushing that day, stood firm in preserving the "W" in one of the most bruising battles in team history.

Now only the Wisconsin Badgers stood in the way of the Gophers' first perfect Big Ten record since 1941. But Wisconsin Coach Milt Bruhn, an ex-Gopher, had a different idea, as his Quarterback, Ron Miller, connected with Pat Richter for two touchdowns in leading his Badgers past Minnesota, 28-21. In the loss, Sandy Stephens and Tight End Tom Hall combined for an 80-yard touchdown bomb, followed by Jerry Jones' 22-yard score. Stephens then connected with Al Fischer with just under two minutes to go, but it was too little too late.

Normally a 6-1 Big Ten record would make a solid case for winning the title, but, in 1961, the undefeated Ohio State Buckeyes would receive that honor. Then, in a bizarre twist of fate, Woody Hayes' Ohio State Buckeyes, who were invited to play the UCLA Bruins in the Rose Bowl, declined the invitation. If an official Big Ten-West Coast agreement had been in effect at that time, Minnesota would have been ineligible to play in the big game two years in a row — but there was no such contract that year. As a result, the Rose Bowl committee selected the Gophers, and for the second time in as many years, they were off to Pasadena for a run at the roses.

"This time," Warmath would later say, "we stayed at a monastery where we were isolated and could get a lot of rest. We were better prepared mentally because it was a team of veterans. We had a more professional attitude, and we wanted to redeem ourselves for what happened the year before. UCLA was not as good a team as Washington the year before, but we played an excellent game."

(Incidentally, the pressure was on to perform well for the cameras during this game. That's because it was the first college football game to be televised nationally in color.)

Reminiscent of the '61 Rose Bowl, when Washington scored a field goal on the opening drive, UCLA would also strike first in 1962. After being held deep in Gopher territory, the Bruins settled for a 28-yard field goal by Bob Smith just seven minutes into the game. The 98,214 fans that had poured into Pasadena's Rose Bowl to see the game could sense early on that Minnesota wasn't just happy to be there. That would be all the scoring the Bruins would do that day against the stingy Minnesota defense. The Gophers, haunted by the previous year's finale, rallied back late in the first on a one-yard touchdown plunge by Stephens, which was made possible by Dickson's fumble recovery a few plays prior. Coach Warmath had decided early that he wasn't going to play as conservatively on this go-round, and his Gophers went for it on several pivotal fourth down plays, picking up a first down on one, and scoring on another. Just before the half, Stephens marched the Gophers 75 yards for a second TD, with Munsey scoring on a reverse.

Dominating the game with their amazing defense, the Gophers looked poised in the second half. Stephens led the Gophers on an incredible 84-yard scoring drive late in the final period, scoring his second touchdown of the game from two yards out. The 19-play drive ate up 11 minutes off the clock, leaving little time for UCLA to do anything but wonder what could have been. The Gophers controlled every aspect of the game, compiling 21 first downs while holding UCLA to eight. Led by the outstanding defensive play of Bell and Eller, Minnesota held the Bruins to a paltry 107 yards of total offense and a mere field goal. Minnesota would not be denied in their second run for the roses, winning the game, 21-3, for the team's first and only Rose Bowl victory. As Coach Warmath was carried off the field, it was

TIMELINE

The St. Paul Saints hockey team wins the IHL's Turner Cup Championship	Gopher swimmer Steven Jackman wins the 100 yd Freestyle National Championship	Tommy Mason, a running back from Tulane, is the first overall pick by the Vikings in the NFL draft	George Keogan, a Detroit Lakes native who coached the Notre Dame Basketball team for 20 years, is inducted into the Basketball Hall of Fame	Gopher Football coach Murray Warmath is named the College Coach of the Year	Gopher first baseman Wayne Knapp is named to the All-American baseball team	The Minnesota Vikings, an NFL expansion team, beat the Bears in their first-ever game	Hall of Famer Lou Brock steals 38 bases for St. Cloud of the Northern League	The Washington Senators baseball team moves to Minnesota where they become the Minnesota Twins

said that his smile could be seen all the way back in Minnesota.

"We went out the year before and lost to Washington, so this year we were going to win the Rose Bowl, no matter what," said Bobby Bell. "We beat UCLA pretty bad, and I'd have to say it was amazing. It was one of the greatest things that ever happened to me in college. I was playing with cracked ribs during the game, but at the time I didn't care because I wanted to win so badly. I can remember our defensive coach was saying to us, 'hey, if you let these guys run three or four yards up the middle, then we are not players at all, we might as well pack up, put our dresses back on, and go home.' Their running back, All-American, Charlie Smith, was a great player, but every time he got close to that line, we were all over him. We shut him down completely. It was great, and when it was over, we were sitting on top of the world."

"It wouldn't have mattered who we would have played this go around," said Big Ten MVP, Sandy Stephens. "I would have died before I lost that game, even if I had to win it all by myself. We just completely dominated UCLA from the point after they made that opening field goal. The game started out similar to the Rose Bowl of the year before, and that shocked us and woke us up pretty quick. That was the first and last time UCLA would score on us that day."

"I don't know if this is something that is very well known," said Carl Eller, "but I think that a lot of the senior players weren't sure if they even wanted to go back to the Rose Bowl in 1961. We actually had a team meeting on whether or not we should even go. Many of the players didn't want to go if Coach Warmath, who was a task-master, was going to lock them up in a retreat again when they were right down the street from Hollywood. Now, I was only a sophomore at the time, so I didn't have a voice on the team like the juniors and seniors did, but I felt like there was a mutiny going on. So, I stepped up and said, 'Hey guys, I don't want you to rob me of my chance to go to the Rose Bowl.' I didn't care what hotel we stayed at, I just wanted to go to the Rose Bowl! I think in retrospect, he (Warmath) probably did relax a little bit on us out there, and we had a great time that year. We had a very strong team in 1961, and we just overpowered UCLA, physically dominating them. It was a tremendous experience."

One of the Gopher's Greatest Ever

Growing up in Shelby, N.C., Bobby Bell played quarterback for his high school six-man football team, until his senior year when he finally piloted an 11-man team. Bobby originally came to Minnesota with every intention of playing quarterback for the Golden Gophers. As a sophomore, he could run as fast and throw farther than all the quarterbacks in practice. But Coach Warmath had already begun to mold the great Sandy Stephens as his quarterback, and since the talented Bell was too good to keep on the bench, as Stephens' replacement, the coach put him in the lineup as an offensive and defensive tackle. Bobby, who just wanted the chance to play, accepted the role and eventually became one of the greatest tackles in Big Ten history.

The 6-4, 220-pounder's transition from signal-caller to tackle was hailed by sportswriters of the day as one of the modern wonders of college football. He led Minnesota to a 22-6-1 record during his tenure, including a national championship and Rose Bowl victory. There aren't many All-American tackles today that could boast to have the same sized 28 inch waist as Bobby did.

Bell is one of only eight Minnesota football players to earn All-America honors in two different seasons, 1961 and 1962. He was awarded the prestigious Outland Trophy his senior year by a landslide vote, recognizing him as the nation's top interior lineman. During his career at the U, Bell won the conference MVP in 1962 and was All-Big Ten in both 1961 and 1962 as well. He was later elected to the College Football Hall of Fame in 1991.

Bell was recruited by several other U of M teams too, including the gymnastics and baseball squads. Wanting to do more, he even became the first African-American to play a varsity game for the Gopher basketball team. Gopher Hockey Coach John Mariucci even tried to talk him into playing goalie. "He told me that I had the quickest reflexes that he'd ever seen and that I was going to be the first black hockey player in the country," said Bell. "Now, coming from North Carolina I had never even seen hockey before. So, when we got out on the ice and someone near-ly took my head off with a puck, I told him that the only way I'd get out there is if he turned the net around in the other direction!"

As a pro in the NFL, Bell made another transition, this time to linebacker, where he guided the Kansas City Chiefs to two Super Bowls. Bell was one of the stars of the team that stopped the Vikings, who were led by his old teammate and friend Carl Eller, in the 1970 Super Bowl. He played 13 seasons, was an all-pro for eight consecutive years, and became the Chiefs' first inductee into the Pro Football Hall of Fame in 1983. Bobby was undoubtedly the greatest lineman and one of the greatest athletes ever to wear the Maroon and Gold.

"I thought I had died and gone to heaven when I arrived at the University of Minnesota," said Bell. "Coming from North Carolina, I remember the first time I ever saw snow, it was so exciting. Being on campus as a Gopher was one of the most exciting things in my life. Playing in those Saturday football games was just so great. The fans and everybody were just really involved in the game. The night before our games we would stay at a hotel in St. Paul. Then, on Saturday, we would drive down University Avenue with a police escort, and it was just wall-to-wall people everywhere yelling and screaming for us. My heart started to pound like crazy. I was so excited, and my stomach was churning. I couldn't wait to get my uniform on. Getting off that bus and seeing all the people hanging out of the frat house windows was incredible. Seeing all that excitement in one place was fantastic. Everybody was so into it! Tickets to our games were nowhere to be found. I had so much fun there, and to this day I have a real love for the University of Minnesota."

Gopher Tombstone? "He gave it his all."

TRIBUTES

"He had great ability and range on the football field," said Tom Brown. "He had so much tenacity, and he was just an incredible ball player."

"Bobby was probably the most versatile player that I ever had the pleasure of playing with," added Sandy Stephens. "I don't know of anyone else who could have gone from quarterback to tackle. When he came in, the only place we had open was at left tackle, and coach Warmath realized that since he was such a good athlete, he had to play him somewhere. Bobby said that he just came here to play and didn't care where it was that he played. He was one of the only guys that could throw a football further than me, and I could throw 80 yards."

Hibbing's Roger Maris hits homer no. 61, breaking Babe Ruth's long-standing single-season home-run record of 60, in the last game of the regular season. The two-time league MVP's record still stands today as one of the greatest records in all of sports.

In 1962, Carl Eller and Bobby Bell stood like two giant oak trees in a forest of outstanding college football players. The two anchored perhaps the greatest defensive unit in Gold Country history. In seven games, the Gophers' Big Ten opponents averaged less than 60 yards rushing per game. Minnesota's defense was so tough that they allowed a mere 61 total points in nine games (34 alone came in a freak loss upset by Northwestern), while five of those nine opponents were even held scoreless. In an era of high scoring, wide-open play, this was truly amazing.

With Sandy Stephens gone, Duane Blaska took over the quarterbacking duties in 1962. He was joined by a solid backfield that year as well, with Bill Munsey, Jerry Jones, Jim Cairns, Bill McMillan, Bill Crockett and Jerry Pelletier. It would be the defense, however, that would be the trademark of this team, which posted an amazing five shut-outs that season.

After opening the season with a tough 0-0 standoff with Missouri, Minnesota went on to blank Navy, 21-0, even holding the Midshipmen to negative 31 yards rushing. From there though, the squad was upset by a pesky Northwestern team. They rebounded to post a pair of 17-0 shut-outs over Illinois and Michigan (Michigan was held to negative 46 yards rushing as well), followed by wins over Michigan State, 28-7, Iowa, 10-0, and Purdue, 7-6. With a 5-1 Big Ten record, the Gophers needed a win at Wisconsin to secure the conference title and a repeat trip to Pasadena. The Badgers, also at 5-1, were ready and waiting when the Gophers came to mix it up at Camp Randall Stadium in Madison.

Unfortunately, what followed could be considered to be one of the most bizarre and disturbing games ever played in college football history. When the dust finally settled, it became clear that the officials, not the players, played a pivotal role in a game that will long be remembered for all of the wrong reasons in Gold Country.

The Gophers opened the scoring in the second quarter with Duane Blaska connecting with Jimmy Cairns on a 15 yard scoring strike. The extra point, however, was no good. Wisconsin Quarterback Ron VanderKelen then rallied his Badgers back with a 65-yard scoring drive to take at 7-6 lead.

In the second half, the game started to turn into a penalty-filled freak-show, capped by the Gophers being penalized 15 yards for illegally aiding the advance of a runner — in this case, Bill Munsey. Minnesota settled for a Collin Versich 32-yard field goal, and the scoreboard read: Minnesota 9, Wisconsin 7. So far so good.

The Gophers later punted, and the coverage team, seeing the ball hit a Badger player, jumped on the loose ball rolling in the end zone, and claimed a touchdown. The officials didn't see it that way, however, and

returned the ball to Wisconsin out on the 20-yard line. The Gophers, dejected, assumed that the refs probably just didn't see it, and figured they would get it right the next time. Wrong! That's when "IT" happened — an event that will live in infamy. On the Gopher 43 yard-line, VanderKelen dropped back to pass and was sacked hard by Bell. The ball then flew into the awaiting arms of Gopher John Perkovich, only to have the referee nullify the interception. Incredibly, he even called Bell for roughing the passer. At this point, Coach Warmath could no longer contain himself. The 15-yard roughing call suddenly turned into 30 when the ref slapped the Gopher bench with an additional 15-yard unsportsmanlike conduct penalty. So, instead of Minnesota having the ball at mid-field, the Badgers now had a first down on the Minnesota 13-yard line with less than two minutes to go. Three plays later Wisconsin scored to make it 14-9.

Then, amazingly, the officials, who were feeling the heat, decided to even things up and let the Gophers back into the contest by first calling the Badgers for a personal foul penalty on the ensuing kickoff, followed shortly thereafter by a pair of pass interference calls. Suddenly, with a minute to go in the game, the Gophers found themselves with a first down on the Wisconsin 14. Then it got weird. Mysteriously, all communications from the press box to the Gopher bench disappeared, and the assistant coaches who had the bird's eye views of the on-field action, were silenced with jammed head-sets. So, on first down, Blaska, not knowing otherwise, went for it all. But, his floater was picked-off in the end zone to kill the rally. Wisconsin had won the Big Ten championship. The irate Gopher fans had just witnessed their third straight Rose Bowl appearance vanish before their very eyes.

"I was called for roughing the Badger quarterback," said Bell, who would go on to receive All-American honors for the second straight year, "but you could see on the film that he still had the ball in his hands, so it couldn't have been roughing. It was a blown call. It was a mess, and they ended up getting about 45 yards out of the whole thing, which ultimately led to them winning the game. It was the craziest game I ever played in. I bet that I've received hundreds of letters and newspaper clippings from around the country about that one play, and people still want to talk to me about it. The referee's name was Robert Jones. I will never forget that guy."

The run was over. For three glorious seasons in the early 1960s, Minnesota had produced a very respectable 22-6-1 record, entitling them to a National Championship, a Big Ten title, and a Rose Bowl victory. Carl "Moose" Eller would stick around for one more year in Gold Country before going on become one of the greatest defensive ends in NFL history as a member of the Vikings legendary "Purple People Eaters" defense of the 1970s.

The Moose

A native of Winston Salem, N.C., Carl Eller went on to star as two-time All-American Tackle for the Golden Gophers from 1961-63. The six-foot-six 260 pound terror was then selected by the Vikings with the sixth overall pick of the first round of the NFL draft. He went on to play 225 regular-season games over 15 years for the Vikings before spending one final season with the Seattle Seahawks in 1979. He was named All-Pro six times, was the NFL's Most Valuable Defensive Lineman twice, and played in six Pro Bowl games. Eller is the Vikings all-time sack leader, credited with 130 quarterback sacks, 44 from

Steven Jackman, a Gopher swimmer, wins both the 50 yd and 100 yd Freestyle National Championships	Virgil Luken, a Gopher swimmer, wins the 200-Yard Breaststroke National Championship	Twins pitcher Jack Kralick throws the only nine inning no-hitter at the Met	Bill McKechnie, a Minneapolis Miller in 1921, is inducted into the Baseball Hall of Fame

1975-77 alone. He also recovered 23 fumbles, a number that still ranks in the top five in NFL history. Eller's leadership and abilities were a big reason for the Vikings 11 division titles and three NFC crowns. He retired after 16 professional football seasons in 1979 but probably could've kept right on playing if he really wanted to. He was just that good. His great speed, power and agility should one day find him a home in the Pro Football Hall of Fame.

Eller has very much become synonymous with football in Minnesota and will always be remembered not only for his big smile, but as a fierce competitor as well. In his first season at the U of M, he even played with a broken hand, tossing aside his cast that he wore in practices come game day. And football wasn't all Carl could do. He once played MacBeth at the Guthrie Theater and was even voted one of Esquire Magazine's "Best Dressed Jocks" in 1972. He also starred in a B-Movie about bikers called "The Black Six," with Mean Joe Greene and Mercury Morris. Eller has also been a huge inspiration and role-model to kids everywhere by speaking to them about the dangers of drugs. Carl went on to make a career working for the State of Minnesota and also operates his own satellite communications company. He has three children and lives in the Minneapolis area.

What Did it Mean for You to Be a Gopher?
"Being a Golden Gopher was great," said Eller. "Going to the U was one of the better choices that I made in my life. Being on a metropolitan campus and being a part of the Saturday football scene at Memorial Stadium were wonderful experiences for me. Sure, it was a culture shock for me because I had come from a segregated town in North Carolina. Everything at the U was a new and incredible experience for me, and it was my first exposure to big-time football. Yes, it means a lot for me to be a Gopher."

What Did it Mean for You to Be a Viking?
"It still means a lot. But, truthfully, I felt I was totally misunderstood by the media. You see, when I played, I felt like I was an artist. I could have easily been the equivalent of a violinist, or a painter or whatever. Football is a mental game and I was a craftsman who had great skill and technique. The culmination of all those things made me a great player. Professional football was a real test of all my skills and I looked at playing as a performance. In other words, when I would do things like putting on a pass rush, or stopping a double-team, or making a tackle behind the play, I had to push and test myself to the limit to do those kinds of things that were just barely humanly possible. I had to be quick off the ball, and I had to beat the opponent to the ball. Sometimes I had to beat two guys, and sometimes I would have to hold one guy off with one arm and try to grab the quarterback with the other, all while trying to maintain my leverage, and all while watching out for the back who was coming to cut me at my knees. You had to do all that in a split second, and I took great pride in being able to do it well."

Does Never Winning a Super Bowl Still Hurt?
"Well, we had four shots at winning the big one. People can look at it whatever way they want to, but the four losses never came off as a negative to me. I can say that we were champions of the National Football Conference three times and NFL once. We went to four Super Bowls, defeated some great teams, and lost to some of the best football teams ever in Miami, Oakland, Pittsburgh, and Kansas City. It wasn't like we took a dive in our Super Bowls, or anything like that. I have nothing to be ashamed of. I have nothing to regret. We lost four games fair and square. But we didn't lose because we didn't put our best effort out there. We didn't lose because we weren't the best team to make it there. Regardless of what anybody says, those were my greatest moments. Those games were great Vikings moments and an unforget-

table part of the great Vikings' history. We never quit. It takes a lot of strength and character to come back time and time again. I think that says a lot more about the Vikings than perhaps some of the teams that actually won the Super Bowl."

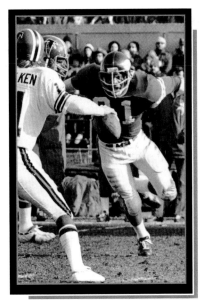

TRIBUTES
"Carl was a very talented football player," said Alan Page. "He was strong, quick and agile, and he was a very intense player."

"Moose was a great talent," said Bud Grant. "He got a lot of sacks and knocked down a lot of balls back then, he was just a dominant player. He played his best against the best players, and would dominate each team's top players that they put up against him."

"He was one of the biggest, strongest, toughest guys to come down the pike," said Jim Marshall. "When he wanted to destroy an opponent, I don't think there was anyone who could stop him. He was a great, great football player and I have so much respect for him. We played throughout our entire careers together. He was my roommate and one of my closest friends."

"These guys, the Purple People Eaters' were household names when I grew up," said Ahmad Rashad. "It was so great to play on the same team with them, because if we scored seven points — it was a blow-out. We would win because the other team wasn't going to score on them. I used to love watching Carl battle. I couldn't wait for the offense to get off the field so I could watch him go up against those huge 300-pound lineman. It was a massive battle of the titans watching them go at it out there, and Carl would usually win."

"He was the enforcer," said Chuck Foreman. "Carl wasn't just a great football player, he was a great athlete. He was also a very bright guy. He was probably the greatest defensive end that ever played the game."

"As great a player as Carl was, I always admired the confidence that he added to our team each time we went onto the football field," said Joe Kapp. "He was like a chieftain out there. He was as big, as fast and as tough as anybody in the league, and yet he had such a will and spirit to win. Confidence is what separates losing teams from winning teams and Carl passed that quality onto our team."

"We named him the moose, because he was a so big and strong," said Sandy Stephens. "Being from North Carolina, he hated the cold, so we had to indoctrinate him to the balmy Minnesota weather! He had so much enthusiasm and was just a great player."

"He was an all-around athlete," said Bobby Bell. "I got recruited with Carl from Winston Salem. He was so tough and strong, that's why we named him the 'Moose'. He was a happy-go-lucky, fun guy, and he was a guy you could coach. I remember playing that great Michigan State team where they had the No. 1 offense in the country and we had the No. 1 defense in the country. I think they were averaging something like 550 yards of offense per game, and at half-time they had like 26 yards — we shut them down. Carl was just unstoppable. We unbalanced the line that game so he could come down to my side and double-down. Carl would drive their guy into the ground every play and our offense took over. He was the greatest."

HORSING AROUND AT CANTERBURY

While Minnesota's most famous horse of all-time would have to be the legendary Dan Patch, a trio of new Minnesota-bred horses have made quite the names for themselves at Shakopee's Canterbury Park: Blair's Cove, Princess Elaine and Timeless Prince.

BLAIR'S COVE

The all-time leading Minnesota-bred money winner, Blair's Cove traveled to 14 race tracks during his career. With 14 starts and seven wins at Canterbury, Blair's Cove became Canterbury Horse of the Year in 1988 and Champion Grass Horse in 1989. His last start and victory came at Canterbury in the inaugural Festival of Championship Classic in 1992. Blair retired with 57 lifetime starts, 17 wins, 10 seconds and 4 thirds. In addition, his total earnings were $533,528 with $197,500 coming from turf victories. Blair's Cove was also the first Minnesota-bred horse to win a graded stakes when he took the Bashford Manor Stakes at Churchill Downs in 1987. And, competing against the toughest horses of his generation, he competed in major stakes races at Keeneland, Gulfstream Park, Colder Arlington, the Meadowlands, Golden Gate and Bay Meadows.

PRINCESS ELAINE

The all-time leading money earning Minnesota-bred filly or mare, Princess Elaine was loved by every Minnesota racing fan, many of whom even traveled to the other race courses to watch her race. With 27 lifetime starts, nine wins, five seconds and two thirds, Princess Elaine earned $232,240. She won nine races at Canterbury from 15 starts, including victories in the USA Handicap, Red Wing Stakes, Lady Slipper Stakes and Minnesota Breeders' Oaks. As Canterbury Champion Older Filly or Mare in 1989 and Champion three-year-old Filly in 1988, Princess Elaine never ducked the "big" mares. Most notably, she ran sixth in the Very Subtle Stakes on the Breeders Cup undercard in 1989. Her rider, Chris Valovich, said Princess Elaine was the best horse he has ridden. When Princess Elaine suffered a life-ending injury during a race at Hawthorne Race Course, Steve Davidowitz of the Star Tribune wrote an obituary. It was probably the only equine obituary ever to appear in a major newspaper. That horse was special and it was a real tragedy when she went down for not only race fans, but for all sports fans.

TIMELESS PRINCE

Canterbury Champion Timeless Prince had many owners throughout his career, ultimately winding up with the St. Paul Police Department, where he went on to serve as a mounted police horse. It is Lester's (Lester Partners) breeder, Mr. Coss of Cannon River Farms, who deserves the credit for finding a new career for Lester. A winner of $327,403 in his racing career, Lester became Champion Two-Year-Old in 1990 and Champion Three-Year-Old colt in 1991. He started 21 times at Canterbury with 10 wins and even strung together five consecutive victories in 1991 to boot. He traveled to 11 race tracks during his career and was claimed by Hall of Fame nominee Steven Herold in 1995. During his prime, conditioner Joey Ruhsam and his owners, Lester Partners, brought Lester out loaded for bear in each of his races, and fans were never disappointed in his courageous efforts.

BOBBY MARSHALL

Bobby Marshall was the first great African American sports figure in Minnesota. The Minneapolis Central High School star went on to become the first man of color to play in the Big Nine (later the Big Ten) as an End for the Gophers. From 1904-06 he led the team to an amazing record of 27-2, while they outscored their opponents by the margin of 1,238-63. In 1906 he even kicked a game-winning 60-yard field goal in the rain and mud to beat the University of Chicago, 4-2 (field goals counted for four points back then). He went on to receive All-Western honors for all three of his years in Minnesota.

In addition to football, he earned all-conference honors as a first baseman on the baseball team and lettered in track as a sprinter. As a professional, he was a star in football, baseball, boxing and even hockey, where, in 1908, he became the first African American to play professionally, when he suited up for the semi-pro Minneapolis Wanderers and later with the Hillsdale Hockey Club in Pennsylvania. In baseball he played for the Colored Gophers and the Chicago Leland Giants professional Negro-League teams, and on the gridiron he played professionally with the Minneapolis Deans, Minneapolis Marines, Duluth Eskimos and Rock Island Independents.

He was such an incredible athlete, that after retiring from playing pro football at the age of 44, he even made a comeback at that age of 50 to play in an exhibition game at Nicollet Park. Marshall was extremely durable and, amazingly, he never sustained a major injury in nearly 30 years of football. He later became a grain inspector for the state of Minnesota and died on Aug. 27, 1968, at the age of 88. In 1971 he was inducted into the College Football Hall of Fame, and several years later was also named to the National Football Foundation's Hall of Fame. He will undoubtedly be remembered as one of Minnesota's greatest ever all-around athletes.

THE MINNEAPOLIS MILLERETTES

"There's no crying in baseball..." That was just one of the classic lines sputtered from Tom Hanks (A.K.A.) "Jimmy Dugan," in the 1992 movie "A League of their Own." The movie focused on two of the teams from the All-American Girls Professional Baseball League (AAGP-BL), the Rockford Peaches and Racine Belles, during the league's inaugural 1943 season. That year the league was started by famed Chicago Cubs Owner Philip Wrigley, who saw girls baseball as a way to keep his ballpark occupied during World War II — while our boys were overseas.

That first year there were just four teams in the AAGPBL: the Racine Belles, Rockford Peaches, Kenosha Comets and South Bend Blue Sox. What many people don't realize, however, is that Minnesota also had a team in the league. That's right, that next year, in 1944, the Minneapolis Millerettes were brought in as an expansion franchise — thus giving the Gopher State its first ever professional women's baseball team. (The Milwaukee Chicks were also added that year as well.)

This, at a time when women were being called upon by the government to take a more active role in the workplace. Rosie the Rivetor was out front-and-center, and America needed them to pick up the slack with the men away. But, while the ladies were being called upon to play the manly game of baseball, Wrigley and other league officials made sure that they remained as "lady-like" as possible. Etiquette classes, charm school, proper posture and appropriate dress attire were all mandated by the league. A code of conduct was highly enforced for the girls, and their every move was scrutinized. Teams even had chaperones, to ensure their behavior. Mrs. Wrigley herself even designed special short-skirted uniforms with satin shorts for the ladies so that they could keep their feminine figures without giving the men any ideas.

The women who wound up making the rosters of these teams were some of the best athletes of their day. Many had been stars in other sports such as basketball, field hockey and softball, so for them to pick up the new game was no problem at all. It was a fun time for women and for the sport as well. Seemingly all of the gals had nicknames and the league, as a whole, gave many Americans a sense of normalcy during this troubling time in history.

After that first season of 1943 was deemed as a success, the Millerettes club was brought together under the tutelage of Manager Bubber Jonnard, a former pitcher for the New York Giants. The team, which played its home games at Nicollet Park, opened its schedule there against the Rockford Peaches in front of around 500 fans. The Millerettes jumped out to a 3-0 lead in this one, only to see the Peaches rally for a 5-4 victory.

The star of our team was Helen Callaghan, who would go on to hit .287 that season with three homers, 17 RBI's and 81 runs scored. (It is also interesting to note that Callaghan, who went on to lead the league in hitting that next season, would later have a son named Casey Candaele — who, in turn, would go on to play for more than 10 seasons of major league baseball with Montreal, Houston and Cleveland.)

And, according to renowned baseball author Stew Thornley, Callaghan wasn't the only member of the squad who would have a relative in the major leagues. Annabelle Lee, the team's star pitcher, was also the aunt of Bill "Spaceman" Lee, who would go on to pitch for the Expos and Red Sox in the 1970s and '80s. (The Spaceman would later even credit his Aunt for teaching him how to pitch!)

As the season went on the ladies got better, but the fan support dwindled. In addition, opposing teams, from as far away as Indiana, were getting tired of taking long bus trips to the Twin Cities, only to have a couple hundred fans show up to watch them. But, the team played on. They knew that they had to make it interesting for the fans to stay involved, so they spiced up their act a bit. One player in particular did this better than the rest, Center Fielder Faye Dancer. Faye was a real crowd-pleaser who oftentimes did somersaults in the outfield between pitches to amuse the fans. Other players stepped it up too. Millerettes' hurler Dorothy "Dottie" Wiltse won 20 games that year while LaVonne "Pepper" Paire dazzled the crowd with her amazing range at shortstop.

That 1944 six-team season was divided into halves, with the winners of each half then meeting in a post-season tournament to determine a league champion. The Millerettes played respectably early on in the season, but then slumped big time. From there the club hit the skids and wound up finishing out the first half of the season in the league basement with a dismal record of 23-36. And, while optimism ran high for the second half, it didn't get much better as the club finished with a nearly identical 22-36 tally in part II. The fans were staying away in droves, the media was ignoring them and the players were playing lousy baseball. When you added it all up, it was a recipe for disaster.

With that, in late July the Millerettes' remaining home games were relocated to other cities. The team, which would then become known affectionately as the "Orphans," played the rest of its season on the road. After the season the franchise was relocated to Fort Wayne, Indiana, where they were renamed as the "Daisies." (The Daisies, incidentally, would go on to play for 10 more seasons, winning league titles in 1948, 1952, 1953 and 1954. And, the star of that 1954 club was St. Paul's Jean Havlish, who would go on to become a Hall of Fame bowler.)

While the AAGPBL would go on well into the 1950s, that would be the end of professional women's baseball for some time. (In 1988, a display of women in baseball opened at the Baseball Hall of Fame in Cooperstown, NY., immortalizing the efforts of the AAGPBL and giving our Millerettes an interesting footnote in Minnesota baseball history.)

The 1944 Minneapolis Millerettes

Back Row: Bubber Jonnard, Dorothy Wiltse, Vivian Kellogg, Audrey Haine, LaVonne Paire, Kay Blumetta, Lillian Jackson, Ada Ryan (team chaperone)
Middle Row: Faye Dancer, Elizabeth Farrow, Marge Callaghan, Audrey Kissel, Margaret Wigiser
Front Row: Ruth Lessing, Annabelle Lee, Helen Callaghan, Betty Trezza

In 1963, a dynasty of sorts officially began. This was the year that football coach John Gagliardi, of St. John's University, in Collegeville, Minn., won his first national championship, barely beating Prairie View A&M in a thriller.

The 1963 Minnesota Intercollegiate Athletic Conference (MIAC) season was very successful for the Johnnies. Gagliardi's team was led by Halfback Bob Spinner, who won his second straight MIAC scoring championship in the season finale during a 32-6 drubbing of rival St. Thomas.

Next, it was off to the small-college playoffs for St. John's, where they met the College of Emporia (Kansas). This one wasn't even close as the Johnnies cruised, 54-0, en route to walzing through the playoffs and advancing to the title game. There, the Johnnies would face Prairie View A&M of Texas in Sacramento, Calif. at the Camellia Bowl.

Prairie View A&M was the dominant black college team in America at the time. They played a big-time schedule against teams like Grambling State and Florida A&M and dominated them all. Prairie View also had some great players on that team who would go on to become stars in the NFL, such as Hall of Famer Otis Taylor, and Jim Carnie, who would later become an All-Pro defensive back for the Kansas City Chiefs.

The Johnnies were decisive underdogs going into the contest. Prairie View had 40 "free-ride" football scholarships for their players while St. John's had none. The only thing the Johnnies did have in their favor was the a-typical California weather on that day, which was a chilly 39 degrees — downright freezing to a Texan.

Prairie View scored first on a 29 yard roll-out by Quarterback Jimmy Hall. The Johnnies answered though, on Bob Spinner's 41-yard punt return in the second, making it 7-6. But the Panthers came right back on Jimmy Kearney's 61-yard pass to Otis Taylor to make it 14-6.

St. John's defensive back John McCormick then returned an interception 44 yards, and Johnnie Quarterback Craig Muyres later hooked up with Halfback Bernie Beckman to make it 14-13 at the half.

Then, in the third, the Johnnies took the lead for good on Muyres' 23-yard pass to Hardy Reyerson. Muyres then hit Ken Roering for the extra point and St. John's led 20-14. Late in the same period Beckman, off a double reverse, hit Roering on an 18-yard touchdown.

The Panthers rallied back in the fourth as Kearney threw a 14 yard TD pass to Halfback Doug Broadus cutting the margin to 26-21. But the Johnnies answered, this time on a 19-yard Muyres to Reyerson aerial, followed by a Spinner extra point catch. Prairie View scored on an Ezell Seals one yard plunge, with only 2:15 to go on the game clock. But it was too

little too late, as Roering recovered the Prairie View on-side kick to seal the deal. The Johnnies had done it, upsetting the mighty Panthers 33-27, as the 12,220 fans, many of whom had make the trek from Minnesota, went wild.

Beckman, the smallest man on the field, ran for 52 yards, caught three passes for 43 passes, including a conversion, and played brilliant defense. For his efforts he was named as the game's MVP.

"It was a tremendous win for us," said Gagliardi. "Prairie View is the best team we played all year. Believe me, we knew we weren't going to be playing St. Catherine's! I mean it, it was like coming back after two nine-count knock-downs. And the second knock-down really had us hanging on the ropes. I give credit to the team. They managed to come through with the big play when it was needed all season, especially Craig Muyres, who I believe is the best clutch quarterback in the United States."

A Living Legend

John Gagliardi was born in 1927, the son of an Italian-born body shop owner in Trinidad, Colo. To fully understand this man's life-long calling of coaching, you have to go way back to Trinidad Catholic High School. Gagliardi's storied coaching career ironically began when his high school coach was drafted into World War II. Without a coach, the school was just going to drop the football program until "Gags" talked the administration into letting him do the coaching. Gagliardi, the teams' captain, took over the reins at the age of 16. Even at that young age people could see the man had a gift for teaching, working with young people, and instilling in them a winning attitude. Upon graduating, he put himself through school at Colorado College, where he coached the high school team for two more seasons. He then took over as C.C.'s head coach for his junior and senior seasons as well. His teams won four conference titles in six years.

After graduation from Colorado College in 1949, the 22-year-old Gags accepted his first college coaching position at Carroll College, a small Catholic liberal arts school in Helena, Mont. He coached not only the football program, but also the basketball and baseball programs as well. Inheriting a Carroll College athletic program in utter disarray, he turned things around in a hurry, leading the football and basketball teams to three straight championships.

His success drew the attention of another small Catholic college — St. John's University of Collegeville, Minn. St. John's needed a coach to succeed the mythical Johnny "Blood" McNally, a former Green Bay Packer and Duluth Eskimo great and a charter member of the Pro Football Hall of Fame. SJU had not won a conference title in 15 years, and Blood, their departing head coach, offered these inspiring words to the new coach: "Nobody can ever win at St. John's."

In 1953, all John Gagliardi was given was a mandate to turn the program around and nothing else that was tangible. Amazingly, he immediately quieted the skeptics by winning the MIAC title that fall with the help of his first great halfback, Jim Lehman, the father of Minnesota golfing great Tom Lehman, who led the country in scoring. Gags also went on to turn around the Johnnies' track and hockey teams too, proving his unique coaching methods and motivational skills could make any team a winner.

There have been more than 25,000 head coaches in college football history. Just five of them have won more than 300 games. They are (ranked by most wins): Eddie Robinson, John Gagliardi,

Gopher swimmer, Steven Jackman, wins the 50yd Freestyle National Championship	Former St. John's University football player and coach, and Duluth Eskimos player Johnny Blood, is inducted into the Pro Football Hall of Fame.	Gopher swimmer Wally Richardson, wins the 100 yd Butterfly National Championship	International Falls native Bronko Nagurski, a Gopher football and Chicago Bears legend, is inducted into the Pro Football Hall of Fame.	Paul Flatley, a Vikings wide receiver, is named as the NFL's Rookie of the Year	Gopher second baseman Jon Andresen is named to the All-American baseball team	Gopher swimmers Alfred Ericksen, Virgil Luken, Wally Richardson, and Steve Jackman, win the 400 Yard Medley Relay national championship	The Minneapolis Millers hockey team, led by player/coach Ken Yackel, who was a former three-sport star at the U of M, loses to Fort Wayne in the International League championship game

Bear Bryant, Amos Alonzo Stagg and Pop Warner. Of them, only Gagliardi are still coaching. Robinson, the head coach at Grambling State University, has the most career wins of all-time with 408, while Gagliardi remains No. 2 with 388 going into the 2002 season.

One of his biggest moments in coaching and perhaps in life happened in 1993, when his Johnnies pulverized Bethel, 77-12, for Gags' 300th win. After that historic event the eyes of the world of sports were suddenly on Gagliardi. The national media invaded Collegeville for words of wisdom from the man who had became known nationwide as a coaching genius. It was quite the scene.

Gagliardi has built one of the nation's top NCAA Division III programs. The attitude and winning tradition he instills in his players is unprecedented. Among this seven-time national coach of the year's many achievements are his three small college championship teams. First, in 1963, then two years later, when they crushed Linfield College of Oregon, 35-0 (Amazingly the Johnnies' defense allowed just 27 points to be scored against them that entire season!), and, in 1976, when they beat Towson State of Maryland, 31-28.

As a collegiate coach Gagliardi's teams have won 24 conference titles and have appeared in 41 post-season games. In the past 39 years, SJU has been nationally ranked 37 times and it owns a 28-13 post-season record as well. From 1962-64 SJU owned the nation's longest winning streak, with 20 wins. Then, in 1993, SJU averaged 61.5 points per game, setting a record that may never be broken.

Among his numerous awards and achievements, Gagliardi has been inducted into the Minnesota and Montana Halls of Fame and is a member of the College Football Hall of Fame as well. He has been the subject of a Sports Illustrated cover story and was awarded the Football Writers of America Citation of Honor. Perhaps his greatest honor will live on forever though. The NCAA honored the coach by naming the Division III equivalent of the Heisman Trophy after him. The Gagliardi Trophy is now given annually to the outstanding NCAA Division III football player. There have even been a couple of books written about him, with more on the way!

The winningest active coach and second all-time in college football history, Gagliardi currently owns a 388-112-11 collegiate career record. Amazingly, he is now just 20 wins away from the all-time collegiate wins record of 408, set by former Grambling's Eddie Robinson. And Gagliardi's teams are still setting the standard for MIAC competitors. In 1993, SJU became the first NCAA team since the 1904 Gophers to score more than 700 points in a season. Then, in 2000 St. John's made the national title game, followed by a national semifinal appearance in 2001. This guy is still going strong!

Gagliardi's success is attributable to more than mere football strategy and tactics. He is an astute judge of talent. He creates an environment of fun along with high expectations, and he concentrates on methods and practices that truly focus on winning football games. John Gagliardi has built a legacy that is unrivaled in college football, and what's frightening for all the other MIAC schools is that he may just be getting his second wind.

Today John and his wife Peggy live in Collegeville and have four children. It's business as usual for the coach though as he enters his 54th season behind the bench and prepares for his emotional journey to instant football immortality — hopefully in 2004. We'll see you all at the festivities, but remember, please, NO Gatorade shower!

St. John's Tombstone:

"I dared to do a lot of things that no one else dared to do — like the way we practice. We've never gone 'full-go' in practice I am proud of the fact that I saved a lot of guys from permanent injuries because of that. I've been a lucky guy and I've always had great athletes to make me look good along the way."

Gagliardi's unorthodox coaching methods have been distilled into a series of: "WINNING WITH NO'S"

THE OVERALL PROGRAM
- No athletic scholarships.
- No big staff, just four assistant coaches.
- No coordinators.
- No freshmen or junior-varsity program.
- No discipline problems.
- No insisting on being called "Coach."
- No players cut.
- No pampering athletes.
- No one persuaded to come out or stay out.
- No hazing tolerated.

THE SEASON
- No staff meetings.
- No player meetings.
- No film sessions after Monday
- No special diet.
- No training table - team eats with other students.
- No special dormitory.
- No signs in dressing rooms.
- No slogans.
- No superstitions.
- No play-books.
- No statistics posted.
- No newspaper clippings posted.

THE PRACTICES
- No practice pants - shorts or sweats worn at practice.
- No agility drills.
- No lengthy calisthenics (about three minutes.)
- No pre-practice drills.
- No practice apparatus or gadgets.
- No blocking sleds or tackling dummies.
- No tackling.
- No laps.
- No wind sprints.
- No special coaching clothes worn.
- No use of the words "hit," "kill," etc...
- No clip boards.
- No whistles.
- No practice on Sundays.
- No practice on Mondays.
- No drills.
- No spring practice.
- No practice in rain, extreme heat or cold.
- No practice if mosquitoes, gnats, etc... are bad.
- No long practices - varies from 30 to 90 minutes.
- No practice under the lights
- No water or rest denied when players want it.
- No practice modules.
- No underclassmen carry equipment other than their own.

THE GAMES
- No big deal when we score - we expect to score.
- No Gatorade celebrations.
- No trying to "kill" opponent.
- No trash talk tolerated.
- No tendency charts.
- No use of headphones.
- No coaches in press-box.
- No player NOT played in rout (143 players once played in a game)
- No spearing allowed.
- No cheap-shots or foul play tolerated.
- No counting tackles.
- No precision pre-game drills.
- No big games pointed to.
- No special pre-game or post-game meals.
- No computer analysis.
- No cheerleaders.

THE OFF-SEASON
- No meetings
- No between season practices or conditioning.
- No captains' practice.
- No study or tutoring program necessary.
- No weightlifting program

THE RESULTS
- No player has not graduated.
- No discipline problems.
- No player lost through ineligibility.
- No class has NOT had at least one prospective pro player.
- No small college has larger crowd support.
- No wider point margin in national playoff history.
- No team has fewer injuries.
- No team has fewer penalties.
- No small college coach has won more games.

TIMELINE

Minneapolis' Bud Wilkinson retires as head football coach at the University of Oklahoma. The former Gopher guard earned All-American honors in football, where he played on three national championship teams and also captained the 1935 hockey team. At one point, his Sooners won 47 consecutive games, en-route to three national championships.

Lake City's Ralph Samuelson was given credit by the American Water Ski Association as the "Father of Water Skiing." Forty-four years after his first "ride" in 1922, around Lake Pepin, Ralph's invention is finally given its due. He took two pine boards, held them over a tea kettle, put them in a vice to curve them upward, and fastened the skis to his feet. Behind his brother's clamming boat, he reached speeds of more than 80 mph.

St. Paul's Tommy Gibbons, known as the Phantom, is inducted into the Boxing Hall of Fame. The light-heavyweight champion once went 15 rounds with Jack Dempsey in 1923.

Minneapolis' Dr. Emmet Swanson wins the Service Bolt division in the National Rifle Championships. One of the greatest marksmen in US history, Swanson competed on four Olympic teams (1948, 1952, 1956 and 1960)

Willow River native Ernie Nevers, a former football player for the Duluth Eskimos, is inducted into the Pro Football Hall of Fame. He once scored 40 points in a game, still an NFL record

While a young right fielder by the name of Tony Oliva was named as the Rookie of the Year in 1964, the big story of the season was that of Harmon Killebrew, who led the American League with 49 homers — his fourth straight season of 45 or more dingers. Major League Baseball's sultan of swat won the home run crown for the third straight year that season, putting him in a very select class. Only seven players had ever led their leagues in home runs for three or more consecutive years up to that point. The Pittsburgh Pirates' Ralph Kiner holds the all-time record of seven straight years, and Babe Ruth had two streaks — four in a row from 1918-21 and six in a row from 1926-31.

Killebrew finished the 1964 season with some other very impressive stats. He hit a modest .270, scored 95 runs and drove in 111 RBIs to boot. With the addition of teammate Bob Allison's 32 homers, the two combined for 81, the most prolific homer-twosome ever for the Twins. At a sports banquet in Baltimore, Killebrew was presented with a crown of jewels, symbolic of the major league home run championship. He would join a select fraternity of prior winners, which included Mickey Mantle, Ted Williams, Ernie Banks, Eddie Mathews, Hank Aaron, Willie Mays and Roger Maris.

"Over my career I led the league six times in home runs," said Killebrew, "but that year was special because it was the first time I hit 49. That was probably one of my best years ever as an individual, but unfortunately we didn't win anything as a team."

Despite the efforts of those two players, however, the team finished with a disappointing sixth-place finish at 79-83. Pitching and defense were again where most of the finger-pointing turned to, as the team finished tied for worst in the league in overall defensive performance. So desperate were the Twins at second base that after trying five different second basemen, they went out and traded Lenny Green and Vic Power for former Gopher star Jerry Kindall. He was decent, but did not solve the answer to their riddle. They did acquire a few new pitchers that year though in Jim "Mudcat" Grant, Al Worthington, and Johnny Klippstein — all of whom would make contributions. Kaat was the ace with 17 wins, while Pascual and Grant added 15 and 11, respectively.

Despite the team's struggles on the field that season, there was some good news. The season was just a warm-up to the fabulous World Series run in 1965 — and Harmon Killebrew would be leading the charge!

Mr. Baseball
Harmon Killebrew grew up playing baseball on the vacant lots of Payette, Idaho. Their, the neighbor kids would emulate the late Hall of Famer Walter Johnson, who had played semi-pro ball just 15 miles away. What set Killebrew apart from other kids though was his intense dedication to the game and

his desire to improve himself. While many boys were content simply to play the game, Harmon would practice for hours in the backyard of his home, swinging his bat at imaginary pitches. From there he would become an Idaho high school football, basketball and baseball sensation. Upon earning 12 high school letters, he decided to accept a scholarship from the University of Oregon to play both football and baseball.

But, after being heavily recruited by both colleges as well as major league baseball scouts, Harmon suddenly was presented with another interesting option. At the time, Idaho Senator Herman Welker was a close friend of Washington Senators owner Clark Griffith, and one of Welker's favorite subjects was talking about a certain local star playing baseball back in his home-state of Idaho. Welker persuaded the Old Fox to check out the kid, Killebrew, so Griffith immediately dispatched scout Ossie Bluege to Idaho. As the story goes, the first time Bluege saw him play, the 17-year-old Killebrew hit a 435-foot shot out of the park and into a sweet potato field, prompting Bluege to call Griffith and say, "Sign him up!"

Harmon truly wanted to go to college that fall, but when Griffith flashed a $30,000 signing bonus in front of him, he just couldn't refuse. So, Harm became the Senators first bonus baby. (The bonus-baby rule meant that players were forced to spend at least two seasons in the big leagues before being sent down to the minors. The rule was notorious for damaging young ballplayers by depriving them of necessary minor-league teaching and experience.)

Harmon spent the required two seasons riding the pines in Washington, D.C., before spending several more years in the Senators' farm system. He received a "last look" in 1959 when he was finally placed on the team's major league roster. Three major league managers had expressed doubt that he would ever make it as a big league ballplayer. They saw his potential as a power hitter, but needed to be sold on Harmon the fielder, runner and thrower.

That's when Calvin Griffith, who had succeeded his uncle as president of the Senators, decided to see what the family money had bought and insisted that Harmon be given an extended shot with the Senators. The new Washington third baseman surprised everybody in 1959 by becoming one of the most feared sluggers in the American League. Harmon led the usually dormant Senators, finishing the season with a surprising 42 homers and driving in 105 runs. Killebrew even tied Cleveland's Rocky Colavito for the home run title as well.

When the Senators moved to the Twin Cities in 1961, Killebrew continued his torrid home run hitting pace, winning three successive home run titles from 1962-64. He rose to Hall of Fame stardom in the early 60s in Minnesota, becoming the primary attraction at old Metropolitan Stadium. On the field, Harmon assumed the position of Twins' team leader. His hustle and tenacity made him the complete player that had eluded him earlier on in his career. He became known as a fierce competitor, a solid fielder and a true gentleman.

"I was really apprehensive about moving to Minnesota to tell you the truth," recalled Harmon. "I liked playing in Washington, I thought it was a great place to play, and I really enjoyed the excitement of seeing and meeting all the presidents, congressmen, senators, and other famous people who would attend our games. Although I didn't like playing in the cold Minnesota weather, the warm hearts of the people made it warm up in a hurry. They were great. I really enjoyed the years I spent playing in the Twin Cities. The fans were just wonderful to me. The 1960s were an exciting time for sports in Minnesota with

TIMELINE

St. Olaf wrestler Dave Schmidt wins the 177 lbs. Division III National Championship	The Gopher baseball team Beats Missouri, 5-1, for the National Championship	Mankato State wrestler Howard Gangestad wins the 123 lb. Division II National Championship	Gopher swimmer Walt Richardson wins the 100 yd Butterfly National Championship	Urban (Red) Faber, a Minneapolis Miller in 1911, is inducted into the Baseball Hall of Fame	Gopher winger Craig Falkman is named to the All-American hockey team	Gopher catcher Ron Wojciak is named to the All-American baseball team	St. Paul's Jean Havlish becomes the first and only Minnesotan to win the top division of the Women's International Bowling Congress Singles Title when she rolled record totals of 690 in the three game singles series and a 1,980 in the nine game events. She was later inducted into the Bowling Hall of Fame in St. Louis.

46

the Vikings' success as well."

Killer went on to win the American League MVP in 1969 when he hit 49 dingers with 140 RBIs and 145 walks, all team records that still stand. In 1974, sensing that the end was near for his aging veteran, Calvin encouraged Harmon to retire and manage in the Twins farm system. Griffith was grooming Killebrew to be an eventual Twins manager. But the old Killer wanted to play just one more season. So he declined Calvin's suggestion and signed on as a designated hitter with the Kansas City Royals. Killebrew's playing career in Minnesota was over.

On May 4, 1975, Harmon returned to Met Stadium, this time as a member of the opposition. His No. 3 was officially retired in a pre-game ceremony, and to top it all off, he smacked a homer to left field in his first at-bat. Minnesota fans went crazy as he rounded the bases in what some have said was the loudest ovation Twins fans have ever have given an opposing player.

"I think that being a Twin meant that I had an opportunity to play on a lot of great ballclubs, and play with some great players over the years," said Killer. "Just putting on that uniform and walking on that Met Stadium field to represent the Twins was about as big a thrill as anything for me."

Harmon Clayton Killebrew, Jr., will be remembered as one of the greatest home run hitters in history with 573 career round-trippers. He was second only to Babe Ruth in the history of the American League to hit more than 40 home runs, (eight times), 30-or-more home runs, (10 times), all while driving in 100-plus RBIs (nine times). Over his career he tallied 1,584 RBIs, while garnering 2,435 hits and playing in 10 All-Star games.

Killebrew was also the consummate team player, always more interested in the team's achievements rather than his own, "You know, it's fine to hit homers, but it's RBIs that mean the most," he said.

Because of his tremendous contributions to the game of baseball, on January 10, 1984, Killebrew became the first Twin ever to be inducted into the Baseball Hall of Fame. At the induction ceremony, he went on to tell the gathering that he attributed much of his success to his father, who had once explained to someone who had commented on the families' sports-worn front lawn, by saying that he was "raising children, not grass."

Harmon was more than just a slugger. He overcame his early fielding problems and emerged as a solid all-around baseball player. Twins manager Sam Mele recognized him as a genuine team leader whose presence in the lineup inspired the other players to do their best. Quiet and unassuming, Harmon was always more interested in his team rather than personal accolades, and he is the first to deny his greatness. He is also quick to give thanks and appreciation to the game of baseball for everything it has done for him and his family.

Just outside the town of Payette, there is a sign that says, "Home of Harmon Killebrew." There also is a street named for him, and his No. 12 football jersey still hangs prominently in the halls of his high school for all the kids to see. His hometown didn't forget him — nor will baseball. Killebrew ranks as one of the greatest right-handed sluggers of all time. "One of the quietest team leaders of all time," remarked a sportswriter, "but a leader nevertheless."

"When they originally told us that we were moving from the nation's capital to Minnesota, I was, frankly, a bit apprehensive about it," said Harmon. "But when it finally happened it was just great. The people of Minnesota immediately embraced me and I grew to love it up there. The fans in Minnesota are as good, if not better, than any fans in baseball. They showed me so much love and respect, and I will never forget that."

"When I came to Minnesota I was already aware of the great baseball tradition that they had here. In fact, I had actually played against the Minneapolis Millers and St. Paul Saints in my earlier days. Old Nicollet and Lexington Parks had a lot of great ballplayers come through their gates through the years and that just added to Minnesota's great baseball history."

"Overall, I can't thank the fans of Minnesota enough for their amazing generosity and hospitality towards me over the years. It is a state with a wonderful baseball heritage and I was truly proud and honored to be a part of it."

"The 2002 Twins were just a wonderful story," added Harmon. "This group of kids played hard and played solid, fundamental baseball — and that is really refreshing to see. I couldn't be prouder of these guys and hope they can keep it together for a long, long time."

TRIBUTES

"He was a steadying influence on our teams," said Rod Carew. "The greatest thing that I learned from Harmon was here was a man who would hit two or three home runs in a ballgame one day, and then maybe strike out four times the next night. But, I never once saw him get upset or gesture to the fans even when they booed him. His whole career was one of dignity. I watched him day in and day out and saw that here was a future Hall of Famer who could handle harassment from the people in the stands and not let if affect him as a player. I knew that if he could do that, then I could, as well. Harmon was a great hitter and a great ballplayer."

"Harmon was just what you would expect," said Jim Kaat. "He was the perfect poster-boy for the Minnesota Twins. He was this big, hulking power hitter, very soft-spoken gentleman in every sense of the word, and he was the perfect person to be identified and associated with the Twins. I respect what he did on and off the field, and it was a great pleasure playing with him. Just the way he carried himself during good times and bad times was a great influence on all of us."

"You couldn't have played with a better person than Harmon," said Tony Oliva. "I think he was almost too nice to be a major league ballplayer. He is just a wonderful person, and I considered it to be an honor to be able to say that I played baseball with Harmon Killebrew."

"I had the dream of being a major-leaguer as a kid and, of course, being from St. Paul and following the Twins, I regarded Harmon Killebrew as the one player who I tried to emulate when I was playing out in my backyard," recalled Paul Molitor. "I was always fascinated by his home-run power and by just what he had meant to the Twins. Harmon is a tremendous gentleman. You know, sometimes you get deflated if and when you are finally lucky enough to get to meet your childhood hero. This was by no means the case when I met him though. If anything, my respect for Harmon has grown by getting to know him well. "

"Harmon is just so loved here in Minnesota," added Kent Hrbek. "He was an idol of mine when I was growing up in Bloomington. He was just a fantastic player and is probably the best right-handed home run hitter of all time."

The 1965 Twins were historic. They came out of nowhere and shocked the baseball world while taking the fans of Minnesota on a ride they would never forget. They opened up the season on April 12th with a 5-4 win over the Yankees — perhaps an omen of good things to come for this promising bunch of kids. The season got off to a great start and by mid-season the team was poised to make a run for its first-ever trip to the post-season.

Meanwhile, on July 13th, the baseball Gods shined down on Minnesota by letting Metropolitan Stadium host the states first-ever All-Star game. And, while the National League won the 36th mid-summer classic, 6-5, local slugger Harmon Killebrew thrilled the 47,000 fans in attendance by smacking a tater for the AL. The AL had rallied back from a 5-0 deficit to tie the contest before Ron Santo's RBI single in the seventh proved to be the eventual game-winner.

From there the Twinks rolled. They had a five game lead in the Division and were playing smart baseball. By season's end the team was hitting on all cylinders. Shortstop Zoilo Versalles led the league in at-bats, runs scored, doubles and triples. Outfielder Tony Oliva batted .321 and won his second straight batting title. Mudcat Grant won 21 games to lead the league and Jim Kaat won 18. To top it off, the Twins had four 20-plus home run hitters: Jimmie Hall, Bob Allison, Don Mincher and Harmon Killebrew. (Mincher came off the bench to hit 22 home runs and 65 RBIs during the pennant drive while filling in for Killebrew, who was hurt following a collision with Baltimore's Russ Snyder.) There was also the bullpen of Al Worthington, Johnny Klippstein, Jim Perry, and Bill Pleis who were, at times, untouchable. The Twins won with smart pitching, a solid defense, and clutch hitting.

On September 26, after battling Chicago and Baltimore for the right to represent the American League in the World Series, the Twins, behind Kitty Kaat, clinched the honor when they beat the Washington Senators on their home field, 2-1. Champagne corks popped following the win as the team knew it was now playing the role of Cinderella. (That Sunday, back at Metropolitan Stadium, the Twins' score was displayed on the scoreboard during the Vikings game against the Lions. When the fans saw it, they rose en masse to cheer them on.) Minnesota finished in first place during that magical year, seven games ahead of the pack with a club-record 102 wins. They would then go on to face the mighty Dodgers of Los Angeles in that fabled October get-together, the World Series. L.A., who had to win 14 of their final 15 games to edge out the San Francisco Giants, were playing red-hot baseball. It would prove to be a study in contrasts as the power of the Twins would challenge the speed, defense and pitching of the Dodgers. The Twins now were

presented with the monumental challenge of facing the heavily-favored Los Angeles Dodgers and their ace pitchers, Sandy Koufax and Don Drysdale, who had won 26 and 23 games, respectively. "The Twins are game, but they are not in the same class as the Dodgers, they'll be lucky if the Series goes to five games," one sportswriter noted.

Finally, on October 6, Game One got underway at the old Met with Vice President Hubert Humphrey tossing out the first ball. From there Mudcat Grant threw the first pitch of the first World Series ever to take place in Minnesota. He would be driven by the familiar chatter of his shortstop, Zoilo Versalles, as he chanted, "Hubba-Hubba-Hubba—Cat!" In a shocker, Dodger ace Sandy Koufax had decided to sit out the opener to attend Yom Kippur — the holiest of Jewish holidays. His place was taken by the almost equally feared Donny Drysdale, a six-foot-six right-hander. The Dodgers struck first with a Ron Fairly home run in the second, but Minnesota answered with a homer of their own, this one from Mincher. Minnesota scored six unanswered runs in the third, highlighted by a Versalles three-run tater. The 47,797 fans watched their Twins take Game One, 8-2.

Game Two featured a pitcher's duel between two of the greatest baseball has ever seen, Koufax and Kaat. Scoreless through five, Left Fielder Bob Allison then made an historic diving, sliding circus catch off of Lefebvre's sinking liner to end a fourth-inning scoring threat. The game was still scoreless until the sixth, when Oliva doubled to score Zoilo, with Killebrew coming in on the next play. In the bottom of the seventh Versalles tripled and scampered home on a Perranoski wild pitch. To add some salt to the wound, Twins Pitcher Jimmy Kaat knocked in Allison and Mincher with an eighth-inning liner. Minnesota was shocking the baseball world, winning, 5-1, and threatening to sweep Los Angeles.

Back at Chavez Ravine in L.A. for Game Three, reality bit as Dodger lefty Claude Osteen faced off against Camilo Pascual. The stars were out in force for this one as well, with Frank Sinatra, Gregory Peck, Doris Day and Milton Berle among the spectators in attendance. The Twins threatened early with Killebrew and Zoilo on the corners, but that would be as close as the Twins got that day, as they were both thrown out in run-downs. The Dodgers' John Roseboro then singled in the fourth, knocking in Fairly and Jim Lefebvre. L.A. added two more runs late, as the Minnesota bats remained quiet. They went on to take Game Three by the final count of 4-0.

Then, in a replay of Game One, Grant and Drysdale were rematched for Game Four. Errors and miscues were the story of the day for the Twins though, as the Dodgers got two easy runs early. Killebrew and Oliva smacked solo taters to make it 3-2, but errors by Hall, Oliva, and Frank Quilici in the sixth, accompanied by a Lou Johnson solo homer in the eighth, opened the flood gates. Los Angeles went on to win the game, 7-2, tying the series at two games apiece.

Game Five featured a rematch of the titans, Kaat and Koufax. This time, Sandy would have the last laugh though as he did something that only one other pitcher had been able to do all season — shut out the Twins at Met Stadium. Koufax went on to take the game, 7-0, striking out 10 for the huge shut-out victory. Maury Wills led the Dodgers with a four-hit performance that equaled the entire Twins' hitting attack. With the win, the Dodgers went ahead three games to two with the series headed back to Bloomington.

The Twins were now 0-for-Osteen in their last seven tries under Mr. Mele. But the Mudcat, despite not feeling very well, had the performance of his life in the sixth game of this epic battle. With Earl Battey aboard, Allison started off the festivities in the fourth by slamming an Osteen offering over the Met's left field wall. In the fifth, Grant masterfully pitched his way out of a bases-loaded, no-outs jam. Then, Mudcat amazed the Metropolitan Stadium crowd by going deep for a home run with Allison and Quilici on board to make it 5-1 in the sixth. Fairly homered for the Dodgers in the seventh, but it was way too little, way too late for Los Angeles. The Mudcat had pitched a six-hit, complete-game gem to tie the series at three games apiece. It would now all come down to the pivotal Game Seven.

In what turned out to be their third World Series go-around, it was Koufax vs. Kaat one last time. No one could believe that Koufax was going to pitch on only two days rest, but he did. In the third, Zoilo singled off Sandy, and then stole second as the hometown fans cheered, only to have the home plate umpire wave him back to first. Dodger announcer Vin Scully, explained the call to the millions of radio and TV listeners across the nation: "Umpire Ed Hurley has just ruled that batter Joe Nossek interfered with Catcher Roseboro's throw. Versalles is going back to first, and Manager Sam Mele is coming out of the dugout." Mele protested, but the call stood. The next batter, Oliva, struck out, ending the potential rally.

In the top of the fourth, Kaat served up a dinger to Johnson, then was abused for a double and then a single, good enough for another run. That would be all for "Kitty," as Relief Pitcher Al Worthington was sent in with the Twins down by the score of 2-0. In the fifth, Twins Second Baseman Frank Quilici doubled off the left field wall. Then Rich Rollins, batting for Worthington, walked, setting the table for Versalles. Zoilo ripped the Koufax offering down the line, only to have L.A.'s Jim Gilliam make the catch of his life, robbing Versalles and the Twins of the World Series crown. Koufax then retired 12 Twin batters in a row before Killebrew could manage a single off him in the ninth. With the tying runner at the plate, Koufax stuck out Battey on three straight. Allison was the last hope. With the count 2-2, the Twins left fielder whiffed. The game ended 2-0, and the Dodgers were World Series champions for the second time in three years. The Twins, who had captured the attention and respect of all baseball, had played their hearts out.

After the season Zoilo Versalles was named as the American League's MVP. There had been some question as to whether or not he would win it, after all, his competition was a regular who's who of baseball: Yankees Pitcher Mel Stottlemyre; Tigers Shortstop Dick McAuliffe; Oriole Third Baseman Brooks Robinson; and Red Sox Right Fielder Carl Yastrzemski. At the annual team dinner, Twins Owner Calvin Griffith gave Zoilo the good news.

"My next announcement should wipe away any last doubts as to why the Minnesota Twins won the pennant this year," he said. "I've just received word from the commissioner's office of the choice for the Most Valuable Player in the American League for 1965. The choice is Zoilo Versalles of the Minnesota Twins!"

Upon receiving the honor, Zoilo was asked to say a few words. He stood silent for a moment, as a hush fell over the audience. Perhaps he was thinking just then of growing up on the dusty streets of Marianao, Cuba, and all he had gone through in his life to get to where he was at that moment. As he stood next to the trophy, he said: "I am just lucky. Lucky to get a base hit, lucky to get a home run, lucky to steal a base, and lucky to be here!" Yet, Zoilo would insist that the honor be given to his best friend, Tony Oliva. "Tony's hitting brought us the pennant," he said. "He was the most valuable to our team."

Zoilo the Great!

Brought into this world on December 15, 1940, in a one-room straw hut in Marianao, Cuba, Zoilo Versalles was born to baseball and pover-

ty. Although he was still small, at the age of 12, he was fast enough to play sandlot baseball. Not being able to afford a glove of his own, he shared a glove from an opposing player when the teams switched sides. At 14, he had all the tools that made up a great shortstop: an arm, the hands, the eyes and speed. As he grew older, Versalles taught himself to read by slowly sounding out the players names on the rosters and in the sports pages of the local paper. Baseball had become his life, and would eventually be his ticket out of poverty.

Zoilo was discovered by "Papa Joe" Cambria, a Washington Senators scout who found him in Cuba. He then helped him come to America where he would become a hero to his native Cubans. Cambria's advice to the young Zoilo: "Eat, sleep, and think baseball." Cookie Lavagetto, manager of the Washington Senators, had a simple formula for his team's success: "Tight pitching and a healthy Zoilo Versalles at short."

Zoilo Versalles was one of the greatest players ever to play for the Twins. From 1961-1967 his Twins career batting average was .252. In addition, he had 1,046 hits, scored 564 runs, belted 86 homers, knocked in 401 RBI's and stole 84 bases in a total of 1,065 games. His greatest season, of course, was that of 1965, when he led the Twins to the World Series and was named as the American League's MVP.

On November 28, 1967, Zoilo was traded to the Dodgers for Pitcher Ron Perranoski and Catcher John Roseboro. He would bounce around for a few more seasons before finally retiring in 1971. Sadly, Zoilo, who made his home in the Twin Cites area, passed away in 1995.

TRIBUTES

"Zoilo was the best Twins shortstop ever," said Tony Oliva. "And, there was nobody better in the league than Zoilo in 1965. He could hit and could catch everything. He covered a lot of ground at shortstop, so nothing got by him. He was a great friend and was like my brother. It was comforting for me to have someone to talk Spanish to, because I too spoke very little English."

"Zoilo had a real fine year in 1965," said Harmon Killebrew. "He played a great shortstop and he hit real well too. He was kind of erratic at times as a young player, but he certainly learned to play the game. He was a big reason we won the pennant that year."

"We had played together in the minors as well, and he was a great talent," said Jim Kaat. "He had as good a year as any ballplayer could have in 1965. I don't know how he did it all, because mentally there was so much additional pressure on him because he was taking care of his family responsibilities on top of everything else. Coming out of Cuba from a situation that we all would consider poverty, and then all of a sudden becoming a star in the major leagues was very difficult for him to handle and his career fizzled out a lot quicker than it should have."

"He was a hero of mine as a kid, so I really looked up to him," said Dave Winfield. "He had a unique style and flare and was just a great ballplayer. I once got a chance to meet him, and it was a genuine thrill for me."

Baseball's All-Star Game is played at Metropolitan Stadium. Hubert Humphrey throws out the first pitch as the National League wins, 6-5

TIMELINE

49

The Minnesota Twins, coming back to earth after their phenomenal World Series run of 1965, encountered some rough luck and caught a few bad breaks in 1966. Led by their ace pitcher, Jim Kaat, who had the season of his career with a 25-13 record, the Twins finished in a respectable second place behind Baltimore in the American League with a record of 89-73.

Injuries hindered Bob Allison and Camilo Pascual, who both sat out for much of the season. In addition, Manager Sam Mele was none too pleased when his overweight catcher, Earl Battey, who after an apparent single, was thrown out at first base from right field by Boston's Lu Clinton. Battey's performance prompted the wry sportscaster Halsey Hall to recall some years later that watching him round second base "looked like he was pushing a safe."

That season, Mele juggled the lineup to shake things up. Harmon Killebrew was moved to third, Don Mincher went to first and Bernie Allen was posted at second. Ted Uhlaender filled in for the injured Allison, and Jimmie Hall and Tony Oliva rounded out the outfield. Killebrew wound up with 39 home runs and 110 RBIs, while Tony Oliva hit .307 with 25 homers and 87 RBIs to boot.

Shortstop Zoilo Versalles, coming off his incredible MVP season, seemed to be only a shadow of his 1965 self, leading the American League not in hits, but in errors. One of the bright spots for Minnesota that season though was the effort of Mr. Versatility, Cesar "Pepe" Tovar, who hit in the lead-off spot, while playing short, second and in the outfield.

The pitching staff was strong in 1966. Along with Kaat's 25 wins, Jim Merritt and Mudcat Grant each added 13, Dave Boswell came up with 12, and Jim Perry, who would win the Cy Young four years later, won 11. Camilo Pascual sat out most of the season with a sore arm, but managed to win eight games as well. In addition, Al Worthington was steady in the bullpen, adding six wins and 16 saves.

With a phenomenal 25-13 record, "Kitty" Kaat was the real story. He posted an impressive 2.74 ERA while striking out 205 hitters. And, in 41 outings he pitched 304 innings, completing 19 games. He was the savior of a pitching staff that struggled to find itself all year long.

"For a pitcher, and all pitchers realize this, sometimes it's not always how you pitch, but when you pitch," said Kaat. "Sometimes you have those years when you pitch mediocre, your team scores a lot of runs, and then when you pitch well, you win 2-1. That's the kind of year I had in 1966. I won a lot of games by blow-outs, but I also won the close ones. I think maybe my best year personally, was probably 1971, when my record was 13-14. But in 1966, it all just came together for me and I just happened to pitch on the right day a lot that year."

Kitty-Kaat

Born in Zeeland, Mich., Jim Kaat was the model of baseball consistency. From 1959 to 1983, the red-headed southpaw become the first pitcher in major league history to ply his trade for 25 years. Winning 20 games several times throughout his career, he was more than just a good pitcher; he ranks up there with the likes of Bob Gibson and Bob Lemon as among the best at all aspects of the game. Though he only had a lifetime .185 batting average, Kaat was nevertheless highly respected as a hitter, considering he belted out 16 home runs over his career. What might be most amazing, however, was the fact that Jim was awarded 16 consecutive gold gloves for his spectacular fielding, a record unlikely to ever be matched by another pitcher.

After a remarkable 25 seasons in the majors, Kaat had appeared in 898 games, placing him fifth in history in the category, and he won 283 of them. With a lifetime ERA of 3.45, Kaat fanned 2,461 batters, had 31 career shutouts, 180 complete games and 18 career saves.

As a member of the Minnesota Twins from 1961-1973, Kaat won 189 games, posted a 3.30 ERA, struck out 1,824 batters, and was selected for an appearance in the All-Star game in 1962 and 1966. The 1961 season was the first year that Jim pitched more than 200 innings for the Twins though. For 10 out of 11 succeeding Twins seasons, he appeared in more than 200 innings for the club and in 1966 he threw in 304 and two-thirds innings to boot. During his stint with the Twins, he also pitched 23 shutouts. He led the team in pitching in 1964 with a 17-11 record and an ERA of 3.22. Two years later, his 25 wins against only 13 losses led the major leagues. He was also the Twins opening-day pitcher in both 1965 and 1967. Kaat even received the Twins Joseph W. Haynes Pitcher of the Year Award in 1966 and 1972 as well.

On August 15, 1973, Kaat was unceremoniously sent packing for the Windy City to join his new team, the White Sox.

"I would have liked to have played my entire career in Minnesota," he said. "I was heartbroken when I heard Calvin Griffith had put me on waivers. Yet, in the back of my mind, I knew what was going on because the Twins had gradually phased me out of being a regular starter and made me into a long reliever. In 1973, I was coming back from a wrist injury that had happened the year before while I was sliding into second base. It took me a while that year to get my stuff back together, and I knew that I was getting stronger and healthier, but could sense the end was near.

"I remember getting a phone call from Calvin while I was golfing at the Minnetonka Country Club, and he told me that the White Sox had picked me up on waivers. That night I went in to clean out my locker and to personally thank Calvin for the years I had in Minnesota. Calvin said 'You know, I really would have liked to have kept you, but my manager told me that he didn't think you could pitch in the big leagues anymore.'

"Then, when I went down to the locker room to pack my bags, I saw Frank Quilici, the manager, and said to him, 'Thanks a lot, good luck, and I appreciated the opportunity.' Frank's words were, 'You know, I would have liked to have kept you, but Calvin didn't think you could pitch in the big leagues anymore.'

"I remember driving to Chicago that day, and it was a very difficult trip for me, reminiscing on my days in the Twin Cities. I really enjoyed it in Minnesota and would have loved to have finished my career there. Looking back, in retrospect, it was a great break for me.

TIMELINE

| Mankato State wrestler Bob Soulek wins the 130 lb. Division II National Championship | Larry Ross' International Falls High School Hockey team wins its third consecutive state championship | Ted Williams, a Minneapolis Miller in 1938, is inducted into the Baseball Hall of Fame | UMD defenseman Bob Hill is named to the All-American hockey team | Eveleth native Frank Brimsek, a former hockey great, is enshrined into the Hockey Hall of Fame in Toronto | Gopher quarterback John McGovern is inducted into the College Football Hall of Fame | St. Paul native Walt Kiesling, a St. Thomas graduate and former guard for the Duluth Eskimos in the 1930s, is inducted into the NFL Hall of Fame | Lou Hudson is drafted as the fourth overall pick in the first round by the St. Louis Hawks. The Gopher All-American forward averaged 20.4 points and 8.8 rebounds per game, ultimately having his #14 retired for eternity. Sweet Lou, a six-time NBA all-star, played for 13 seasons in the pro's and scored nearly 18,000 points finishing 12th on the NBA all-time scoring list. |

Going to Chicago was a stepping stone for me to play another 10 years in the majors, and I got to experience a World Series win with St. Louis in 1982."

After his days as an active player ended, Kaat returned to the Twin Cities as a broadcaster. He teamed with Ted Robinson to do Twins KMSP-TV broadcasts in 1988. The following year, he and Robinson joined WCCO-TV and Midwest Sports Channel on Twins games. He served as a Twins broadcaster until 1993, when he moved to the Big Apple to broadcast Yankees games. He continues to broadcast games and is considered by many to be one of the best in the business. One of the all-time greats, Kitty will be undoubtedly be remembered as one of the best pitchers ever to throw for the Twins.

Most memorable game as a Twin
"Winning Game Two of the 1965 World Series. That was really special."

On playing in the 1965 World Series
"We had such a good team that year. When you're in your mid-twenties, it was so exciting just being there, and I don't think you ever realized how difficult it was just to get there. My feeling at the time was that we were good and going to the Series was going to happen to us more than once. So, maybe I didn't think there was enough sense of urgency. We were enjoying all the festivities, and that may have taken a little of the focus off our winning as well.

"From an individual standpoint, I can remember sitting on the bench next to pitching coach Johnny Sain in Game Two. I had never seen Sandy Koufax in person, and I had heard a lot about him. After seeing him pitch for a few innings, I remember telling Johnny that if we gave up just one run, this game would be over.

"What stands out in my mind is just thinking that there was no way we could win against him, because he looked completely unbeatable. I remember what a dominant pitcher Sandy was. I mean we had a really good hitting ball club that year, and we couldn't touch him at all. Well, it turned out that we scratched out a couple of runs that day off of him, and then they pinch-hit for him later on in the game."

Did you always want to play Baseball?
"Growing up as a kid in Michigan, my first exposure to baseball was the 1945 World Series between the Cubs and the Tigers. From that point on, I just always knew that I wanted to play baseball. It was my dream."

What were your happiest days?
"I was happiest very early on in my career. I can remember a former Twins minor league manager of mine, Del Wilbur, who said to me 'Kid, when you get to the big leagues don't be content to just live there, accomplish something while you're there.' I enjoyed getting there but was driven to make my mark. After you win 20 games, make an all-star team, and play in a World Series, your career kind of settles in from there."

What was it like to win a World Series?
"Winning the World Series with the Cardinals in 1982 was unbelievable. I was 44 years old, and it had been 17 years since I had been in a World Series. I had been given up on a couple of times up to that point, and here I was contributing to a team that won the World Series. I think that was probably as satisfying a year as I ever had."

Were Twins pitchers forgotten heroes?
"The Minnesota Twins have always been known as the lumberjacks,

with all those great home-run hitters through the years, but you have to have pitching to win too. I don't think the pitchers who have gone through that organization have gotten the same high recognition that the Twins hitters have. I'm speaking of pitchers like Frank Viola, Bert Blyleven, Mudcat Grant, Camilo Pasqual, Jim Perry and I. That's not sour grapes on my part; it's a matter of fact."

Which Player of the Modern era reminds you of you?
"I would say probably Yankees Pitcher Andy Pettitte. I enjoy watching him, and when I see him both personally and the way he conducts himself on the mound with his competitive nature, I think I see a lot of him in me, and me in him. There are some similarities; we're both tall lefties. Although, back then, I wish I could have had the poise that he shows now in his early 20s, as well as his unbelievable pick-off move."

Twins Tombstone:
"I think after 25 seasons in baseball, I can look back and honestly say that I never gave less than a maximum effort. Throughout my career, I never had to turn the ball down and was ready to play every day. I take pride in the fact that I never missed a start because of a sore arm, and I felt that I gave the Twins their best days work for their money. I'll never go down as one of the all-time greats, but in my mind I feel good about the fact that I got the most out of my abilities. It meant a lot to me that my teammates had confidence in me, and that I was the guy that they wanted on the mound when we had a big game to win."

TRIBUTES

"Jim was a great pitcher and was always a great competitor," said Harmon Killebrew. "He was one of the finest fielding pitchers that I have ever seen. I mean, he won 16 gold gloves as a pitcher — that's just incredible. He should be in the Hall of Fame."

"Jim was great to be around," said Rod Carew. "He was one of the best hitting pitchers in baseball and one of the top left-handers in the game. Being around Jim and watching him perform day in and day out was an inspiration to me as a young player coming up. He is a very classy person."

"He is a very nice guy and was a good teammate," said Tony Oliva. "He was a pitcher that was great to play behind because if you ever made an error, he would never say anything bad to you about it. He would just say 'come on, let's go!' He was a pleasure to play with, and I really like him."

"I really like Kitty," said Jack Morris. "He was a great pitcher. He does a super job broadcasting and is just a super guy."

"He is a great guy and a great announcer," added Kent Hrbek. "I saw Kitty play at the old Met many times. He had a very unorthodox pitching style, and he would just come right at you with whatever he had. He would tell you to your face that his pitches probably couldn't even break a pane of glass, but, nonetheless, he knew how to pitch and was just a great pitcher."

Mahnomen native Joe Guyon, a former NFL halfback, is inducted into the Pro Football Hall of Fame

On March 11, 1965, National Hockey League President Clarence Campbell announced that his six-team league would expand, creating six new teams for the NHL's Western Division. A group of nine Twin City businessmen led by Gordon Ritz, Bob McNulty, and Walter Bush, Jr., then joined in a partnership to control the new franchise.

Plans were swiftly put into motion and the ground in Bloomington was broken for the new $7 million Metropolitan Sports Center. The structure was erected in less than a year, just in time for the North Stars' maiden season.

On June 6, 1967, the draft was held. Wren Blair, a hockey veteran of junior and minor league coaching, scouting, player personnel, and managing, was named as the team's first GM and later the first coach. It would be his job to set about the impossible task of selecting his team's first 20 players. So, with the first pick, Blair opted to draft a young goaltender from the New York Rangers by the name of Cesare Maniago, who was already known by the locals from his minor league playing stint with the Minneapolis Bruins of the CPHL. Among the other skaters he chose that day included two diamonds in the rough from Boston: Wayne Connelly and Bill Goldsworthy. Goldsworthy, of course, would emerge as the team's first superstar, carrying the franchise on his back for its first decade of existence.

The Stars were anxious to make an immediate impact in the league, and as a result, gambled away a lot of their future draft picks in order to obtain some immediate talent. Because the established clubs had been stockpiling talent in the minor leagues, they were able to pawn off their kids, who were green, as well as their veterans, who were too old, onto the expansion teams. Add to the that the fact that the established clubs could bargain with the expansion teams with the lure of cash and future considerations to entice their counterparts to "pass over" their most coveted unprotected players, and it was a mess. When it was all over though, Blair was a bit skeptical to say the least about his new roster of has-been's and cast-off's.

"Good Lord," said Blair to his scouting staff after the draft on the 20 players he had just obtained for the mere price of $100,000 each, "just look at this mess. This is supposed to be a major league hockey

team. There are only four guys on this list that are major league players. Your job and mine is to unload the other 16 just as fast as we can, any way we can. I'll trade 10-for-one if I have to."

Blair even wanted to stop taking players at one point in the draft, but Clarence Campbell told him that he had to take all 20.

The stage was now set. The anticipation for big-time hockey in Minnesota was immense, and season ticket sales soared even well before the team hit the ice. The team was forced to play their first four games on the road however, because the arena's new

seats weren't quite finished being installed. Then, on Oct. 11, 1967, the Stars hit the ice to play their first-ever contest against St. Louis. The Stars first-ever goal was scored by Bill Masterton, but the team wound up tying the Blues 2-2. On a side note, the first fight in franchise history also took place that night, between the Stars' Bill Plager and Blues defenseman, Bob Plager — who incidentally, was his big brother. *(Mom and Dad must've been so proud...)*

On October 21st the Stars faced off against the Oakland Seals for their inaugural home opener. The packed Met Center crowd, who had seemingly waited a lifetime for the NHL to finally come to Minnesota, was delighted to see a young blonde-haired kid from Kitchener, Ontario, tally the team's first-ever goal in the new arena. His name was Bill Goldsworthy, but they would soon come to know him simply as "Goldy!" The two teams excited the crowd that night with a brand of hockey that Minnesotans had never known before, ultimately skating to a 3-3 tie.

Midway through the season, the Stars would encounter a tragedy that was to influence hockey players of all ages for years to come. On what seemed to be just another normal play in a game that season, Winger Bill Masterton was fatally injured after falling and striking his head on the ice. Masterton, a popular player, was a long-time minor leaguer who was enjoying his first NHL season with the Stars when the accident occurred. (Today every player in the NHL is required to wear a helmet because of that incident some 35 years ago.)

With the memory of Masterton's tragic death on their minds, the Stars played inspired hockey the rest of the way through their inaugural season. They finished the regular season with a modest record of 27 wins, 32 losses and 15 ties — good for fourth in the Western Division, just four points out of first. Wayne Connelly led the team in scoring that first year with 35 goals and 21 assists for 56 points.

It was off to the playoffs for the rookie North Stars, who were matched against Goalie Terry Sawchuk and the Los Angeles Kings. L.A. took the first two games of the best of seven series, only to see Minnesota rally back to even the series. The Kings then went up 3-2, only to see the Stars come back one more time to tie it up. Stars forward Milan Marcetta won the sixth game with an overtime goal, and with the momentum on their side, the Stars went on to rout the Kings in Los Angeles, 9-4. Minnesota, who scored a club record nine goals to win the rugged quarterfinal contest, would now face the St. Louis Blues to determine who would play in the Stanley Cup Finals.

Now, even though the Stars were hot, like any expansion team, they weren't yet exactly commanding a lot of respect around town. Such was the case in the second-round playoff series against St. Louis, when it was announced that five of the seven games had to be played in St. Louis because the Ice Capades had already booked the Met Center for a show. Unphazed over losing their home ice advantage, the Stars marched ahead by winning two of the first three games against the Blues.

Game Four of the series was a grinder. Through the third period the Stars were up 3-0, only to see the Blues tally twice within a two minute span. Then with only 11 seconds to go in the game, Blues Forward Jim Roberts scored his second goal of the game to send it to overtime. Then, only two minutes into the OT, Gary Sabourin scored on a wrister to win it for the Blues.

Excited to finally play in the Met Center, Minnesota got back on track the next night, only to lose another overtime heartbreaker.

TIMELINE

| Mankato State wrestler Bob Soulek wins the 130 lb. Division II National Championship | Mankato State Wrestler Bob Wendel wins the 145 lb. Division II National Championship | Gopher center Tom Kondla is named to the All-American basketball team | Gopher end Bob Stein is named to the All-American football team | Gopher first baseman Dennis Zacho is named to the All-American baseball team | UMD center Keith Christianson is named to the All-American hockey team | The Gopher football team earns a three-way tie for the Big Ten title | George Mikan founds and serves as president of the new American Basketball Association, headquartered in Minneapolis | The ABA's Muskies, coached by former Laker Jim Pollard, play in Minnesota for one season |

52

With their backs against the wall though, the guys in green came back in front of a packed house and crushed St. Louis, 5-1, in Game Six.

The Seventh and final game, which shifted back to the Gateway-Arch City, would go down as a classic. It would come down to which goaltender wanted it more, Cesare Maniago or St. Louis' Glenn Hall. The game was scoreless through the first two periods until Stars Winger Walt McKechnie blasted a goal past Hall with only four minutes to go in the game. But, only seconds later, the Blues would tie it up, forcing the teams to play yet another extra period. Then, just before the end of the game, Stars winger Wayne Connelly broke loose on a breakaway, only to get mugged by a Blues defender. As Connelly went down, the fans back home thought for sure that there would be a penalty shot issued, but it never came. The score was still 1-1 after the first overtime period, which meant double-overtime. Then, only three minutes into the second OT, the Blues' Ron Shock blasted a slapshot past Maniago for the game-winner. After nearly 83 minutes of great "old-time" hockey, it was a bitter pill for the Cinderella Stars to swallow. The Blues, who were absolutely spent by the end of this emotional and physical series, went on to get swept by Montreal in the Finals.

"It was just a phenomenal experience," said Lou Nanne, a Gopher All-American who joined the team shortly after playing in the Olympics that year. "To be able to have NHL hockey right in your own back yard and see it every week was something that I was really excited about. Playing was just a thrill for me and that the first season we had a pretty good year, making a great playoff run. The Stars got some credibility after that playoff series with the Blues."

"Sweet Lou from the Soo"

Lou Nanne has become synonymous with the game of hockey in Minnesota. A native of Sault Ste. Marie, Ontario, Louie grew up playing Junior hockey with hall of famers Phil and Tony Esposito. Originally wanting to go to college to be a dentist, Lou came to Minnesota and played for John Mariucci's Golden Gopher hockey teams from 1961-1963. Nanne refers to Mariucci as his "second father," and is forever grateful to him for giving him the opportunity to play hockey at Minnesota.

Earning Gopher captain and All-American honors in his senior year, Nanne tallied a career-high 74 points, becoming the first defenseman to win a WCHA scoring title. For his efforts the newly naturalized American citizen was named as the league's MVP.

"I loved playing hockey at the University of Minnesota," said Nanne, "it was a real privilege. I had tremendous fun all the way through, and it was just a great experience. I really enjoyed the atmosphere, and it was something I will always cherish."

Upon graduating from the University, Lou was drafted by Chicago into the NHL. Nanne got into a contract dispute with the Blackhawks, however, and ultimately refused to play for them, which led to a five year layoff from hockey. While he sat out, he worked for Minneapolis businessman Harvey Mackay's envelope company and also coached the Gopher freshman hockey team for four years as well. During that time, he played on and off with the USHL's Rochester Mustangs, and also went on to captain the 1968 Olympic hockey team in Grenoble, coached by former Gopher All-American Murray Williamson. When the NHL expanded, Chicago couldn't "freeze" him anymore because of the new Reserve List. So, Nanne became a free agent and decided to play for Minnesota's new expansion team.

Lou quickly earned a reputation as being a good team player for the Stars. Polished at killing penalties, he also developed into a fine checking forward who was often matched against the other teams' top line. Louie, considered as Minnesota's "Ice God," would go on to play defense and winger for the North Stars through 1978, becoming the only player to play with the Stars in all of the first 11 years of the

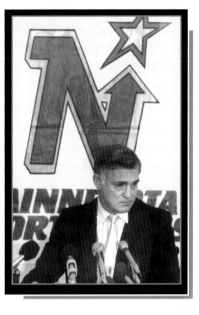

team's existence. He also represented USA during the 1976 and 1977 World Championships, where he served as team captain. In addition, he played for the U.S. in the 1977 Canada Cup series, and later served as GM of Team USA for the Canada Cup in 1981, 1984 and 1987. For his career with the North Stars, including the playoffs, he tallied 72 goals and 167 assists for 239 points.

He then went from player to coach in 1978, and later was appointed as the general manager by Glen Sonmor from 1978-1988.

"It was a lot of fun as a general manager, making very important day-to-day decisions, but there is not a better job in the world than actually playing the game on the ice. Whenever you can play something that you loved as a kid and then they pay you for it, well it doesn't get any better than that."

Of the players on the 1981 Stanley Cup team, only five were left from the team that Nanne took over in 1978. Bobby Smith was his first pick and Mike Modano would be his last. He quickly became known around the league as a shrewd wheeler and dealer of talent. He had clout with the other GM's around the league and parlayed that into his favor. In 1979 he claimed Dave Semenko from Glen Sather's Edmonton Oilers in the expansion draft for the sole purpose of dealing him right back to Sather in a "gentleman's agreement" to leave Neal Broten available for them in that year's upcoming amateur draft. Neal, of course, went on to become a legend in Minnesota. Louie finished his 24-year career with the Stars as the team president from 1988-1990.

Although Canadian by birth, Nanne became a well-known advocate of the Americanization of the NHL. He was one of the first to scout U.S. colleges for American talent and to take an active role in the support of player-development programs, which also included Olympic and international competition. He also wasn't just involved with the North Stars. For his many contributions to USA hockey, Nanne was honored as a recipient of the 1989 Lester Patrick award. And, in 1998 he was inducted into the U.S. Hockey Hall of Fame.

Possibly the most recognized hockey figure in the state, Lou is extremely well liked and respected by his peers. He had been a fixture with the North Stars from start to finish and is the authority on hockey in Minnesota today. His quick wit, colorful sense of humor and knowledge of the game also landed him several TV commentating jobs, including Stanley Cup playoffs and Finals for "Hockey Night in Canada," CBS and NBC. But his favorite colorman gig is still covering the annual State High School Hockey Tournament, something he has done now since 1964. Lou went on to become a very successful businessman with the Minneapolis-based Voyageur Asset Management Co. Later, he even beat prostate cancer. That's Lou, a real winner.

On the North Stars moving to Dallas:

"It was like losing a relative. It was just a really disheartening experience for me."

Gopher/North Star Tombstone: "He always played with the philosophy of never letting anybody beat you because they outworked you."

Twins pitcher Dean Chance throws two no-hitters in the month of August (2-0 over Boston and 2-1 over Cleveland) [One was a five-inning perfect game]

Harmon Killebrew hits the longest home run ever in Metropolitan Stadium: 520 feet

TIMELINE

53

ANN BANCROFT

St. Paul's Ann Bancroft is one of the world's pre-eminent polar explorers, having become the first woman ever to cross the ice to both the North and South Poles. Growing up in Minnesota, Ann loved the outdoors and never seemed to mind the icy cold winters. After receiving her Bachelor of Science degree in Physical Education from the University of Oregon, she went into teaching. Aside from her amazing polar expeditions, Ann has taught physical and special education in Minneapolis schools. She has also coached sports, at various age levels, such as softball, basketball, track and field, volleyball, tennis, cross-country skiing, backpacking and canoeing.

Following her successful ascent of Mt. McKinley in 1983, Ann became the first woman to travel across the ice to the North Pole, when she accomplished the feat in 1986 with fellow Minnesotan Will Steger. Ann, then a 30-year-old schoolteacher from Sunfish Lake, made history when she joined the seven-person team that crossed the Arctic ice pack with Steger's International Polar Expedition. They averaged 20 miles a day on the 500 mile trek, living primarily on pemmican, butter, cheese, peanut butter and oats. The team wasn't totally primitive though. With the aid of homing devices that talked to satellites, they arranged to have some of their 49 sled dogs airlifted out as their load lightened. Bancroft even documented the dogsled journey as a photographer and cinematographer for National Geographic.

"Reaching the North Pole was almost anticlimactic, mainly because we'd just put in a series of 14-hour days and were pretty tired," said Bancroft. "And the North Pole, unlike the South, really looks like the day before and the day before that. It's not like climbing a mountain and reaching the peak. At the North Pole you can look around and not really get the sense that you're at the top of the world. There's no flag, and there's no pole." She went on to add, "The toughest time was when we were in between all the excitement of starting off and the satisfaction of finishing. That's when I'd get flickers of the torch-bearing element — the sense that others, women especially, might be counting on me. I didn't want to be the one turning back. I felt that a lot of people were rooting for me and that there was really some significance for others in my reaching the pole."

The Pole Leader

In 1993, after more than four years of training, which included an Antarctic trip to Great Slave Lake in the Northwest Territories and a traverse of the Greenland ice cap, Ann went to the South Pole. This time she served as team leader for the American Women's Expedition (AWE), a group of four courageous women who skied over 660 miles (averaging 10 miles per day for 67 days), pulling 200-pound sleds through the ice and snow across Antarctica to reach the pole. The group set off from Hercules Inlet and skied into headwinds of up to 50 miles per hour during the constant daylight of the Antarctic summer, in sub-zero temperatures. In so doing, the team became the first all American women's team to ski from the edge of Antarctica to the South Pole as well as the first all women's team to traverse Greenland. They also became the first women to travel to the South Pole without dogs or motorized vehicles

The group's achievements included highlighting the strengths of women as well as providing an educational program for thousands of young people on the environmental challenges in Antarctica. They also conducted physiological and psychological research pertaining to women under extreme conditions and heightened awareness surrounding environmental issues facing Antarctica and their global impact. Ann has brought a much needed awareness to the continent, which represents 70 percent of the world's fresh water supply and is a vital resource for further understanding global warming on our planet.

To top it all off; in 2001, Ann and Norwegian Liv Arnesen became the first women to ice-sail and ski across Antarctica which encompassed a 94 day, 1,717 mile journey.

Today Ann resides in the Twin Cities. Now a busy entrepreneur with interests in film and education as well as outdoor adventures, Ann is very popular on the lecture circuit as a speaker and seminar leader for corporations, schools, and non-profit organizations. Her presentations cover a variety of topics ranging from polar exploration to women's issues. She has also been an active citizen diplomat — working with American/Soviet exchange programs, such as the "Ski for Peace" program, which are designed to foster communication and understanding between people of different nations. Today she can frequently be found in the woods of northern Minnesota, doing what she loves most: exploring and learning. Ann is also an active participant in a number of non-profit and volunteer organizations. A recipient of countless awards and honors, including Ms. Magazine's Outstanding Woman of the Year in 1987, as well as being inducted into the National Women's Hall of Fame, she continues to give of herself and set a positive example for young women everywhere. She is a true Minnesota treasure.

MOOSE GOHEEN

White Bear Lake native Moose Goheen joined the St. Paul Athletic Club in the fall of 1915, and from there went on to become one of Minnesota's greatest hockey superstars. The crowds at his games would chant "Moose" "Moose," to which Goheen would reply by first circling his own net several times to pick up speed, and then make an end-to-end rush, usually scoring. In addition to leading the AC to several McNaughton Cups, Moose also played on the 1920 silver medal-winning U.S. Olympic Hockey team.

He continued to play with the St. Paul team through 1926 when it turned professional and then on through 1932. He was offered pro contracts from both Toronto and Boston, but opted instead to stay in Minnesota and continue working at Northern States Power Company. In 1952 Moose was selected to the Hockey Hall of Fame in Toronto, becoming one of the few Americans ever to have done so. In 1958 he was voted by the Minnesota Hall of Fame as the finest player ever produced in the state.

THE LEGEND OF THE JOHN BEARGREASE SLED DOG RACE

Each January, in an annual Northern Minnesota right of passage, thousands of eager spectators gather on the shores of Lake Superior to cheer on more than a thousand sled dogs and their mushers as they pay homage to the North Shore's most infamous mail carrier, John Beargrease.

Each year more than 30 sled dog teams follow the beautiful North Star Trail from Duluth through Two Harbors and over to Grand Marais and back, for the $10,000 first-prize of what's commonly referred to as "The Beargrease." The route, precariously nestled in between the rugged Sawtooth Mountains and treacherous Lake Superior, makes for a spectacular backdrop. For 500 grueling miles the competitors run around the clock, taking 13 six-hour mandatory lay-overs over the four-to-five day trek, finishing at Duluth's Lester Park.

Though most dogs are Alaskan Huskies, there are a few Greyhounds, Coonhounds and Foxhounds thrown into the mix. On a typical sled dog team, there is either a lead dog or a pair of point dogs out in front. Then there are a pair of swing dogs, followed by the pair just before the sled — the wheel dogs, who are responsible for pulling the sled around tight corners.

As race time approaches and the festivities heighten at Duluth's Ordean Field, the mushers make last-minute adjustments to make sure everything is just right. They untangle their harnesses and ropes, fit their dogs with protective booties, and even pamper their pooches with canine pedicures.

Each team begins the race pulling two sleds, complete with two drivers and a passenger. When the race starts there are two people on the sled. The second passenger, who pays a hefty sum for the privilege of the bumpy ride, serves a purpose. They ride along for the first six miles and then get off at the first check-point. As one of the mushers explained: "These dogs don't have a low gear. It's full speed ahead regardless of the terrain, time, or temperature." With only foot-brakes that drive metal spikes into the snow to slow them down, the mushers can't contain an anxious Husky. When the race starts, the dogs are hyper and excited, and unless there is a lot of weight to slow them down, they will take off and go like hell. The result could be deadly if they took a corner too fast and send the sled crashing into a tree.

Before the race is started, a "Scent team" of 16 Huskies is given a five-minute head start. Much like the pace-car, for the Indianapolis 500, the team lays down its' scent for the first team to follow. With their keen senses of smell, the dogs follow the scent, overriding any smells of humans, snowmobiles, or even a stray wolf or moose.

The dogs can't stand the wait, and it sometimes takes a dozen people just to contain the howling hounds. The mushers also have to be well-conditioned athletes, often having to run for miles at a time through the snow behind their sleds to ease the load.

With their sleds packed with gear, food, and plenty of dog chow, they take off. The snow flies as dozens of paws go for broke through the snow! Some sleds are old and others are fabricated out of space-age polymers, but they all take off to the roar of the crowd in hopes of not only winning, but just finishing the grueling race. When the mushers take off from the starting chute, the first team wears No. 2. That's because No. 1 is always reserved for the spirit of John Beargrease. In addition to basic survival gear, among the standard attire for each musher is a mail bag — in memory of the race's namesake.

The Legend

In 1858, John Beargrease was born the son of Chippewa Chief Moquabimentem, to the Grand Portage Band of Chippewa. John married Louisa Wishcob and together they had 10 children. Beargrease was best known for his legendary mail delivery runs up and down the North Shore. From 1887 to 1900, he hiked, sailed, and rowed, and, in the winter months, traveled by dog sled, devotedly delivering the mail week after week. He was even known by some as "the renown pilot of Lake Superior," often times dangerously challenging its thin and shifting winter ice to get the mail through. Today's postal creed of "Nor rain, nor sleet, nor snow..." mentions nothing about Lake Superior ice, bears, wolves and frostbite — all daily occurrences for old John.

His round-trip, bi-weekly mail route went from Two Harbors to Grand Marais. Known for his dependability and predictability, he provided the only link of communication to the outside world for many of the North Shore's isolated inhabitants. As soon as they heard the familiar sound of the bells on the dogs' collars (worn to scare off wolves), they knew John was coming with good news. Each homestead and settlement depended greatly on him for news and messages from their loved ones.

His ability to drive a dog sled in Minnesota's extreme conditions remains legendary. Averaging 30 to 40 miles a day, he once made the trip from Two Harbors to Grand Marais in 20 hours. More impressive is the fact that he raced with a team of only four dogs, who, at times, were pulling a loaded mail sled that weighed up to 800 pounds. And, that was over ungroomed trails, all while navigating through streams and rocky terrain with only the stars as his guide. Sometimes Beargrease found it easier to trek across frozen Lake Superior to avoid the hilly landscape. Sometimes he even broke through the treacherous ice and plunged into the lake's deadly winter waters, risking his life for others.

In 1895 John was given a two year contract from the government to deliver the mail for the annual sum of $728. In 1897, with the population growing in the northwoods and the trails improving, he traded in his dogs for a team of horses named Red Charley and White Charley. Together they hauled the mail on a new steel sled that weighed 350 pounds. It was John's efficient use of his horses on those trails that convinced Lake County officials to finally upgrade them, eventually leading to the construction of Lake Shore Road. John Beargrease ended his postal duties in 1900 and retired to Grand Portage.

Beargrease lived a heroic life, and fittingly, he died while performing a heroic act. In 1910, as a result of rushing to the aid of another mail carrier whose boat was caught in the high seas off Tamarack Point in Grand Portage Bay, John contracted pneumonia and died. He was laid to rest in Beaver Bay's Chippewa Cemetery.

Today his lore lives on forever, and in some parts rivals that of Paul Bunyan. Through his memory, Northern Minnesota honors and celebrates the man through the annual John Beargrease Sled Dog Marathon. With participants that come to Duluth from all over the world to participate in the event, it has become the main long-distance dogsled race in the lower 48 states. Because of the race's popularity and success, there are also two shorter races from Duluth to Grand Marais (100 miles) and Duluth to Beaver Bay (190 miles).

With a year of Coach Bud Grant's conservative play-calling under their belts, and a new bunch of pieces in place, including the addition of new Offensive Coordinator Jerry Burns, the Vikings came out and posted a much improved 8-6 record in 1968, giving them their first divisional title. Ron Yary, the highly touted Offensive Tackle out of USC, would join the team that year as part of the deal which sent Tarkenton to New York, as would Safety Charlie West, Fullback Oscar Reed and Quarterback Bob Lee. Safety Paul Krause also came over in a trade with the Redskins, while Wide Receiver John Henderson and Linebacker Wally Hilgenberg were claimed on waivers. Krause and West would join an already solid secondary which was led by Corners Ed Sharockman, Earsell Mackbee, Dale Hackbart and Karl Kassulke.

So, after a 3-1 start, Minnesota lost three straight, won its next three, dropped two more, and then needed to win its final two games to have a shot at making it into the playoffs. After beating San Francisco, 30-20, the title hung in the balance as the Vikings went off to Philadelphia to meet Grant's former team, the Eagles.

"We had to win our last game against the Eagles to clinch it, and I remember it was snowing and icy," recalled Grant. "We ended up scoring a couple big play touchdowns on a bad field. Usually teams play conservatively on bad conditions, but I had played enough games on bad fields to know that you can make big plays on bad fields easier than on good fields. So we got a couple big plays and won the game. Then we sat in the locker room and listened to the outcome of the Packers vs. Bears game. The Pack won, 28-17, and we had our first divisional title. (Reporter) Sid Hartman was relaying the information over the phone to us. It was a great feeling."

The Vikes finished the season with a modest record of 8-6, then headed east, to face the mighty Baltimore Colts in the Western Conference Playoff Game. Led by Coach Don Shula, the Colts went on to defeat Minnesota in a rainy and muddy Memorial Stadium by the final of 24-14. Earl Morrall, who had taken over for Johnny Unitas, was the top ranked quarterback in the league that year, made his presence felt. He threw a pair of TD passes on the day, while six-foot-seven, 300-pound Defensive End Bubba Smith tattooed Kapp to force a fumble which was then returned 60 yards for another score by Mike Curtis, to get the Colts up 21-0 in the third quarter. Kapp rallied the troops late in the game though, completing a record 26 of 44 passes for 287 yards, and throwing for a pair of TD passes to Tight End Billy Martin and Running Back "Boom Boom" Brown.

"It was a rough game," said Vikings Quarterback Joe Kapp, who took a bloody beating but played like a hero. "The Colts blitzed us with everything they had, sometimes with as many as a nine men at once, and it caused problems for us."

After the loss, the Vikings went on to play the loser of the Miami vs. Dallas game where they lost to the Cowboys, 17-13, in the NFL's "Runner-up Bowl." In that game, rookie Corner Bobby Bryant returned a punt 81 yards for a touchdown, and Fred Cox kicked two field goals to help Minnesota build a 13-0 lead. But Cowboy quarterbacks Don Meredith and Craig Morton each tossed touchdown passes to rally Dallas to victory.

The Vikings were a team on the rise and one of their emotional leaders, Jim Marshall, played an important role in taking them to the promised land the very next season.

"Winning the divisional title in 1968 was very special." he said. "We worked very hard to get there, and we knew that we had a great core of guys that could go even further. Unfortunately, in our first Super Bowl, we were in a cloud. I think we felt that there was no way we could lose. We were very confident that we could go out, perform, give our best, and win it all. I was deeply saddened at the loss to Kansas City, but it was a wonderful experience just getting there."

The Iron Man
Jim Marshall was born in 1937, in Danville, Ky., and attended East High School, in Columbus, Ohio. He went on to become an All-American Defensive End at Ohio State, and was one of the stars of the 1959 Rose Bowl title team that beat Oregon, 10-7. After playing in the CFL and then with the Cleveland Browns for one season, in 1960, he was acquired by the Vikings, where he anchored one side of the infamous "Purple People Eater" defensive line from 1961-1979. The two-time Pro-Bowler also served as the team's captain, an honor extremely fitting of the type of amazing player that he was.

When it as all said and done the numbers were astounding. From 1961 to 1979, over 19 seasons, he played in an NFL record 270 consecutive games, and 302 consecutive regular season and post season games. Like dog-years, in football-years, that's got to be close to a millennium. And one of the reasons he was able to survive that long down in the trenches was because of Bud Grant's willingness and understanding of what made each guy tick. He knew that Marshall hated to practice and would do anything he could go get out of it. So, every now and then, Bud would accommodate his "mystery" illnesses that would pop up in mid-week to let him take a sauna and get ready for Sunday.

Marshall's legend and lore includes several incredible stories that exemplify the many obstacles he hurdled over the course of his career. For example, a few months before joining the Browns, while stationed at an army training camp, Marshall was stricken with encephalitis. Although he lost over 40 pounds, he still reported to camp and insisted on playing. Jim was a warrior in the best sense of the word. He loved adventure and on more than one occasion it nearly killed him, literally. In 1964, while cleaning his gun, Marshall accidentally shot himself in the side. Once during training camp, he was hospitalized when a grape, of all things, became lodged in his windpipe. Another time, while visiting the American troops during the Vietnam War, he underwent a tonsillectomy that resulted in severe hemorrhaging.

In 1971, Marshall almost died in a snowmobile accident on a trip throughout the Grand Teton Mountains in Wyoming. After his snowmobile went over a cliff and nearly crushed him in the midst of a blizzard, his group was forced to burn $20 bills to keep warm on their three-day ordeal. Marshall later said, "It was the toughest thing I've

TIMELINE

Duluth's John Clawson wins a gold medal on the Olympic Basketball team	Ron Yary, a tackle from USC, is the first overall pick selected in the first round by the Vikings in the NFL draft	Gopher center Gary Gambucci is named to the All-American hockey team	The Edina boy's High School basketball dynasty ends after winning three state championships	Gopher end Ed Rogers is inducted into the College Football Hall of Fame	The ABA's Minnesota Pipers finish second in the Eastern Division. They leave town the next year.	Twins utility player Cesar Tovar plays all nine positions in one game

56

ever encountered in my life, I thought we were all going to die." As a matter of fact, one member of his 16 person group did. Then, in 1980, Jim survived a near-fatal motorized hang-glider accident. He was an enigma, and that's why everybody loved him so much. It was if they wanted to live vicariously through him. It was as if he was Superman himself.

How he played through all of those injuries that would keep 90% of today's players out of the line-up is unconscionable. He played for the love of the game and lived for Sundays. Perhaps former team-mate Ahmad Rashad summed it up best when he described Marshall as "A Viking among men and a giant among Vikings."

One of the initiation rituals for many Vikings rookies was to make the road-trip to training camp in Mankato, with Marshall behind the wheel. For most humans that trip took ninety minutes, but Jim usually made it in about 45 minutes, with the rookies screaming the entire distance. He loved adventure, wherever it presented itself.

But there is also another side of Marshall — the one who studied Oriental philosophy, wrote poetry and even modeled men's clothing. He once took a brokerage test and was given a genius rating. He described life as "wonderful, with so many things to be enjoyed," he said. "I think too many times we restrict ourselves to a small box with a limited wish list on each wall. I like to raise my head above the walls and look out into the horizon and think about all the possibilities that are out there to better enjoy my life. That outlook makes life interesting. It gives you the opportunity to grow as a person. I want to enjoy everything as much as I can while I still occupy this physical body. Because, one day, when I no longer have this earthly vehicle, I want to feel as though I truly had an opportunity to enjoy everything that was available to me."

Jim Marshall, the Captain, will always be remembered as a Vikings legend. Fittingly, on Nov. 28, 1999, in a game against the San Diego Chargers, the Vikings celebrated "Jim Marshall Day," officially retiring his No. 70 jersey in front of a thrilled and appreciative sell-out Metrodome crowd.

On his unbelievable durability and ability to play through pain, Marshall would modestly reply, "I played because I loved the game."

Another way Jim will always be remembered, for better or for worse, is the now infamous "Wrong-Way-Play." In 1964, while playing in San Francisco against the 49ers, Marshall was involved in a play that will forever be a part of NFL film anthologies. During the game, he picked up a San Francisco fumble and ran for the end zone — only it was the wrong end zone! He motored 66 yards right into his own end zone, in the process handing the 49ers two points for a safety. Luckily though, to Marshall's considerable relief, the Vikings still beat the Niners, 27-22.

When asked about the play Jim said, "It was very simple in my mind. It was one of those things where I just got all turned around. I picked up the ball and thought I was going the right way. Of course I wouldn't have run at all if I didn't think I was going the right way. So I crossed the goal-line and threw the ball out of bounds to celebrate, and then, Bruce Bosely, a 49er, ran up to me and said, 'Thanks Jim!' He was giving me the razz, and then it hit me... I had really done something bad. But, what nobody remembers, is that during that game, I went back and caused the fumble that Carl Eller picked up to score the game-winning touchdown. They don't talk about that now do they?"

Today Jim is a cancer survivor and works in the inner city with at-risk youth. He also formed a social service agency along with Oscar Reed, a Viking teammate, called Professional Sports Linkage. Jim described it as, "a service that has programs to help everyone from young people, to senior citizens, to new immigrants, to adjudicated youth — while they are incarcerated, all to create positive, tax-paying, productive members of our society."

Most Memorable game?
"We were playing the Rams in the playoffs, and they were on the one-foot line ready to score the game-winning touchdown. But we dug in, held them, and eventually blocked a kick to win the game. It was an amazing experience."

When were you happiest in your career?
"The early 1970s and particularly 1970, when we lost to the Niners in the playoffs, 17-14. We had our best team that year, maybe of all time. It was unfortunate that one bad call by the referee changed everything. Overall, it was my happiest season and also the saddest season at the same time. I really felt like we were headed back to the Super Bowl."

Vikings Tombstone
"I would like to be thought of as a guy who gave everything he had to give on the football field and did whatever was necessary for his team to help win the game. I had fun doing it, and I tried to give the best that I could give to win."

TRIBUTES
"Jim Marshall was one of the finest athletes I have ever coached," said Bud Grant. "He had durability, and that was the greatest ability you could have. He was one of the finest competitors the Vikings have ever had, period."

"He was the best," said Carl Eller. "He epitomized the term 'Viking.' I am still very good friends with Jim, and I cherish our friendship very dearly. Together we went through a lot out there and he was just a fabulous football player. He was so quick off the ball and was just fearless. I have a lot of respect for him as a player and as a person."

"Jim was a phenomenal football player and a really good friend," said Alan Page. "He is somebody who was dedicated and committed to the game of football and to his franchise. I guess the best way to describe him would be when you look up the definition of professional football in the dictionary, you should find Jim Marshall's name."

"Jim Marshall was our leader," said Chuck Foreman. "A guy that anybody would follow. He is a unique man in that he had the greatest mind control of anybody I've ever seen. He was the heart and soul of the Minnesota Vikings."

"Captain Marshall! Man, he was fearless," said Ahmad Rashad. "He was the epitome of a football captain. He should definitely be in the Pro Football Hall of Fame. No, they should have a separate wing in the Hall of Fame just for him."

"To me, aside from being a magnificent player, Jim was the spirit of the Vikings," said Joe Kapp. "He represented the essence of spirit and leadership. There would be no player who would stand up more for basic, fundamental, consistent values in team sports than Jim Marshall. He was always there for his teammates on and off the field, and he is a wonderful person."

Minnesota finally turned the corner as one of the league's premier teams in 1969, going 12-2 and earning a trip to their first ever Super Bowl. Being seen on Sunday afternoons at the Met was the "in" thing to do by this time, as tail-gating outside of the old stadium took on a life of its own. The fans were crazy for the purple by now and the team was front-page news on a daily basis. Led by their emotional leader, Joe Kapp, the Vikings embraced a new campaign slogan for that season called "40 for 60," which meant that 40 men playing together for 60 minutes, couldn't lose.

The season started out on a downer, however, as the Vikes lost their opener, 24-23, to Fran Tarkenton's New York Giants in Yankee Stadium. Minnesota rebounded to pound Baltimore, 52-14, thanks to Kapp's amazing seven-touchdown performance though. He hit everybody on that "spiritual" day including: Dave Osborn, Bobby Grim, Kent Kramer, John Beasley, Jim Lindsey, and a pair to Gene Washington. That next week against Green Bay, the Vikings made history by playing at the U of M's Memorial Stadium. (The Twins were playing Baltimore in the American League playoffs that day at the Met) No problem though, as the Vikes went on to beat the Pack, 19-7.

From there Minnesota didn't look back, as the team's unstoppable defense led them to a record 12 consecutive victories. In Week Three the "Purple People Eaters" sacked Bart Starr eight times, only to sandwich Chicago's Bobby Douglass nine times just four weeks later. In Week Eight the Vikings scored on their first nine possessions en route to a 51-3 win. In Week 10 Safety Paul Krause picked-off Pittsburgh Quarterback Dick Shiner and took off 77 yards for a touchdown. The score put the Vikes into the lead, and they went on to crush the Steelers, 52-14. In Week 12 they met the Rams out in L.A., who were riding an 11 game winning streak of their own. The Vikes took control early though and went on to beat the Lambs, 20-13. After beating the 49ers the next week, Minnesota found themselves with a 12-game winning streak —the NFL's longest in 35 years. Only a 10-3 loss in a torrential rainfall down in Atlanta, against former Coach Norm Van Brocklin's Falcons, in the season finale (with Grant resting many of his starters for the playoffs), prevented the team from winning 13 in a row.

The Vikings were by far the NFL's best team that year, scoring the most points in all of pro football and yielding the least by an unthinkable 379-133 margin. (Their average of 9.5 points allowed per game was the lowest since World War II.) So, with their Western Conference championship in hand, they prepared to battle the Rams in the playoffs.

On Dec. 27, in front of some 48,000 frozen fans at the Met, the Vikes played the Rams in a game that ranks as one of the most exciting ever in team history. The Rams, guided by their fiery Coach, George Allen, were led by defensive giants Merlin Olsen and Deacon Jones, as well as Quarterback, and NFL MVP, Roman Gabriel. L.A. went up early in this one, scoring early off the recovery of Bill Brown's fumble. Minnesota then rallied back behind a thunderous crowd that the players had never seen the likes of before. With the fans stomping and absolutely going nuts, the Vikes drove 75 yards to tie the score on Dave Osborn's tough one-yard dive up the middle. The Rams answered though, only to take a 17-7 lead on a field goal, followed by a two-yard touchdown pass from Roman Gabriel to Tight End Billy Truax just before half-time. The Vikings roared back in the third behind a 41-yard pass from Kapp to Gene Washington which set up another Osborn one-yarder to make it 17-14. Kapp then took over late in the fourth quarter, capping a 65-yard drive by plunging into the end-zone for a two-yard touchdown. Now, with just a few moments left in the game, Carl Eller crashed into the end-zone to sack Gabriel for a safety to secure the dramatic 23-20 victory.

From there Minnesota went on to beat the Cleveland Browns in the NFL Championship Game, 27-7, to become the first modern expansion franchise to advance to the Super Bowl. The stage was set. The field was slick, the sidelines out at the Met were stacked with snow, and the frigid eight degree temperature made the illusion of Minnesota's cold weather invincibility even more intimidating. Joe Kapp started it off by hitting Gene Washington for a 33-yard pick-up when he beat Cornerback Walt Sumner, who had slipped on the icy field. From there Kapp ran over a couple of Brown defenders to score on a seven-yarder. Shortly thereafter, Kapp scored again on a bomb to Washington, this one covering 75 yards to give the Purple a 14-0 first quarter lead. After Fred Cox nailed a 30-yard field goal, Dave Osborn then chewed off 20 of his game-high 108 yards rushing by finding the back of the end-zone late in the second quarter. Cox then added another 32-yarder late to seal the team's first-ever NFL Championship.

After the game the team, bloodied, cold and battered, cried and celebrated with a champagne party in the lockerroom. For that moment, it was all about a bunch of kids, Black, White and Latino, who had all come a long, long way. They would now go on to face the AFL champion Kansas City Chiefs in Super Bowl IV at New Orleans. More than 80,000 fans crowded into Louisiana's Tulane Stadium on January 11, 1970, to watch the Vikings do battle with the Chiefs in what would prove to be the AFL's last-ever game. That's because the 10-year-old AFL would merge that following season with the NFL, despite the notion by most gridiron fans that the AFL was inferior to the NFL with regards to quality of play. And, because the Jets dispelled that very notion just the year before by shocking the mighty Colts in Super Bowl III, many were expecting Minnesota to restore the balance of power back to the established NFL. The oddsmakers also agreed with that sentiment, declaring the Chiefs, who lost to Baltimore in Super Bowl I, as two-touchdown underdogs.

Kapp, bothered at suggestions made by the media that he lacked a classic throwing style, was quoted as saying: "Classics are for Greeks. Who is a classic quarterback? I think I can play some ball."

Before the game, a hot-air balloon with the Vikings logo on it crashed into the stands, nearly decapitating a group of nearby Sugar Bowl Princesses — a dreadful omen of things to come. The Chiefs, led by Len Dawson's short, precision passing picked apart the now world-famous "Purple People Eater" defense. On the other side of the ball, the Chiefs huge defensive linemen simply out-muscled the smaller

| Vikings center Mick Tinglehoff is named as the NFL's Outstanding Blocker of the Year | North Star winger Danny Grant is awarded the Calder Trophy, honoring the NHL's top rookie | Gopher outfielder Noel Jenke is named to the All-American baseball team | Gopher first baseman Mike Walseth is named to the All-American baseball team | The Twins win the Western Division but lose to the Baltimore Orioles in the playoffs | The Twins win the triple crown: (Carew wins the batting title, and Killebrew wins the homers and RBI's title) | The ABA's Minnesota Pipers finish fourth in the Eastern Division. They leave town the next season. |

Vikings on the line of scrimmage, stuffing Minnesota's highly touted running game. In addition, the Chiefs used an elaborate trapping scheme to neutralize the Vikings great pass rushers, Alan Page and Carl Eller, who were blitzing from the ends. To make matters worse, leading the way for the Chiefs defensively were a bunch of ex-Gophers: Bobby Bell, Aaron Brown and Bob Stein. Very methodically, and without flash, Kansas City dominated the game — capitalizing on five very costly Minnesota turn-overs.

Perhaps the opening kickoff as an indication of how it was going to be that day for Minnesota when Charlie West bobbled and lost the wind-blown offering, giving the Chiefs the ball deep in Viking territory. Jan Stenerud then kicked the first of his three field goals in the first half, ultimately giving the Chiefs a 9-0 lead midway through the second. West then fumbled the ball again on the kickoff following Stenerud's third field goal at the Vikings' 19-yard line. A few plays later Kansas City's Mike Garrett scored on a five-yard run, as the Chiefs went into the locker room at the half up 16-0.

The Vikings came out primed in the second half and appeared to be mounting a rally when they forced the Chiefs to punt, and then capped off a 69-yard, 10 play drive with a Dave Osborn four-yard touchdown run. Kapp drove the team down, hitting John Henderson, who finished with seven catches for 111 yards on the day, for a key first down to keep the drive alive. (Incredibly, Minnesota didn't even get a first down until the second half!) The Chiefs didn't flinch though, as Dawson drove down after the ensuing kick-off and tossed a short five-yard pass to Wide Receiver Otis Taylor at the 41, who then ran right through Vikings' defenders Earsell Mackbee and Karl Kassulke 40 yards and into the end-zone. It would be the final nail in the coffin.

Minnesota had three possessions in the fourth quarter but couldn't capitalize, as each drive ended in an interception. The final blow to the Purple came midway through the fourth, when Kapp, battered and injured, had to be helped off the Tulane Stadium field after badly injuring his shoulder while being sacked — dramatizing the Viking's futility. Back-up signal caller Gary Cuozzo then came in and completed two passes: one to the Vikings and one to the Chiefs. Adding insult to injury was the Chiefs' bombastic coach, Hank Stram, who, while wired with a microphone during the game for NFL Films, said of the Vikings: "They can't figure us out. They don't know what they're doing. It's like a Chinese fire drill out there!" Although the 23-7 loss to the Chiefs stunned the Minnesota faithful and most of the NFL, it did not diminish the accomplishments of a brilliant season.

As Tough as Nails

Joe Kapp grew up as a sports fanatic in southern California and later attended the University of California at Berkeley, where he played football and basketball for the Golden Bears. At Cal he quarterbacked a Rose Bowl team and even played on a couple of championship basketball teams as well. After graduating, he decided to head north of the border to try his luck in the Canadian Football League. There, he would ultimately play for eight years with Calgary and then British Columbia, where he won a Grey Cup as a member of the Lions.

In 1967 Kapp was lured to Minnesota by an old CFL colleague by the name of Bud Grant, who was now coaching the Vikes. Minnesota had just dealt Fran Tarkenton to New York and needed a veteran signal-caller. Kapp obliged and became an instant fan-favorite in Minnesota. He was a throwback to when football was really a game and played because he loved it. He had the mentality of a linebacker and actually loved to punish his would-be tacklers by putting his head down and letting them have it. He occasionally threw spirals, but seemed to be able to will his team to victory on pure emotion and heart alone. The team motto was "40 for 60" that year and that really typified just the kind of team player he really was.

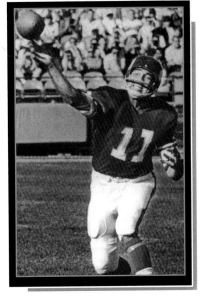

In 1969 Kapp led the Vikings to the Super Bowl and even turned down the team's MVP award, citing the fact that there was no most valuable player on a team of 40 men working together. (Incidentally, Joe bought a Mustang convertible with his Super Bowl bonus money, and still drives it today!)

After three seasons in Minnesota Kapp got into an ugly contract squabble and wound up being shipped off to the Boston Patriots, where he would begrudgingly play one more year before hanging up the cleats for good.

Kapp led the Vikings in passing all three years he was with the team with 4,807 yards on 351 of 699 attempts. He also tossed 37 touchdowns while surrendering 47 interceptions. He left the game, not necessarily on his terms, but will always be remembered as one of the guttiest quarterbacks in NFL history.

He later became head football coach at his alma-mater, Cal. Several years later he got the acting bug, and, after doing some commercials, (including one for Wheaties), he appeared in a number of movies. Today Joe and his wife reside in Los Gatos, Calif., and have four children. Joe later became involved with a family restaurant called "Kapp's," in Mountain View, and does motivational speaking as well.

Viking Tombstone:

"When I played, the effort showed, and I think that's why people appreciated me as a player. You accept the responsibility of playing quarterback for a team and building excellence takes value points such as toughness, determination, persistence, and fortitude. All of the those are things that a player brings with him, in addition to skill, and those are the things that make winners."

TRIBUTES

"Joe was a football player who probably did not have a sense of what was good for Joe Kapp as an individual," said Carl Eller. "In other words, what Joe was about was what was good for the team. It didn't matter whether it was good for Joe or not, he was a true team player."

"Joe is a guy that you would want to be in an alley fight with," said Jim Marshall. "He would do anything that was necessary to get that ball down the field and to make something happen. He didn't throw the prettiest passes in the world, but, he threw winning passes. It didn't make any difference what his passes looked like; they always got to his target. He made some great efforts in the short time he was with the Minnesota Vikings. He is one of my most dear friends, and I am so respectful of his ability and his qualifications. Most of all I'm respectful of the attitude and toughness that he brought to the team. No quarterback that I know of ever had that kind of toughness, period. I've seen him fight linebackers, and come out winning. I've seen him put guys like Jim Houston, one of the toughest all-pro defensive ends in the league, out of a game. He didn't care who you were, he was going to hit you as hard as you were going to hit him. As soon as that ball left his hand he was looking to deliver a blow to someone coming at him. You don't find that anymore. He was a genuine throwback to the earliest days of professional football."

Led by All-Star Right Fielder Tony Oliva, the Minnesota Twins won the AL Western Division for the second year in a row in 1970. This was indeed a wild year for Minnesota baseball, and it all started out with a pre-season managerial change. The popular Billy Martin, who had led the Twins to an impressive 97-65 record and the American League West title only the year before, was fired by owner Calvin Griffith and replaced with former Minneapolis Miller player-manager Bill "Captain Hook" Rigney. (Rigney earned his nickname "Captain Hook" because he used to pull his pitchers early and often when they got into hot water on the mound.)

There was endless speculation as to why the fiery Martin was fired. Maybe it was because he punched the Twins traveling secretary; or maybe it was his fight he got into outside a Detroit bar; or possibly it was because he publicly aired his grievances about the Twins front office management to the press. Regardless of the reason, the fact remained that Calvin canned him. The whole mess didn't bode well with the fans. *"Bring Billy Back"* bumper stickers were everywhere, and there was even a country-western song that uttered, *"Are you leavin' Billy Martin? It's a shame, it's a shame."*

But Rigney, the Twins new skipper, ignored the distractions and went on to guide his team to a 98-64 record and their second straight Western Division title. The season started off well for the Twins. But, midway through the season, Pitcher Luis Tiant broke his shoulder, so the Twins brought up a 19-year-old rookie to replace him by the name of Bert Blyleven. Bert went on to have a pretty good year, winning 10 games for the Twins. One of the highlights that season came on May 20th in a 10-5 win over the Kansas City Royals, when Rod Carew became the first Twin ever to hit for the cycle. (Carew had his knee torn up by a runner at second base early that year though, and sat out for much of the season as Frank Quilici and rookie Danny Thompson filled in for him.)

The pitching staff was led by Jim Perry (the brother of future Hall of Famer Gaylord), who, with 24 wins, a modest 3.03 ERA, and 168 strike-outs, became the first Twin ever to win the Cy Young Award. And, whenever Perry needed help, Closer Ron Perranoski came in to mop up. Ron's American League leading 34 saves, combined with Stan Williams' 15, made up the best bullpen in the league. Throw in Jim Kaat and Tom Hall, and statistically the Twins had the second best pitching staff in the league.

The Twins bats were also hot in 1970, as Harmon Killebrew hit 41 dingers with 113 RBI's, while Rod Carew, Cesar Tovar and Oliva all hit .300 or better as well. As a team, the Twins would go on to lead the American League in batting. Tony-O had another of his fabulous seasons that year, cranking out the most hits in the American

League for the fifth consecutive year, with 204, and once again leading his club to the post-season. He led the team in batting with a .325 average, while driving in 107 RBI's, scoring 96 runs and hitting 23 homers. And don't forget his league-leading 36 doubles as well.

The Twins, champions of the American League West, entered the 1970 playoffs in a rematch of the year before, with, unfortunately, the same results. Being swept by the Orioles the season prior, observers might have thought that some sort of revenge factor would've been motivating the Twins. They were wrong.

On October 3, the Twins opened the American League Championship Series at the Met. Minnesota jumped out to an early one run lead in Game One, but Perry got rocked as the O's went on to beat the Twins, 10-6. Baltimore Pitcher Mike Cuellar hit a grand slam and was later relieved by Dick Hall, the 40-year-old "junk-baller," who came in to mop up by allowing just one hit in the final five innings. Killebrew pounded out a two-run homer in the fifth, but the Orioles hung on down the stretch to take it.

In Game Two it got a lot worse. Baltimore topped their first game power surge by crushing the Twins, 11-3, despite homers by Oliva and Killebrew. Baltimore held a close 4-3 lead after eight and then exploded in the 9th, peppering Perranoski and Luis Tiant for seven runs, including a Johnson three-run homer.

Back in Baltimore for Game Three, Rigney sent Kaat up against Jim Palmer. It wasn't even close, and Earl Weaver's Orioles went on to complete the sweep. Palmer struck out 12 and allowed just six Minnesota hits in this one as Kaat was replaced in the third by Blyleven. Baltimore scored five runs in the first three innings and another in the eighth to ice it. In the first two years of the ALCS the Twins were 0-6 with all six losses coming at the hands of mighty Baltimore. The O's went on to the World Series again that year, this time shutting down Cincinnati's Big Red Machine in just five games.

"Losing two years in a row to the Orioles was tough," said Tony Oliva, who batted .500 in the ALCS. "After the first game, I thought that we had a chance to beat them, but we lost a very tough playoff series to a really good team. That year was a lot of fun and winning the West for the second time was a real thrill. We had a great ball club back then, and it was too bad we just couldn't make it past that next round to make it to the World Series like we did in 1965. There were a lot of great players on that 1970 team, and we were like a family."

Regrettably, for the Twins, this would be the end of the line for a while as the team would struggle over the next several years. For the previous six seasons the team had played outstanding fundamental baseball, but would go downhill quickly from there. After the season Bob Allison retired. Killebrew, although one of the game's best ever, never again hit more than 28 home runs, and Tony-O would go on to suffer a series of knee injuries which hobbled him for years to come. Perry, Kaat and Blyleven were a solid 1-2-3, but the team could never get anything going after that. They had holes in their infield and could not find an effective stopper either. As Minnesota was aging, the Oakland A's were coming of age — it was soon to be their turn to shine.

Oh, Tony-O

Pedro "Tony" Oliva grew up in the western province of Cuba, on his father's farm in Pinar del Rio, about 100 miles from Havana. There, he went to school through the 8th grade in a two-room wooden school-

TIMELINE

Viking halfback Hugh McElhenny is inducted into the Pro Football Hall of Fame	Gopher goalie Murray McLachlan is named to the All-American hockey team	Gopher defenseman Wally Olds is named to the All-American hockey team	UMD center Ron Busniuk is named to the All-American hockey team	UMD center Murray Keogan is named to the All-American hockey team	The state's largest flathead catfish is caught by Garden City's John Robert in the St. Croix River: 70 lbs	The Vikings beat the Chiefs in the "revenge game" following their Super Bowl loss from the season before	The state's largest koho salmon is caught by Coon Rapids' Louis Rhode on Lake Superior near Baptism River: 10 lbs., 6.5 oz.

60

house. He grew up as one of 10 kids — five boys and five girls. (He told his father he was a lucky man because he had hit .500!) Baseball consumed the boys life, and it would be his ticket to prosperity.

"When I was a boy, we would help my father with the work on the farm after school, and then play baseball," said Oliva. "We grew tobacco, oranges, mangos, potatoes, corn, and raised cows, pigs, chickens, and horses. My father loved the game and always found time for my brothers and me to play it. He helped all the kids play and enjoy the game by going to Havana to buy gloves, bats and balls for us. Once, he came back to the farm with nine gloves. We kept them in our house and when the kids came to our farm to play, they used them."

Tony got his big break when he was spotted by Cuban scout "Papa" Joe Cambria, who brought him to the United States for a tryout. His teammates on his Cuban team even chipped in to buy him some clothes for the big trip.

"Since I didn't have a passport, I had to use my brother, Antoine's. So, everyone started calling me Tony," said Oliva. "I found that I liked the name even better than Pedro, so I didn't ever tell anyone my real name."

The newly christened Tony was invited to camp with the Twins, and in 1961, he led the rookie league with a .410 average. After one-year stints in Class A and AAA, he got called up to the majors in 1964. As a Twin Oliva led the league with a .323 average, becoming the only rookie ever to win the batting title. He was even named Rookie of the Year, earning every penny of his lavish $7,500 salary.

That same year, Tony got a new teammate from his native Cuba, Zoilo Versalles. The two became instant pals. "Best roommate I ever had," said Versalles of Oliva. "He doesn't smoke, doesn't drink, and doesn't snore. All he does is eat, sleep, and breathe baseball."

Oliva would go on to become one of the greatest players in Twins history. One of the highlights of his career was when he led the Twins to the World Series in his sophomore year, winning another batting crown en route to being named A.L. Player of the Year.

"It was a great series and something I will never forget," said Oliva. "I look at it this way, there were two champs — one from the American League and one from the National League. But, only one team can win when you play seven games. Anything could've happened that last game, and we got beat by the Dodgers."

Tony won a Gold Glove in 1966 and captured a third batting crown in 1971. In 15 seasons, six of which were affected by a knee injury, Oliva would finish with 1,917 hits, 220 home runs, 947 RBI's and had a career average of .304. His prowess as a hitter was demonstrated in the fact that he led the league in hits five times, and his 220 career home runs rank third all-time among Twins. An eight-time All-Star, Tony's No. 6 was officially retired on July 14, 1991.

From 1962-1976 Tony was simply awesome. He could hit for power and average, as well as run, field, and throw. His versatility made him one of the most feared hitters of his day. If not for knee problems which cut short his career, Oliva would have been a certain choice for the Hall of Fame. After years of agonizing knee problems, Tony finally retired from the game in 1976 and began coaching for the Twins. He has been there ever since. Today, he works as a hitting instructor in the Twins' minor league system and scouts for the club as well.

Tony-O will forever be remembered as one of the Twins all-time greats. From his infectious smile to that Cuban accent that is as strong today as it was 40 years ago, he is a real living legend and a true treasure for Minnesota baseball.

"I would like to be remembered as a ballplayer that gave 100 percent and also a person that was able to get along with everybody," said Tony. "I think the fans here in Minnesota are great, and it was a pleasure to play here for them. I have lived here for over half of my

life, so my family and I am grateful to the good people of Minnesota."

As far as the Hall of Fame goes, Tony knows that had he not suffered through countless knee injuries in the latter stages of his career that he would be a shoe-in for the Hall of Fame. Let's just hope that the Veterans Committee comes to their senses in the coming years so that this outstanding ballplayer and person can be enshrined into his appropriate place in history. Tony, however, has his own views on baseball immortality and remains cautiously optimistic.

"Everybody thinks I should be in the Hall of Fame except for the people that vote. I feel a little bit disappointed. I think I should be in the Hall because I achieved so much. It was too bad that I got hurt, but there were people that did less in the same amount of time than I did that got in. A lot of pitchers now in the Hall of Fame, who pitched against me, have told me over the years that when they were asked by baseball writers who they felt should be in the Hall that isn't, they said me. I had a lot of great accomplishments in my career, and I hope I can still make it in through the back door."

TRIBUTES

"He was like a brother to me," said Rod Carew. "He was the one who took me under his wing when I was a rookie. He even taught me how to tie my first necktie. He allowed me to be his roommate for nine years, and he taught me how to handle myself and how to handle people. He always had that great smile about him. He was never upset at people for anything, and that was one of the reasons that even today the people have a great love affair with this guy. He is a tremendous person aside from being a tremendous baseball player. We knew where we came from. We came from nothing — countries where we wouldn't have been able to make the type of living that we were to make by playing professional baseball."

"Here's a guy that deserves to be in the Hall of Fame," said Harmon Killebrew. "He was a Rod Carew type hitter with power. He was one of the finest hitters that I have ever seen. He could hit the ball all over the park and he was the best off-speed hitter that I ever saw. You could throw him 99 fast-balls and one change-up and he'd hit it out. He was such a great hitter."

"Tony is special to me," said Jim Kaat. "Tony has been short-changed with regards to the Hall of Fame. He was one of the greatest hitters and all-around players in all of baseball. If you were to ask catchers from the 1960s who they feared the most with the winning run on base: Killebrew, Carew, or Oliva, and they would say Tony was the guy pitchers feared most. Jim Palmer and I have talked about that at length and that's how he felt too. Tony was a combination of average, power, speed, and he could drive the ball to produce runs. He was as good a pure hitter as there was."

"I think if you cut his head open, a bunch of baseballs would fall out," said Kent Hrbek. "That's all he knows is baseball. Tony-O was one of my heroes growing up, and I even wore his No. 6 on my first T- ball jersey."

Twins pitcher Jim Perry wins 24 games and is named the American League Cy Young Award winner. Over 17 years in the big-league's, Jim won 215 games. His big brother and fellow pitcher, Gaylord Perry, also won a Cy Young, making them the only brother tandem in baseball history to have won the award.

In 1971 the Vikings reloaded with some new talent. Among the new faces in camp were Defensive Tackle Doug Sutherland, Defensive End Bob Lurtsema, Guard Ed White, Tight End Stu Voigt, Defensive Backs Nate Wright and Jeff Wright, and Quarterback Norm Snead. Snead would prove not to be the solution the team was so desperately looking for that year though. He was brought in to compete with Gary Cuozzo and Bob Lee for the starting job, and thanks to Grant's decision to play musical chairs, they all got to see some action that year.

In the first game of the season Cuozzo got the nod, and responded by sparking the Vikings to a 16-13 victory over the Lions. Then, after a 20-17 rare home loss to the Bears, Snead came off the bench to take over. While Snead led the Vikings to back-to-back shut-outs over Buffalo and Philadelphia, Grant decided to shuffle the deck once more, this time putting Cuozzo back in for the next five games. Lee's number then got called for four of the final five games of the season, assuring Grant of one thing — he needed a new quarterback.

Over that stretch Minnesota went on to win 11 out of 14, even going nine consecutive quarters at one point without surrendering a point. In addition, their defense, which was led by Tackle Alan Page, forced 33 fumbles and 27 interceptions, including seven by Charlie West and six each by Paul Krause and Ed Sharockman, en route to giving up just 139 points — an average of nine points a game. That awesome defense also tallied 49 quarterback sacks for 360 lost yards.

While the team did win their fourth straight NFC Central Division title, the quarterback problem was making more headlines than the team's unbelievable defense, just fueling the debate as to who was going to score the most points each game — the offense or the defense. Clint Jones did rush for 675 yards and Receiver Bob Grim was able to catch 45 passes for a modest 691 yards, but the offense was flat. It was the team's achilles heel, and was about to become exposed.

The purple entered the playoffs that year with high hopes of returning to the Super Bowl. It was Christmas day at the Met, and nearly 50,000 Minnesotans were on hand to watch the Vikes do battle with the hated Cowboys. Dallas jumped out to an early lead in this one, going up 6-3 after an early fumble recovery and an interception, which led to two Mike Clark field goals. After Freddy Cox answered on a 27-yarder, Dallas exploded in the third quarter for a pair of touchdowns. The first of the two scores came on Cliff Harris' interception which was returned 30 yards to the Minnesota 13. Then, on the next play, Running Back Duane Thomas took a hand-off up the middle for a 13-yard touchdown. The Vikes' offense sputtered and was forced to punt again, which led to a Roger Staubach nine-yard touchdown pass to Bob Hayes. Minnesota rallied in the fourth behind an Alan Page safety followed by a

six-yard touchdown pass from Cuozzo to Stu Voigt, but it was too little too late. Dallas hung on to beat the Vikes, 20-12. Once again, it was the team's inability to hold onto the ball that did them in. Five turnovers, including a pair interceptions each from Bob Lee and Gary Quozzo, negated the fact that the Purple actually out-gained the Cowboys in total yardage, 311-183.

The undisputed bright spot of the season though was the inhuman play of Alan Page, who simply took his game to another level. In the Detroit game, Page had a coming out party of sorts. You see, Alan Page was lightening quick, almost to the point that he made everyone else look like they are in slow motion. It would just so happen that in this particular game, the referees weren't that familiar with his ability to get across the line of scrimmage and wreak havoc on the opposing teams' offense. As a result, Page was called on two consecutive encroachment penalties, for what they perceived as him jumping over the line before the ball was snapped. Page went nuts, threw his arms in the air and demanded justice. He would get none, so he took out his rage on the defenseless Lions, who simply had no way of stopping him.

Page released an onslaught of blitzes and bull-rushes that completely destroyed Detroit's game plan. His cat-like quickness proved to be no match for double and even triple teams that were thrown at him. His passion for the game was unparalleled and he hated to lose. That day he blew threw the line time after time and smothered the Lion's quarterback and halfback from sideline to sideline. He caused a couple of fumbles, had a few sacks and simply took all of the rhythm out of their passing attack. They were all so afraid of him that seemingly everyone on the line had one eye on him, which of course let Eller and Marshall have a feast of their own. When the Lions punted the ball away on that day, it wasn't for strategy, it was to get Page off the field and provide a little mercy for the team's offense. Coaches who later saw the game on film said Page's superhuman performance was a never-before seen case of one lineman somehow being able to dictate the flow of the game all by himself. Said one Lion after the game: "They could call this guy murder. We couldn't block him. He played like we weren't even there. He was unreal."

That season Page posted 10 sacks, 109 tackles, 35 assists, 42 hurries and three safeties. It might possibly have been the single-greatest season ever recorded by a defensive lineman. For his efforts, Page made history by becoming the first defensive player in NFL history of to win the league's MVP, something he later downplayed.

"The MVP award was by somebody else's measure," he said. "Certainly 1971 was a good year for me, but there were other good ones in there too. For me, it was trying to be the best that I could be. That was something that was constant for me, and it wasn't something that took place one year and not in others. When I look back, I look on a whole career, not any one season. I had a lot of success in a lot of successful seasons."

The Honorable Alan Page

After starring on the 1966 Notre Dame national championship team, All-American Defensive Tackle Page was selected by the Vikings in the first round of the 1967 draft. The first rookie ever to start for Bud Grant, he would go on to become one of the greatest players the NFL would ever know. Page was selected as a unanimous All-Pro on six different occasions while receiving nine Pro Bowl invitations. From

TIMELINE

Gary Bjorkland, Gopher track and field legend wins the Six-Mile Run National Championship. A former collegiate record holder in the event, he broke 11 cross country and track records at the U, and still holds school records in the 3,000M and 5,000M runs. He won 10 Big Ten titles, and was a five-time All-American. He earned a spot on the 1976 Olympic team, he also competed on two US Pan-Am and 10 US National teams. Today the Grandma's half-marathon is named in his honor.	Mankato State wrestler Ken Stockdale wins the 134 lb. Division II National Championship	Vikings coach Norm Van Brocklin is inducted into the Pro Football Hall of Fame	Dave Bancroft, a Minneapolis Miller manager in 1933, is inducted into the Baseball Hall of Fame	The Gopher Hockey team loses to Boston University, 4-2, in the NCAA Finals	Gopher end Doug Kingsriter is named to the All-American football team	The Minnesota Fighting Saints begin play in the WHA's Western Division at the St. Paul Auditorium	UMD winger Walt Ledingham is named to the All-American hockey team

62

1967-78 the anchor of the "Purple People Eaters" defense posted 108 career sacks, however, unofficial records show that he recorded 173 sacks. (Sacks weren't counted back in the day like they are now.) In addition, he also recovered 23 opponents' fumbles and blocked 28 kicks. Page was even the inspiration for the now common pass-rushing statistic known as the "hurry," which was issued when he forced the quarterback throw the ball before he wanted to.

Page was a nonconformist, often bucking heads with Coach Grant. Later in his career he began to attend Law School at the U of M, and even began running marathons. As a result, Page thinned down to about 230 pounds, which was very small for an NFL defensive tackle. Finally, when he went against the wishes of the coaching staff to keep his weight up, he was released on waivers for $100. Page then went on to play another three seasons with the Bears before retiring in 1981. When it was all said and done, his numbers were staggering. He had played in 236 straight games, was a four-time Defensive Player of the Year, All-NFL nine times, played in nine Pro-Bowls, recovered 23 fumbles, blocked 28 kicks and punts, and recorded 173 sacks.

"There really isn't much to think about on a football field." said Page of his retirement. "Playing the game requires physical ability and a tremendous emotional commitment. Intellectually, it doesn't require much. There are a finite number of things that can take place on a football field. After 10 years, you probably have done most of them. Football to me became repetitious and boring."

When Page's career was over he had a homecoming of sorts. You see, he grew up in Canton, Ohio, the home to the Pro Football Hall of Fame, and actually worked on the construction crew that built the museum one summer during the late 1960s. In 1988 he was inducted into that very Hall of Fame. However, he did it in typical Alan Page style, declining the opportunity to swap gridiron gossip, as most of the football brethren do at their induction's, and instead shocking the pro football establishment by choosing Willarene Beasley (the principal at Minneapolis North High School) as his presenter. Never in the Hall of Fame's history had a person not in the football fraternity made an induction speech. Page selected her because of the fact that she was an educator and, as a black woman, represented minorities. Alan's speech was about the values of education, not football; about learning to tackle issues, not quarterbacks; and about ABCs, not Xs and Os.

"I wanted to take advantage of that recognition and use the day as a mechanism for something meaningful," said Page, who, following her introduction speech, launched the Page Education Foundation from the steps of the Hall of Fame.

On why Page decided to use that forum to speak of education rather than football, Page recalled a pre-season afternoon practice some years ago, when, during a defensive meeting, one of the coaches asked some of the players to read aloud from the playbook. It was at that moment that Page realized that several of his teammates couldn't read, while several others were struggling to just get by.

"In that moment, listening to my teammates unable to read a simple playbook, everything crystallized for me," Page said. "I don't know why it took me so long to realize, but at that moment it became clear that this wasn't a dumb-jock problem, or an athletic problem. These men were supposed to learn to read in first, second, or third grade, long before they were football players. You think about something, and you think about it again, but you can't point your finger at it. Well, that day, I realized the problem I wanted to try to address was education. Pure and simple."

Page has a great outlook on life. "I saw a quote once that read that success is not a place where you arrive at, it's a manner of travel. The success and the joy is in working to get there, not getting there. Once you're there, what's interesting about that? I learned that lesson very early on as a football player. When I was selected as the league's

MVP early on in my career, I felt that's about as good as it gets in professional football. It was at that point that I figured out that the fun was in the journey, not arriving at the destination. The journey never ends."

Today Page sits on the Minnesota Supreme Court. He had always battled adversity, and his journey to the bench would be no exception. By 1979, Page had earned his law degree and moved from the gridiron to private practice. Soon he was working in the attorney general's office. After spending several years there, he decided to seek an even higher

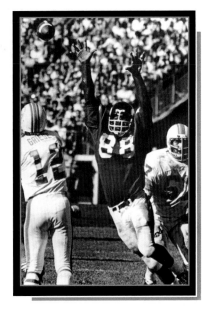

office. Typically, new judges are appointed temporarily and then elected without competition. But, when his opportunity to run kept being denied, he sued then Governor Arne Carlson. A substitute Supreme Court then ruled in Page's favor, allowing him to run successfully, with opposition, in 1992. As a result, he became the first African-American to sit on the state's highest court — or on any Minnesota state appellate court, for that matter. Today, with his spectacles and trademark bow-tie, Associate Justice Page is a member of the Minnesota Supreme Court. He and his wife Diane live in the Twin Cities and have four children. He still logs about 60-miles a week in the sneakers and remains active in his Page Education Foundation, which to date has helped well over a thousand minority students attend college.

Vikings Tombstone:
"If I could choose a way to be remembered, it wouldn't be my association with football. Football is in the past — a good past, but nonetheless it is the past. I'd want to be remembered with children — with my children and other children."

TRIBUTES
"As a football player, I feel very proud to have played with Alan Page," said Jim Marshall. "I think he was one of the guys that truly changed the game. They stopped calling holding (penalties) because Alan was so quick and elusive, and he was so disruptive to the other teams. They (referees) intentionally allowed holding on him, because that was the only way anybody could block him. They gave more freedom to offensive lineman in the way they used their hands, and a lot of that was because of his elusive play. Never in the history of the game, and I have looked at film since the beginning of organized football, have there been any rule changes like they made in the 10 years that Alan was out there. Everything changed with the advent of television, and people wanted to see a more potent offensive representation on the field. That handcuffed the defensive teams. Today football is more of a form of entertainment, rather than the sport that it was back in those days. I think a lot of that had to do with the play of Alan Page."

"Alan had a vision about his own personal life," said Carl Eller. "To a great extent, within his greatness, he saw his own limitations. He felt that he really had to do something significant outside of football. I think that Alan felt consumed by his own greatness on the field, and it was probably too much for him. He was a torch-bearer right from the very beginning."

As a tribute to the town of Eveleth for all of its contributions to the sport of hockey, the U.S. Hockey Hall of Fame is constructed there on Hat Trick Avenue. More than 1/3 of its inductees are native Minnesotans

Central High School's Bobby Marshall, who played for the Colored Gophers professional Negro League baseball team as well as several professional football teams, is inducted into the College Football Hall of Fame.

Marshall, considered to be one of the greatest University of Minnesota athletes of all time, lettered in football, baseball and track. In 1903 he became the first African American to play football in the Big 9 Conference (now the Big 10), as an end for the Gophers.

Minneapolis' Joe Hutton, Hamline University's basketball coach of 34 years, is named the NAIA Tournament's all-time coach. His Piper squads won or shared 19 MIAC titles, 12 times qualified for the NCAA tournament, and won three NAIA national championships (1942,1949 and 1951)

Kent, Minnesota's Jimmy Robinson is inducted into the Amateur Trapshooting Association Hall of Fame. Considered the nation's trap and skeet shooting authority for more than half a century, he was named as Minnesota's Outdoor Sportsman of the Year in 1955.

TIMELINE

The University of Minnesota Golden Gopher basketball program has seen a lot of ups and downs over the course of its history, but one of its most colorful eras involves a coach by the name of Bill Musselman and his unbelievable 1972 Big Ten championship run.

The 1971-72 Gophers, under new Coach Bill Musselman, hit the court with one of the tallest and most talented lineups in the country. In addition to returning upperclassmen Center Jim Brewer, Forward Corky Taylor, and Guards Bob Murphy and Keith Young, Musselman added three junior college transfer players in six-foot-nine swingman Ron Behagen, who had been playing at Southern Idaho Junior College, six-foot-eight Forward Clyde Turner, who came over from Robert Morris Junior College (Illinois), and six-foot-three Guard Bob Nix, from Henderson County Junior College in Texas.

The JUCO transfers that Musselman brought in were not without controversy though. He knew he needed to surround Jim Brewer, one of the best centers in the country, with some talented new players. So, he went outside the system and got some players who could help him right away. While this is practice is commonplace today, back in the early 1970s it was extremely taboo. Back then, it was understood that coaches recruited kids, red-shirted them, and developed them. What Musselman did, in the eyes of many coaches, was to take a shortcut, and "cheat" the system. But Musselman didn't care. He had finally arrived to the big-time and simply didn't want to wait around to someday be a contender. He liked his players to execute a physical, tough rebounding, in-your-face style of basketball, and he now had the tools to do some immediate damage in the Big Ten.

Musselman had the players but knew he still needed to fill Williams Arena with plenty of fans and excitement. So, this consummate salesman and promoter took his players around the state for intra-squad games to sell tickets. In addition, he even instituted one of basketball's greatest pre-game warm-up shows which was similar to that of the old Harlem Globetrotters. The pre-game warm-up saw the players enter into a darkened arena, run through a giant spotlight, and form a circle. There, in addition to basketball finger-spinning, they would pass balls back and forth by zipping them through their legs, behind their backs and off their heads.

The opposing coaches and players hated it, but that didn't bother Musselman.

"It was the greatest exhibition of ball-handling that a lot of people had ever seen," said Musselman. "It was precision ball handling to music like 'Sweet Georgia Brown.' We used to fill up the arena an hour before game time so that people could watch our warm-up."

The Gophers went into their Big Ten Conference schedule with a modest non-conference record of 6-3. They even picked up a new walk-on player early in the season — a young man who

would go on to become a pretty decent athlete in his day. Who was he? Well, in 1971, the U of M intramural basketball champs were a team called the "Soulful Strutters." The Strutters were led by a six-foot-six specimen from St. Paul Central High School by the name of Dave Winfield, who was also a star pitcher on the Gopher baseball team at the time. Now, because the Strutters were the best intramural team on campus, they often-times scrimmaged against the Gopher Junior Varsity team — usually whipping them pretty good. When J.V. Coach Jimmy Williams saw Winfield play during one of those games, he couldn't believe his eyes. So, he told Musselman that he better give the kid a look. He did, and immediately asked him to join the team.

The Gophers opened their Big Ten schedule against Indiana at the old Barn, where the second-largest crowd in school history (19,121) showed up to watch Musselman do battle with his old childhood pal from Ohio, Bobby Knight. Turner, Behagen, Nix, and Young all scored in double figures in this one as Minnesota went on to win the game, 52-51, thanks to a blocked shot by Brewer and a pair of last-second free throws by Nix.

Minnesota added three more victories to make them 4-0 in conference play. Their next opponent was Ohio State. It was a big game, and everyone knew it. There were several sidebars going in as well — including how Buckeye Coach Fred Taylor didn't appreciate Musselman, a fellow Ohioan, recruiting JUCO kids. The media was all over it too. In fact, while the NHL All-Star Game was being played across town at the Met Center that same night, most of the media attention in the Twin Cities was focused on the basketball game. The Gophers had a chance to move into a first-place tie with a victory and the crowd was pumped. What the fans didn't know, however, was that this particular game would go down as one of the most significant games in Minnesota history. This was the game that will forever be remembered as "The Fight" and the beginning of the "Iron Five."

With the Buckeyes leading 50-44 and 36 seconds left in the game, OSU's, star Center Luke Witte broke toward the basket. As Minnesota pressed, Witte outran the field and caught the inbound pass. In the process, he was fouled hard by both Turner and Taylor. Turner was then called for a flagrant foul and was immediately ejected. Then, amazingly and nearly simultaneously, Taylor reached out to help Witte, who was down on the court, up to his feet. But instead of helping him up, he proceeded to knee him in the groin. The crowd was stunned, and subsequent mayhem broke out. OSU's, Dave Merchant rushed over to help Witte, quickly pushing Taylor out of his way. Brewer and Taylor then ran down the court after Merchant, while Behagen, having already fouled out, came off the bench and attacked Witte.

For the next moments, complete pandemonium took over at Williams Arena. The nearly 18,000 fans in attendance were shocked, and many even jumped onto the court to partake in the festivities. Big Dave Winfield even got into the act and it got ugly in a hurry. Several Buckeye players were taken to the hospital, and a near riot ensued. Minnesota's Athletic Director, Paul Giel, then decided, after consulting with the game officials, to simply end the game and declare Ohio State as the winner. Outside, they started to throw rocks at the police cars as they took the players to the hospital. When it was all over, a huge black eye was left on the University of Minnesota basketball program.

The opposing players had much different stories as to what really happened though. "Witte was gong up to take the shot, and Clyde Turner and myself fouled him," said Taylor. "It was really how

| TIMELINE | The NHL's All-Star game is played at the Met Center in Bloomington | Minneapolis's Bruce McIntosh wins a silver medal on the Olympic hockey team | Minneapolis' Charles Brown wins a silver medal on the Olympic hockey team | Minneapolis's Craig Lincoln wins a Bronze medal in the 3M Springboard Diving competition | St. Paul's Franklyn Sanders wins a silver medal on the Olympic hockey team | Warroad's Henry Boucha wins a silver medal on the Olympic hockey team | St. Paul's James McElmury wins a silver medal on the Olympic hockey team | UMD's Keith "Huffer" Christianson wins a silver medal on the Olympic hockey team | Minneapolis' Larry Bader wins a silver medal on the Olympic hockey team |

hard I fouled him that precipitated my helping him up. Basically, it was a situation where he had an easy two points and we were trying to make sure he didn't score. When I went to help Luke up, he spit at me and I got pissed! It was a very tough game, and I kicked him. When I turned around, the entire floor had erupted. It was a scary situation."

To better understand the entire "situation," you have to go back to the end of the first half where an incident took place that may have instigated it all. As the players ran off the court and into the locker rooms, Bobby Nix waved to the pumped-up crowd by raising his fists in the air towards the scoreboard.

"Witte crossed in front of me," said Nix. "There's no question in my mind or anybody's that saw it. It was a deliberate elbow to my face. He just threw it, and he damn near decked me. It was seen by a lot of people, except the officials."

That night, following the incident, replays of the fight were played on virtually every newscast in the country. Every paper ran a story about it, and the next week, Sports Illustrated even featured the brawl as their cover story. Incredibly, all fingers pointed to Musselman as the instigator. They tried to paint a picture that his "win at any cost" attitude had animalized his players into a fit of rage. National media had concentrated only on the game-ending fight, and they never mentioned the half-time incident that precluded the retaliation. Attempts were made to dramatize and polarize Musselman and the Buckeyes' Fred Taylor, the two coaches (both with roots to Ohio). Taylor was a Big Ten coaching legend who built programs traditionally. Musselman, on the other hand, was a rookie who they said took short-cuts to success by obtaining junior college players. Racism and even the Vietnam War were thrown into the stew. People were searching for a scapegoat, and the media had found one in Musselman.

"A lot of things were said in print that were wrong," said Musselman in Bill Heller's 1989 book: "Obsession: Timberwolves Stalk the NBA." "I was blamed for the fight, or for not stopping the fight, yet the fight was the last thing I wanted. My insides were torn up. My hopes and dreams were shattered that night. I couldn't believe life was like that. I believed if you were dedicated and outworked everyone, you'd be successful. That night it seemed like everything I believed in was wrong. I went home and got down on my knees and prayed. And I thought then, 'Well, you asked for this; you wanted to coach in the big time.' Since then, my beliefs have been reaffirmed. But it was my background that got me through that situation. If I hadn't been mentally tough, I wouldn't have survived that incident."

"Obviously the fight was wrong, but I always felt that it was racially motivated," added Musselman several years later. "It was during the early 1970s, and there were a lot of racial overtones. The game got out of hand, and the officials let too much loose play go on. I took a lot of heat for it. It was ridiculous that people would insinuate that I wanted to have a fight. They tried to blame it on my pre-game warm-up routine, saying that it hyped the fans into a frenzy. It was too bad that it happened, but it was an intense heat of the battle thing. The sad part about it was the fact that all the players were good people. Back then our kids never got into any trouble, and they got their degrees. They all made a contribution to society and were all great kids."

Following the game, Behagen and Taylor were suspended for the remainder of the season. (Ohio's governor even suggested publicly that the two ought to be thrown in jail.) The new squad stayed focused though, and even used the suspensions as a personal vendetta to salvage the season. So, Musselman went almost exclusively with a five-man lineup: Turner and Winfield at the forwards, Brewer at center, and Nix and Young as the guards.

The next game was at Iowa. There were plain-clothed police officers everywhere and the fans were skeptical. The Gophers won the game though, 61-50, and just kept on rolling from there. Then, with

Ohio State reeling in a tailspin, Minnesota put it all on the line at Purdue, with a chance to win the Big Ten title. There, behind Jim Brewer and Clyde Turner's 12-point performances, the Gophers hung on to beat the Boilers, 49-48, thus becoming the first Gopher team in 53 years to win an undisputed Big Ten title.

Unfortunately, in their first-ever NCAA Tournament appearance, the Gophers were upset by Florida State, 70-56, in the NCAA Mideast Regional game in Dayton, Ohio. They did manage to come back to beat Marquette, 77-72, in the consolation game though. With the top defense in the nation, the 10th ranked Gophers allowed just 58 points per game that season, finishing with an impressive 18-7 record. Brewer was named as the Big Ten's MVP, and both he and Behagen were named to the All-American team as well. (Incidentally, that next year five Gophers would be drafted into the ranks of professional basketball. Not bad for a program everybody had counted out.)

Musselman, who said going in that he did not believe in "rebuilding years," kept his word and made his first year in Gold Country one of the program's most exciting, and dare we say "eventful" in history.

Coach Muss
A native of Wooster Ohio, Bill Musselman will always be remembered in Minnesota for a lot of reasons. Most importantly though, he will be remembered as a great coach. Attendance nearly doubled at Williams Arena during his four-year career in Gold Country, and he was the impetus, compiling a 69-32 record, for a .683 winning percentage — the best in school history. He rescued the program and for better or for worse got people excited about basketball again. Not afraid to go outside the system and bring in junior college transfers, Musselman left in 1975 under the shadow of allegations and investigations by the NCAA.

Musselman's amazing coaching career included posting a record of 233-84 as a college coach at Ashland, Minnesota and South Alabama. He was also a head coach in four pro leagues as well — the NBA (with the Cleveland Cavaliers and the Minnesota Timberwolves), CBA, ABA and WBA, where his overall career record was 603-426. In addition, he was named as the CBA Coach of the Year in 1987 and 1988, winning four consecutive championships along the way. He later served as an assistant with the NBA's Portland Trailblazers until his tragic and untimely death in 2000, from cancer, at the age of 59.

Gophers & Timberwolves Tombstone:
"I think my teams always played hard and played together," said Musselman. "I think that I have always had the ability as a coach to get the most out of my players, and my teams have always played as hard as they could. I always taught my players to get out of life what they put into it. I think it is important to teach an athlete to be able to face and handle adversity. Mental toughness is important to me, and I always wanted my players to be able to be prepared to handle the good times along with the bad."

| St. Paul's James McElmury wins a silver medal on the Olympic hockey team | International Falls' Mike Curran wins a silver medal on the Olympic hockey team | Minneapolis' Ron Naslund wins a silver medal on the Olympic hockey team | International Falls' Tim Sheehy wins a silver medal on the Olympic hockey team | Gopher diver Craig Lincoln wins the Three-Meter Diving National Championship | UMD winger Walt Ledingham is named to the All-American hockey team | Gopher halfback and Heisman winner Bruce Smith is inducted into the College Football Hall of Fame |

TIMELINE

WILL STEGER

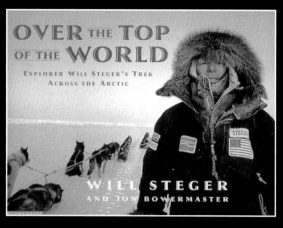

Ely's Will Steger is one of the greatest explorers of the modern era. Steger grew up outside Minneapolis but spent his summers in the Yukon region of Canada as well as in Alaska. A science teacher who also runs wilderness programs in the Boundary Waters Canoe Wilderness Area in Northern Minnesota, he is also an avid Arctic traveler.

In 1986, Steger put together a team of seven men, and one woman — fellow Minnesota explorer Ann Bancroft — that journeyed to the North Pole on foot, something that hadn't been done since 1909, when Admiral Robert Peary accomplished the feat. The unsupported mission was a success and launched both of the Minnesota explorers into the national spotlight. Then, in 1990, Steger raised the bar and aimed at the Antarctic. But he wanted to do more than just reach the South Pole, so he decided to go from the Pacific Ocean to the Atlantic and cross the entire 4,000 mile continent. There were six men and 36 dogs that comprised the International Trans-Antarctic Team. The 220-day journey ended when they crossed a finish line created by an awaiting Soviet welcoming party.

After an Arctic Ocean crossing in 1995, Steger was at it again in 1997. This time, in an effort to increase the awareness of the Arctic region, the 53-year-old explorer set out on an unsupported solo-trek from the North Pole across the Arctic Ocean to Ellesmere Island. With enough food for 50 days, he paddled and pulled a 275-pound, 13-foot canoe alone across 500 miles of ice and water between the Pole to the Canadian Island. To train for the trip, Steger took two 10-day expeditions through the Boundary Waters, where he hauled his loaded canoe through the spring ice. He also spent months training at his Northern Minnesota cabin, where he built his strength and endurance by hauling logs through the snow.

After months of vigorous preparation, he set out to boldly go where no man had gone before. When he disembarked at the pole from the Russian icebreaker, Sovetskiy Soyuz, he was attempting what no other explorer before him had ever dared to begin, a major expedition on the Arctic Ocean during the summer. The ocean is deadly during that time of the year because it is covered with thick fog, cracked ice, and large gaps of open water. Surrounded by a perpetual blanket of thick fog, Will camped on an ice island surrounded by blue ice, water, slush and magnificent pressure ridges. Burning as many as 900 calories per hour hauling the canoe-sled, every day he ate approximately 4,000 calories, or about two-and-a-half pounds of food, to keep up his strength in the bitter cold environment. He also drifted an average of three miles per day due to the constant movement of the sea-ice as well. "The conditions are sobering," he would say. "There is always moisture and an eternal silence that I have never heard."

Unfortunately, because of the extreme weather conditions, Will was forced to abort his expedition midway through. He was plucked from his ice island near the North Pole by a helicopter that he called in though. Although he didn't complete the journey, he was able to communicate his thoughts and pictures through a unique program called "Solo From The Pole." The expedition combined exploration and adventure with technology to create an educational project which allowed him to regularly communicate via a digital camera through the internet to millions of interested people around the world.

Today the Minnesota explorer is a motivational speaker, teacher, and lecturer. Stay tuned to find out just where the exotic adventure enthusiast winds up next!

LUTE OLSON

Coaching legend Lute Olson got his start in Minnesota, when he was a three-sport athlete at Augsburg College from 1953-56. Olson was a six-foot-four forward in basketball, a tight end & defensive tackle in football and a first baseman in baseball. He played under Auggie coaching legends Edor Nelson and Ernie Anderson, and knew early on that coaching was to going to be his life's calling. Olson grew up in tiny Mayville, N.D., and chose Augsburg and its coaches because he wanted to go to school in a similar small-town atmosphere. While at college his life was anything but traditional. He married his high school sweetheart, Bobbi, during his sophomore year, and as a result, had to work the night shift at a local soft drink plant to support his family. He received no athletic financial aid, but worked hard both on the athletic field, in the classroom and at his job.

After college, Olson's first basketball coaching job was at Mahnomen High School, where he spent one season before moving on to teach and coach at Two Harbors High School. His first major coaching gig was at the University of Iowa, where he led the Hawkeyes to six 20-victory campaigns, a league title, and a trip to the NCAA Final Four in 1980. From there he took over as the head coach of the Arizona Wildcats, where his record has been close to phenomenal with a dozen straight 20-win campaigns. He went through a lot at Arizona, losing several times in the early rounds of the NCAA's Big Dance. In 1997, however, he finally got the monkey off his back when his Cinderella Wildcats upset Kentucky to win the National Championship. He made a return home in 2001 when he led his Cats back to the Final Four, this time at the Metrodome, just a stone's throw away from his old stomping grounds at Augsburg. A true coaching legend, Olson has amassed more than 600 career victories and has truly made Minnesota proud.

BUD WILKINSON

Born in 1916, in Minneapolis, Bud Wilkinson attended the Shattuck School in Faribault. There, he quickly emerged as a brilliant student-athlete both on the gridiron, as a quarterback & guard, and on the ice, as a hockey goaltender. So good was Wilkinson as a goalie, that in 1932, he led Shattuck to an undefeated record and in the process, he went unscored upon over the entire season. He graduated in 1933 as Cum Laude with the rank of First Lieutenant, and headed north, to the U of M, where he would emerge once again as one of the school's all-time greats.

Bud distinguished himself in football and hockey in Gold Country, even finding time to also letter in golf. As a guard on the 1934 and '35 undefeated national championship teams, he was termed by the famous writer Grantland Rice as "The best offensive guard in college football." Due to injuries, Bernie Bierman asked Wilkinson if he would switch from guard to quarterback that next year. He did, and in 1936, Bud directed Minnesota to their third straight undefeated national championship.

When it was all said and done, Wilkinson had done it all. Not only was he an All-American goalie on the Gopher Hockey team, but he had also garnered back-to-back All-American honors on the gridiron. In addition, he also won the school's highest honor for scholastics and sports — the Big Ten Medal of Honor.

Following graduation, he played in the college All-Star game, quarterbacking the collegeiates to a 7-0 victory over the Green Bay Packers, the first time in history the All-Stars had beaten the pros. He also played on the Galloping Gophers, an all-star basketball team that traveled around the Midwest playing independent teams, including the Harlem Globetrotters — whom they defeated.

From there Wilkinson went on to Syracuse University, where, in addition to serving as an assistant football coach under Ossie Solem, he earned his Masters Degree in English. He then briefly returned to Minnesota as an assistant to Bernie Bierman before being commissioned in the US Navy.

After the war, he was considered for the Gopher coaching job, but he turned it down instead going to the University of Oklahoma, where he would become the team's head coach in 1947. At OU Wilkinson would forever change the game, and in the process become one of college football's greatest ever coaches.

After tying for the 1947 championship, the Sooners won 12 straight conference crowns. Additionally, in between 1953 and 1957, his teams won 47 consecutive games over five straight undefeated seasons — an all-time national record. His teams also appeared in eight Sugar & Orange Bowl games, and he was named as the Coach of the Year on numerous occasions as well. His record at OU was an astounding 145-29-4, with three national titles to boot. At the time of his retirement, in 1963, Bud had become the winningest coach in college football.

He was also an innovator. He is credited for creating the "Swinging Gate" formation and a 1950s version of the "no-huddle" offense which he called the "Go-Go Offense" He also didn't believe in red-shirting and he even graduated an incredible 90% of his student-athletes. Although his coaching accolades are too many to mention, among his major ones include being inducted into the College Football and National Football Coaches Hall of Fames, being elected president of the American Football Coaches Association and receiving the Sports Illustrated Silver Anniversary All-American Award in 1962.

After retiring, he even ran for senate in 1964, where despite winning the Republican primary, lost the general election. Then, after a career in TV broadcasting, among other business interests, Wilkinson later coached in the NFL for the St. Louis Cardinals in 1978 and 1979. He hung em' up after just two sub-par seasons behind the bench though, and returned to the TV booth, where he served as an analyst for both ESPN and ABC.

In addition to later becoming OU's Athletic Director, Wilkinson led quite a celebrated life after football. He was a consultant to President Nixon and a member of the White House Staff from 1969-1971. He was also a special consultant to President Kennedy on physical fitness from 1961-1964, and he later served as the Republican National Committeeman for Oklahoma during the late 1960s.

Sadly, Wilkinson died in 1994 at the of 77 after battling heart problems. He will always be regarded as one of Minnesota's greatest all-time athletes, coaches and humanitarians.

CINDY NELSON

Cindy Nelson grew up in Lutsen, Minnesota's premier skiing community. And, after a brilliant career on the slopes, she is considered by many to be the greatest skier ever to hail from Minnesota. In 1971, at the age of 15, she made her first U.S World Cup team. That would be the start of an incredible string of 15 consecutive teams that she would be a member of. At only 17, she was selected as a member of the 1972 Olympic team in Sapporo, Japan. However, due to a dislocated hip, she was unable to participate. She remained determined though and went on to win a bronze medal in the downhill competition at the 1976 Winter Olympics in Innsbruck, Austria, in 1976. There, she also served as the U.S. team's flag carrier during the opening ceremonies. She once again skied in the 1980 games in Lake Placid, New York, though she did not place. Amazingly, at the age of 28, she gave it one last hurrah and made the 1984 Olympic team in Sarajevo, but an injured right knee kept her out of the downhill competition.

Called the "Old American" by her European counterparts, Cindy was a member of the U.S. Ski Team from 1971 to 1985, and remains the only woman to ski on four U.S. Olympic teams. One of the most decorated skiers in U.S. history, she won nine World Cup races and skied for the International Skiing Federation world championship team in 1974, 1978, 1982 and 1985. Among her numerous victories are two World Championship medals, including a silver in the combined at the 1980 Lake Placid Games, and a silver in the downhill at the 1982 World Championships. Her World Cup medals, meanwhile, include a bronze in the combined in 1976, a silver in the downhill in 1979, and a silver in the giant slalom in 1983. Upon her retirement from the sport in 1985, she continued to contribute as the director of skiing for Vail Associates in Vail, Colorado.

Minnesota recorded one of the greatest turn-arounds in pro football history in 1973, by posting a 12-2 record and advancing to their second Super Bowl in just four years. Leading the way was the all-purpose wonder, Chuck Foreman, who was named as the NFL's Rookie of the Year for his 1,163 yards both rushing and receiving. The offense was also clicking because the ground game was forcing opposing defenses to respect them. Quarterback Fran Tarkenton took advantage of the situation by throwing for nearly 3,000 yards while hooking up with Wide Receiver John Gilliam 42 times for eight touchdowns.

The Purple jumped out of the gates poised to do some damage in 1973, winning all five of their exhibition games. From there the squad ran off nine straight wins in the regular season before finally losing at Atlanta in Week 10. They rounded out the season by tattooing Chicago, 31-13, getting shut-out at Cincinnati, 27-0, and rebounding to beat both the Packers and the Giants by the identical scores of 31-7, to finish out the regular season at 12-2.

On December 22, 1973, the Redskins came to town to face the Vikes in the first round of the playoffs. It would be a game remembered for two reasons. First, because of the team's great second half comeback, and secondly, because of Carl Eller's half-time motivational speaking speech that ultimately caused the Vikings to have the aforementioned great second half comeback.

Washington got on the board first in this one after Bob Brunet recovered Bobby Bryant's fumbled punt at the Minnesota 21-yard line which resulted in a three-yard touchdown run by Larry Brown. Cox added a field goal in the second, but the lethargic Vikes blew a chance to take a lead at the end of the half when Tarkenton threw an interception.

At half-time, Eller, who played like a man possessed, went ballistic. He screamed, shouted, pounded his fist on metal doors, smashed a chalk board against the wall and challenged every man in that room to give it his all. He was tired of losing big games, and wanted more guts from everyone — right then and right there. The rest of the team sat in shock, staring silently, knowing that they had better step it up big-time, or they were going to have to deal with Carl after the game. And that's just what they did. Minnesota came out and took the lead in the second-half, thanks to Bill Brown's two-yard TD plunge which came on the heels of Oscar Reed's 46-yard scamper into the red-zone. Following a pair of Redskin field goals, Tarkenton capped a 71-yard drive with a 28-yard touchdown pass to Gilliam. Nate Wright then intercepted Billy Kilmer on the team's next offensive play, which led to Tarkenton again hitting Gilliam on an eight-yard touchdown pass. Freddy the foot then came in to nail a 30-yarder late in the fourth to ice it for the Vikes

as they hung on to win, 27-20.

That next week the Vikes headed to Irving, Texas, where they faced the hated Cowboys in the NFC Championship game. Minnesota came out and jumped all of the 'Boys in this one, thanks to an early Fred Cox field goal, followed by Chuck Foreman's five-yard TD run which capped a long, demoralizing 86-yard drive, mostly through the middle of the field. With two of their stars, Running Back Calvin Hill and Defensive Tackle Bob Lilly, out of the game with injuries, Dallas just couldn't get it going.

Golden Richards finally put Dallas on the board early in the third quarter though when he returned a punt 63 yards for a touchdown. Minnesota answered though, when Tark found John Gilliam open behind Cornerback Mel Renfro for a 54-yard touchdown pass. Dallas added a field goal to make it 17-10, but Quarterback Roger Staubach threw two of his four interceptions in the fourth quarter — one of them right into the awaiting arms of Bobby Bryant, who promptly took it 63 yards for a score. Another interception set up a 34-yard field goal by Fred Cox. Walt Garrison then ended a forgettable day for Dallas when he fumbled the ball away at the Minnesota two-yard line late in the fourth to kill their rally and end it at 27-10 in favor of the Vikes.

With that, the Vikings found themselves in their second Super Bowl, this time at Houston's Rice Stadium, where, on January 13, 1974, they took on Don Shula's Miami Dolphins. Yeah, the same Dolphins that had won 17 in a row just the year before to win Super Bowl VII. Their roster was a venerable who's-who of pro football: Bob Griese, Larry Csonka, Nick Buoniconti, Mercury Morris, Paul Warfield, Larry Little, Garo Yepremian and Jim Langer (a native of Little Falls).

Much of the pre-game excitement and controversy the week before the big game centered around the Vikings' miserable practice facilities at Delmar Field in Houston. You see, sparrows had moved in and built nests in the shower room, where most of the nozzles didn't work, nor did they spit out any hot water. The locker room didn't even have any lockers, just a bunch of rusty nails on the wall.

"This is shabby treatment," Grant told reporters at a press conference." This is the Super Bowl, not some pickup game. The NFL sets up the practice facilities, and they had a year to do it right. Go look for yourselves, we don't have any lockers. Our seven coaches have to share one table for spreading out our clothes. These facilities definitely give the Dolphins the advantage."

Meanwhile, the prima-donna Dolphins, on the other hand, were working out at the Houston Oilers' plush practice facilities. Secretly, this was just what Grant wanted. He needed a juicy subplot to distract all of the hounding journalists and their endless questions, so he figured that this headline would be better than that involving of any of his players. Plus, it got his players fired up. They were already underdogs coming in, but now they were plenty pissed off about being treated like second-hand citizens to the glamour boy Dolphins.

The reporters still hounded the players though, including Viking's Tackle Gary Larsen, who found the whole Super Bowl hyperbole to be a bit much. "I hope you don't think I'm a wise guy when I add that we've sweated a long time for this opportunity, and a whole bunch of people will be watching on TV," he quipped. "But there are 800 million Chinamen who don't give a damn about what happens in Houston this Sunday afternoon!"

Maybe Gary was on to something, but all those Americans

TIMELINE

| St. Olaf vaulter Paul DeLaitsch wins the Division III Pole Vaulting National Championship | Vikings General Manager Jim Finks is named as the NFL's Executive of the Year | George Kelly, a Minneapolis Miller from 1930-31, is inducted into the Baseball Hall of Fame | Monte Irvin, a Minneapolis Miller in 1955, is inducted into the Baseball Hall of Fame | Gopher center Jim Brewer is named to the All-American basketball team | Gopher forward Ron Behagen is named to the All-American basketball team | UMD center Pat Boutette is named to the All-American hockey team | Duluth native Frank (Coddy) Winters is enshrined into the U.S. Hockey Hall of Fame | Eveleth native Sam LoPresti is enshrined into the U.S. Hockey Hall of Fame. "Lucky LoPresti," a former Blackhawk goaltender, gained notoriety when his merchant ship was torpedoed in the ocean during WWII. He spent 42 days drifting in a lifeboat before being rescued. |

68

who did care about the game saw nothing more than a good old fashioned butt-kicking, as the Dolphins came out and thrashed the Vikes, thus becoming the second team in NFL history to win back-to-back Super Bowls. On paper, the game seemed to be a mismatch from the opening kick-off. You had the 23rd ranked Vikings run defense up against a relentless Miami ground attack, and Miami wasted little time in exploiting Minnesota's weaknesses. Before the Vikings could manage a first down, the Fish were up by the score of 14-0.

Following two time-consuming 62 and 56 yard drives, Miami Fullback Larry Csonka plowed in first on a five-yard run, followed by a Jim Kiick one-yarder. Garo Yepremian then added a 28-yard field goal to make it 17-0 at the half. The Vikings' only chance to get back in the game came late in the first half when they drove down to the Miami five-yard line, only to see Dolphins' Linebacker Nick Buoniconti crunch Oscar Reed on the next play and force a turnover.

Stu Voigt then got called for a clipping penalty during the kickoff to start the second half, negating John Gilliam's brilliant 65-yard return which would've given Minnesota the ball on the Miami 34-yard line. As a result, they were held on downs, and Csonka scored on a two-yard plunge on the next series to make it 24-0. Fran, who set a Super Bowl record by completing 18 passes, then tried to mount a late comeback by capping a 40-yard drive on a four-yard TD run. He put together another drive with seconds to go, but it was foiled by Curtis Johnson's interception at the Miami goal line to end the game at 24-7.

Just how bad was it? Dolphins' Quarterback Bob Griese had to throw only seven passes that entire afternoon, completing six. The 71,882 fans in attendance that day watched Csonka, named as the game's MVP, set a Super Bowl record by rushing for 145 yards and two touchdowns on 33 carries — doubling the rushing yardage of the entire Minnesota backfield.

"I've never tried to tackle anybody stronger," said Linebacker Jeff Siemon of Zonk. "Once he got going, he just carried you on his back. He has to be the strongest running back I've ever faced."

"I don't have many good memories of that Super Bowl game against Miami," recalled Chuck Foreman. "There's not much to say except that they beat us on both ends of the ball. Of all the Super Bowls I've played in, that was the only one that I could justify losing in my mind. The Miami Dolphins had more talent and a better unit than we had. Personally, it was an incredibly exciting time for me being Rookie of the Year and playing in my first Super Bowl and all. Miami was the only team that I have ever played against that I could honestly say that they were better than us. It was just a tough loss after coming off the great season that we had."

Forty-Fourman
Chuck Foreman was raised just outside of Washington D.C. in Frederick, MD, where he grew up playing football, basketball and baseball. Originally recruited as a defensive tackle, he made the switch to running back at the University of Miami, where he quickly broke all of the Hurricane's freshman rushing records

In 1973 he was drafted by the Vikings as the 12th overall pick of the first round. The transition to the pro's was a smooth one for the powerful running back, who, after rushing for 801 yards, catching 37 passes, and scoring four touchdowns, was named as the NFL's Rookie of the Year. Not only was he a bruising runner, he also had amazing hands — which made him one of the game's greatest all-time offensive weapons. When he had the ball in the open field it was all over. His now infamous 360-degree spins became his trademark, as he often-times left his would-be tacklers dazed and confused in his vapor trail.

"I am sometimes surprised when I look at film of myself," said Foreman of his unorthodox running style in Klobuchar's book: "The First 15 Years." "I just do what's natural out there and live by

instinct. It's like when you're riding your bicycle and all of a sudden, a mad dog starts chasing you. There's a little bit of fear in your heart, and you've got to get away. I look at running as an art."

In 1975, en route to leading the Vikings in rushing, receiving, and scoring, No. 44 also won the NFC scoring and receptions titles by hauling in 73 catches — the most ever by a running back. He followed that up the next year by rushing for 1,155 yards, including a 200-yard game against Philly, to be named as the NFC Player-of-the-Year. Then, in 1978, Foreman, the hub of the Vikings offense for five seasons, suffered a knee injury which would ultimately lead to the premature end of his incredible career. He gained a career-low 749 yards in 1979 and saw his playing time slowly get gobbled up by back-up to Ted Brown. That next season he was traded to New England, where he played one more year before retiring.

Without a doubt, Chuck "Forty-Fourman" was the greatest running back in Vikings history. No one could run the ball with the passion and desire like he did. Sure, Robert Smith was good, but Chuck was special and could do it all. Foreman led the Vikings in rushing for six consecutive seasons, set team records for yards rushing, with 5,879, and also combined yards (rushing and receiving), with 8,936. All in all, he scored 53 rushing touchdowns, while also catching 350 passes for 3,156 receiving yards and 23 receiving touchdowns.

What did it mean for you to be a Viking?
"I was always a big fan of the 'Purple People Eaters' so I had to pinch myself when I was drafted by Minnesota. But, before I came up here to join the Vikings, I actually did a lot of research on the team and on its players. I wanted to know who played there and where they were from. I consider it to be a privilege to have been able to perform there."

TRIBUTES
"I think that Chuck was one of the finest running backs in the history of the NFL," said Jim Marshall. "At the peak of his career, he was one of the most highly skilled running backs that ever played the game of football. He was a great player."

"His talent is still unrecognized," said Carl Eller. "He was one the best running backs ever. Chuck was so good that the Vikings didn't realize how good he was. He was a great player, but as great as he was, I don't think the Vikings ever used his greatness to its fullest extent."

"It was too bad Chuck didn't play the game a little longer," said Bud Grant. "He was the best back in the league for five years. Running backs take a lot of wear and tear, and it was unfortunate that he got hurt."

"Chuck was the best all-around running back that I ever played with," said Ahmad Rashad. "He was an amazing athlete. He could block, tackle, run, catch and score. Chuck Foreman could do everything."

"Chuck was just a great running back," said Alan Page. "He had the speed, talent, the moves, and he always came to play."

Led by their fiery second-year coach Herb Brooks, the 1974 Gophers went on to make history by winning their first ever NCAA hockey championship. After finishing sixth in the WCHA the season before, the Gophers came full circle that season, proving to the world that Minnesota was indeed, the hockey capital of America.

After starting 0-4-1, the Gophers put together a nine-game winning streak that included series sweeps of North Dakota, Michigan State and St. Louis. Minnesota then went on win all but two of it's final 16 home games at Williams Arena. They finished with a 14-9-5 record, good enough for second place in the WCHA, behind Michigan Tech.

The Gophers went on to beat tough Michigan and Denver teams in the WCHA playoffs, and found themselves on their way to Boston, where they would be pitted against the top-ranked, hometown Terriers of Boston University in the NCAA Final-Four. The Cinderella Gophers felt right at home in the Boston Garden though, as they proceeded to knock off BU in the semifinals, 5-4, thanks to Mike Polich's shorthanded go-ahead goal at 19:47 of the third period. They would now face their old WCHA nemesis, Michigan Tech, in the Finals.

The Gophers went back and forth with the Huskies throughout the first period of the big game, until John Sheridan scored late to give the Maroon and Gold a one-goal lead. John Perpich then found the back of the net to make it two-zip in the second. The Huskies came back though, scoring at 3:24 of the same period, to get to within one. It remained that way until the third, when John Harris and Pat Phippen both scored 12 minutes apart to put the Gophers up for good. The Huskies added another one with less than a minute to go, but it was too little, too late. With an impressive 39 shots-on-goal, the Gophers held on to win the title, 4-2. Herbie Brooks had hit the jackpot, and Minnesota had its first NCAA hockey crown.

Brooks had led the Gophers to a 22-12-6 overall record that magical season. It was also the first team in 25 years to win the title with a team comprised exclusively of American players. And, he did it with only two years' worth of talent that he had recruited. For his efforts, Brooks was named as the WCHA Coach of the Year.

Team captain Brad Shelstad, a product of Minneapolis Southwest, was chosen as the tournament's MVP and was also selected as an All-WCHA selection. Les Auge and Hibbing's Mike Polich were named to the All-Tournament team as well. Polich and Harris led the team in scoring that season. Polich went on to a successful career in the NHL, while Harris emerged as a star in another sport, golf, where he won the 1993 U.S. Amateur Golf Championship and later even joined the Senior PGA Tour.

The 1974 team will perhaps be remembered most for their hustle, desire, and work ethic, all reflections of

Brooks' hard-driving motivational style of coaching.

Moving from last place in the WCHA to first could not have been accomplished without unique leaders. "My first year, our two captains, Billy Butters and Jimmy Gambucci, were tremendous leaders who just did a great job of getting the program returned to a good, solid footing," said Brooks. "It was tremendously gratifying getting the school's first championship coming from where we did. The players weren't in awe of anything, and they were extremely strong mentally. Plus they could really compete. They played well on the road and they played against the odds to overcome a lot that season. That first title was very special to me."

Her-bee! Her-bee!

Herbert Paul Brooks was born in St. Paul on August 5, 1937 and grew up in a hockey-crazy family. His father was a well known amateur player in the 1920s, and his brother, David, played for the Gophers in the early 1960s and also on the 1964 U.S. Olympic team. As a boy growing up on St. Paul's tough East Side, a training ground for many future Minnesota hockey stars, Herb was a typical hockey playing rink-rat. He went on to star at St. Paul Johnson High School from 1952-1955. As a senior, the forward led Johnson to a 26-1-2 record en route to winning the state championship. In the title game, Brooks scored two goals in the 3-1 victory over their Mill City rivals, Minneapolis Southwest.

"Winning the state championship, that represented your neighborhood," said Brooks. "I would have to say that it was my biggest thrill ever. It was just the guys in the neighborhood and that was special."

An outstanding athlete, Herb also earned three varsity letters as a first baseman on the baseball team as well. Before long, the colleges were calling.

"I had an interview with the Air Force Academy, because I really wanted to be a fighter pilot," said Brooks. "Unfortunately, because I was slightly color blind, I washed out of the Academy. I also had a scholarship at Michigan, but my dad encouraged me to walk on at the U of M and try to play for Mariucci, so that was the route I took."

At Minnesota, Brooks became known for his blinding speed. "He was one of the fastest, if not the fastest, player in college hockey in that era," said his coach, John Mariucci. Brooks would learn a lot from "Maroosh," saying that he had more to do with shaping his ideas in hockey than any other individual. Brooks wore a Golden Gopher sweater from 1957-59, scoring 45 points over his three-year career. He graduated from the U in 1961 with a B.A. in Psychology.

The next phase of Brooks' life involved his lifelong dream, the Olympics. After graduation, he began to build a successful career in the insurance business, but never fully got away from the game that continued to dominate his life. Herb tried out for the 1960 Olympic team which was played in Squaw Valley. He eluded every cut except the final one, when he was the last player ultimately to be released.

"My father said that they must have cut the right guy, because they won the gold medal," said Herb jokingly.

Brooks then spent nearly a decade playing for either U.S. Olympic or National teams. From 1961 to 1970, he played on two Olympic teams and five national teams — more than any player in the history of United States hockey — captaining the 1965, 1967, 1968 and 1970 teams to boot.

TIMELINE

Hamline's Steve Lindgren wins the Division III Shot Put National Championship	The Gopher hockey team beats Michigan Tech, 4-2, for the NCAA Championship	Little Falls, Minnesota aviator Charles Lindbergh dies at the age of 72. "Lucky Lindy" flew the Spirit of St. Louis on the first solo transatlantic flight from New York to Paris in a time of 33.5 hours.	Minneapolis native Virgil Johnson is enshrined into the U.S. Hockey Hall of Fame	The state's largest rainbow trout is caught by Knife River's Ottway Stuberud on the Knife River: 17 lbs., 6 oz.	The Vikings lose to the Pittsburgh Steelers in Super Bowl IX, 16-6. The purple's only score came in the fourth quarter when Matt Blair blocked a Bobby Walden punt and Terry Brown recovered it in the end zone.	Brainerd International Speedway is born. It is the largest multi-purpose motor sports facility in North America. The three-mile course is the state's largest race track and hosts a variety of venues including motorcycles, superbike, sportscar, go-kart, funny cars and drag racing.

70

"The Olympics were always my goal," said Brooks. "Playing in 1964 and 1968 was really a big thrill, and all things considered, it was one of the biggest highlights of my career."

Herb went into coaching after that, becoming an assistant under Coach Glen Sonmor at the U. At the same time, he pioneered Junior Hockey in the state as the first coach of the Minnesota Junior Stars in the Minnesota/Ontario Junior-A League. Then, in 1971, Sonmor left to become the coach of the WHA's Fighting Saints and Ken Yackel, Sr. was then brought in to finish the season as an interim coach. That next season Brooks was named as the new Gopher coach. The youngest college hockey coach in the country, Brooks would inherit a program that had just off finished in last place.

The chant "Herbee, Herbee" was an all too familiar sound throughout the tenure of the man who would become Minnesota's greatest hockey coach. Brooks instilled a new brand of pride and tradition that next season, starting with his newly designed jerseys which proudly featured the Minnesota "M" on the front. Brooks promised he would bring, "exciting, dynamic people into the program," and he kept his word. In only seven years, he would build a dynasty at Minnesota. More importantly, he did it all with Minnesota kids.

With his extensive knowledge and experience in European hockey, Herb became an advocate of the Russian style of play and in particular, the coaching style of Anatoli Tarasov. He would instill this philosophy in motivating his own players. From 1972-1979, Brooks won the only national championships in University of Minnesota hockey history. There would be three in all: 1973, 1976 and 1979, and his achievements may never be equaled.

While at Minnesota, Brooks won 175 games, lost only 100, and tied 20 for a .636 winning percentage. Herb guided five All-Americans: Les Auge, Mike Polich, Tim Harrer, Neal Broten and Steve Ulseth, while 23 of his protégés went on to play in the NHL as well.

"We went to the finals four of my seven years there, and we made a great run of it," said Brooks. "I think I put a lot of pressure on the players, and I had a lot of expectations of them. I didn't give them an 'out,' and I think I was always able to find the kids who were really competitive. The common denominator of all the guys who played throughout my seven years was that they were really competitive, very hungry, very focused, and mentally tough — to go along with whatever talent they had. I think that really carried us."

Do you believe in miracles? Yes! The next chapter of Brooks' life is the one that made him a household name, the "Miracle on Ice." After coaching the 1979 U.S. National team in the World Games in Moscow, Herb took over as coach of the fabled 1980 U.S. Olympic team. Brooks guided the squad to their incredible upset of the heavily-favored Soviet Union team, setting the stage for the huge win against Finland in the gold medal game. That victory would go down as one of the most memorable moments in U.S. sports history.

After a brief coaching stint in Davos, Switzerland, Herb's coaching success continued with the NHL's New York Rangers, where he gained 100 victories quicker than any other coach before him and, as a result, was named NHL Coach of the Year in 1982. His Broadway stint with the Rangers lasted until 1985.

Then, in an amazing move, Brooks came home and accepted the head coaching position at St. Cloud State University in 1987. He would be revered as the school's savior, leading the Huskies to a third place finish in the national small-college tournament, and more importantly, getting them moved to NCAA Division I status. He stayed for only a year, but with his clout, got the school a beautiful new arena and really got the Huskies' program turned around.

"I've never met Herb Brooks, but I feel like I owe him everything," said Bret Hedican, former Husky and current NHL All-Star. "He's done so much for St. Cloud Hockey, it's incredible."

The next stop in Brooks' hockey resume was Bloomington, to coach the Minnesota North Stars. This was another homecoming of sorts, as Herb took over the reigns from Lorne Henning and became the first Minnesota native to coach the NHL team. The season, however, didn't go well for Brooks. Unable to overcome an enormous number of injuries, the Stars finished in the Norris Division cellar. Then, citing philosophical differences with management, Brooks resigned and was replaced by Pierre Page that next season.

Brooks took some well deserved time away from coaching for a few years after that to embark on a successful business career which included motivational speaking, TV analysis, NHL scouting and occasional coaching. Then, in 1991, he first took over the New Jersey Devils minor league team in Utica, and was later promoted to be the head coach of the NHL team in 1992. He got the coaching bug again a few years later, when he guided the French Olympic team in 1998. Following that he became a scout with the Pittsburgh Penguins, ultimately taking over as the teams' head coach in 1999. He then came full circle in 2002 when he guided the U.S. Olympic team to a dramatic silver medal at the Winter Games in Salt Lake City. Once again, Herbie had made America proud.

One of our nation's most charismatic and inventive coaches, "Herbie" is a true American hero. A member of the U.S. Hockey, U of M, and East Side Hockey Halls of Fame, Brooks also received the coveted Lester Patrick Award for his contributions to American hockey. Throughout his career Herb Brooks has earned great recognition both individually and for his country. Among his many awards and honors, Brooks has been named as Sports Illustrated's Sportsman of the Year, and his 1980 U. S. Olympic team was named as the Sports Achievement of the Century in 2000.

Herbie is a legend in the world of sports and is very much a hockey icon in the United States. Whether he's competing in the business world, on the ice, or even on the diamond of a world championship fast-pitch softball team, he takes the same attitude and intensity to whatever he does, and that's why he's so successful. He is a true Minnesota treasure.

What did it mean to be a Gopher?

"Really, there weren't many options for an American kid or a Minnesota kid in college hockey back then. It was really tough. I always thought it was the toughest time of any Gopher era because of the Canadian kids who were coming down, the competition, and lack of NCAA rules back then. With that, it was very important to play for the U of M. It's not like it is today where there are a lot more hockey schools, and American kids have more opportunities. Playing for the Gophers then, when there were few opportunities, was real special."

Minnesota Hockey tombstone?

"The name on the front of the sweater is more important than the name on the back. They always forget about individuals, but they'll always remember the teams. That has been the cornerstone of my philosophy."

The Vikings team of 1975 was arguably the best ever. The team came out of the gates just smoking, winning its first 10 games. It wasn't until Week 11, when they got upset, 31-30, at Washington, did they even come back down to earth. They then beat Green Bay the following week, lost at Detroit in Week 13, 17-10, and rebounded to finish the regular season with a 35-13 waxing of Buffalo.

In addition to Running Back Chuck Foreman's brilliant season, Quarterback Fran Tarkenton had a career year as well, passing for 25 touchdowns and earning the league's coveted MVP award. Things were looking great for a repeat trip to the big dance. The offense was playing huge and was hitting on all cylinders. They had outscored their opponents, 377-180 and even won nine games by 10 or more points. They were primed to finally win it all that year. That was until the hated Dallas Cowboys came to town and pulled off one of the most infamous plays in the history of the NFL.

On December 28, 1975, the Vikes hosted the Cowboys for the NFC Divisional Playoff game. Minnesota, a veteran laden team which had battle scars from three Super Bowls, was expected to finally win the Super Bowl this year, while the 10-4 Cowboys on the other hand, were a young wild-card team, with a cast of more than a dozen rookies. Sure Dallas had lost Bob Lilly and Walt Garrison to retirement that year, but they did have their hard-hitting "Doomsday Defense," which was led by Ed "Too-Tall" Jones, Harvey Martin, Lee Roy Jordan and Safety Cliff Harris. When this one was all said and done, it would go down as one of the greatest upsets in the history of sports, and without question the Vikings' undisputed worst game of all-time.

The game got underway and after a scoreless first quarter, something pivotal happened in the second quarter that would play an important role in the outcome of the game. Dallas felt that they were jobbed by the refs when Cowboy Safety Cliff Harris, who was waiting to receive a Neil Clabo punt on his own four-yard-line, opted to let the ball sail into the end-zone for a touchback. The ball, however, took a crazy bounce and Vikings Linebacker Fred McNeil jumped on it. Harris didn't know what was going on, but the officials claimed it touched his leg on the bounce, meaning that it was a live ball for anyone to claim. Dallas argued to no avail, and Chuck Foreman leaped over the goal line for a touchdown one minute later, making it 7-0.

After a missed 45-yard field goal attempt by Fred Cox, Dallas came back to tie it up on a Doug Dennison seven-yard TD run. They then took the lead on Toni Fritsch's 24-yard field goal to make it 10-7. But with five minutes to go in the game, Minnesota regained the lead when Brent McClanahan capped an 11 play, 70-yard touchdown drive by taking it in from the one-yard line.

Dallas' offense sputtered on the next series and

was forced to punt. But they held the Vikings in check, thanks to Safety Charlie Waters, who blitzed and sacked Tarkenton for a three-yard loss on a key third down to force the Vikings to punt. The Cowboys then got the ball back on their own 15-yard line with just 1:51 to go. Quarterback Roger Staubach started out his drive by hitting Drew Pearson for seven yards. Then, on fourth-and-16 from his own 25, he found Pearson again at mid-field for another first down. The play, which had Staubach faking a post pattern and instead hitting Pearson angling for the sideline, was aided by Cornerback Nate Wright. Here's why. While the momentum of the pass probably would have carried Pearson out of bounds for an incompletion, the official ruled otherwise, declaring that Wright had forced him out. The Vikings, now frantically pointing their fingers and criss-crossing their arms, claimed it would have been impossible for Pearson to have landed in-bounds. But the referee stood firm, and the drive continued.

Dallas now had a first down at the 50-yard line with 37 seconds left. After throwing a pair of incompletions to Receivers Golden Richards and Preston Pearson, Staubach then mishandled John Fitzgerald's poor snap and was dumped for a six-yard loss. Metropolitan Stadium was rocking. He got up though, and huddled his men at midfield. His bruised ribs from the week before were bothering him and Drew Pearson was exhausted. Pearson thought he could beat Wright, so Staubach told him to do just that. With that, he said a prayer and lined up against the "Purple People Eaters."

Now, with 24 seconds left on the clock, and after a bobbled snap, Staubach dropped back, pump-faked to keep Safety Paul Krause from coming over to offer double-coverage, and let go a desperation heave into the semi-darkness of the late afternoon Minnesota haze. The wobbly pass hung up there and was slightly under-thrown to his sprinting receiver, Drew Pearson. But Pearson, who was shoulder to shoulder with Cornerback Wright in a foot-race down the sidelines, somehow came back, adjusted to ball and miraculously caught the 50-yard ball at the five-yard line and simply fell into the end-zone as time ran off the clock. With the ball pinned awkwardly in between his elbow and hip, the surprised receiver cautiously looked at the official for a penalty flag. But the offensive pass interference call never came. Pearson, who clearly pushed off of Wright, even knocking him down to gain better position on the play, had gotten away with murder. He then turned around, took a running start and fired the ball up at the cowboy hat wearing Marlboro Man billboard ad up on the scoreboard, as a sort of salute to all of Texas.

More than 47,000 fans in the old Met sat in silence, shock, and disbelief. Everyone thought that there would be a penalty called, and there was, only on Minnesota's Wright. The Vikings players went berserk. The fans started booing and screaming: "Pearson pushed off!" Then, in what some crazy zealots later called "justifiable homicide," some drunk lunatic heaved a half-full "Corby's" Whiskey bottle from the 21st row of the Met's right field bleachers and decked the Official, Armen Terzian, square in the noggin. Foreman quickly ran to the aid of the now bleeding ref and pleaded with the fans to remain calm. The game ended a few seconds later, but for Tarkenton, things got much, much worse. Shortly thereafter, he learned that his father, a Georgia Minister whose name was, ironically, Dallas, had died of a heart attack while watching the game on television.

(After the game the whiskey bottle was seized as evidence, and a search for the psychotic fan began. A $5,000 reward was offered;

TIMELINE

St. Olaf vaulter Charles Novak wins the Division III Pole Vaulting National Championship	St. Thomas track and field star Mark Dienhart wins the Division III Shot Put National Championship. Today Dr. Dienhart is the University of Minnesota's Men's Athletics Director.	Billy Herman, a Minneapolis Miller in 1948, is inducted into the Baseball Hall of Fame	Vikings tackle Ron Yary is named as the NFL's Outstanding Blocker of the Year	The Gopher hockey team loses to Michigan Tech, 6-1, in the NCAA Finals	Gopher defenseman Les Auge is named to the All-American hockey team	Gopher center Mike Polich is named to the All-American hockey team	St. Paul native Tony Conroy is enshrined into the U.S. Hockey Hall of Fame

72

the Bloomington Police Department released a sketch of the perpetrator; game tapes were scrutinized and more than a dozen suspects were interrogated. Six months later, a 21-year-old kid from Golden Valley was picked out of a line-up by a couple of witnesses and charged with simple-assault and disorderly conduct. He pleaded guilty and was fined a whopping $100 bucks.)

"It was just a 'Hail Mary' pass," said Staubach very impromptu-like after the game, "a very, very lucky play." "I just threw it and prayed. I'll admit that we were very lucky on that play. But on the other hand, that touchdown we gave the Vikings in the second quarter had to be some kind of a fluke. If you take away that touchdown by the Vikings and our so-called lucky catch, we still would have won by a field goal and I think we deserved to."

"The touchdown pass was a prayer that was answered," said Bud Grant. "From our side of the field, there was no question that Pearson shoved Nate Wright. It was as clear as day and night. He (Pearson) had nothing to lose. If they called a penalty on him, what had he lost? They would just line up and try another long pass. It was one chance in a hundred that he would get away with it, but it was the only chance he had."

In the era of modern football there are several historic and celebrated plays that will forever link certain teams with an era: Green Bay's "Ice Bowl," Pittsburgh's "Immaculate Reception" by Franco Harris, "The Catch" by Dwight Clark from Joe Montana, the Raiders' "Holy Roller" play, and even the Tennessee Titans' "Music City Miracle" to beat the Bills in 1999. But none was as big, or has become so much a part of the NFL's history than has the infamous "Hail Mary."

Fran the Man

Francis Asbury Tarkenton was born on February 3, 1940, in Richmond, Va., and went on to attend high school in Athens, Ga., where he excelled in both football and basketball. From there he became an All-American (and Academic All-American) quarterback at the University of Georgia, where he graduated with a degree in Business in 1961.

Tarkenton was then selected in the third round of the NFL draft by the expansion Minnesota Vikings that same year. He made quite a statement in his first game, torching the mighty Chicago Bears for four touchdowns and running in another en route to leading Minnesota to a dramatic 37-13 win — one of the biggest upsets in NFL history. Fran would play five solid seasons in Minnesota, even having the phrase "scramble" coined after his unorthodox way of running around to evade would-be sackers. He called his own plays and added a new dimension to the quarterback position by refusing to give up.

"Perhaps the best way I can sum up my scrambling activity, and also press home my deepest philosophies about fighting to win, is this way: I was talking to a writer one time, and he wondered why I scrambled. He said, 'I guess there's no sense standing back there and getting clobbered.' You know, I had never thought about that aspect of it, and I quickly corrected him by saying that there was only one reason to scramble — to win a ball game. The only thing I think about on a football field is winning."

Then, in 1966, after five stormy seasons under Dutch Van Brocklin's conservative and temperamental coaching style, Francis was traded to the New York Giants. The final straw came near the end of the 1966 season when Van Brocklin benched Tarkenton before the Atlanta game, apparently out of spite — knowing that his friends and family would be watching back home. Fran demanded to be traded and Vikings General Manager Jim Finks pulled the trigger on a deal that sent him to the New York Giants for two first-round picks. The Giants desperately needed a marquis player much like their cross-town rival Jets had in Joe Namath and they got him in Tark.

Five years later, in 1972, Coach Bud Grant engineered a deal

that brought Fran back to Minnesota. By then Fran was a full-fledged celebrity though and his interests weren't confined to the playing field. Fran was a smart guy and had already started to prepare for his life after football, where he was quite confident that he would become an even bigger star. He owned real estate, had countless major commercial endorsement deals, and he read the Wall Street Journal as avidly as he read his own team's play book. He was handsome, rich and articulate. The Republicans even begged him to run for public office. Yes, Fran had a plan, and football was just part of it.

He was also pretty damn tough. Despite being just six-feet tall and weighing in at a measly buck-eighty, he could take a hit. Once, in a game against the Lions, Detroit Defensive Tackle Dave Pureifory came plowing over the line unscathed and tattooed Tark square in the melon. Fran crumbled. Then, after realizing that three of his front teeth had popped out, he jumped up, put his arm on the giant tackle's shoulder and sarcastically whispered: "No hard feelings, Dave. I'm okay already..." And, just to spite him, he even came back in the second half to lead the Vikes to a 47-7 blow-out. After the game, Tark received nearly 60 stitches and endured several days of oral surgery.

From 1973-1978, Fran led the Vikings to an amazing 62-22-2 record, and guided them to three Super Bowls. Then, in 1978, after 18 incredible seasons in the NFL, 13 of which were with Minnesota, Tark decided to call it quits. At the time of his retirement, he owned nearly every one of the NFL's major passing records: most passing attempts (6,467), most completions (3,686), most passing yards (47,003), most games played (246), and most touchdown passes (342). He had also rushed for 3,674 yards en route to scoring 32 touchdowns, a stat that made him the ultimate double-threat. And, for 15 consecutive seasons, he threw for more than 2,000 yards. He was also a four-time All-NFL selection, played in nine Pro-Bowls, and was named as the league's MVP in 1975. Then, in 1986, Fran was proudly inducted into the Pro Football Hall of Fame.

Fran was an A-typical quarterback who's dogged determination to keep trying in the face of failure, made him a fan-favorite. Back in the 1970s, the Vikings "golden era," he was every Minnesota kids' hero. Because he tried as hard as he did, sacrificed as much as he did, and, at times, carried the team on his back, we loved him. Without question, Fran should be regarded as the best ever signal caller ever to wear the purple. He was just that good.

Today Fran resides in the Atlanta area, where he has four children and three grandchildren. After football Fran tried his hand at just about everything. And, after hosting TV's "That's Incredible," Fran also became an incredibly successful businessman. In fact, over the past 20 years, he has started and built more than a dozen businesses. A highly sought after motivational speaker, Fran is also a board member of several major companies and has countless personal business interests throughout the world. "I'm a capitalist without apology," said Fran. Hey, if you want to see Tark today, just flip on the tube anytime after midnight, you'll probably find him hawking something!

The Vikings had every reason to come out feeling sorry for themselves in 1976. But with the memories of the "Hail Mary" still fresh in their minds, they instead came out and showed their true colors, posting a tremendous 11-2-1 regular season record, and garnering yet another trip to the post-season. On November 21st, with a 17-10 win against the Packers, the defense, which allowed only three teams to score more than 13 points that season, led the team to its eighth division title in nine years. One of the bright spots for the defense was the addition of Cornerback Nate Allen, who loved to tear it up and make big hits. He even posted three of the team's 15 blocked kicks or punts that season. He also fit in well with Safety Paul Krause, who was closing in on the all-time career interceptions record held by Emlen Tunnell.

Foreman, who had his best rushing year with 1,155 yards, and Tarkenton, who, with 2,961 passing yards, surpassed Johnny Unitas as the all-time leader in virtually every major passing category, were again the heroes on the offensive side of the ball. But they were joined that season by a couple of receivers who would make for a wonderful a one-two punch. Sammy White, who would earn Rookie of the Year honors, and veteran Ahmad Rashad, who, after a couple of stints with St. Louis, Buffalo, and Seattle, finally found a home in Minnesota. The team's core group of stars were aging though, and played with a sense of urgency that year. Key players such as Tarkenton, Marshall, Eller, Tingelhoff, Hilgenberg and Krause, all knew that this might be their last chance to get that elusive Super Bowl ring.

The season had its share of highlights, including Foreman's amazing 200-yard game against Philadelphia, as well as the nail-biter in Detroit, where the Vikes hung on to beat the Lions, 10-9, on a blown second half conversion. And then there was the 17-6 win at Pittsburgh, where the Vikings' defense played like they were possessed. They owned the Steelers that day, as Page blocked a field goal and a conversion; Eller blocked a field goal; and Nate Allen picked off a pair of Terry Bradshaw passes — one of which came on the heels of Page's forced fumble which later led to Foreman's game-winning touchdown.

It was now off to the playoffs, where the Purple squared off against the Washington Redskins at Met Stadium. This one proved to be a wild one right out of the gates as Brent McClanahan rumbled 41 yards on the first play from scrimmage. Just three plays later, Tarkenton found Stu Voigt, who plowed his way over two Redskin defenders en route to an 18-yard touchdown. After a Washington field goal by Mark Mosely, Tark hit Sammy White on a key third-and-nine play for a 27-yard touchdown to make it 14-3. From there Chuck Foreman capped a pair of 66 and 51-yard drives by scoring a pair of two and 30-yard touchdown runs. White added another TD of his own in the third, this one being a nine yarder following a 76-yard drive. Washington Quarterback Billy Kilmer rallied his squad back late but came up on the short end of a 35-20 ball game. With the win, the Vikes had earned themselves another title bout with the Rams for the NFC championship.

The Rams flew in to Minneapolis on Christmas Eve for the NFC title tilt with a business-like attitude. L.A. Defensive End Jack Youngblood vowed that this time his team was not going to be psyched-out by the frigid weather. Just how much did they want to make a statement to the Vikings on that 12-degree below zero wind-chilled day? They came out for their pre-game warm-ups in T-shirts, impressing the grounds-crew workers who were out trying to soften up the frozen turf with flame throwers. It didn't do much for the Viking's players though, who just thought that they were nuts.

The Rams came out swinging early in this one, driving the length of the field on the opening series behind the running of Lawrence McCutcheon. Then, after the Vikes held the Rams out of the end-zone on several key defensive stops, Rams Kicker Tom Dempsey came in to attempt a 26-yard field goal. That's when Nate Allen flew over the pile and blocked the kick, leaving Bobby Bryant to scoop up the bouncing ball and race 90 yards in the other direction for a touchdown.

From there Vikings Linebacker Matt Blair took over. First he recovered a John Cappelletti fumble to kill a Ram's drive at the Minnesota 21-yard line, and then proceeded to block a Rusty Jackson punt midway through the second. Freddy Cox gave Minnesota a 10-0 lead at the half thanks to a 25-yard boot, which was then followed by Chuck Foreman's third quarter 62-yard scamper off the right tackle to get down to the Ram's two-yard line. From there he simply ran it in to make it 17-0. The Rams didn't lie down though, as Cornerback Monte Jackson intercepted a Tarkenton offering and got his squad back in the game. They rallied behind McCutcheon's 10-yard score, followed by Quarterback Pat Haden's five-yard TD pass to Harold Jackson to make it 17-13. A monster rush by the Purple People Eaters forced Dempsey to rush his extra-point though and it missed the uprights, wide left.

The Rams kept coming and reached the Vikings' 33 and 39-yard lines on their next two possessions. Wally Hilgenberg blitzed and sacked Haden to end the first threat, and with 2:31 to go, Bobby Bryant killed the Ram's final drive by nabbing his second interception of the day deep in Minnesota territory. A few minutes later, after Tarkenton found Foreman on a critical third down play, reserve Running Back Sammy Johnson ran it in to ice the 24-13 victory for Minnesota.

With that, and to the dismay of millions of football fans across America (much like the Buffalo Bills of the '90s), the Vikings were going back for a fourth shot at the Lombardi Trophy against the perennial AFC playoff bridesmaids, the Oakland Raiders, in Super Bowl XI. The pregame hype was intense, but Grant, who said that he felt his team was as prepared for that game as they could have been for any game he had coached, knew that it was getting to be the end of the line.

The Vikings, attempted to seek redemption from the Super Bowl gods under the scrutiny of an estimated 81 million television viewers along with the 103,438 fans at the Rose Bowl in Pasadena. Minnesota got the first break, when Fred McNeill blocked a Ray Guy punt, and the Vikings recovered at the Raider three-yard line. But the momentum shifted quickly when Oakland Linebacker Phil Villapiano ducked under Minnesota's offensive line and stuck his helmet on the

TIMELINE

The Gopher Hockey team beats Michigan Tech 6-4 for the NCAA Championship	Gopher Wrestler Evan Johnson wins the 190 lb. National Championship	St. John's wins the Division III Football National Championship	Mankato State Wrestler Jack Eustice wins the Division II 134 lb. National Championship	Mankato State runner Peter Pratt wins the Division II Triple Jump National Championship	The Denver Dynamos professional soccer team is purchased by a Minneapolis group and are turned into the Minnesota Kicks. In their inaugural season in Minnesota, playing at the Met, they won the Western Division title, and made it all the way to the Soccer Bowl, where they ultimately lost to the Toronto Metros by the score of 3-0.

74

ball Fullback Brent McClanahan was carrying, popping it out of his arms and into the awaiting hands of his teammate Willie Hall just two plays later. (Incidentally, the player who made the defensive call which helped cause the McClanahan fumble was Oakland linebacker and Bloomington native, Monte Johnson, who grew up worshiping the Vikes — even selling programs at the Met as a kid.) The Raiders, long known for their physical, hard-hitting and even dirty cheap-shot style of play, took it to the Vikes early and often that afternoon. Minnesota hung in there early, but faltered down the stretch.

Led by Quarterback Ken Stabler, who completed 12 of 19 passes for 180 yards, and running back Clarence Davis, who gained 137 yards rushing, the Raiders quickly drove the length of the field to set up an Errol Mann 24-yard field goal. Before half-time they added a one-yard touchdown pass from Stabler to Dave Casper as well as a one-yard Pete Banaszak touchdown run. They were dominating the Vikings, holding them to a mere 86 total yards of offense in the first half, compared to 288 of their own.

In the second half, after another Mann field goal, Sir Francis finally put Minnesota on the board, capping a 68-yard drive by connecting with Sammy White on an eight-yard touchdown pass. However, two Raider interceptions led to another 13 points for the silver and black — one set up a two-yard Banaszak touchdown run, and the other was a record 75-yard pick-off return by Willie Brown to paydirt. Minnesota rallied to get to within 18 points when back-up Quarterback Bobby Lee hit Stu Voigt on a 13-yarder. But it was way too little way too late, as the Raiders went on to crush the Vikes, 32-14. Thanks to the blocking up front by future Hall of Famers Art Shell and Gene Upshaw, Oakland amassed a Super Bowl-record 429 yards, while Fred Biletnikoff, who caught four passes for 79 yards, earned MVP honors.

Nine years after getting spanked by the Packers in Super Bowl II, 33-14, the Raiders had won football's biggest prize. But their victory would be obscured by the shadow of Minnesota's Super Bowl futility — a record four losses in eight years. It would mark the last time that the Vikings would get back to the big dance.

To add insult to injury, Raider Coach John Madden (a native of Austin, Minn.) said that his team had played tougher games in the conference playoffs. Afterward, Tarkenton quipped: "What we're trying to do is run through all the American Football League clubs to see if there's one we can beat..."

"I still don't have good feelings about it," said Rashad. "It was one of those things where I thought we changed everything that we did well during the season to try to do something different for one game, and when it didn't work it was just too late. In retrospect, I guess when you lose a game you don't have many good memories about it. For me, I figured that I had joined a team that had gone to four Super Bowls, so I thought that we'd be back three or four more times. The next thing you know, your career is over. There's something to be said about losing. It teaches you things, and everybody's got to lose at some point. It keeps you going."

As Smooth as Silk

Formerly known as Bobby Moore, Viking's All-Pro Wide Receiver Ahmad Rashad grew up in Tacoma, Wash., and attended the University of Oregon on a basketball and football scholarship. After being drafted in the first round by the St. Louis Cardinals in 1972, Rashad was traded to the Bills two years later. Then, after missing his second season in Buffalo due to an injury, he was acquired by Minnesota in a 1976 trade for, among others, "Bench-Warmer Bob" Lurtsema.

In Minnesota Rashad gelled immediately with Fran Tarkenton, and became a superstar. Rashad still ranks in the top 10 on the Vikings all-time receiving list with 400 career receptions and 5,489

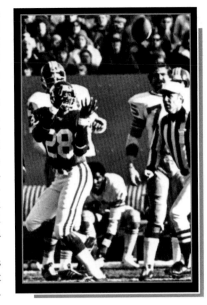

yards receiving. He had 13 100-yard receiving games from 1976-1982, won NFC receptions titles in 1977 and 1979, and from 1978-1981 was named to the Pro-Bowl. Perhaps his best season with the Vikings was in 1979, when he caught 80 balls for nine touchdowns and had 1,156 yards receiving. He even still holds the NFL record for the longest nonscoring pass reception, when he hooked up with Cardinal Quarterback Jim Hart on a 98-yarder in 1972.

Today Ahmad is one of America's most respected sports journalists. A star in the world of television, he hosts several weekly sports and variety shows. In addition he does NFL, NBA and Olympic broadcasting for several networks as well. When he has a spare moment, that is when he's not hanging out with guys like Michael Jordan, he even finds time to come back to Minnesota, where he still has a summer home in Lakeville. Once here, he often goes out with his best friend, Bill Murray, either golfing or to watch the St. Paul Saints, of which Murray is a part-owner. Ahmad, has four children and currently resides in both New York City and Connecticut.

What Did it Mean for You to Be a Viking?

"Minnesota will always be my home because that's where I had the chance to blossom as a player. I had the perfect coach in Bud Grant, the perfect quarterback in Fran Tarkenton, and it was just an ideal situation for me. It was the first time that I had gotten someplace where I felt like I had a kinship with the players and was a part of the team. Anytime you play a sport, you want people to respect your performance. I feel like my years in Minnesota were great, and I was on a real run there. I can't remember ever having too many bad games. I played some pretty good Sundays in Minnesota. Overall, I am a Minnesota Viking. When I look back on my career, I remember only playing for the Vikings. I know I played for St. Louis and Buffalo, but they don't count. The love affair went both ways I felt. I really enjoyed playing there, and I enjoyed the people. It really felt good to actually feel that love from the people because very few athletes get a chance to do that in their careers."

TRIBUTES

"He was the Baryshnikov of wide receivers," said Chuck Foreman. "I remember watching him run patterns, and he was just like a gazelle — smooth and fast. He was a great addition to the Vikings and played a very important role on our last Super Bowl team. He is somebody that I admire and respect. He is a great player and a great person."

"He found a home in Minnesota," said Bud Grant. "He was one of the finest receivers I ever coached. He and Sammy White were a great pair together."

"Ahmad was a great receiver and made a lot of amazing plays for us," said Jim Marshall. "He could catch anything thrown to him. He was unbelievable."

"Ahmad had great hands, great speed, and a great ability to get open," said Alan Page. "He was a great wide receiver."

The Hibbing Curling Club wins the State, National and World Men's Curling Championship.
(The US has only four World titles to its credit, so Roberts' win is an rare achievement.)

*Bruce Roberts - Skip
Joe Roberts - Third
Gary Kleffman - Second
Jerry Scott - Lead

Twins Manager Gene Mauch seemed bound and determined to shake things up in 1977. So, he brought a bunch of candidates into training camp that year and came out with 10 new players on his roster. Complete with youth, speed and hitting, the team had a bunch of young prospects poised to do some damage in the future. The big story of the year though, was that of Rod Carew, who flirted with .400 and became a bonefide superstar before the eyes of the nation.

More than a million fans passed through the Met's turnstiles, that year, mostly to see Rod Carew win the American League's MVP award. He led the league in average (.388), hits (239), runs (128) and triples (16), and also knocked in 100 RBI's to boot.

Carew carried the Twins on his back that year, willing them into a tough pennant race with Kansas City, Chicago and Texas, who were all battling for first place until after Labor Day, when the Royals ran away with it. Carew's hitting was infectious too, as Glenn Adams, Lyman Bostock and Larry Hisle (this group was affectionately known as the "Lumber Company"), also played great, posting .338, .336 and .302 averages, respectively. Hisle led the AL with 119 RBI's as well. In addition, Minnesota native Dave Goltz won 20 games, while Tom Johnson added 16 of his own. As a team, the Twins posted a league best .282 batting average, while tallying nearly 5.5 runs per outing.

But, in the end, the team's solid hitting couldn't make up for pitching depth, and they faltered down the stretch to finish at 84-77, fully 17 games behind first-place Kansas City. Perhaps the highlight of the season, however, came on June 26th, when 46,463 fans, the largest regular season crowd ever to cram into the Met, showed up to watch the Twins, led by Glenn Adams' record eight RBI's, destroy the White Sox, 19-2, to jump into first place in the West. And, in the process, Carew raised his batting average to .403 that day, teasing Ted Williams' legendary record in the process.

"When I went four-for-five against the White Sox and broke .400, that was probably the most memorable game of my career. During that game I received six standing ovations. Their response, by standing up every time I got a base hit, showed me that they cared and appreciated what I was doing."

The Greatest

The son of a Canal tugboat worker, Rod Carew came into the world in a very unique way. On October 1, 1945, in Gatun, Panama, Olga Carew went into labor on a speeding train. As luck would have it, a physician, Dr. Rodney Cline, just happened to be on that same train along with a nurse by the name of Margaret Allen. They delivered Olga's baby boy right there on the train. A grateful Olga then named her son Rodney Cline Carew, after that doctor, while the nurse, Margaret Allen, became the baby's godmother.

As a boy Rod loved playing baseball. He used to listen to major league games on his radio and dreamt of coming to the U.S. to become a big leaguer. One day, Rod's godmother wrote a letter to his mother from New York City. She encouraged them to pack-up and move to New York to pursue a better life. So, in 1962, at the age of 16, Rod, his mother, brother, and sisters, picked up and moved to Harlem, where his mother supported the family by working in a factory.

Speaking little English, young Rod had trouble fitting in at school. He was also wary of the many drug dealers and thugs operating in his neighborhood. Rod spent his afternoons working in a grocery store to help support his family and, in doing so, dearly missed his passion, playing baseball. His luck then changed when he tried out for a weekend sandlot baseball team, the Cavaliers, which played in the shadows of Yankee Stadium in the Bronx.

There, he played shortstop and second base, hitting consistently and with power — and finishing with a whopping .600 average. Word of Carew's skill soon reached Herb Stein, a New York City transit detective, who also scouted young talent for the Minnesota Twins. Stein watched Rod play in several games and was impressed. "He was spraying hits all over the place," said Stein. "He had a pair of wrists that just exploded." Stein told Hal Keller, head of the Twins' farm system, to come see Carew play. That day, Rod went 6-for-7 with two singles, three doubles, and a grand-slam. Rod had been discovered.

When Minnesota came to town to play the Yankees, team officials invited Carew inside for a pre-game tryout. After easily putting two balls into the Yankee Stadium seats, Twins Manager Sam Mele looked around nervously to see if any of the Yankees players had seen the young phenom in action. Then the cautious Mele ordered, "Get that kid out of here before somebody else sees him!"

A month later, in June of 1964, Rod signed his first big-league contract with the Twins. Minnesota agreed to pay him an immediate bonus of $5,000, a minor league salary of $500 a month, and a future bonus of $7,500 when (and if) he made the major league roster. Although other big league teams had started to show some interest in him, Rod was anxious to sign with the Twins. He took the $5,000, gave some money to his mother, bought some new clothes, and put the rest in the bank.

He spent two years in the Twins farm system before Calvin Griffith called-up the 21-year-old for the start of the 1967 season. By the end of that season, he would be named Rookie of the Year and be selected to the All-Star Team. From there he just kept on going, leading the Twins in nearly every offensive category for years to come. Without question though, his best season was in 1977, when he was the biggest story in sports.

After switching over from second base to play first base, Rod had the greatest season of his incredible 19-year big league career that year. He nearly became the first hitter since Ted Williams to break baseball's magic .400 mark. Carew appeared on the cover of Sports Illustrated with the Splendid Splinter, Ted Williams, himself during that season. Rod also appeared on the cover of Time magazine with the headline, "Baseball's Best Hitter." He batted over .400 for the first half of the season, and his final .388 average was good enough to earn him his sixth batting title, while rapping out 239 hits — the most in the majors since Bill Terry hit 254 nearly 50 years earlier. He also scored 128 runs, hit 14 homers and stole 23 bases. In addition, he struck out just 55 times in 616 at-bats. He also had 38 doubles, 16 triples, and

TIMELINE

Carlton runner Dale Kramer wins the Division III 5,000M Run National Championship	Gopher Wrestler Pat Neu wins the 134 lb. National Championship	Sports writer and journalist extraordinaire Hallsey Hall dies at the age of 77	St. Thomas' Robert Grim wins the Division III Discuss Throw National Championship	The Gopher Baseball team wins the Big Ten title	The Minnesota Kicks win the Western Division title	Gopher guard Ray Williams is named to the All-American basketball team	The Gopher Football team loses to Maryland in the Hall of Fame Bowl, 17-7 in Birmingham, Alabama.	Gopher center Mychal Thompson is named to the All-American basketball team	Gopher pitcher Dan Morgan is named to the All-American baseball team

76

drove in 100 runs as well. At season's end Carew had won the MVP award and, for the 11th straight year, was selected for the All-Star team, this time with the biggest number of fan votes ever recorded. In addition, Rod also received the coveted Roberto Clemente Award for distinguished service by a ballplayer to his community.

Afraid that he was going to lose Carew to free agency, Calvin Griffith traded him to the California Angels on February 3, 1979, for outfielder Ken Landreaux and some prospects. And, so it went that Carew would finish his career in California some eight years later.

No true Twins fan will ever forget the graceful power of Rod's smooth hitting style. Carew was a career .328 hitter in 19 big league seasons and won seven AL batting titles (second only to Ty Cobb and Honus Wagner). He hit .300 or better for 15 consecutive seasons, finished with 3,053 hits, scored 1,434 runs, belted 92 homers, knocked in 1,015 RBIs, and stole 353 bases. He was also named to 18 consecutive All-Star teams. Rod's No. 29 was retired by the Twins on July 19, 1987, and then, on January 8, 1991, Rod was elected to the Baseball Hall of Fame. Rod Carew was the greatest pure hitter of his era, and a true wizard with the bat.

"I enjoyed the Twin Cities, and I really enjoyed the people," said Rod. "I came there as a young kid, still learning a lot about playing the game. In the years that I was there I really matured as a person and as a baseball player. I appreciated the Twins organization, Mr. Griffith, and the way the fans there treated me and responded to me."

Some Lesser Known "Carewisms"
There were some oddities to Carew's brilliant baseball career that maybe you weren't aware of. For instance, did you know that he treated his bats with extreme tender love and care, putting them in a hot closet next to the clubhouse sauna to "bake out the bad wood." He also washed his bats in alcohol to clean off the sticky pine tar, because he "loved to use a clean bat." Like a lot of ballplayers, Rod chewed tobacco during games. He said that a big plug of chew would stretch his facial muscles so he could squint more, and as a result, see the ball better. He also used to drink Coca-Cola almost non-stop, sometimes gulping down more than a dozen glassfuls per game. Sometimes. he would ride his bicycle from his home to the ball park, a distance of some 15 miles. He loved to chase balls for the pitchers during practice too, and once, during a game, he even fined himself when he quit running after giving up on a foul ball that blew fair. An amazing bunter, he used to impress his teammates by putting a handkerchief at various spots throughout the infield and dropping bunts onto it.

What did it mean for you to be a Twin?
"I enjoyed the Twin Cities, and I really enjoyed the people. I came there as a young kid, still learning a lot about playing the game. In the years that I was there I really matured as a person and as a baseball player. I appreciated the Twins organization, Mr. Griffith, and the way the fans there treated me and responded to me."

On Minnesota:
"Minnesota to me is still home and I have a lot of fond memories there. The people are what is important. I will always remember the way that they embraced me, even after I went to play for the Angels and came back to Minnesota in a different uniform. They still kept me as one of their own."

When were you the happiest?
"I think it was after my first two seasons with the Twins. I was a little bit of a hot-headed kid. I played for Billy Martin, and he taught me how to stay on an even keel and not get upset at every little thing or every person that made a remark or comment about me. I started mel-

lowing out when I met my wife, got married, and started having children. I found that coming home from road trips or ball games or just a bad day, it didn't really matter, because my daughters didn't care that I was Rod Carew, the baseball player. For them, it was just dad coming home."

Twins Tombstone:
"I came to Minneapolis and played the game hard. I gave people enjoyment, and they responded by showering me with love and respect."

TRIBUTES
"We were roommates for 10 years," said Tony Oliva. "Between the two of us I would tell people that our room was hitting over .700, even though his average was always higher than mine. Rod was a remarkable ballplayer, a great person, and a good friend."

"He was one of the finest hitters I ever saw and the best bunter ever," said Harmon Killebrew. "He used to come out early to the park and practice his bunting. He could drop that ball down the third base line and, with the speed he had, nobody could throw him out. He was just outstanding and just a great, great hitter."

"I followed Rod Carew's career when I was growing up, and I thought he had the best pair of wrists of anybody I ever saw," said Paul Molitor. "The way he could wait and put the ball out to left field was incredible. He was a very gifted hitter who studied the game, knew how to take advantage of pitchers and their weaknesses, and had a remarkable, outstanding major league baseball career."

"In California, we had as close a relationship as any player and manager ever had," said Gene Mauch. "He knew how much I respected him and I felt like he felt the same way about me. It was a great privilege for me to manage Rod Carew. Watching him almost bat .400 was a season of the greatest hitting that I ever saw, and I played with Ted Williams. Watching him operate with the bat was incredible."

"He was such a talented hitter, and I really enjoyed watching him do what he could do," said Jim Kaat. "He was a real magician with the bat. I have a warm relationship with him to this day."

"I remember when I got my first hit, it was against the Angels, and Rod was playing first base," added Kirby Puckett. "I stood on base and said to him: 'How ya doin' Mr. Carew? I just want to tell you that I've been a big fan of yours, and it's my pleasure to meet you, man, because you're awesome, and I'm a rookie so I'm gonna shut up now and be quiet!' 'Please call me Rod,' he said to me. 'I know you're a rookie, and I just want to tell you to just keep playing, keep enjoying yourself, and keep playing the game the way you know how. And, the most important thing you should know, is to learn how to play when you're hurt, and you'll be just fine.' I will always remember that. Rod Carew is the very best there is."

"He was one of the toughest outs to get," said Jack Morris. "I would have to say that he would be in the top five of the all-time best hitters. Aside from Carl Yasztremski, Rod was my toughest out in all of baseball. I felt that every time that he wanted to get a hit off me, he could. It was scary that Rod was so good."

Former UMD Football player Dan Devine wins the national championship as head coach of the Notre Dame Football team

Halfback Bruce Smith, the U of M's only Heisman Trophy winner (1941), had his number 54 retired. The Faribault native led the Gophers to a national championship in his senior year. The triple threat, led Minnesota in rushing, passing and punting. He went on to play in the NFL with the Packers and Rams, and is a member of several football and coaching Hall of Fames.

TIMELINE

77

THE MIRACLE ON ICE

The 1980 United States Olympic Hockey Team will forever remain etched in our memories as one of the greatest sporting events of all-time. There have been numerous books written solely about the historic event. And why not? That single event helped put the sport, which at the time was perceived by many as a "hobby," and by others as merely a regional game found primarily in the North and East, into the national spotlight. It is, in some way I'm sure, partially responsible for the fact that the National Hockey League now has franchises in Florida, Texas, California, Arizona, Tennessee, Georgia and North Carolina. Just how big of a deal was it? Well, it was named as the all-time greatest sporting events of the century. Not bad. And, be honest, whenever you see that replay of the players throwing their sticks up into the crowd, piling on the goalie, and crying to the sounds of Al Michaels saying, "Do you believe in miracles?... YES!" as they upset the heavily favored Soviets in the medal round, do you get goose-bumps? Yeah, me too!

A Dozen Home-Boys

The coach of this fabled squad, Herb Brooks, who had just finished leading his Golden Gophers to the 1979 NCAA National Championship, had the responsibility of selecting 20 players to represent the United States. When it was all said and done, fully 12 Minnesotans had made the cut, nine of whom were players that Brooks had coached as Gophers. These home boys were: Roseau's Neal Broten, Grand Rapids' Bill Baker, White Bear Lake's Steve Janaszak, Rochester's Eric Strobel, Duluth's Phil Verchota, Minneapolis' Mike Ramsey, Babbitt's Buzz Schneider, St. Paul's Rob McClanahan and Richfield's Steve Christoff. The three other Minnesotans on the fantasy team were: Warroad's Dave Christian, who played at North Dakota, and Virginia's John Harrington and Eveleth's Mark Pavelich — both of whom played at Minnesota-Duluth.

"Having played international hockey for so many years, it gives me an awfully warm feeling to be selected as head coach for the 1980 Olympics," said Brooks upon getting the job. "I'm extremely honored and humbled. To be picked when there are so many outstanding amateur hockey coaches in the nation, well, let's just say it's something I never really expected to happen."

In early September, the team began as challenging an exhibition schedule as had ever been organized for an American Olympic Team. Beginning with an initial European tour in early September, the team played a 61-game pre-Olympic schedule against foreign, college and professional teams. The team finished the grueling exhibition season with a 42-16-3 record. The only let-downs during the pre-Olympic schedule were four losses to NHL teams and to the Canadian Olympic team in the late Fall. The highlight of this period was winning the Lake Placid Invitational international tournament.

Entering the Olympic games, the team was a decided underdog, an evaluation that seemed to be confirmed by a 10-3 defeat at the hands of the Soviets in the final exhibition game in New York City. Facing Sweden in the opening game of the Olympics, Bill Baker scored with 27 seconds remaining in the third period to gain a 2-2 tie. The goal acted as a catalyst for the young U.S. team, which then upset Czechoslovakia 7-3. From there they went on to beat Norway, Romania and West Germany, to advance to the medal round.

Do you Believe in Miracles?...YES!

This set the stage for the unexpected showdown in the medal round with the perennially powerful Soviets. The result was an historic 4-3 American victory produced by Mike Eruzione's thrilling goal midway in the third period. The gold medal was won two days later when the miracle Americans scored three goals in the third period to defeat Finland, 4-2. It was pandemonium in Lake Placid, as the team piled on their goalie, Jim Craig. The crowd went nuts and savored the moment, one of the greatest in American history.

Many of the players were visibly moved by what they had done, as evidenced during the singing of the National Anthem, where the entire team gathered on the top podium. Still wringing wet with their jersey's on, goaltender Jim Craig, with an American Flag draped around him, led the chorus. The country went crazy over their newly found sense of national pride. Sports Illustrated named the team, collectively as "Sportsmen of the Year," Life Magazine declared it as the "Sports Achievement of the Decade," and ABC Sports Announcer, Jim McCay, went on to call the amazing achievement, "The greatest upset in the history of sports."

Mark Johnson, son of ex-Gopher, "Badger-Bob" Johnson, led the team in scoring in both the exhibition schedule and the Olympic Games. The line of Schneider-Pavelich-Harrington, all products of Minnesota's Iron Range, led the team's four lines in scoring with 17 goals and 20 assists in the seven Olympic tournament games. Brilliant goaltending by Jim Craig, who played all seven contests, was a big factor in the victory, as was the stellar play of defensemen Dave Christian, Ken Morrow, Mike Ramsey, Neal Broten and Bill Baker.

Instant Super-Stardom

A grateful nation, depressed by the Iranian hostage crisis, hailed the team as heroes. A visit to the White House followed, as well as appearances in cities across the land. Covers of Wheaties boxes, magazines, awards, honors, speaking engagements and a whole lot of hoopla would follow for all the players. In the heart of the cold-war, beating the Russians was a very big deal in this Country. Of particular importance to hockey development in the U.S. was the fact that most of the team went on to have very successful NHL careers. Years later, as part of the new millennium festivities in the year 2000, the "Miracle on Ice" was named as the Sporting Event of the Century. It was simply amazing.

The icy miracle was achieved by enormous ambition coupled with great passing, checking, speed and sound puck-control. Shrewdly, Brooks refused to play the typical dump-and-chase style of the game that was so prevalent in American hockey.

"I didn't want the team throwing the puck away with no reason," said Brooks. "That's stupid. It's the same as punting on first down. The style I wanted combined the determined checking of the North American game and the best features of the European game."

In late February of 1980, everything changed for Herb Brooks. The Olympics success merely added to the American notion that he was some kind of hockey miracle man. He became an instant celebrity, and in the process lived out a life-long dream.

"They were really mentally tough and goal-oriented," said Brooks. "They came from all different walks of life, many having competed against one-another, but they came together and grew to be a real close team. I pushed this team really hard, I mean I really pushed them! But they had the ability to answer the bell. Our style of play was probably different than anything in North America. We adopted more of a hybrid style of play — a bit of the Canadian school and a little bit of the European School. The players took to it like ducks to water, and they really had a lot of fun playing it. We were a fast, creative team that played extremely disciplined without the puck. Throughout the Olympics, they had a great resiliency about them. I mean they came from behind six or seven times to win. They just kept on moving and working and digging. I think we were as good a conditioned team as there was in the world, outside of maybe the Soviet Union. We got hot and lucky at the right times, and it was just an incredible experience for all of us."

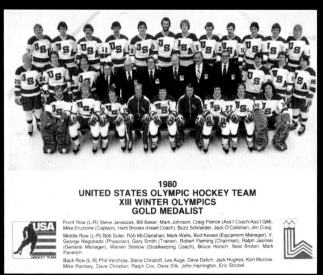

1980
UNITED STATES OLYMPIC HOCKEY TEAM
XIII WINTER OLYMPICS
GOLD MEDALIST

USA
HOCKEY TEAM

Front Row (L-R) Steve Janaszak, Bill Baker, Mark Johnson, Craig Patrick (Ass't Coach/Ass't GM), Mike Eruzione (Captain), Herb Brooks (Head Coach), Buzz Schneider, Jack O'Callahan, Jim Craig
Middle Row (L-R) Bob Suter, Rob McClanahan, Mark Wells, Bud Kessel (Equipment Manager), V. George Nagobads (Physician), Gary Smith (Trainer), Robert Fleming (Chairman), Ralph Jasinski (General Manager), Warren Strelow (Goalkeeping Coach), Bruce Horsch, Neal Broten, Mark Pavelich
Back Row (L-R) Phil Verchota, Steve Christoff, Les Auge, Dave Delich, Jack Hughes, Ken Morrow, Mike Ramsey, Dave Christian, Ralph Cox, Dave Silk, John Harrington, Eric Strobel.

LEROY NEIMAN

Minnesota's very own LeRoy Neiman is one of America's premier artists and is without question the most famous sports artist of the 21st century. He has painted nearly every famous American athlete over his career and is still going strong.

LeRoy Neiman was born on June 8, 1921, in St. Paul, and grew up playing hockey and sandlot football at the Uniondale Playgrounds in the Frog Town neighborhood of the city. He loved sports and painting as a kid, and used to love going to see the Gophers play at old Memorial Stadium. He and his pals would either hitchhike or hop a street-cars to get there, they loved it.

"Bernie Bierman was such a great coach, and Bronko Nagurski was my all-time favorite," said Neiman.. "They were so good in those days during the Depression, and we used to love to watch them whenever he could get the chance."

Neiman attended Washington High School in the late 1930s, until going into the Army. After his discharge from the Service, in 1946, Neiman enrolled in basic drawing technique courses at the St. Paul Gallery and School of Art. There, he learned the principles of composition espoused by the French Impressionist Paul Cezanne, one of his early influences. Neiman later moved to Chicago and entered the School of the Art Institute of Chicago, where he would go on to become a teacher there as well.

It was also in the Windy City where Neiman caught his first big break. You see, while he was an art student, he used to love going to watch the Bears games out at Wrigley Field, where he could watch his boyhood idol, Bronko Nagurski.

Once, at a game, he decided to jump over the railing to get down to the field, where he could take out his sketchbook and draw Nagurski from the sidelines. Suddenly, a cop came up to him and tried to throw him out. But just then, legendary Bears Owner, George Halas, came over and saw what he was painting, and told the cop to back off and let him stay.

Halas loved his artwork and from that point on, he made sure to let him down onto the sidelines to sketch his Bears. That, ironically, was the start of his amazing sports art career.

After gaining recognition early in his career as a contributing artist for Playboy, in the 1950s, Neiman went on to become one of the world's most recognized figures. He is especially well known for his renditions of sports scenes that feature his trademark brushing techniques with vivid color explosions that burst off the canvas. He has been the official artist at five Olympiads, and has become good friends with everyone from Mohammed Ali to Wayne Gretzky. It has been estimated that the more than 150,000 Neiman prints that have been purchased to date around the world have an estimated market value approaching $500 million.

Today Neiman lives in New York City, and continues to do what he loves most, paint, and watch sporting events. He has written nearly a dozen books, given millions to charity and to museums, and shows no signs of slowing down. In 1995 he gave the School of the Arts at Columbia University a gift of $6 million to create the LeRoy Neiman Center for Print Studies.

Plans are currently in the works for creating a museum in his honor that would showcase his paintings in downtown St. Paul — a gesture fit for one of our country's greatest artists, and a true Minnesota treasure.

CHARLES SCHULZ

"Good Grief!" World famous cartoonist Charles Schulz was born in Minneapolis on November 26, 1922, and grew up in St. Paul loving hockey and Gopher Football. After graduating from St. Paul Central High, Schulz went on to art school in Minneapolis. There, he created a comic strip about the adventures of a group of preschoolers (including a kid named Charlie Brown) called "Li'l Folks," which appeared in the St. Paul Pioneer Press in 1947.

United Features Syndicate bought the strip in 1950 and renamed it "Peanuts" because 'Li'l Folks' sounded too much like another cartoon, "Li'l Abner." Seven newspapers carried the original "Peanuts" cartoon strip on October 2, 1950, and the numbers have grown ever since.

He later moved on to California, where he became one of the world's most famous cartoonists. The multiple Emmy winner's cartoons are now read daily by several hundred million people in 68 countries, who speak 26 different languages. He has been one of the top 10 highest-paid entertainers in the U.S., and has built an empire surrounding that lovable pooch, Snoopy.

Today, the Minnesota Cartoonists League meets at O'Gara's piano bar in St. Paul

under an original portrait of Snoopy drawn and signed by Charles himself. The reason they meet there is because that building was, from 1942 to 1952, Charles Schulz's father's barbershop.

Schulz, an avid hockey fan who was later inducted into the U.S. Hockey Hall of Fame, tragically died in the year 2000. A real-life legend, Schulz's memories will live on forever for generations to enjoy.

Janet Karvonen is one of the greatest athletes to ever hail from the state of Minnesota and is considered by many to be the modern matriarch of women's basketball in our state. Back in the late 1970s, she single-handedly put the tiny town of New York Mills on the map. And, in 1978, Janet led her Eagles to their second straight Class A title — confirming a true basketball dynasty was in the works.

After an unbelievable 22-1 regular season record, the defending champions from "The Mills" went on to beat the Perham Yellowjackets, 78-58, at the Sauk Centre gym to win the Region 6A title. In that game, Karvonen, then a sophomore, scored 51 points, pulled down 16 rebounds, and was totally unstoppable. Next, it was off to the Twin Cities and the Girls State High School Basketball Tournament for the Eagles, where they would face the Fertile-Beltrami Falcons in the first round quarterfinals. There, behind Janet's 31 points, New York Mills crushed Fertile-Beltrami, 80-33.

Next up were the Minnesota Lake Lakers in the semis, and the Eagles waltzed to a 59-40 victory in this one behind Karvonen's 21 points. At 6:43 of the first period, she made history when she hit a soft 15-footer to pass Morton's Mary Beth Bidinger and take over the all-time girls scoring record with 1,474 points. She was averaging around 30 points per game and she was only 15-years-old! So, it was back to the Finals for the Eagles, where they would meet the undefeated Redwood Falls Cardinals, who had won the title two years earlier.

The Cards jumped out to a 14-9 lead after the first period in this one, only to see the Mills score 16 straight points to start the second quarter and gain a 33-20 halftime lead.

"I knew we were going to come back," said Janet. "Everyone on the team was hitting really well. I think that's the best we've played all year, in the second and third quarters."

Led by six-foot-one Center Jenny Miller, who grabbed 21 boards, the Rutten sisters, and all-state Point Guard Kim Salathe (who would go on to later become the school's head hoops coach), the Eagles increased their lead to 52-36 after three periods. The Cardinals hung in there and even trimmed the lead to nine at one point, but the Eagles were too tough down the stretch. They went on to win the game, 64-55, earning their second title in as many years.

Peggy Zimmerman's squad had out-rebounded their opponents 46-20, and she set up a zone defense that forced the Cards to shoot from long range. "We knew how to stop them," said Karvonen, "and we did."

Jean Hopfenspirger led the Cards with 19 points while her sister Joan added 10. The 7,000-plus fans were in awe of "Janet the Great," as the six-foot forward scored a game high 24-points and added 10 rebounds of her own. The team also set a tournament record, tallying 203 points.

It was a special time for New York Mills during those four years. Just like in the movie "Hoosiers," Janet recalled how the town "emptied out at tournament time," with many of the local farmers driving more than three hours back home from St. Paul each night to milk their cows. It was a big experience for everyone, including the girls themselves, who made the most of their time in the big city by "watching planes take off and land at the airport and going to Southdale Mall."

Minnesota's Finest
Janet Karvonen grew up in New York Mills, a small Finnish community of just 800 souls near Wadena, approximately 180 miles northwest of the Twin Cities. She was taller than most of her classmates for as long as she could remember, already standing five-foot-nine in the sixth grade. Janet started playing sports at a young age, but was extremely well-rounded. It was no wonder that she would excel at basketball and tennis, seeing as she had a tennis and basketball court in her back yard. But growing up she also was an accomplished pianist, she played the saxophone in the school band, and even she rode Arabian horses raised by her father. Janet also helped out at her father's funeral home and worked at his furniture store as well.

Janet loved to play basketball, and her father often took her to Milwaukee to see the NBA's Bucks play. Before long, Janet started to take the game very seriously. She attended summer camps and, with a lot of hard work, made the varsity basketball team in 1976 as an eighth grader. That same year, girls basketball finally got the respect it deserved in the state, when it was officially recognized by the Minnesota State High School League, and given a tournament format that featured two classes: AA and A. New York Mills would compete in the Class-A bracket, even though there were schools with much larger enrollments in the same class.

In 1977, as a freshman, Janet led the Eagles past Mayer Lutheran High School by one point in the title game to win the state championship. It was an amazing feat for the small town, but the Eagles didn't stop there. They won it all the next year against Redwood Falls and just kept on rolling. In 1979, New York Mills would three-peat as state champs, this time beating Albany, 61-52. Karvonen scored 98 points for the tournament, a new record. As a senior, the Eagles again went to the state tournament to defend their title, only this time it would not have the same outcome. In 1980, New York Mills was upset by Austin Pacelli in the semifinals, 55-43. Although they rebounded to beat East Chain, 59-54, for third place honors, it signified the end of one of Minnesota sports' greatest dynasties. Karvonen set the single season scoring record her senior year with 845 points, averaging nearly 33 points per game.

When it was all said and done, Janet, who was also her class valedictorian, had completely rewritten the recordbooks. She had scored 3,129 points over her high school career, the most ever scored by either a boy or girl in the history of Minnesota basketball. Norm Grow of Foley had previously held the all-time career scoring record with 2,852 points, back in the 1950's. (Janet held the career girls' scoring record for 17 years, until 1998 when Roseau's Meagan Taylor scored 3,300 points. The boys' record was broken in 1991 by Chisholm's Joel McDonald, who put in 3,292 points over his career. To this day, they are the only three players in state history that belong to the prestigious 3,000-point fraternity.)

A four-time all-stater, Karvonen was also a Parade All-

TIMELINE

| Carlton runner Dale Kramer wins the Division III 5,000M Run National Championship | St. Cloud State gymnast John Fjellanger wins the Division II Horizontal Bar National Championship | Hamline's Mark Severson wins the Division III Discuss Throw National Championship | The Minnesota Kicks win the Central Division title | Minneapolis native Hub Nelson is enshrined into the U.S. Hockey Hall of Fame | The state's largest Northern Pike is caught by Mattson's (IL) Robert Quigley on Disappointment Lake: 18 lbs., 14 oz. | Hamline's Mark Severson wins the Division III Shot Put National Championship | UMD defenseman Curt Giles is named to the All-American hockey team | Gopher Gymnast Tim LaFleur wins the Nissen Award, presented to the nations top gymnast |

American first-teamer as well as the U.S. National High School Player of the Year. She even got to appear on the Good Morning America TV show as a guest with O.J. Simpson.

It all happened like a blur for Janet, but she handled her newly-found celebrity with class, never letting it go to her head.

"You have to understand that when I was 14, reporters were asking me what I thought of the ERA and Rudy Perpich — and I'd only just stopped playing with my Barbie dolls! I grew up fast, because I became very mature for my age."

After sifting through more than 150 college offers, Karvonen opted for perennial women's basketball powerhouse, Old Dominion University. Old Dominion had just won back-to-back national championships under one of the greatest female basketball players of all-time, Nancy Lieberman, who had just graduated. Lieberman, who made the Olympic team when she was 16 years old, was also a two-time Wade Trophy winner — women's college basketball's Heisman equivalent. The pressure was on, as some felt that Janet was pegged to be her heir-apparent.

Janet jumped right in and absorbed as much as she could. She made a big contribution that first year and was rewarded when her Lady Monarchs made it all the way to the NCAA Finals. After two years at Old Dominion, however, Janet decided that the college wasn't right for her, so she left the school to enroll at ODU's biggest rival, Louisiana Tech University. She said it was a very difficult decision for her to leave, but one she felt good about nonetheless.

"I left Old Dominion as a starter and had to start over at Tech," she said. "I had to sit out a year, and it took that long before many of the Tech players accepted me."

She eventually cracked the starting lineup and once again helped to lead the school to the 1984 Women's Final Four, this time losing to USC. While there, Karvonen developed a great rapport with her coach at Tech, Leon Barmore.

"I had a lot of respect for him," she said. "He was a great role model and a positive influence in my life." Life wasn't always a picture postcard there for her though. "I remember a game against UCLA," she remembered. "There was this guard I just couldn't handle. She blew by me at every turn and finally my coach called a time-out. He screamed at me to keep an eye on her and later took me out of the game." That UCLA player turned out to be a Jackie Joyner-Kersee, who would go on to become a gold medal winning Olympic sprinter.

Janet graduated with a B.A. in Journalism from Louisiana Tech University in 1985 and then came home to Minnesota. At first she worked as a reporter at a Duluth television station, and later worked in the legislature for Minnesota Commerce Commissioner Mike Hatch. During this time, Karvonen was doing some serious soul-searching and was trying to figure out how she could somehow combine her love of basketball with her newly-found love of public speaking.

"I felt on a gut level that there was a need for female motivational speakers," Janet said. "There were voids that could be filled."

So, in 1988, Karvonen went into business for herself as a public speaker and basketball-camp director — ironic for someone who had dropped out of her college speech class because she was "scared to death" of public speaking. She then established her own educational and sports-oriented company called, Janet Karvonen, Inc. She even established a joint-venture relationship with Reebok and began one of the most successful dual careers in the local sports scene.

As a national public speaker and leadership workshop director, today Janet appears in school, corporate, and civic engagements focusing on areas of drug-free choices, self-esteem, and motivation. She also runs the largest girls basketball camps in the Upper Midwest, appropriately called the Janet Karvonen Basketball Camp. In addition, she has become a household name serving as a television analyst for the high school basketball tourneys as well as Women's Big Ten Basketball games.

"I want to be a friend to youth, a great mother, and someone who leads the way and opens doors for more young women for them to discover their worth," she said. "I want to help girls in their teens as they struggle with sense of self, with issues such as suicide, eating disorders, alcohol and drug abuse, and teen pregnancy. In my speaking, I am able to make a difference, and that's been rewarding."

Karvonen was inducted into the National High School Hall of Fame in 1987, the Minnesota Sports Hall of Fame in 1989, and the Minnesota High School Hall of Fame in 1996. Today, she is also recognized as one of the all-time great female basketball players. She has spent the better part of her life playing and promoting the game and has had a significant role in increasing the popularity of it in the state. From the French-braided naive teenager that Minnesota fell in love with, to the mega-powerful, successful businesswoman today, she is a wonderful role-model for young girls everywhere.

What did it mean for you to be a pioneer of sorts?
"At the time, I really didn't think about it; you just enjoy what's happening. Obviously, I brought a lot of positive attention to a very small and relatively unknown Minnesota community, which, prior to girls basketball, was famous for being the home of Lund boats. When I look back now it's really surprising how many people remember my high school days. It was real special not only for the Eagles, but for the community of New York Mills as well."

On teaching young girls today and making a difference:
"My philosophy is that we're developing young women and young women's skills in life. We're not just limiting it to girls basketball. We want them to feel good about themselves and send them home feeling more confident — ready to take on new challenges and start applying themselves. Academics are really the foundation, but athletics enhance who you are."

Minnesota sports tombstone?
"As someone who brought girls sports to a new level in Minnesota and who helped people across the state gain a greater appreciation for girls' talents and the importance of opportunities for girls in sports. Also, people knew that I could play. I had a jump shot, I had skills, and I was worthy of being appreciated. Girls basketball isn't a joke anymore. In the early days, it was pretty rough going, and I think it will be the same way for girls hockey now. Girls hockey is a much slower game, and it takes time to appreciate it, but more and more people will like and appreciate the sport as time goes by."

On women's professional basketball today:
"I think it's a really exciting time for women in basketball right now. Girls growing up now can be drafted into the professional ranks and can have something tangible to look forward to. I think it's great."

Led by centerfielder Shelly Medernach, who still holds 12 school records including batting average, RBIs, and runs, the Gopher women's softball team finishes third at the College World Series. It is the highest national finish in department history.

Mychal Thompson becomes the first Gopher Basketball player ever to be chosen first overall in the NBA draft. The Portland Trailblazers selected the forward but later traded him to the L.A. Lakers where he won two World Championships. Thompson remains the Gophers' all-time leading rebounder and second leading scorer. His #43 was later retired at Williams Arena.

TIMELINE

In 1979 Herb Brooks' Gophers got back to the promised land yet again. It was smooth sailing in the early going of the season as the Gophers found themselves ranked No. 1 in the country. They hit a slump in January, losing five of six, but rebounded to win six of eight in February. The final series of the season featured a tough North Dakota team coming to town in what would prove to be a WCHA championship showdown. The Gophers took the opener, 5-2, but the Sioux rallied to take the title in one of the best series ever witnessed at Williams Arena.

In the playoffs, the Gophers went on to sweep both Michigan Tech and then the University of Minnesota Duluth at home. They then knocked off Bowling Green, winners of the CCHA, earning a trip to Detroit and the NCAA tournament.

In the first game of the Final Four tournament, led by Eric Strobel's hat trick, Minnesota held on to beat New Hampshire, 4-3. It was now on to the Finals, where they would meet their neighbors from North Dakota. Minnesota jumped out to an early lead in this one on goals from Steve Christoff, John Meredith and team captain Bill Baker, to make it 3-1 after the first period. The Sioux then rallied in the second, narrowing the gap to 3-2. Then, early in the final period, Neal Broten, the freshman sensation from Roseau, scored on a fabulous, sliding chip shot in what would prove to be the game winner. UND added another goal late, but the incredible goaltending of Gopher senior netminder Steve Janaszak proved to be the difference as the Gophers held on to win, 4-3, and claim their third national crown.

With 35 saves, Janaszak, fittingly, was voted as the tournament's MVP. Three other Gophers also made the all-tournament team including, freshman Defenseman Mike Ramsey and Forwards Steve Christoff and Eric Strobel. Additional honors would cascade down to a couple of other future Gopher legends as well. Billy Baker, who scored a then single-season record of 54 points by a defenseman, was selected as an All-American, while Broten was named as the WCHA's Rookie-of-the-Year. As a team, the Gophers won 32 games and simply rewrote the record books that season, scoring an amazing 239 goals in 44 games. Leading the charge were Steve Christoff and Don Micheletti, who both tallied 36 goals apiece that year.

"We were playing against a tremendous North Dakota team," said Coach Herb Brooks. "I think they had 13 guys that turned pro that next year. Broten scored a dramatic goal, sliding on his stomach and hitting a chip-shot over the goalie. It was incredible. I remember speaking at a Blue Line Club meeting the year before and saying that we were going to win it all that next season. It leaked out in the press and went across the country, putting a lot of pressure on our team. I kind of wish I wouldn't have said it now. But I just felt really strong about that team. I put a lot of pressure on those kids and I really raised the bar. But, because of their mental toughness and talent, we won the championship."

"I remember playing at the old Olympia Arena in Detroit," said Broten. "Just being in there and thinking about Gordie Howe and all those old Red Wings teams that had played there was really neat. North Dakota was our biggest rival back then and beating them in the Finals was a great win for us. That year was great, and I have a lot of great memories of my teammates from that season. It was special."

The Pride of Roseau

Neal Broten was born on November 19, 1959, in the hockey-crazy town of Roseau, and grew up loving hockey with his two brothers, Aaron and Paul. Roseau, which is located just south of the Canadian border, is a town of just 3,000 people, yet the city has three hockey arenas. Roseau has also sent more teams to the State High School Hockey Tournament than any other in the state and has won six state titles along the way. This tiny community has one of the richest hockey traditions of anywhere in the country, and much of that can be attributed to the three Broten brothers: Neal, Aaron, and Paul — who each played for the Roseau Rams, Gophers, and then in the NHL.

For the Broten brothers, it started at sun-up, when their parents would awaken before sunrise on frigid winter mornings to drive them to hockey practice.

"When he was a pee-wee, he was scoring five, six, seven goals a game," said Gary Hokanson, Broten's coach at Roseau. "You could see then that he was going to be something special. He was a little guy who could handle the stick and put it in the net like nothing I'd ever seen."

"Roseau is such a great town, with so much hockey tradition," said Neal. "We used to always watch Hockey Night in Canada on TV, and basically all we did was go to school and play hockey. Mom used to make us grilled cheese sandwiches after school, and then it was off to the rink. High school hockey was the biggest thing to do up there. We'd pack all 3,000 people in that arena, and the whole town would root us on. With so many people involved in hockey up there, it was a really special place to grow up."

From there Neal opted to head south, to the U of M, where he quickly took Gold Country by storm. In 1979, as a freshman, Broten easily exceeded everyone's expectations when he broke John Mayasich's 25-year-old school assist record by dishing out 50 helpers to his teammates. In the process, he led the Gophers past North Dakota en route to winning the national championship.

The next chapter of Neal's life story proved to be the one that may well have linked his name to the sport of hockey forever. That off-season, Neal was selected to be a member of the much-celebrated 1980 gold medal winning U.S. Olympic Team that shocked the world. Neal would play center and finish as the teams' fourth-leading scorer.

After the Olympics, Neal could've easily turned pro, having been drafted by the Minnesota North Stars. Instead he returned to the U of M to be reunited with his two former linemates from Roseau, his brother Aaron, and his high school pal Butsy Erickson, who had recently transferred to the U of M from Cornell.

"I needed to work on the weights and get a little stronger before I started pro hockey," Broten said. "Besides, the North Stars had a lot of centers at the start of the year, and I didn't think my chances

TIMELINE

Concordia Moorhead's Dave Bergstrom wins the Division III High Jump National Championship	St. Cloud State gymnast John Fjellanger wins the Division II Horizontal Bar National Championship	Hamline's Mark Severson wins the Division III Discuss Throw National Championship	St. Thomas runner Paul King wins the Division III 3,000M Steeplechase National Championship	Mankato State Wrestler Scott Madigan wins the Division II 150 lb. National Championship	UM Morris Wrestler Tom Beyer wins the 190 lb. Division III National Championship	Twins' second baseman John Castino is named as the American League's Rookie of the Year	Willie Mays, a Minneapolis Miller in 1951, is inducted into the Baseball Hall of Fame	Gopher defenseman Bill Baker is named to the All-American hockey team	UMD defenseman Curt Giles is named to the All-American hockey team

82

of breaking in right away would be so good. And, I thought it would be fun to play with Aaron and Butsy again."

New Gopher Coach Brad Buetow quickly assembled the three to make up one of the most feared scoring lines in all of college hockey. In 1981 the trio then led the Gophers to the NCAA championship game for the second time in three years. There, at the Duluth DECC, the Gophers came up short against Wisconsin, losing 6-3 in the Finals. Neal went on to earn All-America honors that year and was also selected as the first-ever recipient of the Hobey Baker Memorial Award, which recognized the nation's top collegiate player.

"I felt terrible winning the Hobey Baker over my brother Aaron," said Neal. "He deserved it more than I did. I mean he had 106 points and had a lot better year than I did. Aaron had always been in my shadows growing up, and he had a great year that season. He deserved the award way more than I did, and I still feel bad about it to this day."

While that season marked the end of Broten's collegiate career, for Minnesota hockey fans it would only be the beginning of his professional career. Neal left the U just in time to join the Cinderella North Stars as they were heading into the Stanley Cup playoffs that year. The Stars had even traded Center Glen Sharpley, freeing up Neal's lucky No. 7 jersey. The Stars made it all they way to the Finals that year, before losing to the New York Islanders in five games.

"Glen Sonmor was a great coach, and he just let us play the game," said Broten. "It all happened so fast, I had only played three games for the Stars' when we went to the Stanley Cup Finals. I was so wet behind the ears, I didn't really know what was going on. Things happened so fast and the next thing I knew I was playing with guys like Bobby Smith, Steve Payne, Al MacAdam and Freddy Barrett. It was a great experience and I will always remember that first run at the Cup."

For 11 seasons Broten dazzled the Minnesota faithful as a member of the North Stars. He later led them to their only other Stanley Cup Finals appearance in 1991, where they ultimately lost to Mario Lemieux and the Pittsburgh Penguins. Neal was a legend. Period. He became the first U.S.-born player to score 100 points in a season when he tallied 105 in 1986, and never slowed down. The perennial all-star also led the Stars in scoring from 1982-1986, and went on to set the team records for games played (861), points (793) and assists (544).

When the North Stars moved to Dallas, Broten played two seasons in Texas before being traded to the New Jersey Devils during the 1994-95 season. There, Broten became the final piece in the Devils' Stanley Cup puzzle. He ignited New Jersey's offense by scoring seven goals, including four game-winners, while dishing out 12 assists during their amazing playoff run to become the first Gopher player ever to have his named inscribed on Lord Stanley's Cup.

"I can remember sitting there in the locker room with him after they won it," said Neal's father Newell. "He looked at me and said, 'Dad, can you believe it after all these years?'"

Neal went on to play with the L.A. Kings and Dallas Stars yet again before finally retiring for good in 1997. His career numbers are outstanding, and should warrant him a place in the Hall of Fame someday. In 1,099 games he scored 289 goals and dished out 634 assists for 923 career points. He also added 98 career playoff points as well.

For the kid Herb Brooks called "The best player I ever coached at the U of M," the circle was now complete. Three trips to the high school tournament, a Gopher title, a Hobey Baker, an Olympic Gold medal, two Stanley Cup runs with his native Stars, and finally winning a Cup of his own with New Jersey. Broten lived out a hockey dream as only John Mariucci might have dared to imagine it. Known and loved by every hockey aficionado in the state, Neal will forever be the measuring stick, the hockey player against which all oth-

ers will be judged. From his laser-guided passes, to his amazing sense of improvisation and remarkable peripheral vision, Neal Broten is Minnesota hockey.

What did it mean for you to be a Gopher?

"They way I feel about the Gophers can be summed up in two words: Pride and Tradition. There is just so much class there, and to be a part of that was really a humbling experience. Just the feeling of putting on that big "M" sweater with all those other Minnesota kids, and to play in front of such great fans was something I will always cherish. And getting the chance to play on the 1980 Olympic team was an experience I will never forget as well. Just making that squad was an accomplishment. It's something that I always look back on proudly, because there were 12 of us Minnesotans on the team. That just showed the world what kind of kids come from Minnesota, and we were all really proud of the way we represented our state."

What did it mean for you to be a North Star?

"It meant a lot to be playing for the home state team. It was pretty special for me to have been able to have played with all those great players in front of all the great Minnesota fans. I feel spoiled that I got to be here for so long, and that the fans for some reason treated me like a king. I just can't thank them enough. To come home and retire, and to be treated so well by the people here is something I can't explain. I am so humbled by everyone's generosity and am just proud to have been able to have brought joy to their lives through the game of hockey."

Most memorable game:

(In 1990, on the weekend when Roseau won the state high school hockey tournament, the North Stars had a "Broten Brothers Day," at a game against the Rangers at the Met. Neal and Aaron were both playing for the Stars, and Paul was playing for the Rangers.) "It was great supporting the Rams, the town, and to see them win the championship like that was incredible."

On the Stars' move to Dallas:

"It was tough for me to take. A lot of people took it pretty rough, and it was a real big deal. I remember this strange feeling and thinking that this can't be happening to me. You didn't really think it was going to happen until it happened, and then you're moving to Texas."

Gopher / North Star Tombstone:

"I just want to be remembered as an unselfish team player that thought of his teammates before himself."

Where are they now?

Today Neal, his wife Sally, and their two daughters live in scenic River Falls Wis., where they have a 75-acre horse farm. When he's not golfing, hunting or working as a public relations guru for the Minnesota Wild, Neal is talking about hockey — something that will remain near and dear to his heart for the rest of his life.

| The Kicks win the Central Division Conference title | UMD center Mark Pavelich is named to the All-American hockey team | St. Paul native Bob Dill is enshrined into the U.S. Hockey Hall of Fame | The state's largest walleye is caught by Hermantown's Leroy Chiovitte at Seagull River at Saganaga Lake: 17 lbs., 8oz. | Twins second baseman John Castino wins the American League's Rookie of the Years Award | Gopher Football legend, Bronko Nagurski's number 72 was officially retired. The "Bronk" has long been considered to be the greatest and toughest football player of all-time. An All-American at three positions: tackle, end and fullback, in the late 1920's, he also led the Chicago Bears to three titles. He is a member of the NFL and College Hall of Fames. The International Falls High School honored their native son by renaming their schools' teams after him, the Broncos. | TIMELINE |

83

The 1980 Cinderella Gopher Basketball team was all about a kid from Hibbing by the name of Kevin McHale, who would guide this young team all the way to the NIT Finals.

McHale, the team captain, had taken the young group under his wing the year before when he found himself starting alongside of four freshmen: Forward Trent Tucker, Center Gary Holmes, and Guards Mark Hall and Darryl Mitchell. In addition, Lake City's Randy Breuer, a seven-footer, was on the squad and getting better by the day. The Gophers opened their non-conference schedule by reeling off four straight wins before losing to both Tennessee and Florida State. After beating Kansas State, Minnesota won the Pillsbury Classic tournament. Then, they dropped their conference opener, 71-67, at Michigan, but rebounded two nights later with an impressive 93-80 win over the defending Big Ten and NCAA champs from Michigan State. It was up and down for the young Gophers though, as they lost several close games on the road after that. Included were three rough overtime defeats from the Illini, Buckeyes, and Boilermakers, as well as a 73-63 set-back at the hands of Iowa for their only home loss. Minnesota did, however, go on to beat Indiana, 55-47, as well as Ohio State, 74-70, Purdue, 67-61, Illinois, 79-75, and Michigan, 68-67.

All in all, it was a good season for the Gophers and a great senior season for McHale. Minnesota would ultimately finish the regular season with a 17-10 record, tied for fourth place in the Big Ten with Iowa at 10-8. Although they didn't make the NCAA Tournament, the Gophers did get an invitation to the 43rd annual post-season N.I.T. tourney. There, in the first round at Williams Arena, the Gophers rolled over Bowling Green, 64-50, and followed that up with wins over Mississippi, 58-56, and Southwestern Louisiana, 94-73, thanks to Tucker and Breuer, who had 18 points apiece, while Hall and McHale added 16 and 15, respectively. Next, it was off to the N.I.T. 's version of the Final Four at New York City's famed Madison Square Garden.

In the semifinals, behind Breuer's 24 points, the Gophers avenged their overtime loss to Big Ten rival Illinois in a nail-biter, 65-63. In so doing, they now set the stage for the championship game against seven-foot sensation Ralph Sampson and the Virginia Cavaliers.

The Gophers jumped out to a 21-12 lead in the first 10 minutes of the title game behind the strong play of McHale, Tucker and Breuer. But, behind Sampson, who had 15 points and 15 rebounds, the Cavs took the lead at halftime.

It was a back and forth affair for both squads throughout the second half. Then with 1:31 to play, Sampson sank two free throws to put Virginia ahead, 54-53. Now, with 1:06 remaining in the game, McHale's pass to Breuer was intercepted. So, with only 33 seconds on the clock,

Minnesota fouled Virginia's Terry Gates. Gates missed the one-on-one, but the Cavaliers came up with the rebound. Jeff Lamp, a Cavalier guard, was then fouled and proceeded to sink both shots and go up by three. With 11 seconds left, McHale, in desperation, drove for a dunk on Sampson and was fouled. He made both shots to get the Gophers within one point. Minnesota was then forced to foul immediately. It was Lamp who would go to the line again, only this time he sank them both to ice it for Virginia, 58-55.

"We just got too cautious," said Dutcher, whose squad finished the year with an impressive 21-11 record. "We didn't push the ball down the floor and look for any fast breaks. And we got so conscious of getting the ball inside that we didn't take the outside shots we had."

"I remember the game very well," added McHale who scored eight points in the game. "We got all the way to the Finals and, unfortunately, we didn't play particularly well that night. I was sad on a lot of levels. Besides losing the game it was also my last game as a Gopher. I felt a lot of anxiety at that moment because there were some big, big changes coming my way in a hurry."

Mitchell, who had a game-high 18 points, along with Breuer, were both named to the all-tournament team. McHale, meanwhile, who averaged 17.4 points and 8.8 rebounds per game that season, was named to the All-Big Ten team. He would finish his illustrious career in Gold Country averaging 16.7 points and 10 rebounds per game — good for 1,704 points, 950 rebounds and a record 235 blocked shots. He would, of course, go on to become a Hall of Famer as a member of the famed Boston Celtics.

"Kevin is one of the premier big men in the nation," said Coach Jim Dutcher. "He has the ability to score inside or outside. We feel he is one of the most complete players in the country. He can rebound, score, block shots and run well."

From Hibbing to the Hall of Fame
Kevin McHale is without question the greatest basketball player ever to hail from the state of Minnesota. With his patented fade-away jumper and silky smooth touch, he was simply unstoppable in the low post. His hoops legacy was in fact a rather unique form of basketball artistry. From jump-hooks to baseline reverse lay-ins, McHale was a true artist whose canvas was the hardwood.

After an amazing Hall of Fame career with the Boston Celtics, Minnesota was blessed when its most prodigal of native sons decided to return home for good to begin his second career as an executive with the upstart Timberwolves. An avid outdoorsman, Kevin couldn't wait to get back to the Land of 10,000 Lakes to resume fishing and hunting, which, outside of the basketball court, is where he probably feels most at home.

McHale's story is a long and fascinating one though, which has roots that extend all the way up to Hibbing, where he grew up learning the values of a strong work ethic from a father who was a miner on the great Mesabi Iron Range. It was up in the great northwoods where this kid learned to love and appreciate the power of sports. At first, Kevin played them all. And who knows? Had it not been for that lanky six-foot-ten frame of his, perhaps he would've gone on to greatness as a winger for the North Stars instead!

But fortunately for us, he decided to pursue his calling on the hardcourt, where he has certainly made us all so very proud. From

Minnesota's Scott Ledoux, after earning a draw with Ken Norton in 1979, loses a heavyweight boxing title match to the heavyweight champion, Larry Holmes at the Met Center.	Gopher center Tim Harrer is named to the All-American hockey team	The Carleton men's cross country team wins the Division III National Championship	UM Morris wrestler Dennis Koslowski wins the Division III 190 lb. National Championship	The Gustavus Adolphus men's tennis team wins the Division III National Championship	The Mankato State Hockey team wins the Division III National Championship	Hamline's Mike Manders wins the Division III Shot Put National Championship	Minneapolis' Walter Bush, a former North Stars owner, is inducted into the US Hockey Hall of Fame

what began as a hobby at the Green Haven Elementary School, became an obsession for a kid who dreamt of one day playing for his beloved Golden Gophers. As a youngster Kevin would oftentimes even go down to the Hibbing library to read about the Gophers in the Minneapolis Newspapers. He had to have his fix, and every time he read about guys like Jim Brewer, Corky Taylor, Ron Behagen, and Clyde Turner, it made him even hungrier to pursue his dreams.

Kevin worked hard as a prepster and went on to earn All-State honors as a junior at Hibbing Senior High. He led his club to the post-season that year as well, only to get upset in the first round of the play-offs by Little Falls. Then, as a senior, he led his Blue Jackets to the 1976 Class AA State Basketball Tournament title game against Bloomington Jefferson. They ultimately lost that big game to the Jaguars, but not before making believers out of every "David vs. Goliath" fan in the state. And, when Kevin outplayed Jefferson's All-State big man, Steve Lingenfelter, many of the nation's top collegiate recruiters knew that they were witnessing something special.

Kevin, who went on to win the coveted "Mr. Basketball Minnesota" award after his senior season, modestly turned away all of the scholarship offers, and opted to instead pursue his dream of wearing the maroon and gold at the U of M. Gopher fans everywhere rejoiced when they heard the news, and tabbed him as the savior of a program that was on the rebound. McHale then came in and simply took Gold Country by storm, becoming an instant fan-favorite.

Kevin became synonymous with Minnesota basketball, and from 1977-1980, he averaged 15.2 points and 8.5 rebounds per game, while accumulating an incredible 1,704 points — then second all-time in school history. A two-time All-Big 10 selection, McHale was also the U's career record holder for blocked shots with 235, and had also amassed the second most rebounds of all-time with 950 as well.

After his illustrious career in Gold Country, McHale was selected with the third overall pick of the first round of the 1980 NBA Draft by the Boston Celtics. Before he joined the club though, he played on a pair of gold medal-winning U.S. Pan-Am teams in both Puerto Rico and Mexico.

Kevin then headed east to join one of the greatest teams in all of sports, the Celtics. There, he would help make up one of the most formidable front-lines in the history of the game, alongside Larry Bird and Robert Parrish. He made an impact his rookie season too, garnering All-Rookie team honors en route to leading the team to the NBA title. He led Boston to two more championships in both 1984 and 1986, as well as five Eastern Conference titles and eight Atlantic Division crowns. He was given the NBA's Sixth-Man Award both in 1984 and 1985, and among his seven trips to the All-Star game, he was selected to the All-NBA First Team in 1987. He was also named to the NBA All-Defensive First Team in 1986, 1987 and 1988 as well.

Over his incredible 13-year NBA career he scored 17,335 points, while averaging 17.9 points, 7.3 rebounds, and 1.7 assists per game. He ranks 10th all-time in the NBA in career field goal percentage with .554, and also shot a remarkable 79.8 percent from the free-throw line. Twice he led the league in field-goal percentage, and he remains the only player in NBA history to shoot over 60 percent from the field and 80 percent from the free throw line in the same season when he did it in 1987. And, his 56-point effort against the Detroit Pistons on March 3, 1985 still ranks second all-time in Celtics' single-game history.

In 1993 Kevin quietly retired from the game. Perhaps famed Boston Globe writer Bob Ryan put it best: "The long-armed wonder from Minnesota's Mesabi Iron Range won his way into the hearts of Beantowners with his lunch-bucket approach to the game and his uncanny ability to play Tonto to Larry Bird's Lone Ranger."

Danny Ainge, McHale's former teammate laughingly called

him "the black hole," because once you got a pass to him inside, the ball was not coming back out.

"He just struck fear in the hearts of the defenders," said Ainge.

"During the height of his career he was easily the best power forward playing the game, and I'd rate him in the top three of all time," said Celtic great Bob Cousy.

"Kevin was a great college player but I think he turned out to be a better pro. As a low-post player he's the best I've ever seen," added Larry Bird.

Kevin came home to his beloved Minnesota in 1993 and began working with the Minnesota Timberwolves. For two years he worked as the assistant G.M. and also served as a TV analyst for Wolves' games. In May of 1995, he took over the team, becoming the general manager as well as vice president of basketball operations. In that role, McHale has become responsible for the franchise's entire basketball op's department — overseeing player personnel decisions, scouting and the coaching staff. One of his first moves with the Wolves was selecting high-school phenom Kevin Garnett with the fifth-overall pick in the 1995 NBA Draft. He wasted little time in retooling the entire Wolves roster and soon made his presence felt. In 1997, the team made its first-ever playoff appearance under McHale's former Gopher teammate and pal, Head Coach Flip Saunders. Since then the Wolves have made five consecutive post-season appearances and have emerged as one of the NBA's brightest up-and-coming teams which is on the verge of taking that next step.

McHale's legacy will include many things. Most importantly though, will perhaps be his reputation as the most unstoppable NBA low-post scorer of his era. His hard work and desire to win, coupled with his creativity with the ball down in the paint truly revolutionized the game for generations to come.

His list of honors and accolades is even more impressive than his stats. In 1997 McHale was named as one of the NBA's Top 50 Players for the league's first half-century, and in 1999 he was immortalized forever when he was inducted into the prestigious Basketball Hall of Fame. In addition, in 1995, Kevin was honored as the best player in 100 years of Gopher Basketball, as his No. 44 was officially retired up into the rafters of Williams Arena.

Today Kevin continues his never-ending quests of shooting that perfect round of golf, landing a 10-pound Walleye, watching and hoping that his Vikings will someday win the Super Bowl, and most importantly, leading his Timberwolves to that elusive NBA championship. He is happy to be home though, pursuing both of his passions of the great outdoors and basketball with his wife and their five kids.

What did it mean for you to be a Gopher?
"This was a great time in my life. I had a ton of fun going to school at the U and met so many good people. I still have a lot of great friends from my years there. We had such a good time playing ball. At that time I didn't even think about a future in the NBA. I was just happy to have fun and get an education. It was the whole atmosphere at the U that I just loved."

Dollar Bay native Frank Kahler, founder of the Minneapolis Millers, is enshrined into the U.S. Hockey Hall of Fame	Legendary North Star goaltender, Gump Worsley is inducted into the NHL Hall of Fame. Famous for his refusal to wear a face-mask, the Gumper asked rhetorically: "Would it have been fair not to give the fans the chance to see my beautiful face?"	New Prague's Les Bolstad, a legendary Minnesota golfer, and Gopher Golf coach from 1947-1976, is inducted into the Collegiate Golf Coaches Hall of Fame. As a player he won every state championship during his career. Les won the U.S. Public Links title in 1926 as well as two Big Ten titles. The U of M Golf Course was renamed after him in his honor.	Gopher center Clayton Tonnemaker is inducted into the College Football Hall of Fame	Minneapolis' Gary Hoakanen wins the John Beargrease Sled Dog Race	Two hockey playing brothers from Bloomington, Brennan and Scott Olson, invent an off-season training tool that features a straight-lined roller skate. They name their invention - Rollerblades, and today the global sporting goods company based in Minnetonka generates hundreds of millions of dollars in annual revenues, and owns more than a 50% market share in the in-line skating industry.	TIMELINE

The 1981 North Stars season will forever be remembered as one of the all-time greats in Minnesota sports history. It was our first taste of Stanley Cup Finals hockey, and it literally took the state by storm. A combination of youth and veteran experience played a big role in the Stars compiling a solid 35-28-17 record that season, and leading the way was Center Bobby Smith, who scored 93 points on 29 goals and 64 assists.

The team also got a late boost that post-season when former Olympian Neal Broten, who had just completed a Hobey Baker Award winning season with the Gophers, was added to the roster, adding even more quickness to an already speedy squad. The Stars had even traded away Glen Sharpley, thus freeing up Neal's lucky No. 7 jersey.

Much to the approval of the Minnesota fans, the Stars opened the first round of playoffs on the road against rival Boston. Now, coming in to this best-of-five playoff series, the Stars were a collective 0-28-7 in Boston, having never won a game in the Garden. There was clearly no love-loss between these two clubs, who, earlier in the year had beaten the hell out of each other at Met Center for a combined 406 penalty minutes (a record that still stands today!). So, the Stars headed to Beantown expecting another blood bath. What they found however, was that Boston wanted to play some serious hockey, and with that, the fans were treated to a great series.

In Game One, with the score tied at 4-4 the end of regulation, Steve Payne scored the dramatic game-winner at 3:34 of the first overtime period to give the Stars a 1-0 lead in the series. With the Boston "monkey" now off of their proverbial backs, Minnesota followed it up with a 9-6 victory in Game Two. The series then shifted back to Bloomington for Game Three, and in what would play out to be a classic, the Stars, brimming with confidence, beat the Bruins 6-3 to sweep the series. "That had to be the biggest upset in Stars history," said legendary radio colorman Al Shaver after the game.

Next up for Minnesota were the Adams Division champion Buffalo Sabres, who were sporting a gaudy .619 winning percentage. Steve Payne once again set the tone by scoring yet another overtime game-winner in Game One. The Stars didn't look back from that point on, winning both Games Two and Three, only to drop a Game Four double-overtime heart-breaker by the score of 5-4. They rolled on to win the series four games to one.

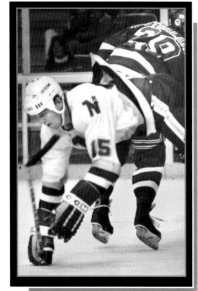

In the semis, the Stars found themselves pitted against another surprise team, the Calgary Flames. With Goalies Gilles Meloche and Donny Beaupre trading off in net, the Stars were proving to be a formidable force. Minnesota made a statement in the series opener by crushing the Flames, 4-1. Calgary came back to win Game Two on a late third period goal, only to see Minnesota win the next two games, 6-4 and 7-4.

The Flames rallied to win Game Five 3-1 back in Calgary. But the Stars hung in there and behind Brad Palmer's game-winning wrister in the third, took Game Six, 5-3. Protecting their home ice throughout the series, the Stars simply outplayed the Flames and ultimately won the series four games to two. With that, after several disappointing semi-final losses over the past decade and a half, the North Stars, for the first time in franchise history, had finally made it to the Stanley Cup Finals.

"Getting the opportunity to play in the Stanley Cup Finals was incredible," reminisced Bobby Smith years later. "I can still remember standing on the bench as the conference finals game against Calgary was winding down, and Brad Palmer had just scored an insurance goal for us. Just realizing that you had spent your whole life watching the Stanley Cup Finals and now you were going to be playing in them, was tremendously exciting."

The Finals would prove to be a classic case of Cinderella vs. Goliath. Goliath, in this scenario, was the defending Stanley Cup champion New York Islanders, whose path to the Finals went through Edmonton, and then the Big Apple, where they swept their cross-town rival Rangers, in the semis. The Stars were now in uncharted territory as they geared up for the Isles, who were no strangers to the hoopla surrounding Lord Stanley's Cup.

Minnesota, primed on speed and enthusiasm, opened the best-of-seven series in New York City. There, in front of some 15,000 fans, the Stars prepared to make history. It wouldn't be easy. The Stars, visibly nervous and looking scruffy (from not having shaved [superstitiously] in weeks) took the ice with aspirations of winning professional hockey's most coveted prize. Things got off to a bumpy start for Minnesota as New York jumped out to a quick 1-0 lead on a goal by Anders Kallur. The Stars then caught a break when Bob Bourne was assessed a major penalty for spearing. Unfortunately, the Islanders jumped right back as Kallur and Brian Trottier scored two unanswered shorthanded goals during the five-minute disadvantage, and the Stars were never able to regain their composure. A pair of third-period New York goals on only three shots secured an easy 6-3 Isles victory.

Game Two got off to a better start for Minnesota as Dino Ciccarelli scored a power-play goal to go ahead early. (Dino emerged as a star in the playoffs, scoring 14 goals and 21 points in 19 games — both NHL playoff records for a rookie.) Then, precisely one minute later, Bossy tied things up for New York. Shortly thereafter, both Potvin and Nystrom each scored one of their own as well. But the Stars rallied and came back to tie it at three apiece in the second, on goals from Palmer and Payne. The defending champs got nervous, but their experience prevailed as Potvin, Ken Morrow, and Bossy each scored in an eight-minute stretch to mirror the result of the 6-3 series opening win.

Game Three brought puck mania to the then so-called hockey capital of the world, Bloomington, Minn. The Met Center was the site of countless tailgate bashes as the adoring North Star fans welcomed home their heroes from the Big Apple. The Stars jumped out to a 3-1 lead after the first, and the crowd went crazy. But Goring tallied twice in the second as the Islanders took a 4-3 lead into the final period. Again, the Stars rebounded, tying the game at the 1:11 mark of the third, only to see the Islanders regain the lead less than a minute later. With New York up by one, Goring put the final dagger in the collective hearts of Minnesota, scoring again at the six-minute mark for the hat-trick to all but seal it up. The Isles added an empty-netter and came

TIMELINE

Rush City's Dick Beardsley wins the first ever Grandma's Marathon and sets the course record which still stands today at 2 hours, 9 minutes and 37 seconds. He would go on to repeat as champion in 1982 as well.	UM Morris Wrestler Duane Koslowski wins the Division III Heavyweight National Championship	Gustavus Adolphus tennis doubles partners Shaun Miller & Jim Hearn wins the Division III National Championship	Hamline's Todd Wallert wins the Division III Shot Put National Championship	The Minnesota Kicks Soccer team folds	Gopher winger Steve Ulseth is named to the All-American hockey team	The Gopher Hockey team loses to Wisconsin 6-3, in the NCAA Finals which are held in Duluth	The Vikings abandon Midway Stadium as a practice facility and move into Winter Park in Eden Prairie, named after former Vikings and Lakers owner, Max Winter

86

away with the 7-5 victory.

Refusing to lie down and be swept, Minnesota played brilliantly in Game Four. Utility man Gord Lane opened the scoring for the Isles to silence the crowd early in the first period. But then, midway through the period, controversy struck. With Minnesota on a power play, Brad Maxwell tallied on a blistering slapshot from the blue line. Or so he thought! Referee Andy Van Hellemond apparently never saw the shot, which was later seen on the replay to rip right through the goal netting. The crowd went nuts over the no-goal call, but they were eased just seconds later when Craig Harstburg's shot from the point beat Billy Smith to tie it up. This time the red light was turned on and the crowd went berserk. With the score tied up at two apiece, Minnesota took the lead on Steve Payne's top-shelf slapper midway through the third. Bobby Smith then added an insurance goal late in the game to seal the deal, and insure a 4-2 victory for the Stars.

The 19-year-old phenom goaltender, Donny Beaupre, played huge, turning away shot after shot against the mighty Islanders, who had been held to fewer than five goals on only three occasions in 18 post-season games. The Stars kept their cool during the game and it paid off. Of the four North Star goals scored in the game, two came on power plays and a third was scored three seconds after an Islander penalty had elapsed.

With the win, the Stars had lived to skate yet another day. The series once again shifted back to Uniondale, Long Island for Game Five. Unfortunately for the Stars though, New York came out flying. And, once again it was Butch Goring who would do most of the damage. At 5:12 of the first period a North Star clearing pass deflected off referee Bryan Lewis and right onto the stick of Bob Bourne, who promptly fed the rushing Goring for the goal. Then, less than a half a minute later, John Tonelli and Bob Nystrom dug the puck out from behind the Minnesota net and fed it to a wide open Wayne Merrick, who beat Beaupre to make it 2-0. That line was amazing. It was their 18th goal of the playoffs — all of which came while at even strength against their adversaries' top lines. A few minutes later, Goring, who would capture the Conn Smythe Trophy as the playoff's MVP, scored again on a wrister, putting the game out of reach. Behind legendary Coach Al Arbour, the Isles went on to win the game, 5-1, and the series. It would be the second of four-straight Cups in the Islanders' dynasty.

The Savior
Bobby Smith grew up playing hockey in Ottawa and went on to play major junior hockey for the Ottawa 67s in the Ontario Hockey Association. In the 1978 he scored 69 goals and 123 assists for an amazing 192 regular season points, and then added another 30 points in the playoffs alone. He topped the OHA in both assists and points, and won the Canadian Major Junior Player of the Year award. His stock rose as the young scoring machine was projected to be the No. 1 player selected in that year's upcoming NHL draft.

For the Stars, finishing dead last in the Smythe Division at the conclusion of the 1978 season may have been a blessing in disguise, for they were rewarded with that very No. 1 overall pick in the draft. It was a tumultuous time for the organization. Against the background of several losing seasons, there were serious financial problems facing the struggling franchise. So the North Stars' management merged their franchise with the Cleveland Barons.

The North Stars were saved from extinction by the merger. Now they needed to get the fans excited about hockey again in Minnesota. They needed a savior, and they got Bobby Smith. Lou Nanne, the long-time North Star who had moved from the ice up to the front office, was overjoyed to obtain the rights to select the 20-year-old, six-foot-four phenom.

Smith established a torrid scoring pace in Minnesota in his

first year, scoring 30 goals and 44 assists en route to winning the Calder Trophy, as the NHL's top rookie. The Stars also improved by 23 points under the tutelage of veteran Coach Glen Sonmor. Bobby instantly became a fan favorite in his new home. He led the Stars in scoring four of his first five years with the club. Perhaps his finest season with Minnesota, however, came during the 1981-82 campaign when he notched career highs in games played (80), goals (43), assists (71), and points (114).

In 1984, Smith was involved in one of the team's most talked-about trades ever, when be was dealt to the Montreal Canadiens for Keith Acton, Mark Napier and a third-round pick. Smith played seven seasons north of the border, recording 70-plus points in five of those years. In 1986, he led the Canadians to a Stanley Cup victory, even scoring the game-winning goal in a 4-3 win over the Calgary Flames. It was a dream-come-true that came to life in the grandest of fashion.

In 1991, Smith, then a 33-year-old veteran, returned to his beloved Minnesota to lead the Stars back the Stanley Cup Finals, this time against Badger Bob Johnson and the Pittsburgh Penguins. Unfortunately that series had all too familiar results, as Mario Lemieux and Jaromir Jagr beat the Stars in six games. Nevertheless, Smith's leadership and guidance, both on the ice and in the locker room, to the younger players was immeasureable. He contributed eight goals and eight assists in that playoff run after a 46-point regular season, proving that he hadn't lost the edge that had always made him special in the minds of North Stars fans.

For 15 seasons Bobby ruled the red line. He played in 1,077 games with the North Stars and Canadiens, scoring an amazing 1,036 points. Smith also played in 184 playoff games, where he scored 64 goals and 96 assists for 160 points, ranking him 12th on the NHL's all-time playoff point leaders list. Smith also played in four NHL All-Star Games (1981,1982, 1989 and 1990), and from 1981 to 1990 served as the vice president of the NHL Players' Association.

When the North Stars were hijacked to Dallas in 1993, Bobby promptly retired, ending two wonderful chapters of Minnesota hockey. After retiring from the game Smith fulfilled a lifelong dream and went back to college at the U of M to obtain his MBA. That experience would pay quick dividends, when, in 1996, he became the Phoenix Coyotes' first Vice President of Hockey Operations.

Bobby was one of the greatest hockey players to ever lace up the skates representing a Minnesota team. He had incredible instincts, an amazingly accurate shot, and a great passing touch. He was the ultimate competitor and team player, always putting his teammates first.

North Stars Tombstone:
"I would like to be remembered as a guy who always competed to the best of his ability and became as good a hockey player as he could have become. And, as a guy who played his best hockey in the playoffs, when it was the most important, as well as when it was the most difficult to play your best."

Winona's Tracy Caulkins wins the Sullivan Award. At age 15, she is the youngest ever winner. She also wins the 1982 Sportswoman of the year. She won her first national title at the age of 14.	Duluth's Tommy Williams, a former Boston Bruins great, is enshrined into the U.S. Hockey Hall of Fame	Former Laker guard Slater Martin is inducted into the Basketball Hall of Fame	Minnesota native Tom Hoover wins his fifth annual Crown Auto Funny Car Championship at Brainerd International Speedway	On November 18th, the Dome deflates due to a blizzard that dumps 10-inches of snow in Minneapolis	Gopher diver Chris Curry, the U of M's first woman athlete to receive an athletic scholarship based on athletic ability, wins the AIAW National 3-Meter diving title. Curry went on to receive the Big Ten's Medal of Honor for her athletic and academic achievements.

TIMELINE

TRENT TUCKER
THE GOPHERS WIN THE BIG 10 TITLE

The Minnesota faithful had good reason to be optimistic for the upcoming 1981-82 season. After all, the team was returning all of its starters and even opened the year ranked in the top-10 in the nation. Led by Trent Tucker, Randy Breuer, Darryl Mitchell, Mark Hall, Gary Holmes, Jim Petersen and Tommy Davis, the Gophers won their first five non-conference games that year, including victories over San Francisco State, Dayton, Loyola, Drake, along with an impressive 76-54 win at Marquette. After losing to Kansas State, they returned home to the friendly confines of Williams Arena, where they first crushed Army, 79-37, and then the Arizona Wildcats, 91-62, en route to capturing their eighth consecutive Pillsbury Classic holiday basketball title.

In their final non-conference game, the brilliant Trent Tucker led the way with 22 points, as Dutcher's contingent easily handled Cal State Long Beach, 75-67. With an impressive 8-1 record, the stage was now set for the start of the 1982 Big Ten Conference race. Unfortunately though, the Gophers lost the opener to a very tough Ohio State team, 49-47, in Columbus. Minnesota bounced back two nights later, however, with a 64-58 victory against Michigan State at East Lansing. The next stop was Williams Arena and the hated rivals to the south, the Iowa Hawkeyes. There, more than 17,000 zealous fans jammed the barn that Thursday night to watch the Gophers upend the Hawkeyes. Behind Randy Breuer's 22 points, Minnesota did just that, winning the game, 61-56. Two nights later, Tucker stepped up by pouring in 21 points en route to leading his Gophers past the Michigan Wolverines, 67-58.

Minnesota continued to build its confidence throughout the season, with Tucker and Breuer shouldering much of the load. The fans were turning rabid as the Gophers started to show signs that they were for real. That next week, the now 5th ranked Gophers simply outplayed the Badgers in Madison, winning in a blowout, 78-57. Their next opponent, Illinois, would give them trouble all season. The Illini came to town on January 23rd and knocked off Minnesota, 64-57. The loss could have been a turning point for the team, but they would have little time to dwell on it as they traveled to Evanston, Ill., and Bloomington, Ind., the following week. But, in what was starting to become a trend for the squad, they rebounded from the Illinois loss by beating the Northwestern Wildcats, 61-53, and Bobby Knight's Indiana Hoosiers, 69-62, in a game where all five Minnesota starters scored in double figures.

They followed this up with a 73-50 drubbing of the Purdue Boilermakers at home, but stumbled against the Hoosiers at Williams Arena, losing a squeaker, 58-55. Unfazed and determined, the Gophers sucked it in and won three in a row against the Badgers, Boilermakers, and Wildcats, to set up the much anticipated rematch with the Illini in Champaign. There, in a game that was closer than the final score would reflect, the Gophers once again fell to Illinois, 77-65.

It was now crunch time for the Gophers as they headed into the final two-week stretch of the season. The Gophers, of course, were still very much in contention for the Big Ten title. First, they invaded Michigan, where they hadn't beaten the Wolverines since 1963. That 0-16 record fell in a big way on that day though, as Minnesota prevailed, 60-51. With their confidence higher than ever, the Gophers then traveled to Iowa City to do battle with the Big Ten front-runners, in what turned out to be the biggest game of the year. The implications were enormous as Iowa led Minnesota in the conference standings.

This one was back and forth throughout the entire contest. It seemed that everytime Minnesota struggled to gain the lead, the Hawkeyes found a way to pull ahead. It was a thriller that went down to the wire, and the two teams ultimately wound up going into overtime. Then another overtime and amazingly, one more. Finally, in the third exhausting extra session, Darryl Mitchell, who led the Gophers with 21 points, sank two huge free throws with no time showing on the clock to clinch a stunning 57-55 Minnesota win.

"That triple overtime game against Iowa was probably the most memorable game I ever played in — it was just unbelievable," said team captain Trent Tucker. "It was a really tough situation in a very hostile environment, but we got a total team effort to win it. I'll always remember Randy Breuer's big blocked shot to save us to get us back into it, and then Darryl Mitchell's two free throws to seal it. The whole thing was just incredible!"

The Gophers, now deadlocked with Iowa for the Big Ten lead, returned home to host Michigan State the following Thursday. In front of a packed mob of excited fans, the Gophers did not disappoint. Despite only shooting a paltry 35 percent from the floor, they upended the Spartans, 54-51, in another nail-biter, highlighted by a pair of Gary Holmes free throws with 11 seconds remaining to seal the deal. Mitchell led the way with 16, while Breuer added 14 and Tucker put in 13 as well. In an interesting side-bar, Illinois beat Iowa to put Minnesota in the driver's seat on the road to the championship. Then, in the final regular season game of the year, Breuer lit it up by scoring a career high 32 points and 12 rebounds while Tucker added 23, as the Gophers beat Ohio State, 87-75, to win the 1982 Big Ten title.

"For me, it was seeing all my expectations and goals come true," said Tucker. "I came to Minnesota in 1978 as a part of the biggest and most celebrated recruiting class in the history of the program. So the pressure was there from day one, and we were expected to someday win a championship. Now, it was year four, and we had matured to a level where we could win it all. To hear the final horn go off and to see the jubilation of the fans, the coaches, and the players was just great."

"It was a tight race all season long, but we held on to win it," added Breuer, who led the team in scoring, rebounding, and blocks. "It was amazing. It was tremendously gratifying because we were the team that was predicted to win it all from the beginning. We had a lot of seniors on that team, but it was a tough fought battle all season long. You couldn't relax for one game because the whole season was tight all the way."

Minnesota ultimately finished 14-4 in the conference that season, good enough to win their first Big Ten title in 10 years. For Dutcher, the 1981-82 team was his third team in seven years to win 20 or more games in a season. And for the first time ever, his squad also

Hamline runner Dennis Hensch wins the Division III Long Jump National Championship	UM Morris Wrestler Duane Koslowski wins the Division III Heavyweight National Championship	The Gustavus Adolphus men's tennis team wins the Division III National Championship	Rush City's Dick Beardsley wins his second Grandma's Marathon	Hamline's Mark Manders wins the Division III Discuss Throw National Championship	Hamline's Mike Manders wins the Division III Shot Put National Championship	Minneapolis' Dave Eckstrom wins the Twin Cities Marathon Wheelchair Division	Gustavus Adolphus doubles tennis partners Shaun Miller & Rich Skanse win the Division III National Championship	Gustavus Adolphus tennis singles player Shaun Miller wins the Division III National Championship	The St. Thomas Women's Country Team wins the Division III National Championship

earned an NCAA post season tournament bid.

After receiving a first-round bye, the team flew to Indianapolis to play the University of Tennessee-Chattanooga in the Mideast Regional. There, the Gophers, who were led by 20 points from Tucker, 17 from Breuer, and 16 from Mitchell, squeaked by UTC, 62-61, in a thriller. Next it was off to Alabama, where they would have to take on Denny Crum's tough Louisville Cardinals. This time, despite 22 points apiece from Breuer and Tucker, the Gophers lost to Louisville down the stretch, 67-61. (Perhaps the team fell victim to the "Sheraton Jinx." You see, the Gopher basketball team was staying at the Sheraton Hotel in Birmingham, the same hotel that the Gopher Football team stayed at when they were beaten by Maryland in the Hall of Fame Bowl only five years earlier!) It was a disappointing loss and a sad ending to a fabulous season for the Gophers, who finished with an impressive 23-6 overall record. (They should also be given credit for being a "Sweet 16" team, because back then the "Tourney" was only comprised of 32 teams.)

Post-season honors were highlighted by the naming of Tucker to the All-American team. He would go on to be drafted in the first round by the New York Knicks, who took him sixth overall. Breuer and Mitchell were also named to the 1982 All-Big Ten team as well. Breuer, a native of Lake City, was selected in the first round of the NBA draft by the Milwaukee Bucks and later played for the Minnesota Timberwolves. And, in a testament to Gopher basketball success, Hall, Holmes, Peterson, and Davis also went on to be drafted too.

Tuck

Trent Tucker grew up in Flint, Mich., absorbing everything he could about sports. He played basketball and baseball at Flint Northwestern High School, just north of Detroit. There, the six-foot-five guard averaged 29 points and 12 rebounds per game, good enough to be named as a high school All-American. Out of high school he was heavily recruited throughout the Big Ten, especially by his home state Wolverines at the University of Michigan. Tucker had always been a big-time Michigan Football fan. But, luckily for Gold Country, he was recruited by Jesse Evans, an assistant coach with the Gophers who was his junior high school basketball coach. And, as luck would have it, when Trent came to Minnesota on a recruiting trip, he watched the Gophers upset his Wolverines at Memorial Stadium, and from that point on he knew that he wanted to be a Gopher.

Tucker wore the maroon and gold from 1978-1982. He went through a lot during his tenure in Gold Country, including learning the game from a couple of pretty good teammates — Mychal Thompson and Kevin McHale. For his career, he remains at or near the Top 10 all-time in nearly ever offensive category, including scoring, with 1,445 points, assists with 219 and steals with 153. He averaged 12.5 points and 3.4 rebounds per game over his four-year career, while shooting 50 percent from the field and nearly 80 percent from the charity stripe.

After his brilliant career at the U, Tucker went on to play 11 seasons in the NBA, nine of them with the New York Knicks, but also with Michael Jordan and the Chicago Bulls, where he won a championship ring in 1993. He retired from active competition after that season and went on to become a TV analyst for the Timberwolves. For his career in the NBA, Tucker averaged 8.2 points, 2 assists and 2 rebounds per game. He also tallied 6,236 career points, of which 1,725 were from three-pointers. He was a solid two-way player for many years.

Tucker was one of the greatest pure shooters ever to have come out of Minnesota. His jump-shot was legendary, and one could only imagine what he would have done if they had a three-point line back then. He will always be remembered not only for being an incredible basketball player who led the school to a Big Ten title, but also because he is a genuinely nice person who always played team basket-

ball. The common denominator found most often when describing Tuck was that everyone just thought he was a great guy.

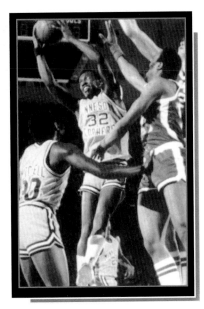

Gopher Tombstone?
"Trent Tucker was a guy who came out and gave everything he had every night and played the game the way it was supposed to be played."

What did it mean for you to be a Gopher?
"As a freshman, I didn't understand what it really meant to be a Gopher because I was too young to understand. But as I progressed and got older, the significance of being a Gopher and what it meant to the community became apparent to me. It was an unbelievable experience and something I will always treasure. I looked upon my teammates just like we were a family. You'd go through the ups and downs with your teammates and when the last game was played, all you have is memories. I miss those moments of guys pulling together, trying to overcome all the adversity, and then finding a way to win as a team. Aside from furthering my education, the University of Minnesota also afforded me the opportunity to fulfill my lifelong childhood dream of playing in the NBA. Knowing that all that hard work had paid off was very gratifying to me."

Where are the pure shooters in the NBA today?
"Michael Jordan could be the reason why guys can't shoot basketballs anymore. He transcended the game to a level where no one else can reach. Most kids today want to put the ball between their legs, dribble behind their back, and dunk the ball. Although dunking brings big excitement from the crowd, it won't get them very far in basketball. Kids don't focus enough on the fundamentals like the jump shot, it is a lost art in the NBA game, but it's also a huge part of basketball. I run basketball camps, and the first thing I tell kids is that if they can make jump shots, then they have a chance to play at any level."

On that patented Tucker jumper:
"I was born to shoot a basketball, like some guys are born to hit a baseball. I had the knack from day one. I had the proper technique and the proper balance as a player to shoot the jump shot. I was a natural shooter and I honed the skills that I was given."

TRIBUTES
"Trent is such a nice guy," said Willie Burton. "He is someone you would look up to and follow. He was a heck of a competitor. We played against each other a few times in the NBA, but I had already developed a tremendous amount of respect for him back when I was in college. Off the court he was the nicest guy around, but on the court, whoaaa!"

"He is a great guy and was a great basketball player," said Randy Breuer. "He also had a great family. I remember his parents and brothers coming up to Minnesota to watch us quite often when we were playing, and I thought that was really neat. I enjoyed playing with him a lot, and, boy, we had a great time."

TIMELINE

| The North Stars win their first-ever Norris Division championship | Gopher catcher Greg Olson is named to the All-American baseball team | Gopher gymnast Robin Heubner is named to the All-American team for her second time. The former two-time Big Ten all-around competition champion also holds several school records. | Gopher diver Chris Curry wins the women's 3-Meter Diving title at the AIAW Swimming & Diving Championships | Actor Paul Newman wins the Pepsi Trans-Am race at Brainerd International Speedway -- his first pro victory | The Twin Cities Marathon was founded. Organizers realized that a marathon between downtown Minneapolis and downtown St. Paul, combining the spectacular autumn beauty of both cities, would be a much greater attraction than two marathons on both sides of the Mississippi River competing against each other. That year, the TCM attracted more than 4,500 entrants, which was a record for a "first-time" race. The first race had 3,511 finishers. (The 1996 event had 5,478 finishers.) | Gopher runner Cathie Twomey sets the women's world record in the 20K. |

89

BILL GOLDSWORTHY

William Alfred Goldsworthy was born to Art and Manetta Goldsworthy on August 24, 1944 in the town of Kitchener, Ontario — located just northeast of Detroit. Art Goldsworthy was one of the city's best known athletes during the 1930s and early 40s, having made a name for himself as a star baseball pitcher. The Goldsworthys had two children, Ken, and his baby brother of five years, Bill. The two brothers, who shared a small bedroom with one bed, grew up playing together. One of the things that the two brothers looked forward to most, was sitting down with their parents in front of the TV once a week to watch "Hockey Night in Canada."

At the age of six Bill laced up his first pair of skates. As a youngster, he displayed a lot of raw talent for the game. Within a year he was playing league hockey against the best kids in the city. Wanting to emulate his childhood hero, Detroit Red Wing's star right winger Gordie Howe, Goldy insisted upon playing on the right side.

Eventually Bill was selected to play on a traveling Kitchener All Star team, which kept the mischievous youngster out of trouble. Playing on the team was a big commitment, having to carry his hockey bag for more than a mile to catch a bus each time the team played. And, occasionally, if the road was icy enough, Goldy would simply put on his skates and skate to the rink.

Billy later starred as free safety on his high school football team as well. Having to practice football after school, walk home, eat, and then go to hockey practice at night, kept him in prime physical condition. Soon he was noticed by some of the local scouts. In addition to liking this skinny, temperamental blond kid's good speed and quick shot, they liked his unbridled spirit. Even back then, he was one tough S.O.B.

Goldy played his way through the Canadian amateur leagues, first with the Waterloo Siskins, and eventually for the Niagara Falls Flyers, a Junior A team in the Ontario Hockey Association that was affiliated with the Boston Bruins organization. By 1964, at the age of 20, Goldy was signed by the Bruins. However, although he was considered to be one of the organization's hottest prospects, he was only able to get called-up for three brief stints with the NHL team. It was a rough couple of up-and-down years for the six-foot, 190-pounder, who was unable to earn a regular spot on the strong Bruins roster.

He finally caught a break on June 6, 1967, when former Bruins scout turned North Stars GM Wren Blair selected him from Boston in the NHL's expansion draft. Wanting to make the most of his opportunity, the 23-year-old worked hard to make the club's opening-day lineup. He played in 68 games with the Stars in his first season, scoring a modest 14 goals and 19 assists. However, at the end of the regular season, Goldy caught fire in the playoffs and led all scorers with 8 goals and 15 total points. Figuring he could parlay that success into a break-through sophomore campaign, Goldy came back that next year with another average 14-goal season.

Goldy came into camp in the best shape of his life that following season, and thanks to North Stars' Coach Jack Gordon putting him on the same line with Center Jude Drouin and Left Wing Danny Grant, Goldsworthy scored 28 goals in 28 games in the second half of the season. One of the biggest reasons for his turnaround was due to the constant pushing and prodding by Blair.

"I remember one day in our first year at Minnesota I told Goldy I would make a hockey player out of him if it killed us both," said Blair. "And right then I wasn't sure I was going to make it!"

Goldy continued to excel for the Stars, becoming the team's first superstar. One of the reasons why the fans seemed to love this kid so much was because of his now infamous post-scoring dance, affectionately called the "Goldy Shuffle." Yes, the "Shuffle" had taken Minnesota by storm by this point, and the fans couldn't get enough of it. You see, every time Goldy scored, he would immediately skate down the ice with one leg tucked up by his chest, and at the same time, holding his stick up in the air with his left arm, he would pump his right arm like he was trying to start a chain saw. Hard to describe, the little jig became a thing of beauty.

"I think I did the shuffle for the first time in my first year with the North Stars," he explained in his book when asked about how it all began. "We were fighting for a playoff spot, and were playing Pittsburgh at home right near the end of the season. We needed a tie or a win. We tied 2-2, and I think I got both goals. I was so happy at the time that I did a little dance on the ice. Jeez, I got all kinds of letters from people who liked it. Then the press began to call it the "Goldy Shuffle." So now I do it whenever we're winning. When we're losing though, management doesn't like to see it too much."

Goldy was a strong veteran voice in the locker room, and the players genuinely liked him. One of his closest allies on the team was former linemate and Duluth native, Tommy Williams, whose guidance and friendship helped Goldy's career immensely. "You know, as far as I'm concerned, Goldy is one of the best players in this whole league," said Tommy, who also started his career in Boston. "If he were with the Bruins now, he'd be a potential 50-goal scorer. I'm not kidding. Maybe more. Put him on Esposito's line for example. I'd say he'd score 50. He's that good."

Never one to shy away from a melee, Goldy endured himself to the fans not only because he could find the back of the net, but also because he was willing to take a few stitches every now and then for the team. Always one who could be counted upon to dress for every game, his reckless, driving, thumping style of play made him a fan favorite for more than 11 seasons in Minnesota.

Goldy finally hung em' up in 1977, but not before becoming the first player on a post-1967 expansion team to score 200 goals and the first to score 250. In 1971, Goldy became the team's leading scorer (a mark he held for more than a decade), and his 48-goal season in 1973-74 was the club's best ever — until Dino Ciccarelli broke the mark eight years later. Known as a solid team player who could play at both ends of the ice, Goldy was the first North Star ever to reach the 500-point plateau, totaling 267 goals and 239 assists for 506 points over 670 games with the team. And, in addition to his five All-Star game appearances, he was also selected as a member of Team Canada's much celebrated "Summit Series" roster that defeated the Russians in 1972.

On February 15th, 1992, during a memorable ceremony in front of a sell out crowd, Goldy's No. 8 was retired into the Met Center's rafters. Tragically, only two years later he was diagnosed with AIDS. On May 29th, 1996, at the young age of 51, Goldy died.

Goldsworthy's untimely death from complications related to AIDS and alcoholism in 1996 is now the inspiration behind a new non-profit program called "Reality Game." With the slogan, "In the game of life, you make the call," the group is headed by Goldy's daughter, Tammy Goldsworthy Loheit. Today Loheit speaks to groups about communicating the importance of choices toward alcohol, drugs and sex.

BABE WINKELMAN

Babe Winkelman is undoubtedly Minnesota's most famous outdoorsman. He found a way to be a very successful entrepreneur doing what he loves to do most — hunting, fishing, and enjoying the great outdoors. Babe grew up on a small family farm near the tiny town of Duelm, in central Minnesota, tromping around, kneeling in the mud, fishing, hunting, and observing wildlife. He began fishing at the age of six, along tiny Stoney Brook which ran through his family's farm. During the 1960s, every possible moment was spent at the family cabin on Hay Lake near Brainerd, where he taught himself a "pattern" approach to fishing that he continues to teach others today.

In the early 1970s, Babe spent several years as a guide and fished in competitive tournaments. He co-founded the Minnesota Bass Federation, serving as its president in the early years, and also co-founded the Masters Walleye Circuit. Around that same time, after helping build a successful construction business with his father and brothers, Babe listened to his true calling and took a huge risk by starting Babe Winkelman Productions. It would be a company bearing his name and his personality. Its mission: To teach others how to be successful when fishing and hunting while always remaining respectful of the natural world.

"I would have been comfortable and made a good living for the rest of my life in the construction business," said Babe. "But it's not what I wanted to do."

Twenty-five years later, Babe Winkelman is a world-renowned fisherman and hunter. He is also a highly successful businessman. Since 1975 he has been a professional, full-time fisherman, and since 1980, he has been on television promoting the sports he loves. He has hosted also two very successful television programs seen throughout North America on both broadcast and cable stations, "Outdoor Fishing" and "Outdoor Secrets."

His most memorable trip, in fact, was a deer hunt to Idaho a few years back. "I love the challenge of hunting a critter on his terrain," Babe says, "and spending the time it takes to understand him. We passed up about 350 deer and never pulled the trigger in seven days of hunting. I was after a specific deer and never found him. I don't go hunting just for the sake of dispatching an animal, and for a lot of reasons that was a great hunt."

Babe Winkelman Productions produces everything from video titles, comprehensive guide books, and instructional audio cassette courses, to newspaper and magazine articles, as well as major television commercials for companies as big as Chevrolet trucks. The company has won scores of awards, and Babe himself has been individually honored with two prestigious Cindy awards for on-camera charisma. A truly motivational speaker and dynamic on-air personality, he has also served as corporate spokesman for a host of major corporations including: Chevrolet, S.C. Johnson & Son, Cobra Electronics, Remington Arms, Leatherman Tool, and Ray-O-Vac. (In the case of Ray-O-Vac, Babe is in very elite company: Arnold Palmer and Michael Jordan are the firm's other spokesmen.) He is also a member of the Freshwater Fishing Hall of Fame, and in 1992 he was inducted into the prestigious Sports Legends Hall of Fame by the Touchdown Club of Columbus, Ohio. Reserved for the world's best athletes in baseball, football, boxing, etc., Babe is the only outdoors figure to be so honored.

For Babe, the biggest reward is hearing from his countless enthusiastic viewers who find success and satisfaction and become better caretakers of the land. "We know we've turned tens of thousands of people on to fishing and hunting, because we've got their letters," said Babe. "We've helped millions of anglers not only understand how to catch more fish, but to understand more about nature and develop their appreciation for the environment. And now we're doing the same thing with hunting."

Currently Babe, his wife, Kristeen, and their five girls live in Brainerd. It's business as usual for Babe and his amazing production company in Nisswa, Minnesota.

JILL TRENARY

Charm, grace, beauty, and talent all fit Minnesota's greatest figure skater to a tee. Born on August 1, 1968, the Minnetonka High School graduate grew up figure skating on our icy lakes and ponds.

During a very successful amateur skating career, Jill won her first U.S. National Championship in 1987, upsetting World Champion Debi Thomas. A year later, she qualified for the Olympic Team and finished fourth at the Winter Games in Calgary. She earned her second National Championship in 1989 in Baltimore and that same year won a Bronze medal at the World Championships. In 1990, Jill won her third U.S. National Championship, and, later the same year, she won the World Championship at Halifax, Nova Scotia, by defeating the reigning champion Midori Ito. She added a U.S. Open Championship in 1992 as well.

Since her incredible amateur career, Jill has toured professionally with the "Tour of World and Olympic Champions," Torvill and Dean's "Face the Music and Dance Tour," "Skate the Nation Tour,"and also the "Discover Stars on Ice Tour."

In recent years, Jill has begun television and broadcast commentary for several major networks. Jill maintains homes in Colorado Springs and London with her husband, former skater, Christopher Dean.

the greatest athlete ever to play and coach in the history of Minnesota sports, retired as the head coach of the Vikings. The gray-haired, crew-cutted warrior's exit from the game signified an end to one of the greatest sports eras of all time.

The early 1980s were a tumultuous time for the Vikings. Much of the teams' infrastructure, personnel and personality were about to change. The Purple People Eaters were all gone, and in 1982, the Vikings lost much of their mystique when they moved indoors to the Metrodome, something Bud could never really get used to. The cold weather had always given Minnesota a psychological advantage.

"We knew we could play with numb fingers and frozen feet, which gave us an edge," said Pro Bowl Receiver Ahmad Rashad. "A lot of times I caught passes without ever feeling the ball, just this heavy thump against my frozen hands."

Bud never allowed his players to use heaters on the sidelines or even wear gloves or turtlenecks under the jerseys. He wanted them to stay focused, and theorized that if his players were thinking about getting warm then they weren't thinking about football.

"The Vikings always ran out for the warm-ups with this big facade, like we weren't cold," said Rashad in his book of the same name. "Of course, we were freezing. But the other teams didn't know that, not for sure. They would be looking at us out of the corners of their eyes, thinking 'How come these guys look so warm?' They must be some bad dudes..."

"The things that bothered me about going into the dome is that it took some of the coaching out of it," said Grant. "Outside I could use the elements to my advantage. Things like the wind, sun, rain, snow or a even a frozen field."

At the end of the 1983 season, the Vikings had finished with an 8-8 record, good enough to place fourth in the NFC Central. Shortly after that season, Bud announced his resignation as the team's head coach. Not only was the entire state of Minnesota shocked by his announcement, but so too was the entire world of football. Bud simply decided it was time to get out. He wanted to spend more time with his family and enjoy more of the outdoors in the summer and fall, hunting and fishing.

"In my mind, timing is the most important thing," said Bud. "I decided this was the time to quit. There wasn't any pressure on me. There are a lot of things I want to do while I still have my health."

Grant was happy to be getting out on his terms, and he could now enjoy life from the stands, rather than from the sidelines. He was replaced by assistant Les Steckel, who had a drill sergeant's mentality and, unlike Bud, ran preseason training like boot camp. Steckel had issues and the team struggled, big-time.

Steckel's Vikings had

racked-up an embarrassing 3-13 record that season, something that was hard for Grant to take. So, after helplessly sitting by and watching the team he had built crumble before his eyes, Bud got angry.

So, on December 18, 1984, fully 327 days after calling it quits, and after owner Max Winter and G.M. Mike Lynn begged him to resuscitate some life back into their franchise after its' disastrous season, Grant promptly un-retired. With Lou Holtz packing the Dome for Gopher games, Lynn needed a sure thing.

"It's unusual, but we're in an unusual business and you have to have the opportunity to be unusual," said Bud. "I think I'm old enough now to claim a little senility."

Grant's team rebounded in 1985 by going 7-9 and finishing third in the Central Division. Bud wanted to rehabilitate his team and get it back on track. He succeeded. So, on January 6, 1986, only 384 days after his return, Bud shocked the world one more time by announcing his re-retirement for the second time in as many years.

"I've been in professional sports for 36 years," said the 58-year-old Grant. "I think I'd like to enjoy the fruits of those endeavors."

His replacement this time was long-time assistant coach and friend, Jerry Burns. Determined to hang em' up for good, he even turned down several other high-buck offers to coach in the NFL.

From Superior Upbringings

Harry "Bud" Grant was born on May 20, 1927, and raised in Superior, Wisconsin. His father Harry, was the Superior Fire Chief. Bud grew up playing sports and became a tremendous prep athlete. After playing football, baseball and basketball at Superior's Central High School, Bud joined the Navy in 1945 and was stationed at the Great Lakes Naval Station outside Chicago. Bud continued his athletic prowess at Great Lakes, where his team played Big Ten clubs under football Coach Paul Brown and basketball Coach Weeb Ewbank, both hall of famers. In 1946, Bud was discharged and enrolled at the U of M.

There, even without a scholarship (because he was in the service, the G.I. bill paid for his tuition), he would excel in three sports, earning nine letters from 1946-1949. He was a two-time All-Big Ten End on the gridiron, starred as a forward and was the team MVP on the basketball team, and also played centerfield and pitched for the baseball team — where he even led the team in hitting as a freshman. Under Bernie Bierman, Bud played with Gopher greats such as Leo Nomellini, Clayton Tonnemaker, Gordie Soltau, Billy Bye, Jim Malosky and Vern Gagne. To earn spending money in the summers throughout college, Grant became creative. Since he could pitch three days a week and bat clean-up, he played baseball as a "ringer" for several small town-teams around Minnesota and Wisconsin, where he could mop up as much as $250 bucks in a good week.

"Being a Gopher kind of grows on you a little bit," said Bud. "It wasn't anything that I felt particularly strong about when I got there, but now it means a lot. Back then, the Gophers were the only game in town, and we always played before a packed house. It was a tough time, with no scholarships and little money, but we had a lot of fun."

By 1950, Bud had finished his tenure at the U of M, and was considered by most to have been the most versatile athlete ever to compete there. (That was affirmed when he later beat out Bronko Nagurski and Bruce Smith to be named as the "Top Athlete at the University of Minnesota for the First 50 Years of the Century.") From there he joined George Mikan and Jim Pollard as the newest member of the mighty

Minneapolis Lakers dynasty. In joining the Lakers, Bud also became the NBA's first "hardship case," meaning he could leave college early and play professionally. (Lakers G.M. and longtime friend Sid Hartman petitioned the league and made it happen for him.) As a Laker, Grant averaged 2.6 points per game in each of the two years he played for the club, both of which were NBA championship teams.

Anxious to try something different, Bud then joined the NFL's Philadelphia Eagles, who had made him their No. 1 draft pick that year. So talented was Grant, that in 1952, after switching from linebacker, where he led the team in sacks, to wide receiver, he finished second in the league in receiving and was voted to the Pro Bowl. After two years in Philly, he decided to take a 30% pay-raise and head north of the border to play for the Winnipeg Blue Bombers of the Canadian Football League. In so doing, Bud became the first player in NFL history to play out the option on his contract. He dearly missed hunting and fishing, something he figured he could readily do in up in Winnipeg.

There, he played both ways, starting at corner and at wide receiver. He led the league in receiving for three straight years and also set a record by intercepting five passes during a single game. Then in 1957, after only four years in the league, and at the prime of his career, the front-office offered the 29-year-old the teams' head-coaching position. He accepted and proceeded to lead the Blue Bombers to six Grey Cups over the next 10 years, winning four of them.

On March 11th, 1967, Grant came home again, this time to take over the Minnesota Vikings. "I enjoyed Winnipeg very much, but coming to Minnesota was coming home for me," said Grant. It was a position that former Lakers owner, Max Winter, who now ran the Vikings, had originally offered to him, but had declined, back in 1960. Bud took over from Norm Van Brocklin, and although he only won three games in his first season, that next year he led the Purple to the division title. The year after that, in 1969, they made it to the Super Bowl, and Bud was named the league's Coach of the Year. It would be his first of four.

That was the beginning of one of the greatest coaching sagas in all of sports. Bud could flat out coach, and his players not only respected him, they also liked him. Bud treated them like men, didn't work them too hard in practice, and his players always knew they could count on that post-season playoff check.

Grant, who went on to coach for 28 years, won a total of 290 regular season and post-season games, 122 as coach of the Winnipeg Blue Bombers of the CFL from 1957-66 and 168 as coach of the Vikings from 1967-83 and 1985. At Minnesota, his teams made the playoffs 12 times, and won 15 championships: 11 Central Division (1968-71, 1973-78, and 1980), one NFL (1969) and three NFC (1973, 1974 and 1976). In 1994 Bud was inducted into the Hall of Fame. With it, he became the first person ever to be elected to both the NFL and the Canadian Football League Hall of Fames.

"It's something that they can't take away from you," said Bud, who's presenter at the event was his old friend, Sid Hartman. "Usually in sports there is a new champion crowned every year, but this is forever."

Today, Bud and his wife Pat live in Bloomington. They have six children and many grandchildren. And, although he is officially retired from football, he still has an office at the Vikings headquarters and still consults with the team from time to time. Now, when he is not spending time either with his family or in the great outdoors, hunting or fishing, he has championed many causes that are near and dear to his heart. Among them is the fight against commercial fishing with nets and spears on Minnesota lakes. Bud is a zealous activist when it comes to preserving our natural resources and does all that he can to help conserve them for future generations.

Gophers/Vikings/Lakers Tombstones:

"There were people who could run faster, jump higher, throw harder and shoot better than me, but I don't think anybody competed any harder than I did. I felt that I always had an advantage over my opponents because I never got tired. The longer we played, the stronger I got. Then I could beat you. And I applied that same theory to coaching. That was the type of player who I was always looking to get to play for me. Also, one thing that most coaches can't say, is that I've never been fired. I've always left whatever I was doing on my own accord, and I am proud of that. Every dollar I have ever made was from professional sports. I've had no other business or profession, and the only investments that I've got are six kids with college education's. Other than that, I don't have much."

TRIBUTES

"Bud should go down as one of the most intelligent coaches in the game," said Jim Marshall. "He understood how to deal with men. He had a unique sense about him that he could get the best out of every one of his players. He was a great organizer, he put together the team, ran a tight ship, and he brought true discipline to the team. He knew how to harness the talent and the energy that we as players had. I feel very respectful towards him for understanding that and not trying to change that part of what we had. He was not an egotist. He was a winner."

"Bud was the greatest professional coach that I have ever been around, he treated you like a man," said Ahmad Rashad. "He never wasted words. Bud was one of these guys that used to say: 'You practice, you prepare, you play, you go home, you have dinner.' He was a no-nonsense guy. And just a great person."

"I came to know, understand, and appreciate Bud much later in life," said Carl Eller. "My affection for Bud has actually grown more since I left football. He was not a person to get close to his players, yet he cared deeply for his players. He had a great charisma, knowledge, and skill of the game. I appreciate his strengths and qualities much more now."

"He commanded respect as well as anyone I've ever known, and he did it without yelling or intimidating or chewing people out," said Fran Tarkenton. "He never put himself up as an offensive or defensive genius. But everybody knew that he was the leader. He just wasn't overbearing. He's a very wise man."

"I played football the old fashioned way, and I believe I was a great student of Bud Grant," said Joe Kapp. "He didn't coach a lot about X's and O's, but rather with an attitude. There was a deep fire in Bud that you never saw."

"He was very tenacious, a great defender, and he could shoot from the outside," said Laker great George Mikan. "He was always assigned to guard the opposing team's best scorer. One of his great talents was his ability to throw me the ball into the pivot. I loved him!"

"Bud didn't tell you what you wanted to hear, he told you what you needed to know, and that's a big difference," said Chuck Foreman.

Since its first official game back in 1931, the University of Minnesota Duluth has established a hockey tradition that has become synonymous with success. For many, hockey is a religion in northeastern Minnesota, and the UMD Bulldogs have gained a tremendously loyal following.

There have been a lot of Bulldog hockey stars over the years, including the likes of: Tom Kurvers, Bill Watson, Bret Hull, Norm MacIver, Curt Giles, Derek Plante, Chris Marinucci, Jim Johnson, Chad Erickson, Tom Milani, Mark Pavelich, Murray Keogan, Chico Resch, Dave Langevin, Walt Ledingham, Ron Busniuk, Dennis Vaske, Bob Mason, Dan Lempe, Jim Toninato, Brett Hayer, Pat Boutette, and Keith "Huffer" Christianson, to name a few.

In 1984, the Dogs finished with an impressive 29-12-2 overall record, the best in school history. They also posted a 19-5-2 mark in the WCHA, good enough to win their first-ever conference title in the 20 years that they had been in the league. Then, led by All-Americans Tom Kurvers and Bill Watson, the Dogs came as close as a team could possibly come to winning a national championship, only to come up just short. That national championship game was, by most accounts, the greatest ever.

UMD Coach Mike Sertich's team, fresh of their first-ever showing in the NCAA playoffs against Providence the year before, started out their magical season by receiving a lesson in humility when they got spanked by the U.S. Olympic team, 12-0. Winger John Harrington of Virginia and Goaltender Bob Mason of International Falls were both former Bulldogs who played on that 1984 squad. Another highlight that season came in December, when the Dogs split a two-game exhibition series with the Junior Red Army Team in Leningrad and in Moscow to become the first American collegiate ice hockey team to tour the Soviet Union.

UMD settled down after that and kicked off the WCHA season by sweeping Colorado College. From there, the Bulldogs won eight of nine and finished the regular season losing only four of their final 16 games. They swept Wisconsin at the season's end to win their first McNaughton Cup, signifying the conference title.

Forced to host a "home" series at Williams Arena in Minneapolis due to a scheduling conflict with the Duluth Arena, the Dogs slaughtered North Dakota, 8-1 and 12-6, before near-capacity crowds in the WCHA championship series, to advance to the NCAA quarterfinals at home against Clarkson College. There, they split with Clarkson and in so doing, earned themselves a trip to Lake Placid to face North Dakota in the NCAA Final Four. UMD did not disappoint either, beating the Fighting Sioux, 2-1, in an overtime thriller.

Their opponents in the title game were the champions of the CCHA, Bowling Green, who had knocked off Michigan State in the other semifinal. This epic game would be a tale of two teams and two different playing styles. Bowling Green, whose lineup was dominated by Canadians, had only four Americans on the squad. Duluth, on the other hand, comprised mostly of home-grown Minnesotans, had only four Canadians. The sell-out crowd of nearly 8,000 people had no idea that they were about to be a part of college hockey history when the opening puck dropped. They were though, and this one was nothing short of spectacular.

For the first time in two games, UMD fell behind early on as Bowling Green Defenseman Garry Galley crashed into Bulldog Goalie Rick Kosti, and went top-shelf on a backhander at 5:58 of the first. The Dogs came back, as they had done so often that season, when Aurora's Bob Lakso stole the puck in the Bowling Green zone, and slipped a pass to Chisholm's Mark Baron, who flipped the biscuit under the crossbar to tie it up at one apiece.

Then, after being stymied on their first three power-play attempts, Hoyt Lakes' Matt Christensen directed a face-off to the left point where Billy Watson proceeded to tip in a Kurvers blast to go up by one. In the third, Lakso, who would be named to the all-tournament team, spurted between two Falcon defensemen and fired a low wrister to beat Goaltender Gary Kruzich on the short side. Things were looking pretty good for UMD as they were now up 3-1. It didn't last long though, as Falcon Forward Jamie Wansbrough, pressured by Bulldog Defenseman Jim Johnson, drove in and went five-hole on Kosti. UMD answered right back, however, at 11:55 on a wrister by International Falls' Tom Herzig.

As it went back and forth throughout the third, Bowling Green scored once again at 12:42. Kosti stopped a blue line blast by Mike Pikul, but got caught up in traffic in front of the net as he tried to recover. Forward Peter Wilson put in the garbage goal to make it 4-3, still in favor of Duluth. Then with 1:37 to go, Bowling Green tied it up on a fluke goal. With their goalie pulled, the Falcons dumped a long, off-target shot into the zone from beyond the red line that many people felt was off side. Oddly, the puck bounced off the end boards and past Kosti, who had stepped behind the net to control a puck which would never arrive. The puck hit a crack in the dasher board, deflected to the net, hit the left post and stopped in the crease. With Kosti way out of position, John Samanski, who had sprinted down the slot, tapped in a "freebie" to tie it up.

"I've never seen it happen, but I've heard of it happening," said the goaltender on the tough-luck bounce. "However, it never happened to me. It happened so fast that I didn't know what to do. I felt helpless."

From there the teams went to sudden death. And not just one overtime, in fact, there would be a total of four! Save after save, both goalies battled to stay alive. In the blur of the overtimes, Kruzich and Kosti, both freshmen goalies, played out of their heads. Kruzich stopped three UMD break-aways while Kosti stopped 19 shots in the final 37 minutes. Time stood still. It was unbelievable. Both teams were visibly fatigued and seemed to be skating on adrenaline alone.

Finally, at 7:11 of the fourth overtime, it ended, breaking the collective hearts of UMD hockey fans forever. Falcon Winger Dan Kane sped into the Bulldog end from the neutral zone and, from the high slot, threaded a pass to Gino Cavallini, who broke in all alone on Kosti. Cavallini took the puck from the left to the right, and put a back-

Osseo's James Martinez, a Gopher wrestler, wins a bronze medal in the L.A. Olympics	St. Paul's Stephen Erickson wins an Olympic gold medal in Star Class Sailing	Bemidji State beats Merrimack College for the Division III hockey National Championship	Wayzata's Greg LeMond wins the Tour de France and earns Sports Illustrated's Sportsman of the Year honors	St. Thomas runner Nick Mancui wins the Division III 10,000M Run National Championship	St. Thomas University wins the National Division III Indoor Track Championship	St. Thomas University wins the National Division III Women's Cross Country Championship	Augsburg Wrestler Steve Gliva wins the 118 lbs. National Championship	St. Olaf hurler Todd Nash wins the Division III Triple Jump National Championship	Gopher Women's tennis player Claudia Brisk wins the Big Ten Player of the Year Award

hander in to make college hockey history. The dream season was over.

Kosti, who tied a tournament record with 55 saves, really had no chance on the game-winning goal. Kane made the perfect pass, and Cavallini made the perfect shot. That was it. As soon as the puck hit the back of the net, Kosti skated straight to his bench, where he was met by his teary-eyed teammates, who sat motionless in disbelief.

The Bulldogs and Falcons had skated for 97 minutes and 11 seconds at Olympic Arena, in a game that took nearly four hours, while taking part in the (then) longest and most memorable game in college hockey history. The historic arena in Lake Placid that housed the famed "Miracle on Ice" Olympic team four years earlier, had now played host to the "Marathon on Ice."

"The thing I remember most about the overtimes was being really tired and gasping for air during the whistles," said team captain Tom Kurvers. "I think we only played four defensemen for most of the game. After a while, you didn't take any chances. You just played your position and tried not to make a mistake. The whole overtime was confusing. I hardly remember any of it. I was hugely disappointed at the loss, but it was an incredible game."

"Just to be going into overtime was a huge letdown, and we didn't feel that we had to be there," added Bill Watson. "It's one thing to score late to get into overtime, and it's another thing to squander the lead to get into overtime. The excitement level was incredible. The overtimes went on and on and on, and it just became a situation of survival and mind over matter as to just how much you wanted to win. It was tough playing on the much bigger Olympic ice surface too. It was probably my toughest loss ever as a hockey player."

UMD turned the corner that night in the world of college hockey though. No longer were they just the second-best team in Minnesota. Bulldog hockey had arrived big time.

Then, in an ironic twist, UMD returned to the Final Four again the following year. This time, led by a young freshman named Brett Hull, they lost a three-overtime heart-breaker 6-5, to RPI in Detroit. They rebounded to finish third in the nation by winning the consolation game 7-6 over Boston College, in, you guessed it, overtime. For his team's efforts, Coach Mike Sertich was selected as the WCHA's Coach of the Year for an unprecedented third season in a row.

A Pair of Hobeys
Over those two fantasy seasons, two Bulldog players: Tom Kurvers and Bill Watson, each stood out to capture college hockey's highest honor, the Hobey Baker Memorial Award.

Tom Kurvers was born on September 14, 1962, and grew up skating in the shadows of the Met Center in Bloomington. In 1980, his Bloomington Jefferson Jaguars were knocked off in the Minnesota State High School Hockey Tournament by Grand Rapids, who were led by future North Star Goalie, John Casey.

During his tenure in the Port City Kurvers scored 43 goals and 149 assists for 192 total points. For his efforts he was named as a first-team All-American. He went on to play for seven teams over 11 seasons in the NHL where he scored 93 goals and added 328 assists for 421 career points. He retired from pro hockey in 1995.

Bill Watson, meanwhile, was born on March 30, 1964, and grew up playing hockey in Powerview, Manitoba. From there he went on to star on back-to-back national junior hockey championship teams in Prince Albert, Sask. He came to UMD in 1982, and by the time he had left, the right-winger had scored 89 goals and 121 assists for 210 points. He still holds the record for most assists in one season with 60. For his efforts he was twice named as a first-team All-American in 1984 and 1985. Watson then went on to play with the NHL's Chicago Blackhawks for five seasons before retiring in 1990 because of a shoulder injury. He scored 23 goals and added 36 assists for 59 career points

in the Windy City, playing tough, two-way hockey all along.

What did it mean for you to be a UMD Bulldog?
Kurvers: "Just remembering how much I had missed college hockey was awesome. I love the connection that I feel towards Duluth. There's a pride and bond there because of all the success that we had."

Watson: "There is such great hockey pride and tradition there. Duluth has always had a reputation of producing great players. We have had not only great individuals, but we had some great teams as well. We went out there every night under the lights and play hard to win. Great players make a great program."

Bulldog Tombstones:
Kurvers: "He was one of the best hockey players to come out of Minnesota. Obviously not the best, but I am honored when my name gets tossed around with a Mike Ramsey, Reed Larson, Neal Broten, or Phil Howsley — not as a comparison, but just in the group. It means so much to me to be thought of in the same breath as those guys, who I have a lot of respect for."

Watson: "My career was more than the Hobey Baker Award and the individual trophies. It meant a great deal to play in Duluth. It was very tough for me that we didn't win that national championship. As close as we came, we probably should have won back-to-back national championships. I felt that I was on a team that was probably as good as any team that college hockey has ever seen — and that was probably the biggest honor that I could ever have bestowed upon me."

Both of Watson and Kurvers remain loyal Bulldog fans and both are still heavily involved in the game of hockey. After receiving his Masters in Business Administration from the University of St. Thomas in 1997, Kurvers went on to became a radio broadcaster and later a scout with the Phoenix Coyotes. Watson, meanwhile, went into coaching, first at Duluth's St. Scholastica, and then at Western Michigan University. He later moved back to Duluth, where he currently has a successful insurance business. Tom and Bill remain friends and still reminisce about those glory days back in the early 1980s when they came oh so close to winning it all.

"As a teammate, he really evolved into a great leader," said Watson of Kurvers. "When our class came in, I think it helped Tommy a lot that we could take a little bit of the burden off of his shoulders. Our friendship grew more and more as the team kept on winning. He is a great guy and a tremendous hockey player."

"Billy Watson was our best player," said Kurvers. "Even the year that I won the Hobey Baker, he was our MVP and go-to guy. If he had played another year at UMD, he could have possibly scored the most points ever for a college player. I've always said that if we were playing a pond hockey game and could draft anybody in the universe to be my teammate, Bill Watson would be the one — he was that good of a hockey player."

| Winona's Tracy Caulkins wins three swimming gold medals in the: 200M Individual Medley, 400M Individual Medley and the 400M Medley Relay. (By the time Caulkins retired, she had earned 48 national titles and had set 61 American and 5 world records.) | Calvin Griffith sells the Twins to banking mogul Carl Pohlad | The state's largest green sunfish is caught by Waconia's Richard Kunze on Scheuble Lake: 1 lb., 2.7 oz. | Grand Marais' Kevin Turnbough wins the John Beargrease Sled Dog Race |

In 1985 the upstart Gophers greatly improved to finish with a 7-5 record, which included the program's first post-season bowl appearance in nearly a decade. Leading the charge once again was Rickey Foggie, who tore up the Big Ten that year. There have been quite a few memorable T-formation quarterbacks at the University of Minnesota, but none of them was as versatile a performer as was Rickey Foggie. Foggie could run, pass, scramble, and wreak havoc on opposing defenses — making up the rules as he went along.

Led by Foggie, who scored three touchdowns on 140 yards rushing while throwing for another 157, the Maroon and Gold kicked off the season with a 28-14 win over Wichita State. From there, the Gophers crushed Montana, 62-17, as Foggie again played masterfully. The Gophers piled up over 500 yards of offense in this one as Valdez Baylor rushed for 89 yards and a pair of touchdowns, while Foggie scored three TDs of his own and passed for another to Mel Anderson.

Minnesota, despite Foggie's TD pass to Kevin Starks late in the game, then lost a heartbreaker to the top-ranked Oklahoma Sooners, 13-7, in Week Three. The team rebounded though by pouncing all over Purdue, 45-15, as Foggie threw for 212 yards and a TD, while rushing for 47 yards and another touchdown. The Gophs went on to beat Northwestern in Week Five, 21-10, behind nearly 300 yards of total offense from Foggie, in addition to 102 yards receiving and a TD from Tight End Kevin Starks. In Week Seven they beat Indiana, 22-7, in a game that featured Valdez Baylor rushing for a career high 141 yards and a TD, along with three Chip Lohmiller field goals.

Minnesota then lost a pair of nail-biters, one to Ohio State at Homecoming, 23-19, and the other to Michigan State, 31-26. Foggie scored the only two touchdowns in the Buckeye game, and then sat out the Spartan game with a pulled groin, as backup QB Alan Holt came up just short in leading the team back from a huge deficit. In Week Nine, the Gophers beat Wisconsin, 27-18, in a game that was highlighted by an 89-yard record-setting TD bomb from Foggie to Mel Anderson. The Gophers finished out the season on a huge downer though, getting pummeled by Michigan, 48-7, who was led by Quarterback Jim Harbaugh, and by Big Ten champion Iowa, 31-9. Despite finishing only fifth in the Big Ten with a 4-4 record, the Gophers were invited to once again go "bowling," something that hadn't occurred since 1977, when they played in the Hall of Fame Bowl.

With that, Minnesota was off to Shreveport, La., to meet the Clemson Tigers in the 10th annual Independence Bowl. Nearly 43,000 fans, many of whom made the trip from the Gopher State, crowded into Independence Stadium to watch the big game.

Now, in a bit of off-the-field drama, Coach Lou Holtz controversially opted to exercise a little-known secret clause (which would later become known affectionately as the "Notre Dame Clause") in his contract which entitled him to step down to take the head coaching position at Notre Dame, should it become available. It did, and he went, leaving his Defensive Coordinator, John Gutekunst, to take over as head coach of the team. "Gutie," who had served as an assistant at both Duke and Virginia Tech before joining Holtz at Arkansas and then Minnesota, was eager and excited to make the most of his "golden" opportunity.

"Lou's got to be one of the top five greatest college coaches of all time, without question," said Foggie of Holtz's decision to leave. "Everywhere Holtz has been, he's won. He turned our football program around and got people in the stands. He was able to recruit good athletes to come in and make us competitive again. His greatest asset was to be able to recruit and to motivate his players to go out and win at all costs. I just wish he would've stayed at Minnesota longer, because there's no telling where the program would be today if he had."

"This was a big change for us, but, because Gutie was already on the staff, we were familiar with him, and we kind of knew what to expect," Foggie added. "But, going from Lou Holtz, who was a fiery, up-tempo guy, to Gutie, who was a more laid-back kind of coach, was a big change. Gutie wasn't the motivator that Coach Holtz was, but he knew the X's and O's of the game, and he was a good guy."

With "Gutie" at the helm, the Gophers took to the field and made a statement on the game's first play from scrimmage. That's when Clemson QB Rodney Williams hit Wide Receiver Ray Williams on a screen pass. Williams, upon being tattooed by Gopher defender Doug Mueller, then proceeded to cough up the ball at the Tiger 39-yard line. Minnesota then took over and began to drive downfield behind Ed Penn's 25-yard run, which got the Gophers down to the Clemson five-yard line. But after a holding penalty, they could only muster a field goal attempt. Kicker Chip Lohmiller came in, but was wide-right on a 22-yarder, keeping the score at 0-0. But two plays later, Clemson again fumbled on their own 26-yard-line. After a failed attempt to get the ball in the end-zone, Lohmiller came in and this time drilled a 22-yarder straight through the uprights to put the Gophers up 3-0.

In the second quarter, after forcing the Tigers to punt, the Gophers put together an impressive drive that started with two David Puk nine-yard scampers up the middle. Foggie then hit Tight End Craig Otto on another nine-yarder to get to their own 43, followed by 15 and 20-yard runs by Baylor. Finally, on third-and-four, at the Tiger nine, Foggie hit Anderson on a nine-yard scoring strike, and the Gophers went up 10-0. Clemson rallied back in the third though, thanks to a pair of Jeff Treadwell field goals to make it 10-6. Then, behind the running of Clemson Tailback Kenny Flowers, the Tigers drove and scored on a Jennings touchdown catch to take a three-point lead, 13-10.

The valiant Gophers came back in the fourth though, behind their leader, Rickey Foggie, whose running and passing sparked an 85-yard drive that was capped by another Lohmiller "Chip-shot" to tie the game at 13 apiece. After the Gopher defense forced the Tigers to punt, Foggie came out and lined up in the shotgun formation. He started out the drive with a 10-yard pass to Anderson, followed by a 16-yard Baylor run to the Clemson 36. Foggie then hit Flanker Gary Couch on a 14-yarder, quickly followed by a Baylor run that gave him 12 more of his team-high 98 yards. Now, with the Gophers at the seven-yard line, Fullback David Puk rumbled down to the one. That was all Baylor

TIMELINE

| St. Thomas runner Erik Rosenkranz wins the Division III Decathalon National Championship | St. John's runner Jim Gathje wins the Division III 3,000M Steeplechase National Championship | Macalaster runner Julia Kirtland wins both the 3,000M and 5,000M Division III Indoor Track National Championships | b St. Thomas runner Lisa Koelfgen wins both the Indoor and Outdoor Division III 1,500M Indoor Track National Championships | St. Thomas runner Nick Mancui wins the Division III 10,000M Run National Championship | St. Thomas University wins the Men's Division III Indoor Track National Championship | Hoyt Wilhelm, a Minneapolis Miller from 1950-51, is inducted into the Baseball Hall of Fame | Gopher winger Pat Micheletti is named to the All-American hockey team | Baseball's All Star Game is played at the Metrodome, as the American League beats the National League, 6-1 |

96

needed to launch himself into the end-zone as the Gophers took a seven-point lead.

But the Gophers weren't out of the hot water yet. Faced with a fourth-and-six at their own 39, Clemson faked a punt to stay alive. Then on fourth and 12, Williams completed a 21-yarder to Jennings to reach the Gopher 31-yard line. So, with 90 seconds left in the game, the Tigers tried a trick play. Williams tossed a long, backward pass to Receiver Ray Williams, who then turned around and lofted a pass of his own to Tight End Jim Riggs near the goal line. That's when Cornerback Donovan Small dove, and just barely got his finger on the ball, deflecting it out of bounds and preserving the Gopher victory.

"When they first threw that ball out wide," said Small, who was named the Defensive Player of the Game, "I was going to come up to try to tackle the guy. I thought it was a screen pass. But just out of the corner of my eye I saw this Clemson guy running really hard downfield. I wondered why that guy was running so hard, so I decided I'd better try to catch up to him."

"I have fond memories of that game because I always wanted to attend Clemson," added Foggie, who threw for 123 yards and a touchdown in the game. "But the Clemson coach told my high school coach that I was too slow to run their offense. So there was a definite revenge factor there for me personally. I knew a lot of the guys that played for Clemson, and to go out and play well and to beat those guys was just really satisfying for me. Minnesota hadn't been to a bowl game for a while, so to win it was a special experience for everyone."

For the season Foggie accounted for 1,821 yards of total offense and was named to the All-Big Ten team. Baylor led the team in rushing with 680 yards, while Lohmiller led the team in scoring with 75 points. In addition, Linebacker Peter Najarian was the Golden Gophers' top tackler (for the third straight season) with 133 total hits.

The most versatile quarterback in Gopher history, Rickey Foggie could do it all. He could pass, run, scramble, and wreak havoc on opposing defenses, all while leading his club to victory. When his tenure was over in Gold Country, there were quite a few pages in the record books that had to be rewritten.

The Fog Rolled In

Rickey Foggie was born on July 1, 1966, in Waterloo, S.C., and grew up as one of nine siblings in a family that loved playing sports. At Laurens High School, he was an all-conference and all-state performer in both football and basketball, and, in his senior year, he led his high school football team to the South Carolina state championship.

After being heavily recruited in both sports, Foggie came to Minnesota in 1983, following the disastrous 1-10 Gopher season under Joe Salem. As a freshman, he led the team in both rushing and passing, and showed great promise by redefining the conventional rules of the quarterback position. For his career Rickey was twice named as the team's MVP and twice he earned All Big Ten honors as well. He accounted for nearly 2,000 yards in offense in his senior season alone, passing for 1,232 yards and 8 TDs and rushing for 714 yards and 6 TDs. He posted numbers that won't often be equalled.

Foggie left Minnesota as the school's all-time leader in total offense with 7,312 yards. In addition, he ranks in the top 10 all-time in rushing with 2,150 yards and 25 TDs as well. He also scored 160 points, threw a record 34 touchdowns, and ranked No. 2 all-time behind only Marquel Fleetwood in career yards passing, with 5,162. He was also later named as the Outstanding Offensive Player in the 1986 Liberty Bowl. Considered a threat every time he touched the ball, he became only the third quarterback in college football history to run over 2,000 yards and pass for more than 4,000 yards.

When Rickey finished his tenure at Minnesota, he headed north of the border to play in the Canadian Football League, first with

the British Columbia Lions, then the Toronto Argonauts, and lastly with the Edmonton Eskimos. From there he headed to Memphis, when the CFL expanded to the United States, and then to the Hamilton Tiger Cats. Then Rickey had a homecoming of sorts when he came home to Minnesota in 1996 to play for one season with the upstart Fighting Pike of the Arena Football League.

"I felt like I had a good reception from the fans, and it was great to be able to come back to the Twin Cities," said Rickey of the Pike. "We had a lot of fun that year, but it was unfortunate that we didn't get to win any games at home. I was disappointed that my Pike experience wasn't a successful situation, but I was glad to get back into the atmosphere of having the fans come out and watch me perform again."

When the team folded that next season Foggie headed east and began his 10th year of professional football with the New Jersey Red Dogs of that same arena league. All in all the Fog spent nine years in the CFL and another seven in the Arena Football League, where, after playing with the Florida Bobcats and Detroit Fury, he still is going strong with the Toronto Phantoms in 2002.

With his amazing ability to run the option attack like no other before him, Rickey will go down as one of the best Gopher quarterbacks ever. He electrified the fans in Minnesota and was pivotal in turning a shattered football program around. When Foggie left Gold Country the Gophers had not only gone to two bowl games, but they had also returned to a semblance of their former glory.

What did it mean for you to be a Gopher?

"Once I learned the great tradition of the school and its winning success, it all kind of sunk in. Coach Holtz brought back a lot of the tradition. To be able to play in front of sell-out crowds for our first two years was great. I felt that we brought a college football atmosphere back to the U of M. The fans were great, and it always meant a lot to me that they supported me the way that they did. Maroon and Gold is something that I will never be able to get out of my system, and I am always proud to say that I am a Gopher."

Gopher Tombstone:

"I would hope to be remembered as a guy who went out and just had fun playing the game, was part of rebuilding a program that had been down for a couple of years, and helped bring the excitement and respectability back to Gopher football."

TRIBUTE

"Rickey is a really good guy," said teammate Darrell Thompson. "I remember that when I was a freshman, he was so nice to me and really helped me through a lot. Throughout all the pressures of the games, he was good at keeping things fun and light. He even used to give me little gifts before games and, when he wasn't joking around with me in the huddles, he was giving me tips on how to improve my game. I appreciated it and we still keep in touch today."

| Canterbury Downs horse track opens in Shakopee and that next season nearly $135 million is wagered at the track | Baseball's All Star Game is played at the Metrodome | UMD goalie Rick Kosti is named to the All-American hockey team | UMD defenseman Norm Maciver is named to the All-American hockey team | Minneapolis native Harold Trumble, former head of the Amateur Hockey Association, is enshrined into the U.S. Hockey Hall of Fame | Freeport's Janice Ettle wins the Twin Cities Marathon in a time of 2:35:47 | Grand Marais' John Patten wins the John Beargrease Sled Dog Race | Hibbing native Louis Robert Blake is enshrined into the U.S. Hockey Hall of Fame | Moose Lake's Annie Adamczak, arguably one of the state's greatest all-around athletes, is named as the Big Eight Female Athlete of the Year after earning All-American Volleyball honors at the University of Nebraska. |

TIMELINE

The University of Minnesota Golden Gopher Football program has a long and epic history dotted with peaks and valleys. Minnesota has always been known to represent the "three yards and a cloud of dust" mentality of Big Ten football, which was anchored by a sound running game. There have been so many great running backs through the years in Gold Country including legends such as Bronko Nagurski, Bruce Smith, Paul Giel, Pug Lund, Bill Daley, Marion Barber, Rick Upchurch, Bob McNamara and even Chris Darkins as of late. But none of them could run like Darrell Thompson, who rewrote the record books during his tenure at the U. In 1986, Darrell, as a true freshman, led the Maroon and Gold to the Liberty Bowl in Memphis, where they lost a heart-breaker to the Tennessee Volunteers.

In 1986, the Gophers were anxious to show the world that their Independence Bowl victory over Clemson the year before was no fluke. It was John Gutekunst's first full season as head coach at the University of Minnesota, having taken over the reigns from Lou Holtz, who went on to coach at Notre Dame just prior to the 1985 Independence Bowl. (Holtz had a "Notre Dame Clause" in his contract that gave him the green light to jump ship to South Bend at any point should the Irish come calling.)

The beginning of the 1986 season brought more hype and hoopla to campus than perhaps every before. That season a kid from Rochester hit campus by the name of Darrell Thompson, and by the time he was done four years later, he would own most every rushing record in the books. "Darrell and Rickey (Foggie)" became quite the dynamic duo that year, as the upstart Gophers earned their second straight post-season trip to a bowl game.

Coach Gutekunst had emerged from the shadows of Holtz and was now anxious to show the football world that his team was for real. He also wanted the world to know that their 1985 Independence Bowl victory the year before was no fluke.

The season got underway against Bowling Green, as Thompson made an immediate impact by rushing for 205 yards and scoring four touchdowns en route to a 31-7 victory. Thompson was for real. But, the Gophers hit a few bumps in the road from there, including a giant pothole in the shape of the University of Oklahoma, who crushed the Gophs by the ugly score of 63-0. Minnesota followed that up with a 24-20 loss to tiny Pacific University, despite two more touchdowns by Thompson. From there the Gophers rebounded and went on a roll, first beating Purdue, 36-9 (as Rickey Foggie scored three rushing touchdowns and passed to Mel Anderson for another), then Northwestern, 44-23 (led by Thompson's 176 yards rushing and two touchdowns, as well as Mel Anderson's 90-yard kickoff return for another), and final-

ly Indiana in a squeaker, 19-17. Thompson ran wild for 191 yards in this one to set up Chip Lohmiller's game-wining 21-yard field goal with two seconds to go on the clock.

Minnesota ran into some more trouble in Week Seven when they got shut-out by Ohio State, 33-0, thanks to the Buckeye's defense, which was led by future NFL star, Chris Spielman. The squad then lost to Michigan State that next Saturday by the final of 52-23. But the Gophers rebounded as they had done all season long in Week Nine, this time defeating the Wisconsin Badgers, 27-20, to retain Paul Bunyan's Axe. In that game, Foggie threw a 27-yard strike to Dennis Carter for the go-ahead touchdown, while Thompson rushed for 117 yards to become the first Gopher frosh to run for 1,000 yards.

Next up, No. 2 ranked Michigan, who had beaten Minnesota the past eight seasons. The Michigan game, in all of its pomp and circumstance, would prove to be one of the greatest ever for the University of Minnesota. After back and forth scoring the entire game, it all came down to the wire in this one. Down 17-16 with just over two minutes to go in the game, Michigan Coach Bo Schembechler opted to go for the tie instead of a two-pointer to win. He succeeded, and with the game now all tied-up, Minnesota drove the ball downfield. Then with 47 seconds left, Foggie took off from the Michigan 48 and ran for 31 yards to the Michigan 17. The stage was now set for Woodbury Kicker Chip Lohmiller, and the "Chipper" came through in a big way. He nailed the 30-yarder as time ran out to give the Gophers a dramatic 20-17 victory, as well as the coveted Little Brown Jug. In addition, Linebacker Larry Joyner, who sparked the defense with 11 tackles and forced two fumbles, was named as the Defensive Player of the Week.

"I knew once we got it inside the 40, Chip could put It through," said Foggie. "He's got a great leg."

Next, Despite Lohmiller's record 62-yard field goal, the Gophers finished out their season by losing to Iowa, 30-27. It didn't matter though, as the Gophers still earned a berth in the Liberty Bowl, where they would face the University of Tennessee, right in the Vols' own backyard of Memphis.

The game got underway with the Volunteers jumping ahead 14-0 on two Jeff Francis touchdown passes. The first came to Joey Clinkscales in the left flat as he beat both Cornerback Matt Martinez and Safety Steve Franklin to scoot into the end zone for an 18-yard touchdown. After a second quarter Foggie fumble at midfield, Francis dumped a screen pass to Fullback William Howard, who promptly took it to the house to make it 14-0. The Gophers came close twice in the half — once getting to the Vols' six-yard line, where Foggie came up short on a sneak, and then again when Thompson fumbled on the Vols' 33-yard line. Minnesota's only points came on a Lohmiller 27-yard field goal that capped a 70-yard drive at the end of the half.

When the third quarter opened, Foggie appeared to be a man on a mission. The junior quarterback led Minnesota on a 10-play, 88-yard drive that was highlighted by an 11-yard quarterback-keeper for a touchdown. Then, Thompson added a two-point conversion to make the score 14-11. Still in the third, behind 38 of Thompson's game-high 136 yards, the Gophers started a long march down to the Tennessee 14. But, a holding call nullified their touchdown hopes, and Minnesota had to settle for another field goal by Lohmiller.

Tied at 14-apiece in the fourth, the Vols cruised upfield on a 67-yard drive that was capped by Clinkscales' second TD catch of the game less than two minutes later. So, with Tennessee up, 21-14, the

TIMELINE

| Bemidji State beats Plattsburg State for the Division III hockey National Championship | UM Morris Wrestler Dan Lewandowski wins the Division III 190 lbs. National Championship | St. Thomas runner Jeff Hyman wins the Division III 5,000M Run National Championship | St. John's runner Jim Gathje wins the Division III 3,000M Steeplechase National Championship | Macalaster runner Julia Kirtland wins the Division III 5,000M National Championship | St. Thomas runner Lisa Koelfgen wins the Division III 1,500M Indoor and Outdoor National Championships as well as the Women's Cross Country National Championship | St. Thomas University wins the Men's Division III Cross Country National Championship | St. Thomas University wins the Women's Division III Cross Country National Championship | Vikings quarterback Tommy Kramer is named as the NFL Comeback Player of the Year |

98

Gophers tried to mount a rally. Their next drive got stalled on their own 49-yard line, but after an exchange of punts Minnesota got the ball back at midfield largely because of two great plays by freshman Linebacker Jon Leverenz — who forced a two-yard loss on a first-down play, and then broke up a key third-down pass. So, with Foggie and Thompson poised for the upset, they tried one last drive to win it all. The final push, a seven-play drive, started out well, but unfortunately ended near midfield when Foggie's fourth-down pass to Waconia's Ron Goetz fell incomplete. Tennessee took over with 16 seconds left and simply ran out the clock to win it. Minnesota out-gained Tennessee in the game 374-324, but, in the end, the final score read 21-14 in favor of the Vols.

The Gophers played well, despite having to do battle deep inside enemy turf. For the season, they finished at 6-6 and tied for third in the Big Ten with a 5-3 record. Thompson, who led the conference in rushing that year, also set a new Gopher single-season rushing mark with 1,240 yards. He was something special.

"It was a big deal because you grow up watching the bowl games on TV, and when you finally get to play in one, it is a very special event," said Thompson, who was named to the All-Big Ten team. "I mean, only the year before I was playing for Rochester John Marshall High School, and now here I was starting at running back in the Liberty Bowl, it was an exciting time."

"Daaaa-rrrr-ellll!" "Daaaa-rrrr-ellll!"

Darrell Thompson was born on December 23, 1967, and grew up playing several different sports in Rochester. His parents encouraged their children to play a lot of sports and to be well-rounded athletes. After all, his dad played basketball at Clark College in Atlanta and his mom was a three-sport star at Alcorn State University in Mississippi. Thompson's younger brother and sister also went on to earn scholarships playing volleyball as well.

At Rochester John Marshall High School, Thompson was a three-sport star. Along with being a forward on the basketball team, Darrell also earned all-state honors in track. There he ran the 100, 200, and 400 meters, and even anchored the 1985 state championship mile relay team. But his main sport was football. His senior year he rushed for over 1,000 yards, scored 102 points and averaged an amazing 9.7 yards per carry. Not only was he all-state in football, he was also an All-American. In fact, Darrell was the state's most highly recruited football player ever, and was wooed by nearly every major college in the country.

For his career at the University of Minnesota, Darrell rushed for 4,654 yards on 936 attempts, and scored 40 touchdowns, making him the school's all-time career rushing, attempts, and touchdowns leader. He also scored 262 total points, placing him second on the all-time scoring list behind only teammate Chip Lohmiller — a kicker. From 1986-1989, his teammates voted him the teams' MVP. He is the only running back in Big Ten history to go over 1,000-yards as a freshman and a sophomore. In 1987, he became the first player ever to gain more than 200 yards in a game against Michigan. In that same game he dazzled the sellout Metrodome crowd as well as the national TV audience with a 98-yard touchdown run, the longest run from scrimmage in Big Ten history. He also threw two passes for the Gophers, both good for touchdowns.

After a phenomenal senior season, Darrell was drafted in the first round by the Green Bay Packers. He went on to play for five seasons with the Pack, before hanging up the spikes for good in 1995. Because he was hampered by injuries throughout much of his pro career and was often forced to play out of his natural position, he was never able to truly showcase his talents in the NFL.

Statistically speaking, Darrell was the greatest running back that has ever played at the University of Minnesota. With his six-foot-

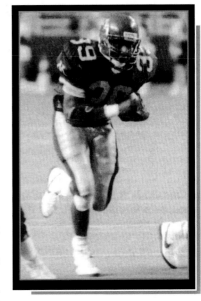

one, 220-pound frame combined with his 4.4 speed and acceleration, he was an elusive yet punishing back.

"Darrell can get into another gear at any time," said Coach Gutekunst. "It's phenomenal. He has quickness and shiftiness laterally. He can step out of things, change direction, and get back to full speed in a hurry."

One of the only things tougher than trying to tackle Darrell Thompson was trying to get him to talk about his amazing accomplishments. "I don't see it as that big a deal," said Darrell of his gridiron talents. "I can run a football, but some other guy can hook up a stereo. God gave everybody their own thing."

Darrell was not only an incredible athlete, he was also one of the nicest guys you could ever meet. He was definitely the big man on campus, but when you got to know him, it became readily apparent that he was just a modest guy from Rochester who happened to be pretty darn good at carrying a pigskin.

What did it mean for you to be a Gopher?
"I took a lot of pride in it. I really enjoyed playing for the U, and I'd like to see more kids from Minnesota experiencing the same pleasure that I had there. Athletes can carve out a real nice niche in the community here."

Why did you select the U of M?
"At the time I didn't think that pro football was a very realistic expectation, so I figured that I would rather end up working in Minneapolis when I was through playing at the U. When I was being recruited, I went to schools like Nebraska, Wisconsin, and Iowa, but I didn't think that I would want to live in those towns after my football career was over. They were all great football towns, but Minneapolis is a great city to live in. I see a lot of Big Ten football players from all over the country living here now because it's just a great place to live."

On being the Packers' first-round pick:
"I was really happy and I was blessed. It was something that I never thought was even that realistic, but when it happened it was special. We were a pretty close knit family, and it was neat that they could all drive up to Green Bay from Rochester to see my games."

On Kids and the Future
Thompson has been retired from the game for a several years now, and currently works in Minneapolis where he manages youth programs and charitable foundations. "I tell kids today that they can play in the pros if they work really hard at it — but I tell them to be realistic," said Thompson. "Since there's only a one-in-10,000 chance of making it in the pros, I tell them that they need to study and make other plans in life so that they can be successful even if they don't make it."

Gopher Tombstone:
"I'd want to be remembered as a guy who played hard, loved to compete, and was someone that commanded respect from his teammates."

| Vikings quarterback Fran Tarkenton is inducted into the NFL Hall of Fame | Wayzata's Greg LeMond wins the Tour De France Bicycle race | UMD defenseman Norm MacIver is named to the All-American hockey team | St. Paul native Kenneth Yackel, a former Gopher great, is enshrined into the U.S. Hockey Hall of Fame | Squaw Lake's Robin Jacobson wins the John Beargrease Sled Dog Race | Ultra Wheels In-line Skates, a division of First Team Sports, is founded. It was the brainchild of three men: John Egart, Dave Soderquist and Ron Berg, who started the company out of a garage in Anoka. The company went public on, ironically, Wall Street's Black Monday, in October of 1987. Today, with annual sales at $75 million, it remains one of the top three in-line skate companies behind Rolleblade. The skates are manufactured in an Alexandria plastics molding plant. |

TIMELINE

The 1987 Minnesota Twins were, in a word, awesome, and their story is perhaps one of the greatest in all of sports. It all began during that off-season when GM Andy MacPhail set the early tone by acquiring ace Reliever Jeff Reardon. Was he the missing piece of the puzzle? Heck, most baseball pundits predicted another season of mediocrity for these Twins, probably no better than fourth in the AL West. Boy were they wrong!

The Twins took baseball by storm in 1987, featuring a lineup that was comprised of Minnesota's own "Fab-Four," the quartet of Herbie, Kirby, Bruno and the G-Man. They even added a new kid by the name of Dan Gladden, a hard-nosed left fielder who was full of grit and determination. The team played up and down that season but overall, played solid fundamental baseball under Manager Tom Kelly.

One of the highlights (or lowlights) that year came on August 3rd, when Pitcher Joe Niekro was ejected from the Twins 11-3 win in Anaheim. Niekro, a crafty old vet, got caught with his hand in the cookie jar in this one as he coughed up a five inch emery board out his pocket after being accused of doctoring knuckle-balls. Busted!

The Twins finished the regular season with a modest 85-77 record, but it was good enough to win the West. Frank Viola began to show great consistency as a starter along with veteran Bert Blyleven, who, believe it or not, was with the Twins the last time they were in the American League Championship Series back in 1970. Leading the charge was Kent Hrbek. After being stiffed for the All-Star Game, Herbie took out his anger on opposing teams, finishing with a career-high 34 home runs and adding 90 RBI's to boot.

So, in the first round of the post-season, the Twins prepared to do battle with the Detroit Tigers. Detroit, with the best overall won-loss record in the bigs, was predicted to crush the Twins. The Twins thought differently though and took the first two in Minnesota and then went on to win two of the final three in Detroit. Tim Laudner's double off Tigers ace Jack Morris was the difference in Game Two, and in Game Four they took the lead for good on Greg Gagne's fourth-inning home run. Leading the way in the series was Gary Gaetti, who was named as the ALCS MVP.

Now it was on to the World Series, where the Twins would face the St. Louis Cardinals. The first two games weren't even close. In Game One, the first World Series game ever played indoors, the Twins blasted St. Louis, 10-1, thanks to Dan Gladden's grand slam. The second game was another cakewalk, an 8-4 victory, highlighted by homers from both Gary Gaetti and Tim Laudner. Then, just when it looked like a series sweep for Minnesota, the Cards came back and took the next three games in St. Louis. The Twins hung in there in Game Five on Gaetti's eighth-inning, two-run triple, but the Cards held on for a 4-2 win. Now, just one victory for the Cardinals at the Metrodome, and St. Louis would be crowned as world champions.

Game Six was a wild one. Down in the fifth, the Twins retaliated behind DH Don Baylor's three-run homer, and then slammed the door on the Cards thanks to Kent Hrbek's childhood dream-come-true. With the Twins up 6-5 in the sixth, Herbie would make history that night when he proceeded to hit a 439-foot grand salami over the center field wall, and into a sea of white homer hankies. The series was now even at three games apiece. As the Bloomington native circled the bases with his fists pumping and his mouth wide open, he remembered playing out that very play a million times before in his own back yard – just a stone's throw from the old Met. The Twins, behind Puckett's four hits and four runs, went on to take Game Six, 11-5, to even it up at three games apiece.

Said teammate Roy Smalley after Game Six: "Before Kent went up to bat I looked at Frank Viola and said, 'You watch... This is too set up. This is too much like a storybook. It's too perfect.'"

"It is something I will never feel again," said Herbie after the big game. "People talk about thrills in baseball. Just making the big leagues was a thrill. Hitting a home run at Yankee Stadium in my first game in the big leagues was a thrill. Hitting a grand slam in the World Series in your home state — that is indescribable."

Game Seven had all the drama you could ask for. The Cardinals scored first in this one with a pair of runs in the second, but the Twins rallied with runs in the second and fifth, and then took the lead on three walks and an infield single in the sixth. Frankie V. then held St. Louis scoreless on just two hits after the second, and ace reliever Jeff Reardon came in to retire the Cards in order in the ninth to bring Minnesota its first world championship. It was truly a wild one. Three Twins were thrown out at home plate. Greg Gagne drove in the winning run on an infield hit. Frankie "Sweet Music" Viola pitched eight beautiful innings, giving up only two runs early on. And, fittingly Jeff Reardon came in for the ninth, getting the final out on McGee's ground ball to Gary Gaetti. When the G-Man threw the ball across the diamond to Herbie at first, the Twins had won the game, 4-2, earning the title of baseball's World Champions. As Carl Spackler (alias: Bill Murray from the classic movie Caddyshack…) said so prophetically, it was truly a "Cinderella-Story."

In the series finale, the Minnesota fans had actually grown quite fond of the parachute-topped edifice better known as the "Homerdome," a true testament to its' inexplicable magic it had provided the Twins. Frank Viola would earn Series MVP honors, and for Herbie, there would be ticker-tape parades, presidential meetings, and even Late Night with David Letterman.

"I just step back and think of the guys that I played with back then," Hrbek would later recall. "Great guys, like Viola, Gaetti, Brunansky, Laudner and Bush. We grew up in the big leagues together, we lost in the big leagues together, and then, in 1987, we were the best in the world together. I can still remember sitting on the clubhouse floor after the game. Everybody thought we all were drunk as pigs, but we weren't, we were all just mentally and physically spent. It was something that we had all worked so hard for, and had so much fun doing. And when it was over we just soaked it all in and enjoyed it."

"That team was the closest-knit group of guys I've ever been around," added Kirby Puckett. "It was unbelievable. I mean win or lose, every night you could find at least a dozen of us eating together at a restaurant. We hung out together and we won together. I still remember, after we won Game Seven, a bunch of us were just sitting there on the floor in the clubhouse, drinking champagne, and staring at each other like, 'What did we just do?' I've had a lot of people ask me since then, 'How did it feel?' And you know what? I can't tell them. It's something you have to experience for yourself to get it. It was something only the people in that room could understand."

"Being it was my first full year as a manager, it was a very special thing," said Manager Tom Kelly. "It was a new experience for me getting into the playoffs and into the World Series. Typically, we are somewhat afraid and apprehensive about new experiences because we don't know what to expect. There was a lot of cautious optimism surrounding the whole experience. The playoffs were a little more nerve-racking than the Big Dance, but, all in all, it was an incredible experience."

Herbie

Kent Hrbek was born on May 21, 1960, and grew up in the shadows of Metropolitan Stadium in Bloomington. There, he loved to follow the Twins and loved to play baseball. Herbie went on to Bloomington Kennedy High School, where he batted .480 his senior year.

"He was an excellent fielder," said Buster Radebach, his high school coach. "He was a student of the game and he studied it."

However, it was in American Legion ball that summer where Hrbek started to get noticed. His coach, Red Haddox, recalled that fans were simply in awe of his massive home runs. "He could handle the glove and could run for a big man," added former Twins Owner Calvin Griffith, who went to see one of Kent's American Legion games. "I could see that his stroke alone was sufficient to gamble on him." So, in the 17th round of the 1978 draft, Herbie became a Twin, accepting a $30,000 offer.

After a brief stint in Visalia, where he was voted the MVP of the California League, he got the call to come up to the show. He finished second to Cal Ripken in the Rookie of the Year voting, and was the lone rookie on the All-Star team that year as well. "My sister probably sent in 10,000 votes on her own!" Kent quipped regarding that years All-Star balloting. He even made the cover of Sports Illustrated with the title: "Best of the Worst," and also appeared on the ABC-TV's Good Morning America show. He had arrived in the big time.

While Herbie was most appreciated by his teammates and the fans for his upper-deck power and agility, he will also be remembered as one of the best fielders ever to play first base. A .282 lifetime hitter over his 14-year career, Hrbek finished second in the 1984 MVP race when he hit .311. He is among club leaders in nearly every offensive category: 2nd in home-runs (293), 2nd in RBI's (1,086), 4th in hits (1,749), 4th in runs (903), 5th in total bases (2,976), 2nd in walks (838), 3rd in total games (1,747), 5th in at-bats (6,192) and 3rd in doubles (312). He finally hung em' up and retired in 1994 and his No. 14 was formally retired on August 13, 1995. Herbie will go down as one of the all-time greatest fan-favorites in Minnesota sports history. Bar none.

What did it mean for you to be a Twin?

"I thought being a Twin was just about the greatest thing in the world. Being from Minnesota, and being just a huge sports fan, I have always rooted for our teams, whether it was the Twins, Vikings, North Stars, Timberwolves, or Gophers — I just wanted our teams to win. I don't think there is anybody that wanted to win a ball game more than Kent Hrbek, and there probably never will be."

On Minnesotans:

"I just think the people up here are great. I don't know, and people

might think I'm a dink for saying this, but I think East Coast people could care less about family, and West Coast people, they don't even know if they have a family! When you can walk into a mom & pop restaurant in the middle of Iowa while you're out pheasant hunting, and everybody knows everybody, and they all care about each other, that to me is home."

Twins Tombstone:

"I had a great time playing. I liked to put on a show and have a good time and make people think that I wasn't so much different than they were, just because I was a major league baseball player. People always thought that I had too much fun on the field, but having a good time was the only way I played well. I'd like to think that I was a fun-loving guy who felt like 'Hey, don't look at me badly because I could drink a beer and I was a major league baseball player.' There are too many guys now that thought they were so much better than others because they were major league baseball players, and I could never stand that! Let me tell you, you're not better than me because you can hit a 90 mph fastball, and because you make $6 million a year! Don't think that your sh-- doesn't stink, because it does!"

On retirement:

"I just want to be Kent Hrbek, have a family, and be able to stop at Super America and pump my gas without worrying about signing this or that. I want to be able to walk around with my fly down, or with spit dribbling off my chin, because I'm human, and everybody else has done that before. I don't want to be Kent Hrbek, the Minnesota Twin, I just want to be 'Joe Blow,' because that's who I am."

TRIBUTES

"He was awesome," said Kirby Puckett. "He was the best first baseman that I ever played with. He was one of the best teammates that I ever had. He was a great person, fun to be around and he made every day special coming to the ball park. I always felt that he should have won several gold gloves and been on more all star teams. He's like me, just care free and just wanting to play the game. He loved what he did and he played hard every day. He got hurt a lot at the end, I think he separated that shoulder like three or four times, but they were all tough injuries during the call of duty. You knew that whenever you had Herbie and me in the same clubhouse, it was going to be loud and something would always be going on. Herbie always made me laugh, and he didn't even have to try."

"Kent is a fun-loving guy and he always played and conducted himself that way whether he was on or off the field," said Tom Kelly. "He was such a talented hitter and player, and he enjoyed playing the game. He probably wanted to win more than any other player I have managed. He had such a desire and will to win. He was a home grown athlete who was just a great player."

"He grew up with me," said Tony Oliva. "I coached him all the way through the minor leagues and into the big leagues. He was a wonderful player and a great person."

VERNE GAGNE

Verne Gagne was born in Corcoran, Minn., and grew up in Hamel during the Depression, attending a one-room school house. A tremendous athlete, he grew up loving sports. "At the age of 10 I knew that I wanted to be a football player and a wrestler," said Gagne. Later he transferred to Wayzata High School for one year, ultimately graduating from Robbinsdale High School in 1943. There he earned all-state honors in football, and, even though he weighed only 185 pounds, he also won the state heavyweight wrestling championship.

During the early 1940s, because of World War II taking so many young men overseas, the University needed football players. So, Gagne was recruited by Bernie Bierman to play for the Gophers. But his main sport quickly became wrestling. After winning the Big Ten heavyweight wrestling title in 1944 as a freshman, he went into the Marine Corps. There, Gagne also played football for the El Toro Marine team in 1944 and 1945. He returned to the U of M to continue playing football, where, in 1949, the star defensive end was selected to play in the College All-Star Game. And, as a wrestler, Verne became arguably the greatest grappler to ever come out of Minnesota. He went on to win the Big Ten heavyweight championship four times and won two NCAA national championships as both a heavyweight and as a 191-pounder. The two-time All-American also wrestled on the 1948 Olympic team.

"Gopher Football was pretty exciting back in those days," added Gagne. "When we were growing up as kids and listening to the Gopher Football team winning the national championships in the 30's and 40's, every kid wanted to play football for the Gophers. I never dreamt that I would have a chance to go to college. I was very fortunate."

After college he was drafted by the Chicago Bears. But, because Halas wanted him to give up a year of eligibility and sign a contract as a junior, Gagne passed. That next season, however, he signed with Curly Lambeau's Green Bay Packers. Verne played for the Pack throughout the 1949 pre-season, but just before the first regular season game, Lambeau informed him that because the Bears still owned his rights and wouldn't release him, he was ineligible to play. Gagne then said "to heck with football" and went into the sport that would make him one of the most celebrated and recognizable athletes of his day, professional wrestling.

Verne spent a life-time participating and promoting the sport that he loved, a sport that was born in Minneapolis, "All Star Wrestling." Verne was a local celebrity and became a local hero to a lot of people around the country. He was a daily feature in all the newspapers and became synonymous with the sport.

"In pro wrestling back then, there were a lot of great wrestlers like myself, who came out of major universities and wanted to continue," said Gagne. "Sure there were famous guys we wrestled, like Gorgeous George back in the late 40's and early 50's, but back then it was more like collegiate wrestling. Today there are no 'wrestlers' in wrestling."

"We did a TV show called "All Star Wrestling" that we broadcasted from the old Calhoun Beach Hotel, starting in 1950 and going all the way until 1992, never missing a week. The program was syndicated all over the United States, in the far east and all over the world. During the 60's, 70's and 80's it was the highest rated television show in Twin Cities, period. With a 26-share rating, we beat every sit-com, the Vikings, the Twins, everybody. We had no idea that it would grow as big as it did. We even drew the biggest crowd ever at Madison Square Garden. I was traveling the country and making more money than Joe DiMaggio and Mickey Mantle."

The grand grappler retired in 1981 but had more than a few come-backs with his son, and tag-team partner, Greg Gagne. Verne was an entertainer and one of the most successful ones at that. In addition, Vern was always one of the "good guys," making him one of the sport's all-time favorites. Not much has changed either. Still going strong, Vern is still one of the "good guys."

TONY DUNGY

As a Gopher quarterback from 1973-76, Tony Dungy finished his career in Gold Country near the top of almost every passing category. In addition to his incredible on-field performance, he was also a two-time Academic All-Big Ten selection. And, he played Gopher basketball as well. From there Dungy went on to sign with the Pittsburgh Steelers, where he played safety for two seasons. His best season was in 1978, when he posted six interceptions (second in the AFC) and helped to lead his Steelers over the Dallas Cowboys in Super Bowl XIII.

In 1980 Tony returned home to Minnesota, where he took over as the team's defensive backs coach. Soon after that he returned to Pittsburgh, where after a stint as an assistant, he became the league's youngest defensive coordinator at the age of 28. He would stay with the Steelers under Coach Chuck Noll for eight seasons before finally moving on as an assistant with the Kansas City Chiefs. After three years in KC, he came back to Minnesota, this time as a the Vikings' defensive coordinator. From 1992-95 Dungy worked his magic, ultimately turning the Vikings' defense into one of the league's best. His trademark for forcing turnovers became legendary and, as a result, it wasn't long before he got a call from the struggling Tampa Bay Buccaneers, asking him to serve as their head coach. Tony obliged and immediately turned the program around. In 1999, after leading his team to a pair of playoff appearances, he guided his Buc's to the NFC Championship game. Then, in 2002 Dungy left Tampa and headed north to Indianapolis, where he took over as the head coach of the Colts. Dungy, who is as modest as ever, has quietly emerged as one of the league's brightest young head coaches.

"The University of Minnesota is really where I got my start," said Dungy of his alma mater. "I owe a lot to Head Coach Cal Stoll. He helped shape some of my values and some of the things I wanted to do in my life. The 'U' is where I developed a lot of the values that I carry with me today"

Linda Roberts

Linda Roberts was one of the best players ever to perform in Gold Country. During her tenure she held 11 Gopher records, the most of any athlete to play for the Gophers. Linda, who played from 1977 to 1981, competed in 129 games during her career, starting 126 of them, the most of anyone in Gopher history. She also held the career records for most free throws made (426) and most rebounds (1,413). In 1977-78, Roberts pulled down a team record 387 rebounds and also attempted a team record 254 free throws that same year. The next season, Linda sank 21 of 25 free throw attempts against Rhode Island, both team records.

Roberts was twice nominated for the coveted Wade Trophy, was a three-time recipient of the team's MVP award, and three times she won the Minnesota Gopher Award. In 1996 Roberts was rewarded for all of her accomplishment when she was inducted into the Minnesota Women's Athletics Hall of Fame.

Laura Coenen

With 2,044 points, Laura Coenen was, at one point, the all-time leading scorer among both men and women at the U of M. What's even more impressive is the fact she did it all while overcoming a thyroid problem that limited her to just 299 points during her junior season. Coenen still holds several Gopher single-game, season and career records. She scored in double figures in 91 of 102 games and had 10 or more rebounds in 53 games. She earned first team All-American honors in 1983 and 1985, and was also a District IV Kodak All-American as well.

In 1983, as a sophomore, Laura was named as the Big Ten MVP, and in 1985 she was named the Comeback Player of the Year. She was also a Wade Trophy finalist as a senior, emblematic of the nation's top player. In 1986 the women's basketball program made her No. 44 the first jersey ever to be officially retired.

Upon graduation, Coenen played professionally in Germany. Then, wanting to try something different, she returned to the US. and competed on the gold medal winning U.S. handball team at the 1987 Pan Am Games, as well as at the 1988 and 1996 Summer Olympics.

Deb Hunter

Many consider Deb Hunter to be the greatest all-around player in Gopher women's basketball history. Known for her quickness, Deb was always quick to steal the ball and unselfishly dish it to her teammates for the bucket. She owned nine Minnesota records including most career assists and steals. She also held the record for most assists in a game (15), most assists in a season (241), most steals in a game (12), and most steals in a season (139). She also held the records for best field goal percentage in a season (.600), best career field goal percentage (.519), and best career free throw percentage (.829).

The guard could also shoot the ball with great accuracy, as evidenced by her career-high 34 point outburst against Purdue in 1983. That same year, the two-time team MVP received first-team All-Big Ten honors. In 1982 she received honorable mention All-American honors, and in 1983 she was named as a Kodak Region IV selection.

Carol Ann Shudlick

Apple Valley's Carol Ann Shudlick is one of the greatest women's basketball players ever to hail from Minnesota. One of the most highly recruited prep stars in state history, she went on to attend the University of Minnesota. By the time she finished her tenure in Gold Country, she owned eight school records and became the Gophers' all-time leading scorer with 2,097 points. During her senior campaign in 1994, Shudlick became Minnesota's first-ever winner of the Wade Trophy, awarded to the nation's most outstanding senior basketball player.

The three time all-academic Big Ten selection was also the first Gopher ever to be named as a first team Kodak All-American. To top it off she was named as the Big Ten's Player of the Year, the Sports Channel-Chicago Player of the Year, and the Chicago Tribune Silver Basketball Award winner. The Patty Berg Award honoree also received the Big Ten Medal of Honor Award and was even named to every all-tournament team that she participated in that season.

After graduating with a journalism degree, Carol Ann played professional basketball overseas in Madrid, Spain and also with the upstart Columbus franchise of the ABL. She later signed with her hometown WNBA Minnesota Lynx, where she briefly played before retiring.

By 1988, all of Minnesota was still dizzy and hungover from the World Series hoopla that had swept through the state during that magical season a year earlier. So, that next season, people were more interested than ever to see if the club could repeat as world champs. Fans turned out at the Metrodome in droves. In fact, the Twins became the first American League team ever to draw three million fans, as 3,030,672 people passed through the Metrodome turnstiles to watch the reigning champs defend their title. The faithful wanted to see up-close a part of the history, that for many of them, had unfolded before their eyes only on television.

On the field, the 1988 Twins finished with a quite respectable 91-71 record, en route to a second place finish in the American League West. In fact, it was the team's first 90-win season since 1970. Minnesota battled Tony LaRussa's Oakland A's for the better part of the season, but in the end the Athletics were too tough and won the AL crown with an amazing 104 wins.

As a group, the Twins placed second in the major leagues with a collective .274 batting average. Kirby Puckett had another monster year, batting .356 (the highest by a right-handed hitter in the A.L. since Joe DiMaggio's .357 back in 1941), while leading the league in hits with 234. Gary Gaetti hit .301, Hrbek hit .312, and previously-unheralded pitcher Allan Anderson, who was called up from Portland (AAA), won 16 games — while producing the league's lowest ERA at 2.45. In addition, Closer Jeff Reardon notched a club-record 42 saves, good for second in the Majors as well.

As for their skipper, the remarkable Tom Kelly, he reaped the benefits of leading his ballclub to the 1987 World Series and was honored by managing the 1988 All-Star game. He was joined at the All-Star festivities in Cincinnati by Kirby Puckett, Tim Laudner, Gary Gaetti, Jeff Reardon, and Frank Viola — who also just happened to be the starting and winning pitcher for the AL, as they beat the NL, 2-1.

Viola's heroics weren't confined to the 1988 All-Star Game though. He picked up right where he left off in 1987, when he won the World Series MVP, this time winning the coveted Cy Young award as the league's best pitcher. The 1988 season was a dream for Viola as he led the league with 24 wins, posted a 2.64 ERA, and struck-out 193 batters. He also set the Twins record for the all-time best winning percentage that season at .774.

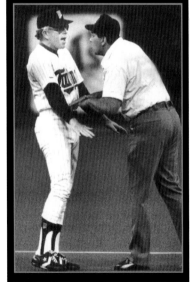

The man ultimately responsible for the success of the team, however, was Manager Tom Kelly. The Twins skipper never made a lot of noise in the dugout, yet was able to lead his team all the way to the promised land occupied by baseball's world champions. Kelly's soft-spoken, 'lead-by-example' attitude filtered throughout the club-house and became infectious with all of his players. He was a stickler for the fun-

damentals, and it was no coincidence that his team committed a league record for the fewest errors (84), while posting a gaudy .986 fielding percentage. T.K. had a reputation of being a fan favorite, a media darling, and all-around good guy. Perhaps the biggest compliment paid to him though was that he was referred to as a "players' manager."

T.K.

Tom Kelly's career has been a long and winding one, with roots that begin right here in Minnesota. Jay Thomas Kelly was born on August 15, 1950, in Graceville, Minn. Baseball had always played a big role in his life because his father, Joe, was a Northern League pitcher during the 1940s and later played in the New York Giants system. His family ultimately moved east, where Tom grew up in New Jersey. He went on to become an outstanding ballplayer at St. Mary's High School in South Amboy, N.J. From there he went on to attend Mesa Community College in Mesa, Ariz., and also Monmouth College in West Long Branch, N.J. Baseball remained a big part of his life as he continued to get better and better at each level that he played at. By now he was getting looked at by scouts and knew that he had a good shot at making it in the big leagues if was just given the opportunity.

T.K. fulfilled a boyhood dream in 1968 when the expansion Seattle Pilots selected him in the fifth round of the Major League Baseball free agent draft. So, he reported to Newark to play in the minor leagues. In his first year he hit an impressive .317, led the league in stolen bases and became an all-star. From there it was off to Clinton and then Jacksonville, until 1971, when he was signed as a free agent by the Minnesota Twins. After spending a year in Charlotte, he began a four-year stint in Tacoma, the Twins triple-A club.

Then, in 1975, Kelly got the call he had been waiting for his entire career — he was going to the show. On May 19th, he got his first major league hit when he singled off Detroit's Joe Coleman. It wasn't a very long stint in the bigs, 127 at bats in 49 games to be exact. But it was something he had dreamed of during his entire career as a ballplayer. So, for a career minor leaguer, the entire big league experience was pretty special to him. He ended up with 23 hits, while driving in 11 batters, scoring another 11 runs and batting a buck-eighty-one. Kelly's lone dinger of his career came off Tigers Pitcher Vern Ruhle.

"It's something you always dreamed about, to play at the major league level," said Kelly. "As a minor leaguer, you were always working towards that goal. I got the opportunity, but I wasn't good enough to stick around. At least, I did have a chance which was great for me, and it is something I will always remember."

After a season at triple-A Rochester, Kelly caught another break. This time he found his calling as he would spend the next three years in Tacoma and Toledo as a player/manager. In 1979 and 1980, he managed a Twins' farm team in Visalia, where he led the club to two consecutive divisional titles. He was also named the California League Manager of the Year for two years in a row. He was then promoted by the Twins to Orlando, where he was named as the Southern League Manager of the Year after guiding his team to the league championship.

In 1983, he got another call to the majors, this time as the new Twins' third base coach, becoming the first Minnesotan to ever

TIMELINE

Watertown's Dennis Koslowski wins a bronze medal on the Olympic wrestling team	Minneapolis' Robert Seguso wins a gold medal on the Olympic doubles tennis team	Laker center Clyde Lovellette is inducted into the Basketball Hall of Fame.	Stewartville's Bart Bardwell wins his third consecutive Twin Cities Marathon - Wheelchair Division	Carleton runner Anna Prineas wins the Division III 3,000M Indoor Track National Championship	Augsburg's Carolyn Ross wins the Division III 400M Dash and 400M Hurdles Indoor Track National Championship	The Concordia Moorhead women's Basketball team wins the Division III National Championship	Augsburg wrestler John Beatty wins the Division III 134 lbs. National Championship	Bemidji State's Liz Mulvihill wins the Division III Indoor Track Shot Put National Championship

104

become a member of the Twins' managerial staff. Then, in 1986, T.K. took over the Twins' managerial duties from a faltering Ray Miller. It would be the start of an historic ride.

In 1987, Kelly became only the fifth manager in baseball history to win a pennant as a rookie when his Twins beat the Cardinals in the World Series. For his efforts the 37-year-old was named as the American League Manager of the Year. It was a tremendous victory for all of Minnesota and T.K. was given much of the credit. And deservedly so, for it was he who acted as the glue which held those players together.

Kelly's heroes won their second World Series over the Atlanta Braves just five years later. Tom thus became first Twins manager ever to lead his club to two divisional titles (and subsequent world championships), and the third manager ever in baseball history to have won two World Series while losing none. In 1991, Kelly again was again named as the American League Manager of the Year. In 1992, Kelly managed the American League All-Star team to a 13-6 victory in San Diego. Fittingly, Kirby Puckett was named as the All-Star Game MVP.

In 2001 T.K. stepped down as the Twins manager and handed the reigns to long-time coach, Ron Gardenhire. When the dust had finally settled, Kelly's career resume was simply amazing. Very quietly he became entrenched as baseball's longest-tenured manager, managing 2,385 games in his nearly 20 years behind the bench in Minnie. In addition, he also became the all-time winningest manager in Minnesota history, having won 1,140 games.

TK also won a pair of World Series' in a span of five years. This may not sound impressive until one realizes that the Chicago Cubs have not won a single World Series since 1908, or the Red Sox since 1918. Kelly will no doubt go down in history as the greatest Twins manager of all time. Period.

"In 1975, I was just so happy to be in the big leagues that it didn't mean much to me right away," said Kelly. "But after being in the organization for 20-some years, I think it's very special, and I put more credence to it now than I did then. The Minnesota Twins have been good to me and my family. I feel like a part of the organization, maybe not an intricate part, but a piece. I feel like it's more of an honor now. We try to convey that point to the players, that it is an honor to wear the Twins' uniform. We think it's important that they represent the uniform as well as they represent themselves and their families."

On his longevity as Twins manager, T.K. was humble: "It just shows that I have had a lot of good players here over the years, and good players make managers look good. You have to remember that a manager is only as good as his players, and I've been very fortunate. I think it's the result of a good Twins minor league system, good scouting and good coaching. It's not just one person, and there are a lot of people involved. The game itself can beat you up. All the time I spent playing and managing in the minor leagues with the bus rides, the traveling, and the wear and tear was tough. I am starting to feel the 'longevity' of the game maybe a little more — it's catching up to me. But I am grateful to be where I am, and I do think it is an honor to be the manager of the Minnesota Twins."

On the 1987 World Series:
"Being it was my first full year as a manager, it was a very special thing. It was a new experience for me getting into the playoffs and into the World Series. Typically, we are somewhat afraid and apprehensive about new experiences because we don't know what to expect. There was a lot of cautious optimism surrounding the whole experience. The playoffs were a little more nerve-racking than the Big Dance, but, all in all, it was an incredible experience."

On the 1991 World Series:
"By 1991, we knew what to expect, so I think I enjoyed that one a little bit more because I knew what was going on. I wasn't as nervous this go around as I was in 1987. I frequently use the phrase 'storybook-like' to describe the games that series, because each game was like turning a page in a book to find out what was going to happen. Having the games come down to the ninth inning and the last at-bat was incredible. We were very fortunate to win, because either team could have easily won. What was really rewarding was the fact

that we went from last place in 1990 to first place in 1991. It was also very special to me because we proved that smaller market teams could still win it all."

Twins Tombstone:
"He was someone who worked hard to get where he got, all the time knowing that good things can happen to someone who works hard."

TRIBUTES
"T.K. will always be my favorite manager," said Kent Hrbek. "He's such a great guy. He was like my mother at the ballpark. He knew how I was feeling when I walked in the door just by looking at me. I just think he is an awesome manager, and I just love the guy."

"I consider Tom to be the most fair manager that I ever played for," said Jack Morris. "He let everybody know that there were no superstars on his team, and the players respected that."

"We go way back," said Kirby Puckett. "I played for T.K. back when I was in the instructional leagues, and we always got along well. All he ever asked of me was that I gave a 100 percent, and I've always listened to whatever he had to say."

"Even before I came here I had the greatest respect for Tom Kelly," said Paul Molitor. "The way that his teams would perform in last-place seasons, or in championship seasons, was remarkably consistent, and that definitely relates to the manager's control and leadership. Coming to the Twins, he surpassed my expectations as a manager in the manner of how he handles teams, rosters, and the ups and downs of a typical season."

"We played together for a season, and we had a very good relationship," said Rod Carew. "I liked him then, and I like him today. I like the way that he goes about getting his players ready to play. He's a player's manager, and all of the players that have played for him, speak very highly of him. He allows his players to enjoy playing the game, and I think that is important. Tom goes about handling all the personalities on the team in a very professional and fun way, and that's why he is successful."

"He is a great person," said Tony Oliva. "He wants you to work hard, and he knows a lot about baseball. I don't have enough good words for Tom Kelly, he is just a great man."

"I have the utmost respect for him, and I think he was the best manager in the game," said Jim Kaat. "I think the way he molded that 1987 team was incredible."

Doug Woog has become a coaching icon at the University of Minnesota. Perhaps the Minnesota equivalent to the Notre Dame football coach, Woog achieved great success in Gold Country, and he did it all with Minnesota kids. That alone may have been the single greatest tradition in all of college sports, yet it was something that was constantly used against him as the reason why his teams never won the NCAA championship. Always the bridesmaid, never the bride.

Woog sent six Gopher squads to the NCAA Final Four, but none was able to bring home the hardware. One thing is for certain though, the closest the Wooger ever came to getting that monkey off of his back came in 1989, when the Gophers lost a heart-breaker to Harvard at the Civic Center in St. Paul.

The Gophers were coming off of their first WCHA championship under Woog and were expected to finish even better than the previous year's Final Four semifinal loss to Maine. Things looked promising for the team at the start of the season. Dave Snuggerud and Tom Chorske had returned from the Olympics and led the team in scoring; the reigning Hobey Baker Award recipient, Robb Stauber, was in goal; and returning leadership could be found in such players as: Randy Skarda, Todd Richards, Lance Pitlick, Luke Johnson, Jason Miller, Ken Gernander, Dean Williamson, Peter and Ben Hankinson, Larry Olimb, Sean Fabian, Grant Bischoff, Jon Anderson and David Espe. In addition, there were two highly regarded freshmen in Tom Pederson and Travis Richards, who both made decent contributions.

The Gophers opened the season by winning 12 of their first 14 games, including sweeps over Wisconsin, Denver, North Dakota and Colorado College. The team was awesome that year, losing back-to-back games only once. They went on to win the WCHA crown by a seven-point margin over Michigan Tech, making it back-to-back McNaughton Cups for the first time in the history of Gopher hockey. With an impressive 34-11-3 overall record (26-6-2 in conference play), they then went on to meet Colorado College in the first round of the WCHA Playoffs. There, they swept the Tigers, 5-4 and 7-1. Then, at the WCHA version of the Final Four at St. Paul's Civic Center, Denver and Wisconsin both upset the Gophers, each winning by a goal.

Minnesota then swept the Badgers in the ensuing NCAA playoffs, also in the Civic Center, by a pair of matching 4-2 scores. This now set up a rematch with their old adversaries from the East — Maine, in the NCAA Final Four. Revenge was sweet for the Maroon and Gold, as they crushed the Black Bears, 7-4, behind Jon Anderson's hat trick.

So, the stage was set. The Gophers, on their home-ice, would now face Harvard for all the marbles in the NCAA hockey championship game. Minnesota jumped out to a 1-0 lead when Jon Anderson went downstairs,

stick-side, off a sweet Benny Hankinson pass at 6:24 in the first. Then Harvard's Ted Donato and Lane MacDonald each scored in the second to pull ahead by one. Bloomington's Jason Miller evened it up at two apiece when he scored his fourth goal in three games, off a Lance Pitlick rebound. In the third both teams exchanged power-plays until Ted Donato tallied again to put the Crimson back on top. But, like so many times before that season, the Gophers came back. This time on a Pete Hankinson wrister to make it three apiece. The buzzer sounded and with that, both teams headed to overtime.

Now, just as the fourth period got underway, Randy Skarda skated down the ice, made a move and took a slapper at Harvard Goalie Chuckie Hughes. All you could hear was a dull plunk. That could've only meant one thing: "Skarda hit the pipe. Half an inch and we're champions," said Coach Woog. Then, at 4:16 of sudden-death, Harvard's Ed Krayer got a gift. After Stauber stopped a missile that took him out of position, Krayer picked up the rebound that landed on his stick and slid a back-hander under his sprawled out pads. It was a dagger sent right into the collective heart of Gopher fans everywhere.

Stauber, who stood on his head the entire game, stopping 24 shots and earning every bit of his Hobey Baker award from the year before, sat motionless on the ice in utter disbelief. As the nearly 16,000 Minnesota fans sat in silence, shock set in as they pondered just how close they had come to winning it all. Many in the large crowd thought that the 4-3 decision might have been the best college hockey game that they had ever viewed.

"I don't like to think about it," said Stauber, who led the WCHA in goaltending. "I remember the shot, and I reached for the rebound but missed it. There were so many things in that game I would've done differently. Sometimes in big pressure games you tend to be more reserved and play more conservatively than you'd like to. But, that was a great year, and we had nothing to be ashamed of that season at all."

Randy Skarda had come within one inch of getting that 900-pound gorilla off Doug Woog's back on that fabled day in April. "It was probably the most crushing defeat of my life," said Skarda. "Kenny Gernander set me up, and I hit the inside of the pipe. Afterwards I couldn't leave my house for two weeks, I was devastated."

As for the Wooger, the thought of coming that close was something he will never forget. "We had the advantage of being at home in St. Paul that year, and the disadvantage of not getting to bed the night before until 3:00am because of all the fans," said Woog. "I remember Hankinson scoring late and tying it up for us as we came back, and I can still see Randy Skarda making a rush on their goalie and the sound of hitting the pipe. That one pipe changed the history of Gopher hockey forever. It delayed the inevitable that we will win a national championship. There is always something that puts humility into the pot, and that's the one you gotta answer every week: 'When will we win the big one?'"

The Wooger

Doug Woog grew up playing hockey in St. Paul. Before graduating in 1962 from South St. Paul High School, he earned all-state hockey honors for an amazing three consecutive years. He also starred in football and was a good student to boot. From there Doug fulfilled a life-long dream by accepting a scholarship to play for the U of M and learn the game from one of the all-time great coaches, John Mariucci.

Carleton runner Anna Prineas wins the Division III 5,000M and 10,000M National Championships	Augsburg's Carolyn Ross wins the Division III 400M, 400M Dash & 400M Hurdles Indoor Track National Championship	Vikings tackle Keith Millard is named as the NFL's Defensive Player of the Year	Wayzata's Greg LeMond wins his second Tour De France Bicycle race	St. Paul native Robert H. Paradise is enshrined into the U.S. Hockey Hall of Fame	Warroad native Roger Christian, a former hockey great, is enshrined into the U.S. Hockey Hall of Fame	The state's largest brown trout is caught by Smithfield's Landis Bullock on Lake Superior: 16 lb., 12 oz.	The Vikings pull the trigger on the worst trade in the history of sports, sending the Dallas Cowboys five players and eight draft picks for Herschel Walker.	The Gopher Basketball team makes it to the Sweet Sixteen before ultimately losing to the Duke University Blue Devils

Woog went on to a fabulous career in Gold Country, earning All-American honors his junior season after leading the team in scoring. He was named as captain for his senior season en route to leading the team to a 16-12-0 record, and a second place finish in the WCHA. For his efforts he was named the team's MVP. From 1964-1966 the speedy center scored 48 goals and 53 assists for 101 career points. Doug graduated with honors from the U of M in 1967.

From there he went on to play for the 1967 U.S. National Team and was a candidate for the 1968 U.S. Olympic team. It was now off to the real world for the Wooger though as he began teaching Geography while coaching football and hockey at Hopkins West Junior High School. Then in the fall of 1968, he took a job at his high school alma mater, where he became the head soccer coach as well as an assistant on both the hockey and baseball teams. While coaching at South St. Paul, his soccer program won six conference titles and twice finished as runner-up's for the state championship.

From 1971 through 1977 he branched out to coach the St. Paul Vulcans and the Minnesota Junior Stars, who he led to two U.S. Junior National titles. During that time, in 1973, Doug fulfilled another dream when he earned his Master's Degree in guidance and counseling from St. Thomas University.

In 1978, Woog was chosen to lead the West Team in the U.S. Olympic Festival, where his squad won the gold medal. At the 1989 Olympic Festival Woog duplicated that feat by winning the gold medal with his South squad. He was the assistant coach of the 1982 U.S. National Junior Team and then served as an assistant coach for the 1984 Olympic team that competed in Sarajevo, Yugoslavia as well. In 1985 Woog coached the U.S. National Junior Team; in 1987 he served as the assistant coach for Team USA in the 1987 Canada Cup; and in 1989 he was the head coach of the of U.S. Select 17 team.

In 1985 the "Wooger" returned to his college alma-mater. There, he guided the Golden Gophers to seven league championships (four regular season and three post-season) over his illustrious 14-year career. During his tenure in Gold Country the Gophers were among the nation's very best, garnering WCHA Final Four/Five and NCAA appearances in 12 of 14 seasons, posting seven 30-win seasons, and appearing in six NCAA Final Fours. In 1999 Woog resigned as the University of Minnesota's head hockey coach to take an assistant athletic director position at the school. He would leave as the all-time winningest coach with a gaudy 389-187-40 record (.664).

Today, in addition to his work at Minnesota, Woog is a television analyst for Gopher Hockey games and also runs his own summer hockey camp in Breezy Point, Minn. In addition, he served as a national committee member for the AHAUS and was chairman of the National Skating Committee for USA Hockey. Woog has also been the chairperson for the Wakota Arena Board, along with being a past president of the South St. Paul Coaches Association. He has been instrumental in initiating and maintaining youth athletic organizations in his community and is an overall good friend to hockey.

Doug has been involved with amateur hockey, his community, as well as local charities at all levels throughout his career. He is a solid coach, a wonderful person, and a great supporter of Minnesota hockey. In 2002 Doug was honored by being inducted into the U.S. Hockey Hall of Fame in Eveleth. Presently, Doug and his wife Jan reside in St. Paul. They have three children: Amy, Steve and Dan.

What did it mean for you to be a Gopher?
"It was a life-long dream come true for me to be able to play for the Gophers. The fact that we had scholarships was just a means to an end. Back then there weren't that many opportunities for us after college as far as hockey was concerned, with only six NHL teams and all. So, we played for the love of the game and were happy to get to school to be

able to make a living. Yeah, being a Gopher was pretty special."

On Coaching:
"To see how it has grown and prospered and how the people of Minnesota have grasped on to hockey is unbelievable. People realize that Gopher Hockey is associated with quality, and to be the coach of that was a real honor. There's a pedigree and an aura for kids to play Gopher hockey. Starting with Herbie in the 70's, our program has been consistent and we have had a lot of wins. This program was doing fine as far as their ability to win before I got here, and it didn't need me to come over.

"What I have gave the program is a level of respectability in terms of how I communicate to the public. I think I gave some consistency to the educational value of the sport and brought some credibility to the program in terms of the media and television. It has also become very profitable for the University in terms of dollars, and our program alone generated television revenues that probably exceed the entire WCHA put together. The new rink was a statement to the people and to thank them for their support."

On only recruiting Minnesota kids:
"I was committed to going with the Minnesota kid as long as I was the coach. We provided opportunities for Minnesota kids to get professional jobs, and we got more kids than any other school in the country playing professionally. I'm proud of the fact that kids in Minnesota grow up dreaming about being Gophers, and they have great role models to look up to and watch. But, it got tougher with Duluth, St. Cloud, Mankato and Bemidji all competing for Minnesota kids. A kid might rather have played on the first line somewhere else rather than to play on our third or fourth. That's how we were recruited against, but I wouldn't change a thing."

Gopher Tombstone:
"I want to be thought of as someone that won with dignity and performed with dignity."

TRIBUTES
"I coached Doug on the Gopher freshman team, and he was a great player," said Lou Nanne. "Doug has been a very successful coach at the U and he's a guy that's really committed to the program. He had his own feelings on how he wanted to develop it with Minnesota kids, but he was successful for the most part and he had a wonderful run."

"They don't have to win the title to be successful," said John Mayasich. "I would say there are American born players out there who could help him. I wouldn't say don't go out and get them to have them contribute, but I think we can be competitive with the Minnesota kids. It takes 20 players, and a hot goalie to win it.

"I played for Doug with the Vulcans," said former NHL star Paul Holmgren. "He was a terrific coach as well as a tremendous player. For a small guy, he could be really intimidating. I enjoyed playing for him, and I think he's done a great job with his teams."

Expectations were at an all-time high for the 1989-90 Gophers, a team which entered the season ranked 20th in the nation — the program's first national ranking since finishing seventh back in 1982. After a summer exhibition tour of Australia, the team, which was pretty banged up, returned home to begin its non-conference schedule. They also returned home to face another distraction — this one from the ever-probing NCAA, which this time alleged that former University administrator Luther Darville had misappropriated University funds by issuing payments to both football and basketball players. The case lingered on and proved to be a real distraction.

Moving on, the team went out and posted a 9-1 non-conference record that year — losing just their season opener on a buzzer-beater, 66-64, to the Bearcats of Cincinnati. From there the Gophers, led by Melvin Newbern's 27 points, went out and crushed the No. 4-ranked Illini, 91-74, in the Big Ten opener. They dropped two straight after that to both Purdue, 86-78, and Michigan, 87-83, but rebounded to spank Northwestern, 97-75, and Ohio State, 83-78. Their momentum was short-lived though, as the team got upset that next week in Madison, 77-75, on a last-second Badger dunk. Back at the Barn three nights later, Minnesota upended Iowa, 84-72, thanks to Willie Burton's 21 points and 10 rebounds, and Richard Coffey's 14 points and 13 rebounds. They followed that up with a huge 108-89 home win over the Hoosiers on Super Bowl Sunday, with Burton, Coffey, Lynch, Newbern, Shikenjanski and Bond, all scoring in double figures. It was the most points ever scored against a Bobby Knight-coached team.

After losing to Illinois, Minnesota came home to the old Barn where they knocked off Purdue in one of the season's best games. Newbern was the hero du jour, nailing a turn-around jumper in the final seconds to seal a 73-72 victory for the nearly 17,000 Gopher faithful in attendance. The Gophers then climbed up to the No. 17 spot in the AP poll after beating Michigan State, 79-74, but once again fell to earth following a 99-72 spanking by the Illini. After edging Purdue, 73-72, on yet another Newbern jumper in the game's final seconds, Minnesota was beaten by Michigan, 77-73, to abruptly end their impressive 12-game home winning-streak. They rebounded to beat Northwestern, 90-72, followed by Iowa, 102-80, and Indiana, 75-70, to make it 20 wins for the season. But, they wound up losing their final two conference games of the year to eventual Big Ten champion Michigan State, on Senior Night, in an overtime heartbreaker, 75-73, and also to Ohio State, 93-83, despite a career-high 31 points from Willie Burton. (The five Gopher seniors — Burton, Richard Coffey, Connell Lewis, Newbern, and Jim Shikenjanski took a farewell lap around Williams Arena on Senior Night, and Willie whooped it up big-time by getting up on a chair and waving a towel to all the

fans for his final curtain call.)

With that, the No. 6 seeded Gophers received another NCAA bid for the Big Dance. Their first opponent: the University of Texas-El Paso, at the Southeast Regional in Richmond, Virginia. There, behind Kevin Lynch's 18 points and Coffey's 11 rebounds, the Gophs hung on to win ugly, in overtime, 64-61.

"It was awesome because everything that Coach Haskins had said and told us began to really come true," said Burton. "The hard work, running in the mornings, being put down all the time by the fans at the other schools, it was tough. But it all came together and we were a force to be reckoned with."

Two nights later the team faced the Northern Iowa Panthers in the round of 32. There, behind Burton's 36 points and 12 rebounds, Minnesota rolled to an 81-78 victory — earning their second trip to the "Sweet 16" in as many years. With the loss of Duke still fresh in their minds from the year before, the Gophers then headed to the New Orleans Super Dome, to take on the mighty Syracuse Orangemen. Led by future NBA stars Billy Owens and Derrick Coleman, the Gophers knew they would have their hands full.

"My club has come a long way," Haskins said before the game. "They've shown great improvement and they remember getting to the Sweet 16 a year ago only to get whipped by Duke. They haven't forgotten that and they'll carry that memory into the Syracuse game."

What happened next though, was pure magic. Down by four at half-time, the Gophs came back and shot nearly 80% from the field in the second half, en route to an impressive 82-75 victory. Five players scored in double figures, including 20 from Newbern, 18 from Lynch, and 10 from seven-foot Center Bob Martin of Apple Valley. Even the ex-paratrooper, Richard Coffey, got into the act, snatching 12 boards as well.

The next step for the Cinderella Gophers was their first-ever appearance in the Tourney's "Elite Eight," where they would face off against the Georgia Tech Yellow Jackets, and their "Lethal Weapon Three" trio of sharpshooters: Kenny Anderson, Dennis Scott and Brian Oliver. In what would go down as one of the greatest games in Gopher history, Minnesota came out and played valiantly.

"I finally realized, in my heart, that if we lost, we would never play together again as a team," said Burton. "We didn't want it to be over, so we went out there with destruction on our minds. We just didn't want the ride to end."

It was a back and forth contest all day, but in the end, the Jackets came out on top — thanks in large part to the fact that the referees wound up issuing an unbelievable 35 free throws to Georgia Tech, compared to just 11 for the Gophers. That disparity would ultimately cost the Maroon and Gold the game. Despite that fact though, the team battled down to the wire, and refused to roll over.

Willie led the Minnesota attack, and the Gophers jumped out to a 12-point lead. But the Yellow Jackets closed the gap and trailed by only two at halftime, 49-47. Later in the fourth, now down 93-88 with just seven seconds left on the clock, Burton dribbled down and pulled up from the top of the circle to nail a dramatic three-pointer to make it 93-91. Then, when Tech got the ball in-bounds, the Gophers quickly fouled Guard Kenny Anderson. Anderson, who would go on to NBA stardom, stepped up and nervously missed the front end of the one-and-one free-throw.

With that, Richard Coffey, the rebounding machine, grabbed

TIMELINE									
St. Thomas' Ben Bautch wins the Division III 35 lb throw Indoor Track National Championship	Hamline runner Betty Hansen wins the Division III 800M National Championship	St. Olaf's Christy Aker, Andrea McCarty, Amanda Mason & Julie Keller, win the Division III 200 yd Medley Relay National Championship	St. Thomas runner Gretchen Farkas wins the Division III 5,000M National Championship	Gustavus Adolphus wins the Division III Women's Tennis National Championship	Concordia's Kristin Kuehl wins the Division III Discus National Championship	St. Thomas runner Michael Brown wins the Division III 1,500M Run National Championship	St. Thomas runner Trish Tinucci wins the Division III 400M Hurdles National Championship	Beth Daniel wins the LPGA's Northgate Classic, played at Brooklyn Park's Edinburgh Golf Course	The expansion Timberwolves set the NBA's all-time attendance record with over one million fans seeing them at the Dome

the ball and heaved it to an awaiting Mario Green, who in turn, tossed it to a streaking Kevin Lynch at mid-court. Lynch then dribbled down to the right corner of the court, and with time running out, stopped and fired an off-balanced three-pointer over the top of the outstretched Forward Johnny McNeil's fingertips. At that moment, it was like slow-motion. The ball just hung in the air for what seemed like an eternity. Then, as the buzzer sounded, the ball bounced harmlessly off the front of the rim — crushing the collective dreams of the millions of Gopher fans who were tuned in across the nation. Minnesota's Final Four dreams were over as the team watched in disbelief.

It was a sad ending for an otherwise brilliant season. The improbable 23-9 Gophers had shocked the world and emerged as a real contender. And, for seniors Willie Burton, Melvin Newbern, Jim Shikenjanski, Richard Coffey, Connell Lewis, as well as Coach Haskins — the collective group of newcomers who came into a program in shambles back in 1986 — it was the end of an amazing ride. They had joined a ravaged and ragged Gopher program, and, as seniors, stepped down from active intercollegiate play as saviors, giving Gold Country fans two magical back-to-back trips to the Big Dance.

For Burton, who emerged as one of the program's most beloved all-time players, it was a very sad and emotional ending to an incredible career in Gold Country. "It almost went in... It really bothers me because it was a good shot, and he barely missed it," said Willie B., who, after averaging 24.4 points per game, was named to the All-Big Ten Team and received honorable mention All-American honors. "Personally, I think that the last shot was just too much pressure for him (Lynch) to take. I mean at the time he was open, going top speed and he had a look at the hoop, but it was a lot of pressure to deal with. When Kevin missed, I was so bummed out because I didn't want it all to end like that. I remember, after the game, I stopped and looked hard at everyone. I took a picture of everybody together in my mind for one last time."

"They shot 25 more foul shots than we did, and they won by two," added Burton, when asked about the blatantly lopsided refereeing during that game. "I had 35 points and never took a foul shot the entire game. Maybe it was because those refs were from the ACC, Georgia Tech's home conference? We just couldn't get a break that night, and it was frustrating because the referees just wouldn't blow their whistles for us."

Several thousand fans showed up at the Twin Cities International Airport following the Georgia Tech loss to show their appreciation for an unbelievably entertaining and exciting season. The Gophers had captured the hearts and imaginations of the state of Minnesota that season, finally putting the program back on track and into the national spotlight.

Willie B.
Born on May 26, 1968, Willie Burton grew up in inner city Detroit playing baseball, basketball, football and track. Solid in both athletics and academics in high school, he graduated with a 3.6 GPA. His prep athletic credentials were also impressive. He earned three letters in basketball and two in baseball. In basketball, where he averaged 22 points and 12 rebounds per game his senior year, he was a two-time All-Stater as well as an All-Detroit selection.

From there Willie decided to attend the U of M, where, after four glorious years, he was named to the All-Big Ten Team, received honorable mention All-American honors, and for three straight years was voted as the team MVP. Willie finished his Gopher career averaging 19.3 points per game with 6.4 rebounds. Upon graduation, he ranked ninth in career rebounding (705), sixth in career blocks, (79) and was third on the all-time scoring list, with 1,800 points, behind only Mychal Thompson and Voshon Lenard.

"The reason I went to the University of Minnesota was because it had more to offer after basket-ball," said Burton. "I took a recruiting visit to the Twin Cities and just fell in love with the region. I thought it was a beautiful place. The people got along, I loved the mix of the cultures that were there, and it was just a dream place as far as where I would like to live once my basket-ball days were over. I knew in my heart that it was the place that I wanted to be. I signed a letter of intent for Coach Dutcher one month before the program's troubles in Madison. But, through it all, I never said I would leave because my goal was to be a Gopher and to live in Minnesota. Coach Haskins and I started out together and we just started the basketball program over. All of us seniors came in together when Clem took it over, and that's why we were so close to each other. We went through a lot of scrutiny after all that happened, but when it was all over we showed the world we could go a long way."

After his memorable career with Minnesota he went on to become a first-round NBA pick, where he was selected with the ninth overall pick of the first round by the Miami Heat. He would later find himself playing for the Philadelphia 76ers, where he scored a career high 50 points during a game in 1995. He bounced around with several teams after that, including Atlanta, San Antonio and Charlotte, and has been a steady pro player ever since, averaging better than 10 points and three rebounds per game over his career. His quick first step and fine post-up ability made him one of the best-ever to hail from Minnesota.

What did it mean for you to be a Gopher?
"Playing at the University of Minnesota was the most meaningful thing in my life. The time I spent on campus was the best four years of my life. My teammates and I were like brothers who all genuinely cared about each other. I loved it there. I lived in Centennial Hall for all four years that I was there, and it was great. I still proudly wear a University of Minnesota baseball cap because I've earned the right to wear it. I can't put into words what the University of Minnesota meant to me. The experience was just awesome."

On Minnesota fans:
"My relationship with the Gopher fans was incredible. I think I bonded with them because they genuinely cared. When I came to Minnesota, in my freshman year, we were getting clobbered, but the fans still came and filled up Williams Arena. I will never forget that, and neither did my teammates. That was the reason we went out and we played the way we played."

Gopher Tombstone:
"I want to be remembered as being a good person with a good heart. Someone who genuinely appreciated the game, the fans, and the every-day people of the Twin Cities. You could say that I was one of the nicest guys in the world until the game started, and then I had a hockey player's mentality. I didn't want the spotlight, I just wanted to play."

| The Gopher Men's Gymnastics team finishes as runner-up's in the NCAA Finals hosted at Williams Arena | Gopher second baseman Brian Raabe is named to the All-American baseball team | Gopher catcher Dan Wilson is named to the All-American baseball team | UMD goalie Chad Erickson is named to the All-American hockey team | Eveleth native Connie Pleban, former Olympian and National Team member, is enshrined into the U.S. Hockey Hall of Fame | The Twin Cities hosts the U.S. Olympic Festival | Wayzata's Greg LeMond wins his third Tour de France Bicycle race | The Gund brothers sell the North Stars to a group that ultimately sells the team to Norm Green | Eveleth native Willard Ikola, a former goaltender great, is enshrined into the U.S. Hockey Hall of Fame. The former Olympian coached the Edina Hornets to an amazing 600-140-38 record, making him the state's all-time leader. | TIMELINE |

Well, the good thing about finishing in last place, is that the only place to go from there is up. And that is exactly what the 1991 "worst to first" Twins did. These Twins were a full-circle success story that will forever be remembered for Jack Morris' World Series heroics.

After the teams' best pre-season ever at their new spring training facility, the Lee County Sports Complex in Ft. Myers, Fla., (they moved after playing 55 years in Orlando), the squad slithered to a pathetic 2-9 start, courtesy of a pair of ugly West Coast swings. They rebounded though, and stayed strong under Manager Tom Kelly. Early on in the season, many Twins fans had a good feeling about this new bunch of kids. Some even went as far as predicting an inkling of destiny when the Twins tore through the American League that summer, reeling off 15 wins in a row en route to winning the West. One of the reasons for the clubs' success was due to the unbelievable pitching of Scott Erickson, who, at one point, won a club-record 12 consecutive games en route to closing the gap on first-place Texas.

The 95-67 Twins then went on to easily win the ALCS, beating the Toronto Blue Jays four games to one, to earn a trip back to the World Series. One of the highlights of the ALCS came in Game Three, when pinch hitter Mike Pagliarulo won it for the Twins on a home run to right in the 10th inning. Kirby then homered in Games Four and Five to seal the deal for Minnie.

Now, in the World Series, the Twins would face another cellar-dwelling team from 1990, the resurrected Atlanta Braves, who had beaten the Pittsburgh Pirates, 4-3, in the NLCS. The World Series got off to a great start for Minnesota. The Twins won Games One and Two at the Metrodome, 5-2, and 3-2, respectively. Game Two was highlighted by Kent Hrbek's now infamous all-star wrestling tag-out of Atlanta's Ron Gant on first base. In addition, Chili Davis hit a two-run homer in the first inning, while Scott Leius added one of his own in the eighth. The Homer Hankies were back and so were the Twins.

The series then shifted south, to "Hot-Lanta" where the Braves won three straight, highlighted by a 14-run shellacking of the Twins in Game Five. Up three games to two, the Braves then returned to the Dome to try and wrap it up. Kirby Puckett thought differently though and played the game of his life in Game Six. First, Puck robbed Braves outfielder Ron Gant of a home run in the third on a Ringling Brothers-like grab off the center field Plexiglas. Then, after a Terry Pendleton homer to tie it up, Puckett regained the lead for his twins on a sacrifice fly. Atlanta knotted the score again in the seventh to send it into extra innings, only to see Kirby take over in the 11th. There, with the game tied at three, Kirby stepped up and hit a towering shot off Atlanta's Charlie Liebrandt that was without question the greatest home run in Twins history, giving

Minnesota a thrilling 4-3 win and evening the series at three games apiece. "We'll see you tomorrow night!", said legendary broadcaster Jack Buck following the big hit.

The locker room was surprisingly calm before Game Seven. In fact, the clubhouse television sets were all tuned to football games when the players arrived — so they could set their fantasy football line-up's, believe it or not. Manager Tom Kelly had named Jack Morris as his starter in the most important baseball game of 1991, while Atlanta's Bobby Cox countered with John Smoltz, a Detroit native who grew up worshipping that very Jack Morris.

The game was a back and forth pitching duel that went scoreless into the top of the eighth. That inning would prove to be one of the most tense of the series. With Lonnie Smith on first, Terry Pendleton hit a liner to the gap. Then, Smith, who was running on the pitch, mysteriously eased up and slowed down as he was rounding second. Replays showed that Twins Second Baseman Chuck Knoblauch put on a fabulous deke, faking that he was going to catch the ball coming in from the outfield. Little did Smith know however, that the ball was, in reality, still rolling around in the outfield at the time. By this time he realized what was going on he could only advance to third. Gant then hit a squibber to Hrbek for an easy out, followed by Sid Bream who hit into a 3-2-3 double play to end the inning. Morris leaped into the air pumping his fist up to the sky as the Twins had dodged a huge bullet.

Through the tenth, the Twins and Braves matched donuts on the scoreboard. It had now become only the second Game Seven in World Series history to reach extra innings. Kelly would later say: "There was no thought of changing pitchers. Morris could rest in November; the outcome of October was his to decide."

Dan Gladden then led off the last of the 10th with a broken-bat base-hit that he somehow managed to stretch into a double. Knoblauch, who would be named Rookie of the Year that season, had just one sacrifice bunt all year. He got his second on that night though by moving Gladden to third. The Twins were now 90 feet from their second title ever. After intentionally walking Kirby and Herbie to load the bases, Gene Larkin now stood at home plate for the at-bat of his life. Larkin jumped on the first pitch and then hit a fly ball to left-center. Atlanta Left Fielder Brian Hunter, who was playing in, could only look on helplessly as the ball flew over his head and landed on the turf. The rest, they say, is history.

"The Twins are gonna win the World Series!", shouted announcer Jack Buck after the huge hit. "The Twins have won it!"

Fittingly, Morris was the first to grab Gladden as he touched the plate. Two mobs of players, one at home and the other at first, eventually merged in the center of the diamond in a sea of chaos. The hated Atlanta Braves had been tomahawk-chopped by the Minnesota Twins in one of the greatest World Series' ever.

With five games decided by a single run, this series was, in a word, incredible. In front of 55,118 rabid fans under the teflon tent, Morris had pitched a seven-hit, 10-inning, 1-0 shut-out gem. Jack won two pivotal games for his Twins in the Series, and they were the most important — the first and the last. His performance in Game Seven will go down in baseball lore as possibly the greatest ever. His two wins coupled with an amazing 1.17 ERA, earned him the Series MVP.

"I wasn't really aware of what was going on historically when I was in that game, because my focus was strictly on getting out the Atlanta Braves and making sure that the fans at the stadium and every-

Augsburg College wins the Division III wrestling National Championship	St. Thomas' Ben Bautch wins the Division III 35 lb throw Indoor Track National Championship	Augsburg wrestler Chester Grauberger wins the Division III Heavyweight National Championship	UMD runner Jodi Swenson wins the Division III High Jump Indoor Track National Championship	Concordia Moorhead hurler Kristin Kuehl wins the Division III Discus National Championship	St. Thomas runner Leonard Jones wins the Division III Long Jump Indoor Track National Championship	Twins general manager Andy MacPhail is named as Major League Baseball's Executive of the Year	Gophers Wrestler Marty Morgan wins the NCAA's 177 lb. National Championship	Deephaven's David Wheaton makes it to the U.S. Open Tennis semi-finals before losing to Boris Becker	The St. Thomas University Women's Basketball team wins the Division III National Championship

one else watching would not go away disappointed," said Morris. "I've only watched the replay of Game Seven a few times because I get kind of choked up. I've recognized and realized that as soon as the game was over that it was probably my best day ever. Nothing else would compare in my career, and I recognize that I could never do any better than that, so I should just take it and appreciate it."

Amazingly, when Jack was asked just what was going through his mind when he took the mound in that 10th inning, it was something all Minnesota sports fans could relate to. Here's what he had to say: "I don't mean this in any derogatory way, but Fran Tarkenton had a big influence in that game. I remember growing up in Minnesota and watching the Vikings lose their third Super Bowl. I know that it is unfair for me to say that Fran was the reason they lost, because obviously it's a team sport. But you know, I think there were so many people that were disappointed in the Vikings, and particularly in Tarkenton, because he was the leader. The quarterback and the pitcher are considered to be the team leaders, and they are the people with the most influence on the outcome of a game. As I sat there, and the game progressed, I just couldn't help but think of the Vikings and those Super Bowl losses. During that seventh game, I looked up in the Metrodome crowd and saw all these people, just exhausted from screaming and cheering, but going absolutely berserk, wanting a winner so bad, and a sort of calmness came over me. It was like something was driving me from that point on, and I just refused to let the fans of Minnesota go home disappointed. I knew that we were going to win, if it took all night long. We weren't going to be losers, we weren't going to be the Vikings."

Tiger Jack
From the sandlots of St. Paul, Jack Morris attended Highland Park High School and then went on to play college ball in Utah, at Brigham Young University. From there he was drafted by the Detroit Tigers, and went on to become one of baseball's all-time greatest pitchers. He was the only pitcher to have won 14 or more games in each year of the 1980s and three times he won 20 or more games in a season. Although some were critical of his perennially high ERA, Jack would shrug and say that he was paid to win games, and that his contract did not stipulate that the margin of victory be by a shut-out or by a score of 6-5.

The winningest pitcher of the 1980s, Jack Morris was a workhorse, notching double-digit wins in 14 of his 16 full seasons in the majors, while finishing in the top 10 in Cy Young Award voting seven times. He won a trio of World Series titles as well, winning his first in 1984 with Detroit, his second in 1991 with his hometown Twins, and his third in 1992 with Toronto. He was also very durable, being relegated to the disabled list just twice in his 18-year career. He had a solid fastball, a hard slider, and excellent split-finger to make his pitching arsenal one of the best ever. Morris even hurled a no-hitter against the Chicago White Sox on April 7, 1984, matching the earliest date in a season a no-no was thrown. Among the most reliable pitchers in history, he holds the AL record with 515 straight starts, once going more than 10 seasons with just one missed start. An excellent all-around athlete who was often used as a pinch runner, he also holds the major league career record for put-outs by a pitcher, with 387.

"Every ballplayer whether they signed out of high school or college probably has some kind of dream of playing with their hometown team," said Jack of his return home to Minnie. "And I was no different. After being drafted by Detroit and playing there through the years, I thought I might finish my career there. But as the political football of baseball goes, you gotta do what you gotta do, and when the opportunity arose to come play for Minnesota, it was like a dream come true. The 1991 season was a fairy tale."

Jack had spent 14 seasons with the Tigers before coming back

to Minnie — where he wound up staying for just one year.

"As players, we don't always recognize what points of light come across our paths until after they're gone," said Jack. "I never had any intention of leaving Minnesota when I was here. I never wanted to, but I understand what happened. Mr. Pohlad had to save his money for a guy named Kirby Puckett. He lost several great players and really the nucleus of a ballclub because of the fan appeal of one player. I'm not blaming anybody, Kirby did what he had to do, and he was justified in doing it. Carl Pohlad did what he had to do, and all of us players who left the Twins did what we had to do. It was just unfortunate that we couldn't have kept it together because I wanted nothing more than to win it all again with that same group of guys."

After his heroics with the Twins, Jack signed with Toronto, followed by stints in Cleveland and Cincinnati before finally hanging up his spikes at the tender age of 40. In 1994 Jack opted to come home yet again and become the ace of the Northern League's St. Paul Saints, where he ended up leading the league with a 2.61 ERA. He retired during that season in St. Paul though, to spend more time working his ranch in Montana. When it was all said and done Jack finished his illustrious career with 254 victories and 175 complete games. He will hopefully find his way to the Hall of Fame. He is definitely worthy.

Twins Tombstone:
"I think people need to know that I loved the game of baseball. I really appreciate and respect the game and had fun playing it. I realize that I am rough around the edges. I've never really been well versed enough to be smooth and sensitive to everybody, because I was so driven in one direction — and that was to win. I blocked out a lot of distractions. It was the price of winning. In the process I turned off a few people. I just want people to know that I gave it all I had, and winning was most important to me. I think that when you are a perfectionist like myself, the only way you're justified in your effort is to win. It creates a huge burden on you — and you become your own worst enemy as well as your own worst critic."

TRIBUTES
"Jack was a very competitive player," said Tom Kelly. "He was intense about his job and was very workman-like. He knew how to win and took the ball every four or five games. He was a great pitcher."

"His game seven performance was the most jacked up I have ever seen a pitcher pitch in a ballgame, and I don't think there will ever be another game pitched like it," said Kent Hrbek. "To me that was the single most gutsy performance by a pitcher that I have ever seen."

"Tiger Jack was probably one of the most intense people that I have ever been around," said Kirby Puckett. "He was a warrior and gave you everything he had. Whatever he had going, he would use to get it done, and that's the mark of a great pitcher. He protected us as well. If another pitcher threw at us, he would throw at their players — and that is the way the game is supposed to be played. He took the ball no matter what and wouldn't miss a start. I respected that."

TIMELINE

| St. Thomas runner Trish Tinucci wins the Division III 400M Hurdles National Championship | St. Cloud's Janice Ettle wins her second Grandma's Marathon | Payne Stewart wins the U.S. Open over Scott Simpson at Chaska's Hazeltine National Golf Course | Gopher shortstop Brent Gates is named to the All-American baseball team | Twins' second baseman Chuck Knoblauch is named as the American League's Rookie of the Year | Eveleth native John Matchefts is enshrined into the U.S. Hockey Hall of Fame | Gustavus tennis doubles partners Dave Jussila & Ryan Skanse win the Division III National Championship | Unbridled, owned by Bloomington's Frances Genter, wins the Kentucky Derby (sired Derby winner Unbridled's Song, as well) | After beating Chicago, St. Louis and Edmonton, the North Stars lose the Stanley Cup to Pittsburgh, four games to two. | Jan Stenerud, a Vikings kicker from 1984-85, is inducted into the Pro Football Hall of Fame |

KIRBY PUCKETT
THE PUCK INKS THE DEAL OF A LIFETIME

In 1992 the Twins made big news even before the season started when the finally signed Kirby Puckett to a new, fat contract during a live, made-for-TV extravaganza. There had been Kirby sightings in Boston, New York, and even one in Des Moines. Would he stick around and finish his illustrious career with Minnesota? That suspenseful question was answered on December 4th, when, in a circus-like atmosphere, he inked a five-year, $30-million deal that made him the highest paid player in baseball. (Incidentally, that dubious honor ended just for a few hours later when Barry Bonds signed with the San Francisco Giants.)

That season was, by all accounts, a success. The Twins went 90-72 to finish in second place, but just couldn't catch the Oakland A's down the stretch. They did, however, achieve several record-setting individual and team accomplishments. Among them was Tom Kelly winning his 523rd game, the most of any Twins manager in team history. There was also Kirby Puckett's fabulous year which included reaching 200 hits for the fifth time; knocking in 100+ runs and 100+ RBI's and hitting over .300 for the seventh time in nine seasons. In addition, he also belted out three grand slams en route to twice being named as the American League Player of the Month. Other Twins to notch the 100-run plateau included Shane Mack and Chuck Knoblauch, who each had good years as well. Finally, Reliever Rick Aguilera got his 109th save to become the Twins' all-time saves leader as well.

The Puck

Kirby Puckett was born March 14, 1961, in Chicago. He grew up in the Robert Taylor Homes, a public housing project on Chicago's tough South Side, just down the road from the White Sox's Comiskey Park. Kirby's dad, William, was a postal worker, and his mom, Catherine, stayed at home in their 14th floor apartment to take care of Puckett's nine brothers and sisters. Kirby usually came home from school, did his homework, and then went out to play ball.

"It was a long haul, coming from where I came from," said Kirby. "I can remember as a kid I broke up so many lamps and windows up in my room hitting the ball around — even with a wadded up sock ball. I was just playing baseball, just doing what I loved to do."

In 1973, his family moved out of the projects and into a better neighborhood outside of the city. Kirby would begin school at Calumet High School where he would emerge as a star third baseman. Kirby found it hard to get noticed by any scouts or college recruiters though.

"Not too many scouts came to the ghetto to see me play." said Puck. "We didn't even have a field, so we just played in a forest preserve that didn't have any fences or anything."

Kirby persevered through it all though and graduated in the top 20 per-cent of his class.

That summer, Kirby took an assembly line job working at the Ford Motor Plant on 130th street in Chicago. "There were only two buses a day that went out there," said Puckett, "so if you missed one, you were done for. It took 90 days to get into the union, and I remember I was there for something like 89 days, and then they laid me off."

Kirby's luck would soon change. At a Kansas City Royals free agent try-out camp, amongst several hundred hopeful kids, Bradley University Coach, Dewey Kalmer, offered him a scholarship. Puckett did well at Bradley, even making the all-conference team. Then, one year later, in 1982, tragedy struck when his father died of a heart attack.

Kirby wanted to be closer to home and his family, so he left Bradley and enrolled at Triton Community College in River Grove, Ill. Puckett came into his own there, finally getting the attention of some scouts. But most of them just weren't impressed. They thought he was too short to play in the big leagues. Then his luck changed again when Jim Rantz, the Twins' director of minor leagues, took a chance on the fireplug-shaped ballplayer.

"He stood out," Rantz said. "It wasn't because he had a home run, a double, stole two bases, threw a guy out at home, or had a shaved head, either. What stood out was the enthusiasm he had for the game on a miserably hot night, when everybody was dog tired. That was the thing you noticed."

Once he was in organized baseball, Kirby tore up the minor leagues — first in Elizabethton, then in Visalia and finally in Toledo. Virtually everywhere he went, he won the league's MVP award. The Twins soon realized that they had themselves a diamond in the rough.

Then, while playing for Toledo in Old Orchard Beach, Me., Kirby got the call to come up to the "show." Mud Hens Manager Cal Ermer called him in to tell him the good news and that he had to get on a plane to Los Angeles right away.

"I was called up, and I was so nervous," said Kirby. "The plane was five hours late and by the time I finally got to the airport, there was nobody there to meet me. I had no idea how far the stadium was, and I only had $10 to my name. So when I got in a cab and told the driver that I needed to get to Anaheim for my first game, the driver gave me a funny look. By the time we got there, the fare was $60. So, I left all my stuff in the cab, and he waited for me to run in and get some money. I ran in and got my meal money from the Twins, telling them it was $85, so I could tip the driver $25 bucks. I still wish I had remembered to get the taxi driver's name because I was really grateful."

Kirby didn't disappoint either. On May 8, 1984, Puck became the sixth player in AL history to get four hits in his big league debut. He had arrived. Puckett's career was a storied one. There were two World Series and two ticker-tape parades down the streets of Minneapolis. There was Game Six in the 1987 "Cinderella-Series," against the Cardinals, when he got four hits and scored four runs to carry the Twins. And there was the "Worst-to-First Series" of 1991, when, in that Game Six, Kirby had one of the greatest games of his life. He first robbed Braves Outfielder Ron Gant of a home run on a Ringling Brothers-like grab off the plexiglass, and then, in the 11th inning, with the game tied at three, Kirby stepped up and the greatest home run in Twins history off Atlanta's Charlie Liebrandt to ice it.

His bat didn't always make for heroics though. There was the Tony Oliva-inspired home-run epiphany during spring training in 1986, when, during batting practice in Orlando, Puck hit 10 consecu-

Minnetonka's Janice Klecker wins her second consecutive Twin Cities Marathon	The Metrodome hosts Superbowl XXVI as the Redskins beat the Buffalo Bills	The NCAA Basketball Final Four is held at the Metrodome and Duke beats Michigan for the National Championship	St. Paul's Amy Peterson wins an Olympic Short Track Speedskating silver medal in the 3,000M Relay	Watertown's Dennis Koslowski wins a silver medal on the Olympic wrestling team	Garden Grove's Janet Mulholland wins a bronze medal on the Olympic Volleyball team	Mankato State's Charles Zheng wins the Division II Pole Vault Indoor Track National Championship	Mankato State runner Dale Bahr wins the Division II 800 Meter Run Indoor Track National Championship	Gustavus Adolphus tennis player Jon Lindquist wins the Individual Division III National Championship

tive balls over the fence. However, after each hit, he heard a strange sound. "Little did I know that they had some kind of auto show going on next door," said Puckett. A motorcycle cop then drove out onto the field where he told Kirby, "Swing at one more pitch, and I'll put you in jail!" Kirby's monster fly-balls had been smashing windshields!

Kirby was incredible. Only Willie Keeler had more hits in his first 10 years in the big leagues (2,065) than Puckett (2,040). In 12 seasons and 7,244 at bats with Minnesota, Kirby finished with a career batting average of .318, which included 2,304 hits, 1,071 runs, 1,085 RBIs and 207 homers. He won a league MVP, played in 10 All-Star games, was named an All-Star game MVP, finished with a .989 fielding percentage, and earned six Gold Gloves. He was also awarded the treasured 1996 Roberto Clemente Man of the Year Award by Major League Baseball for his outstanding community service.

Tragically, in 1996, Kirby's career was ended due to irreversible retina damage in his right eye. Amazingly, his last trip to the disabled list was also his first. "I knew that baseball wasn't going to last forever," said Kirby. "It was great living in a fairy tale for 12 years, and I enjoyed every minute of it. I just thank God that I got the chance to live out the dream I had since I was five years old. Isn't that the way life's supposed to be?"

Puckett went on to add that he found it remarkable that anyone could feel sorry for a man who, in 1997, despite not being able to play, was in the final year of a $6-million contract. He grants himself but one regret, he would have liked to have reached 3,000 hits.

His trademark smile, goatee, and bald head, are only some of the reasons why Kirby is the most popular athlete in Minnesota sports history. His boyish enthusiasm for baseball is his greatest trait and his positive attitude not only inspired his teammates but the fans as well. From his patented after-the-hit "bat-flip," to his in-depth explanations on his hitting style, which included: "I'm just trying to get my hacks man..." and "I'm just seeing the ball good man...", he was the best.

Maybe it had to do with his cartoon-like physique, or possibly it's his funny-to-say name which was highlighted in his appearance on the the Late Show with David Letterman, where he read the "Top 10 Ways to Mispronounce Kirby Puckett" (Number Seven: Turkey Bucket). There were two Wheaties boxes and even "Kirby Puckett Pancakes." "Man, those pancakes were good," said Kirby, "just add milk and eggs, and you're ready to go..."

Perhaps former Twins General Manager Andy MacPhail put it best when he said: "If Kirby Puckett had played his career in New York or Los Angeles, they would be building statues of him today."

Then, in August of 2001, Kirby, who went on to serve as the Twins' Executive Vice President of Baseball, was inducted into the Baseball Hall of Fame in Cooperstown, N.Y., alongside his teammate and friend, Dave Winfield. It was an amazing day for all of Minnesota baseball as the Gopher State was thrust into the national limelight for all to see. For Kirby, it was a fitting tribute to one of the best ever.

"My first love was always baseball, and it still is baseball," said Kirby. "I've lived a dream, man, and being a Twin means everything to me." "I was a gamer, and I came to play every day. I never took the game for granted. Not for one day. I had a smile on my face, but when I stepped between the white lines, I tried to hurt you because that was my job, man. I took my job very seriously because I knew that people paid their hard earned money to come see me play, and I wanted to give them the best possible show that I could every time I stepped onto a baseball field. I always did the little things that could give my team the edge, and that's why my teammates loved me."

"No matter what, with the game on the line, I wanted to be the man," he added. "I thrived on that, and that's what made me the player that I was. I never thought of myself as a superstar or anything like that, I'm just Kirby. My mom used to always tell me what goes up has

to always come down, and sooner or later, all those people that you treated badly on the way up, you see again on the way down. I've remembered those words."

TRIBUTES
"I loved to play against this guy because he would be your friend just before the game, but when you got on the field he would do everything he could to try to stop you," said Paul Molitor. "That's what I liked about him. That and because he had fun doing it. I could see the positive affect that he had on other players who he had played with over the years. For him to have to prematurely retire was such a strong disappointment for me, knowing that I wouldn't have the chance to play with him. He was just a great player and is a tremendous person."

"He is one of the most energetic, giving, influential playmakers that I ever played with," said Dave Winfield. "He was a dynamite player, who was ready to go every day. He was always up and always a positive influence. I think it hurt me more when he couldn't play than when I couldn't play any more. He was one of my best friends in the game, and I really enjoyed working with him. I understand now why he was able to carry that franchise over all these years."

"I have played with a lot of great guys and a lot of great players over the years, but never have I played with anybody more popular than Kirby," said Jack Morris. "Pitching against him you always felt a sense of accomplishment if you got him out because he wanted to hit you every time. Just by his actions he could show the whole world his love and appreciation for the people and the game of baseball."

"He's in a class by himself," said Tom Kelly. "He added more charisma on and off the field to the game than any player, maybe ever. He is such an outgoing and friendly person, and always had time to say hello to everybody he had contact with, and I think that is a very special quality. He was a terrific player, worked very hard and had a lot of good things happen for him. He has a magical quality about him that will always be remembered."

"He loved to play the game," said Kent Hrbek. "I watched him hit for 12 years from the on-deck circle, and I don't care what they threw at him, he could hit everything. He was definitely the best hitter I ever saw in baseball. Kirby is a great friend, and what more can I say about a player who was the greatest there ever was?"

"He is just a great person, and it was a real pleasure and a gift from him for me to be his coach," said Tony Oliva. "He would always come to the ballpark ready to work, smiling all the time. He is great, just great. I don't have enough words to describe Kirby because he is so special to me."

"Kirby and I have developed a very good friendship over the years," said Rod Carew. "He's made a name for himself on and off the field, and he does so much for the community. He is such a happy-go-lucky, fun-loving guy, and he went out and enjoyed playing the game of baseball. Kirby is the type of individual who never forgot who he was or where he came from. He never thought he was better than anyone else because he was a baseball player and an athlete."

TIMELINE

JOHNNY "BLOOD" MCNALLY

Born on November 27, 1903, in New Richmond, Wis., Johnny "Blood" McNally was one of football's all-time greatest players. He was also one of the game's most colorful characters, playing the game on his own terms and having fun every step of the way.

At six feet and 185 pounds, McNally was a lightning quick running back with hands that made him one of the finest receivers in the National Football League. He could throw, catch, run and punt with the best in the business. And, on the other side of the line, he was a ball hawking mad-man and a deadly tackler. He played pro football for a total of 22 years, but is most remembered in Minnesota football history for his exploits both as a student at St. John's University and also with the Duluth Eskimos in the late 1920s.

McNally grew up in New Richmond, Wis., the son of a wealthy family of newspaper publishers and paper mill owners. Incredibly, he never played any organized sports throughout high school, primarily because he was too small. He graduated at the age of 14, and after a year of prep school, was shipped off to St. John's University for some good Catholic disciplinary teachings. His father had also attended the school in the late 1800s, but ironically, was expelled for a harmless tobacco spitting incident which inadvertently found the back-side of an unsuspecting professor.

Johnny sprouted at St. John's and quickly got involved in sports. After three years, he had earned letters in football baseball, track and basketball. But then he decided he needed a change of pace, so he transferred to Notre Dame.

In the spring of 1924 he received a 60-day suspension from Notre Dame for disciplinary problems, so he decided to make it permanent. From there he headed back to Minneapolis, where he and one of his football buddies from St. John's, Ralph Hanson, got jobs at a local newspaper. But it didn't pay much. So they decided to pick up some extra money by playing football in a semipro city league for a team called the East 26th Street Liberties. But McNally didn't want to lose his remaining year of college eligibility by playing pro ball, so he assumed an alias.

"I used to get around town on my own motorcycle then, and so we both hopped on it and headed out to where this team practiced, some playground in back of a factory," said Blood. "On the way there, we passed a movie theater on Hennepin Avenue and up on the marquee I saw the name of the movie that was playing, 'Blood and Sand with Rudolph Valentino.' Ralph was behind me on the motorcycle and I turned my head and shouted, "That's it. I'll be Blood and you be Sand!" And so we went to the practice, tried out, and made the team, as Johnny Blood and Ralph Sand. And, of course, I kept it as a football name from that time on."

After helping the Liberties win the city championship, Blood ventured up to Michigan's Upper Peninsula to play a year of pro ball with the Ironwood Panthers. From there he signed with his first NFL team, the Milwaukee Badgers, in 1925. Blood continued to bounce around after that, with his next stop being in Duluth, where he and Ernie Nevers forged one of the greatest backfields in history.

"Signing with the Duluth Eskimos is one of my great memories," said Blood, "because it was there that I got to play with Ernie Nevers, who was the star. No, he was the team! Ernie was a fine man, I admired and respected him. He was a fiery kind of guy, a different specimen really, and we had a pretty good football team up there, considering it was Duluth and not Chicago or New York."

He remained with the Eskimos for two seasons, and then signed on with the Pottsville Maroons. After a year there he joined the team that he would become most synonymous with, the Green Bay Packers, where he was a fixture on several NFL championship teams for some nine seasons.

In negotiating his first contract with Packers Owner Curly Lambeau, Blood asked for $100 a game. Lambeau countered with an even better offer of $110 a game, provided he agreed to a clause in his contract that forbade him from drinking after the Tuesday of each week there was a game scheduled. Blood had a compromise of his own. He would accept $100 if he could booze it up through Wednesday. Lambeau agreed.

Blood tore up the league, and even scored 13 touchdowns in 1931, a single-season record at the time. Before Don Hutson joined him on the Packer roster, Blood owned nearly all the major NFL pass-receiving records. It was also in Green Bay where Blood became famous for his soldier of fortune antics as well. It was said that he broke as many training rules as he did tackles, and ignored team curfews just as he did Prohibition.

"I was reckless on the football field," confessed Blood. "Reckless in a lot of things, I guess. I liked to have a good time back then: women, travel, a little drinking, loved to spend money. I had a lot of experiences. I was very uninhibited, that way all my life, even as a little kid. My mom would teach me Shakespeare and my dad taught me sports. So I was a semi-split personality."

Once during a game, Blood checked into the huddle with a pass play directly from Lambeau. He then turned to Quarterback Arnie Herber and said: "Arnie, throw it in the direction of Mother Pierre's whorehouse." Herber, like Blood, was no stranger to the Green Bay nightlife, and knew he was going to be headed for the goal post at the northeast end of the stadium. The pass was there, and so was Blood for the touchdown.

Missed curfews and broken rules were just part of his daily routine though. One time, when the Packers were leaving for a pivotal game in Chicago against the Bears, Lambeau realized that Blood had missed the train. Then, shortly after pulling out of Green Bay, the train came to a sudden halt. The players then opened their windows and saw Blood, who had parked his car right smack in the middle of the railroad tracks to stop the steaming locomotive. With that, he moved his car, and jumped on board as if nothing had happened.

In 1937, Blood, after one too many run-ins with old Curly, moved on, this time to Pittsburgh. There, he became the player/coach for the Pirates (they would later be known as the Steelers). His debut was something the steel city fans will never forget, as he took the opening kickoff 92 yards for a touchdown against their cross-state rivals, the Philadelphia Eagles.

After a couple of years in Pittsburgh, Blood drifted to Kenosha and played there in 1941. From there he found himself in the Air Force, which took him to the China-India-Burma theater of operations as a sergeant and cryptographer. He returned to Green Bay in 1945, and at the age of 42, played what would be his final season of pro football.

Blood was a newspaper man's dream come true. Whether he was hopping freight trains for kicks, or gallivanting to all hours of the night, he was a character. From all of his travels and exploits he was eventually dubbed as the "Vagabond Halfback," a nickname that appropriately stuck for a man who had wandered all over the world. Whether in China, or in a Havana jail (for only one night), he was a legend.

When it was all said and done, he had managed to cram in 22 years of professional football. In addition, the four-time All-NFL halfback tallied 59 touchdowns both rushing, receiving and passing and nearly 400 points in 15 seasons with five NFL teams. With that, he decided to go back to school. That's right, 26 years later he returned to St. John's to finish his degree and begin his new career as a teacher and coach. He was later replaced by another legendary football coach, John Gagliardi, who came to Collegeville 1953 and has been there ever since.

A fabulous athlete and notorious free spirit, Blood was later enshrined as a charter member of the Pro Football Hall of Fame in 1963. Once referred to as a "Peter Pan who would never shed his eternal youth," Johnny Blood was a legendary figure in the early days of pro football. A proud playboy of the pro football world in the '20s and '30s, his slashing runs and amazing pass-catching abilities were simply ahead of his time. He died the day after his 82nd birthday on November 28, 1985, in Palm Springs, Calif.

ERNIE NEVERS

Ernie Nevers was one of the greatest football heroes our country has ever known. The speedy blonde-haired fullback could do it all. He ran, passed, kicked, punted, returned kicks and punts, called signals, and played a mean cornerback position on defense. He revolutionized the game, and even saved the once fledgling NFL from going broke way back in 1926, when he came home to play in one of the most storied football seasons of all time with the upstart Duluth Eskimos.

Born on June 11, 1903, in Willow River, Minn., Ernie later moved to Superior, Wis. It was at Superior Central High School where he blossomed into a three-sport star in football, baseball and basketball. At the age of 16 his folks moved to California, where Ernie graduated from Santa Rosa High School. After graduation he attended Stanford, and soon became a featured triple-threat fullback in Pop Warner's explosive double wing offense. The once timid teenager was now a household name throughout America.

"As a youngster I was very shy," confessed Nevers. "I was scared to death of people. But football gave me an outlet for my emotions. You get the chance to go man-to-man and see if you can stand up against the best they can throw at you. On a football field I was just a different person."

Nevers, a two-time All-American selection, had been a headliner all through his collegiate career, but he reached superhuman status during the 1925 Rose Bowl against Notre Dame and the vaunted Four Horsemen. There, against the better wishes of his doctor, he played through one sprained and one broken ankle. With a pair of tin-snips and a hammer, Coach Warner concocted a crude artificial ankle brace out of sheet aluminum and rubber inner tubing, and taped it to Nevers' lower legs. Amazingly, Ernie played the entire 60 minutes, rushed for 114 yards on his two bum-hoofs, and even registering half of the team's tackles on defense. He played valiantly, but came up short though, as the Irish won, 27-10. That next year, against California, in his final college game, the workhorse handled the ball on every offensive play but three.

Pop Warner, who coached both Nevers and the legendary Jim Thorpe, was once asked who was the better player of the two. "Nevers," Warner quickly replied. "He could do everything Thorpe could do and he tried harder. No man ever gave more of himself than Ernie Nevers."

By the time the football season was over with during his senior year, Ernie was in big demand. So, with a semester of school remaining, he decided to turn pro. His first gig was for $25,000 to play in a series of all-star games against the New York Giants in Florida. Shortly thereafter, he signed a pro basketball deal for a Chicago team in a league that was a forerunner to the NBA. Then, that Spring he signed a $10,000 pro baseball contract as a pitcher with the St. Louis Browns. But after a year, he decided to get back to the gridiron and suit up for his old high school pal, Ole Haugsrud, and his upstart NFL Duluth Eskimos. There, he got a $15,000 contract plus 10% of the gate, to serve as the team's player/coach. Haugsrud even renamed his team as the "Ernie Nevers' Eskimos" in his honor. More importantly though, his presence, credibility and star-power single-handedly saved the NFL from going broke.

Ernie's two-year stint in Duluth was epic. In 1926 alone, the Eskimos played 29 games, 28 of them on the road, and traveled nearly 20,000 miles. Nevers played all but 29 of the total minutes for that season, with those idle minutes coming after he ruptured his appendix. Nevers set five league marks for rushing, passing, and scoring that year, as the team barnstormed throughout the country. The Eskimos folded in 1928 (they became the Washington Redskins) and Ernie headed back to coach for a year under Pop Warner at Stanford. He came back in 1929 though, this time with the Chicago Cardinals.

Nevers played for the Cardinals from 1929-1931, also serving as player/coach for the latter two years. His most memorable moment in the Windy City came on Thanksgiving Day, 1929, when the Cards played the cross-town Bears, and their star running back, Red Grange, at Comiskey Park for the City Championship. Nevers came out, smashed over the Bear's goal-line six times, and kicked four extra points. The final score: Nevers 40, Bears 6. That's right, he scored all 40 points by himself! And, to prove it was no fluke, he scored all of his team's points again in a 19-0 win over Dayton that next Sunday.

"Ernie was probably the first of the triple-threat backs," said Grange. "He could run, kick and pass. He was a star through and through. Guys like Nevers and Bronko Nagurski would have played the game for nothing."

In 1931, after suffering too many nagging injuries, the five-time All-NFL star hung up the cleats for good. He stayed on as a coach though, through the 1937 season, and again in 1939. His final numbers were awesome. In his five NFL seasons, he passed for 25 touchdowns, rushed for 38 touchdowns, kicked seven field goals, nailed 52 extra points, and tallied 301 career points. Not bad for just 54 games of work.

He made one final coaching stint in 1946, when he led the ill-starred Chicago Rockets in the All American Football League. He later moved to California, where among other business interests, he became the director of the California Clippers, Oakland's pro soccer team.

Once referred to as "America's all-time one-man team," Ernie Nevers was, in a word, amazing. He was to the NFL what Gale Sayers, Walter Payton and Emmitt Smith later exemplified. In 1963 Nevers was inducted as a charter member of the Pro Football Hall of Fame. Many years later Sports Illustrated called Nevers the "best college player of all time." He died on May 3, 1976, in San Rafael, Calif., at the age of 73, ironically, just six weeks after his old friend, Ole Haugsrud, had passed away.

In 1993 Minnesota saw the return of one of its most incredible native sons, Dave Winfield. The greatest all-around athlete to ever hail from the Gopher State, "Winny" came home that year to get the 3,000th hit of his illustrious career. Fresh off his World Series run north of the border in Toronto, Winny was the lone bright-spot on an otherwise mediocre Twins season. The big day came on September 16th, when Dave got hit No. 3,000 off Oakland's ace closer, Dennis Eckersley, becoming only the 19th player in major league history to achieve that coveted plateau.

"It was great," said Winfield. "I was so glad to come home and to have been able to accomplish such a major milestone in front of my home crowd in the Metrodome. That was definitely a special event for me in my career, and it's something that I will always remember."

Winny's achievement wasn't the only highlight, however, as Kent Hrbek reached 1,000 RBI's, and Brian Harper became just fourth catcher in more than four decades to hit .300 in three consecutive seasons as well. To top it off, on July 13th, in Baltimore, Kirby Puckett earned All-Star Game MVP honors by hitting a homer and an RBI double in the mid-summer classic. Closer Rick Aguilera also pitched well in the bullpen, but Scott Erickson led the Majors in losses, with 19. Overall, Minnesota finished with a 71-91 record, which left them tied for fifth place with the Angels.

Winny

Dave Winfield is the greatest athlete ever to hail from the great state of Minnesota. Dave grew up in St. Paul loving sports and after a phenomenal prep career at St. Paul Central High School, Winfield opted to stay close to home and attend the University of Minnesota. There, he went on to pitch for legendary Coach Dick Siebert on a baseball scholarship. He was eventually "discovered" by Gopher Basketball Coach Bill Musselman while playing in an intramural basketball league on campus. The Gopher junior varsity basketball team needed some tough competition to practice against, and since Winfield's intramural team, the "Soulful Strutters" were campus champs, a scrimmage was arranged. There, upon seeing Winfield's incredible athleticism, Musselman immediately made the six-foot-six forward a two-sport star at the U of M.

"I switched from a baseball scholarship to a basketball scholarship," recalled Winfield. "Baseball was only partial, and I needed a full ride. A poor kid from St. Paul… so I switched, and the rest is history."

Making the jump to the hardcourt, Winfield played two seasons with the Gopher basketball team, becoming a starter on the 1971-72 team that went 18-7 and won the Big Ten championship — the school's first in 53 years. His big break though, ironically enough, came on the heels of the now infamous "Ohio State Brawl," in which several players were suspended from the team. Thrust into the starting lineup as a member of the notorious "Iron-Five" squad, Winny went on to average 6.9 points per game that season. Then, in 1972-73, he averaged 10.5 points per game en route to leading the Gophers to a 21-5 record — good for second in the Big Ten.

"Dave is one of the most extraordinary athletes that I have ever been around in my life," Coach Musselman later recalled. "He is one of the hardest working people, and one of the most sincere athletes that I have ever seen. For 20 years, the first thing that I checked every day during the baseball season was Dave's box score from wherever he was playing. We are good friends, and I think the world of Dave. I have so much respect for him, because he was on a Gopher baseball scholarship and didn't have to play basketball. What he sacrificed knowing that he had a career in baseball was incredible. I mean he could have gotten injured. I have never seen anybody play harder than Dave Winfield. He had the most incredible endurance and was the best rebounder I have ever seen. When he was 28, he told me he was going to play baseball until he was 45, and I think he finally retired at 44. He took great care of himself, and his combination of speed and strength was just awesome."

Winfield's Gopher sports career was nothing short of incredible. On the diamond Winfield was a three-time All-Big Ten pitcher and was a career .353 hitter. In 1973, he led the Gophers to the Big Ten title, and was selected as an All-American as well as the MVP of the College World Series. As a pitcher, his 19-4 career record afforded him an amazing .826 winning percentage. He finished with 229 career strikeouts, second only to Paul Giel's 243, and his single season record of 109 strikeouts stood for nearly 25 years. (The University of Minnesota baseball program has since honored the former great by giving the Dave Winfield Pitcher of the Year Award to the team's top annual hurler.)

"For me, I was a baseball player first," said Winfield. "But I loved playing basketball for the Gophers as well, and I was lucky enough to play both sports. I really liked all the guys on the basketball squad, and we had a lot of good competitors on that team. Mentally and physically I thought I was ready, and each game I thought I got better. It was here and now, and we just had a good time. That's why we were successful."

"He is truly an amazing athlete and, as our captain, he was a strong team leader," recalled Dick Siebert. "I don't know of any sport he can't excel at. I remember when David asked for a half-hour off from baseball practice to compete with his buddies in an intramural track meet. He had never before high jumped, and all he did was place first, going 6-foot 6-inches while still in his baseball uniform. He may be the finest all-around athlete I have coached, or for that matter to ever compete for Minnesota. To top it all off he was also a fine student."

Upon graduating from the U of M in 1973, Winfield found himself with several post-graduate options. He is one of the few persons in the history of sports to be drafted in all three professional major sports. He was taken in baseball by the San Diego Padres, in basketball by the NBA's Atlanta Hawks as well as the ABA's Utah Stars, and in football by the Minnesota Vikings.

"In football, they drafted me strictly as an athlete," said Winfield. "I was six-foot-six and 230 pounds with good hands, speed, and strength. The Vikings officials figured they could make me into a

TIMELINE

The Gopher Basketball team beats Georgetown University for the N.I.T. Championship In New York's Madison Square Garden	The Augsburg University Wrestling team wins the Division III National Championship	Bemidji State beats Mercyhurst College for the Division III Hockey National Championship	Augsburg wrestler Gary Kroells wins the 158 lb. National Championship	Augsburg wrestler Joe Hoialmen wins the 134 lb. National Championship	Edina's John Harris wins golf's National Amateur Championship	St. Thomas runner Kelly Copps wins the Division III 10,000M National Championship	UMD hurler Kerrick Johnson wins the Division II Discuss National Championship	Augsburg wrestler Nick Fornicoia wins the 118 lb. National Championship	St. Thomas' Pat Ahern wins the Discuss and the 35lb throw Indoor Track National Championships

116

tight end. Who knows? It would have been great to have caught some of those Fran Tarkenton passes! There's no question that I made the right choice though, and I would have had a short career playing football."

Not surprisingly, Winfield chose baseball, going directly to the big-leagues to join the Padres, where he batted .277 in his first year. (Not bad for a guy drafted as a pitcher!) In 1979, he became the first Padre voted to the All-Star Game starting lineup. Then, in 1980 he signed with the New York Yankees and became the richest man in professional sports. He stayed with the Bronx Bombers until being traded to the California Angels in 1990. He signed with the Toronto Blue Jays in 1991 and won a World Series with that club in 1992. Then, in 1993, he came home to join the Twins, where, on September 16th, Dave got his 3,000 hit off of Oakland's vaunted relief pitcher, Dennis Eckersley.

"He was just a super athlete and a classy human being," said Tom Kelly of his time in Minnesota. "He was very, very athletic, and the things he could do at his age were remarkable. He conducted himself and carried himself with such class. He has such a wonderful attitude and so much professionalism. I really enjoyed having him here as a Twin. His 3,000th hit was another new experience for me. We were trying to get him to get it at home by spacing out his at-bats, and when it finally happened, it was a thrill for all of us."

And, while he opted to leave that next season to pursue another pennant with the Cleveland Indians, he certainly made Minnesota proud. Spanning nearly a quarter of a century, two countries, two leagues, and six cities, Winfield has done it all. The 22-year veteran of six teams and 12-time all-star won seven Gold Gloves and six Silver Bat awards. He amassed more hits (3,110) than Babe Ruth, more home runs (475) than Joe DiMaggio, and more RBIs (1,833) than both Mickey Mantle or Reggie Jackson. He is one of only five players with over 3,000 hits, 450 homers, and 200 stolen bases.

In the summer of 2001, Winny was finally given his due when he was inducted into the Baseball Hall of Fame, alongside fellow Minnesota sports icon Kirby Puckett. It was a special day for all of Minnesota as Winfield spoke eloquently about his life and the game of baseball. His amazing career had finally come full circle and his good teammate and friend, Kirby Puckett, was right there by his side. An all-star and fan-favorite who played hard well into his forties, Winny will always be remembered as one of the game's great ones.

"I always looked at baseball three ways," said Winfield. "It was a game, a science, and a business. I used it as a springboard to do the other things that I am doing in life such as the Dave Winfield Foundation. I met a lot of people, traveled the world, and have done a lot of great things. I have become a role model, if you will, for a lot of young people. I think I have become someone that people listen to and they respected the way I went about my work, and I am proud of that. It seemed that the better I played, the more I was able to accomplish."

Off the field, his accomplishments are equally impressive: He served on the board of President Bill Clinton's National Service Program. He was a Williams Scholar at the U of M. He received the first Branch Rickey Community Service Award, and he was given baseball's coveted Roberto Clemente Award.

Now Dave devotes much of his time to what might be considered to be his crown jewel of achievements, the Winfield Foundation — a non-profit foundation, which for more than a quarter century has been a reflection of his commitment to children. Winny has always been a very popular athlete and role model and has given of himself long before it became fashionable. His foundation's message to kids isn't "be a superstar" but rather "be the best that you can be." His generous monetary gifts, contributions of time, creativity, and commitment are immeasurable. He has traveled coast to coast to conduct drug-prevention assemblies and seminars. His organization has gener-

ated and distributed millions of dollars, and worked with four presidential administrations, government, organizations, corporations, media, celebrities, and every-day people to bring forth grassroots pro-grams that have touched countless thousands on a one-to-one basis.

One of Minnesota's most precious of native sons, Dave Winfield is without question the greatest all-around athlete to ever hail from the Gopher State.

On Coming Home
"It was a real pleasure to play for the Minnesota Twins. Minnesota is a place that I really wanted to play at during some point in time over my baseball career. I just didn't know if it would ever happen, but luckily it worked out. It was easy playing and working in Minnesota, and I was really glad that I got a chance to do it."

TRIBUTES
"When I was in 8th grade, Dave was a senior in high school," said Paul Molitor. "I saw him play, but I never had a chance to play with him. I think in a lot of ways I owe him a lot, because as a member of the Gophers when he was drafted, he opened some eyes about Minnesota baseball. That gave kids like myself a lot more opportunities to get some exposure. The parallels of our careers are somewhat remarkable in that we grew up on the same playgrounds, played for the same American Legion team, competed at the same University, and we both had to go north of the border and wait until the latter stages of our careers to win a World Series championship. For two guys who grew up five blocks apart in St. Paul to end up both accumulating 3,000 hits with their hometown teams is pretty remarkable, I think. I marveled at Dave's play for many years. He was a tremendous, tremendous athlete. I consider him to be a good friend, and whenever we see each other, we always reminisce about our past and growing up in St. Paul."

"When I was a rookie, Winny took me under his wing," added Kirby Puckett. "I'll never forget going to New York City and talking to him. I remember saying 'Hello Mr. Winfield,' and I remember him saying to me, 'I've heard a lot about you, rook.' I was just in awe. He's like six-foot-six and so intimidating. Then he sent me a note in the clubhouse inviting me to dinner with him that night after the game. I remember just talking to him. He was so nice to me. That was really special to me."

"It was fun playing with him toward the end there," said Kent Hrbek. "I know that, playing against him, I was scared to death of him. He could hit a baseball as hard as anyone ever has. I was always afraid that he was going to kill somebody out there when he hit the ball. I remember one time when he hit a line-drive bullet right between shortstop Lenny Faedo's legs, and poor Lenny didn't even have time to get his glove down on the ball. For a big, huge, opposing figure-of-a-guy like he is, he's very gentle at heart and is really a super-nice, sweet guy."

"Dave is a first-class gentleman," added Jim Kaat. "He has so much professionalism and was just a great athlete. He used his great athleticism to turn himself into a Hall of Fame hitter.

Gopher diver Pat Bogart wins the NCAA's Platform Diving National Championship	Gopher track & field star Martin Eriksson wins the NCAA's Indoor pole-vaulting National Championship	Austin's Lee Janzen wins the U.S. Open Golf Tournament	Gopher second baseman Mark Merila is named to the All-American baseball team	The North Stars are uprooted and moved to Dallas, where they become the Dallas Stars	UMD defenseman Brett Hauer is named to the All-American hockey team	UMD center Derek Plante is named to the All-American hockey team	The Hibbing Curling Club Women's team wins the U.S. Women's Curling Association National Bonspiel Championship. Georgean Glumack - Last Rocks Susan Vesel - Skip Gail Murray - Second JoAnne Baratto - Lead

TIMELINE

In 1994, the Minnesota Vikings finished with a respectable 10-6 record, good enough to stay ahead of the Packers, Lions, Bucs, and Bears to win the NFC Central Division. The team's hopes of getting past the first round of the playoffs though, something Head Coach Denny Green had yet to do, were dashed when they were spanked by the hated Bears, 35-18, at the Metrodome.

The bright spot that season, however, was the spectacular play of Vikings Wide Receiver, Cris Carter. In 1994, CC had the biggest season of any wide receiver in the history of the National Football League, snagging a then league-record 122 balls, shattering Sterling Sharpe's record of 112 catches set with Green Bay the year earlier. Carter also set a team record for receiving yards in a season with 1,256, breaking former teammate Anthony Carter's record of 1,225 yards in 1988. The 1,256 yards receiving were fourth best in the NFC and seventh in the NFL. He averaged 10.3 yards per catch that year while finding the end zone seven times to boot.

With the addition of Jake Reed's 85 catches, the dynamic duo set an NFL record for receptions by a receiving tandem with 207, breaking the previous record held by Houston's Haywood Jeffires and Drew Hill of 190 receptions back in 1991. Interestingly, both tandems had the luxury of Quarterback Warren Moon throwing them the ball. Moon wasted little time in torching the competition in 1994, shattering nearly every one of the team's major single-season passing records in the process. His league-leading 4,264 yards and 371 completions were simply huge.

Carter emerged as a superstar that season, at times carrying the team on his back. On September 9th, C.C. caught three touchdown passes in the first half of a game against the Dolphins. Less than a month later, on October 2nd, he single-handedly took care of the Phoenix Cardinals when he caught a team record 14 passes for 167 yards. Then, against the Bears, Carter had two touchdown catches, including the overtime game-winner on a 65-yard bomb from Moon, thus earning NFC offensive Player of the Week honors. He also scored the first ever two-point conversion in team history on September 18th against those same Bears, and he led the team in 100-yard receiving games that year with five.

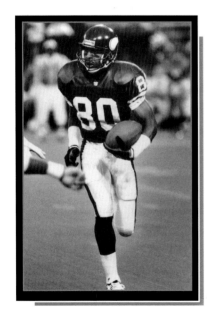

Carter became the first Vikings player in history to have three seasons with 70-or-more receptions, and at season's end, he had caught at least one pass in 54 consecutive games, including the playoffs. For his efforts, No. 80 was selected to the Pro Bowl for the second straight season, his first as a starter, as well as earning All-Pro and All-NFC recognition.

"It was nice to break the NFL record, but, for me, I wasn't all that wrapped up in it," said Carter. "It was a great year for us as a team, and winning the NFC Central was a great accomplishment

for everyone. It was especially great to have Warren Moon with us as well. It was Warren's first year and we were experimenting and getting used to one another on the field. We put together 244 balls, which is still a record for back-to-back seasons. Our timing and cohesiveness was just great. Warren was just a phenomenal quarterback."

Just how tough was the Central that year? With Minnesota being joined by Chicago, Detroit and Green Bay in the playoffs, it marked the first time in league history that a division had placed four teams in the post-season. And, it would be those same gritty Bears that the Vikes would host in their first-round wild-card playoff game at the Dome. This would be a cake-walk right? I mean they had beaten Chicago six straight times. Think again.

Despite their fourth-place conference finish, Chicago was not to be taken lightly. They were led by Quarterback Steve Walsh, a Cretin High School alum who would play huge in front of his home-town fans, completing 15 of 23 passes for 221 yards and two touch-downs. Minnesota jumped out to a quick 3-0 lead in the first on Fuad Reviez's" 29-yarder. But the Bears, who had turnovers on their first two possessions, came back with a pair of second quarter scores from both Lewis Tillman, who capped a long drive with a one-yard dive, and by Walsh, who hit Tight End Keith Jennings on a nine-yarder in the end-zone. The Vikings then cut Chicago's margin to 14-9 just 19 seconds before the half on Moon's four-yard touchdown pass to Cris Carter. But the Bears roared back in the third on Raymont Harris's 29-yard touchdown run. After another Reviez field-goal, Walsh made it 28-12 late in that same quarter when he found Jeff Graham with a 21-yard touchdown pass.

Vikings' third-down specialist Amp Lee came in and tried to mount a late rally when he caught an acrobatic 11-yard TD pass from Moon midway through the fourth, but when Bears DB Kevin Minniefield scooped up a fumble and raced 48 yards for a touchdown, the 35-18 upset was complete. The Vikes had really stunk up the joint. Their defense, which logged seven touchdowns and had held its opponents to only 68 rushing yards per game up to that point — the fourth lowest in NFL history — simply couldn't shut down Walsh. Even John Randle, who registered 13.5 sacks that year was neutralized. They just couldn't capitalize — as evidenced by their two turnovers which produced just three points in the ball game. Conversely, the Bears shut down Minnesota's running game, and forced Moon, who was playing injured, to go to the air far too frequently — 52 times to be exact.

With three straight playoff defeats, including a pair in the Dome, everyone began to wonder if Green had what it took to get this team to the next level.

Arguably the Greatest Ever

Cris Carter was born in Troy, Ohio, on November 25, 1965. He went on to graduate from Middletown High School in 1983, where he caught 80 passes for over 2,000 yards, and earned Parade All-American honors as a senior. He also excelled as an all-state basketball player, scoring over 1,600 points during his prep career. (His older brother Butch went on to play for seven years in the NBA and later became the head coach of the Toronto Raptors.)

Heavily recruited out of high school, Cris chose to go to Ohio State, where he earned first-team All-American honors in 1986. When it was all said and done, Carter would finish as the Buckeyes' all-time leader in receptions, with 168, and touchdown catches, with 27, while

TIMELINE									
Twins pitcher Scott Erickson throws a no-hitter in a 6-0 win over Milwaukee	St. Paul's Amy Peterson wins two bronze medals in the 500M and 3,000M Relay in Olympic Short Track Speedskating	The Bemidji State Hockey team beats Alabama Huntsville for the Division II National Championship	The state's largest lake sturgeon is caught by Hinckley's Kim Bergston in the Kettle River: 94 Lbs., 4 oz.	St. Thomas' Leonard Jones wins the Division III High Jump and Long Jump Indoor Track National Championships	Concordia's Renee Erickson wins the Division III Javelin National Championship	Gopher Second Baseman Mark Merila is named to the All-American baseball team for the second straight year	UMD winger Chris Marinucci is named to the All-American hockey team	Roseville's Randy Bartz, arguably the state's greatest ever speed skater, wins an Olympic silver medal on the 5,000M Relay Short Track Speedskating team

ranking No. 2 in receiving yards, with 2,725.

Cris went on to be selected in the fourth round of the 1987 supplemental draft by the Philadelphia Eagles. After three productive years in Philly, then Head Coach Buddy Ryan, for some insane reason, released Carter, citing irreconcilable differences. C.C. was then immediately claimed off the waiver wire by the Vikings. Philadelphia's blunder was Minnesota's gain. Now the Purple had two Carters, Cris and long-time Viking great, Anthony, to form one of the most lethal receiving tandems in the league. Cris got some sweet revenge against his old mates on November 15th that year as well when he nabbed six receptions for 151 yards, including a 78-yarder for a TD.

"I was really excited about the possibility of playing in Minnesota because I knew about the tremendous tradition that the Vikings had built over the years," said Carter. "But I was most excited about the opportunity to play with Anthony Carter."

In 1991, Cris led the Vikings in receptions with 72 and added 962 receiving yards to go along with his five TDs. That next year, after leading the club in receptions, receiving yards and TD's, he knew he had made it to the big-time when he was selected as a member of John Madden's notorious "All-Madden" team. In 1993 he played in his first Pro Bowl, and in 1994 he set the NFL's all-time receptions record, with 122. Showing that 1994 wasn't a fluke, CC went on to catch another incredible 122 balls for the second consecutive year in 95', giving him the most catches ever in the NFL over a two-year span.

"I think that season I accomplished even more than in 1994 by catching 122 again, as well as catching 17 touchdowns," said Carter. "That might be the best year that I have ever had as a pro."

In 1996, Carter made his fourth Pro Bowl team in his eighth season with the Vikes. Perhaps his biggest accomplishment that season came during the off-season, when he was ordained as a minister. Since then he simply dominated the world of professional football. Week in and week out he continued to amaze fans everywhere by making spectacular one-handed finger-tip catches. He had a sixth sense as to where the sideline was, and always seemed to somehow drag both feet in order to make sure he was in bounds.

In 1998 the Vikes took a gamble on a wide receiver with some baggage by the name of Randy Moss. Cris took on the role of tutoring the rookie, showing him the ropes along the way. As a result, the duo went on to become the most feared in the NFL. In 1998 the team made it to the NFC Championship game, only to lose a heart-breaker to the Falcons, and in 2000 they made it back to the Final Four, only to get embarrassed by the New York Giants. Nonetheless, this awesome duo was simply awesome and struck fear in every defense it faced.

Carter retired from the Vikings following the 2001 season. The team was on the downside and C.C. wanted out. He expressed his desire to sign with a winning team, but when he interviewed with the Browns, that idea was thrown out the window. In fact, Carter negotiated with several teams that off-season, including the Rams, but wound up getting no deal. So, he retired and took over as a TV analyst on the HBO show, "Inside the NFL." Then, in October of 2002, Carter un-retired when the wide-receiver depleted Miami Dolphins came calling. Carter makes his home in South Florida, so it was a good fit for him to be close to his family while still being able to play the game he loves. And why not? Jerry Rice was still going strong in Oakland at the tender young age of 40 — fully four years older than Cris.

As for the Purple, Cris owns virtually all the Vikings receiving records. For his career, he scored 129 touchdown, caught 1,093 passes and racked up 13,833 receiving yards. He is a virtual lock for the Hall of Fame and ranks second only to Jerry Rice in those same stats. He is a living legend and will go down as one of the all-time best ever. Period.

Aside from his on-the-field stats, Carter is also very proud of

his achievements off of the field. In 1999 Carter was honored by being named as the NFL's Man of the Year — receiving the Walter Payton Award. He was also honored for his efforts in the community with his Cris Carter's CAUSE (Christian Athletes for Spiritual Empowerment), as well as for his tireless work with inner-city schools, the Special Olympics, the Boy Scouts and the Make-A-Wish Foundation. In addition, Carter frequently speaks to kids about drug awareness and is actively involved in the Big Brother-Big Sister program. He also joined with fellow player, William White of the Kansas City Chiefs to establish the Carter-White Charitable Foundation, which sponsors numerous activities for underprivileged children.

On Owning all of the Vikings Receiving Records:
"It's really nice because those records are pretty substantial, and the players who played before me were phenomenal. That gives the records a lot of credence and value in my mind. It's always nice to be compared to great people of the past and also with people who are still playing in the league. Growing up and watching Ahmad (Rashad) and Sammy (White) catch passes in those blustery days at old Metropolitan Stadium, to me is unbelievable. It's nice to have been able to have seen some of their incredible careers, along with guys like Anthony Carter, and know that I was be able to pass them up. This means a lot to me."

On Minnesota's Fans?
"I really enjoy the fans in Minnesota. They're great, and I love playing before them. It seems that they have warmed up to me as my performances have gotten better. I feel that they have shown their appreciation toward me and have always been very respectful of me. It has always given me a sense of confidence in my ability knowing that during tough situations, the fans are behind me. Because a lot of times in certain situations, they know that I'm going to get the ball, and it's nice knowing they are behind me. In Minnesota, the fans really know their sports, are very knowledgeable, and they know the history of their sports heroes. There is just a great football tradition here — which makes rivalries like against the Packers even better."

On Minnesota?
"I'm not a big fan of the Minnesota weather, and I only live here during the season, but I can definitely see the appealing aspects of guys wanting to live here as far as the quality of life goes. When my family and I are here, we definitely love it, and we have become very comfortable in our second home. I really wouldn't want to play anywhere else besides Minnesota. The people are very cordial, and it's a pleasure for my family and I to be with Minnesotans."

Vikings Tombstone:
"I would like to be known as a strong competitor and for my ability to compete. I think that would be the thing that would make me the most proud."

Plymouth's Pol Vanwinkel wins his third Twin Cities Marathon - Wheelchair Division	The state's largest largemouth bass is caught by Austin's Joseph Johanns on Lake Tetonka: 8 Lbs., 12.75 oz.	St. Thomas runner Kelly Copps wins the 5,000M and 10,000M Outdoor as well as the 5,000M - Indoor Track National Championships

TIMELINE

119

In 1995, the Minnesota Timberwolves astonished the basketball establishment when they became the first NBA team in more than 20 years to draft a player directly out of high school. With the fifth overall pick of the first round, Wolves' GM Kevin McHale gambled on the raw talent of a 19-year-old named Kevin Garnett. Less than a month removed from his senior prom, Garnett, the most highly recruited prep player of maybe all-time became Minnesota's lottery prize. The Wolves, who were entering their seventh sad year of mediocrity, had always seemed to be just one ping-pong ball away from drafting a superstar. Minnesota simply had nothing to lose by drafting a high schooler.

To fully understand why this gamble was so big, and why the story was equally as big, one has to go back to the franchise's infancy and look at the evolution of mishaps and draft-bungles that put the team in a position to take such a risk.

After a 29-year hiatus, the NBA returned to the Gopher State in 1989 with the granting of an expansion franchise to Harvey Ratner and Marvin Wolfenson. It was a big deal having a new professional team in town, and basketball fans came out in droves to see the fledgling Minnesota Timberwolves. The Timberwolves built their new franchise around their first two draft picks Pooh Richardson of UCLA and Villanova's Doug West. Led by former Gopher Coach Bill Musselman, the Wolves played their first two seasons in the Metrodome, and at the end of their inaugural season, had set a new all-time NBA attendance record with well over a million customers walking through the Metrodome turnstiles. Unfortunately, that was the only worthwhile record the franchise would set. From 1989-1995, the Wolves won only 126 games and lost 366. By 1995, the honeymoon had clearly worn off, and the fans were growing weary of being the league's doormat. Minnesota's sporting public wanted a winner and were growing inpatient. NBA expansion teams were notorious for slow starts and growing pains, but, by that time, the three other expansion franchises that came into the league around the same time that the Wolves did had all made the playoffs, with Orlando even making it to the Finals.

The Timberwolves had experienced more than their share of tough luck, but much of the blame had to be put on poor drafting and inadequate management. Along with two ownership groups and an aborted move to New Orleans, the head coaching position had been a regular revolving door. After Musselman came Jimmy Rodgers, then former Wolves Guard Sidney Lowe, followed by Bill Blair who was succeed by present Coach Phil "Flip" Saunders. The Wolves had chosen six consecutive lottery picks — Richardson, Felton Spencer, Luc Longley, Christian Laettner, Isaiah Rider, and Donyell Marshall. By the time young Garnett came on board, only Laettner and Rider remained, and both were shipped elsewhere shortly after.

The word on Garnett come draft day was that he was a seven foot beanpole with terrific all-around talent. Sports Illustrated even went as far as saying that he just might be the best athlete in the draft. He was described as a cross between Indiana Guard Reggie Miller and a kinder, gentler version of Miami Center Alonzo Mourning. He could run, leap like crazy, block shots, monster-dunk, handle the ball like a guard, and shoot 20-footers with ease. He represented the most elusive of all commodities for the league's bottom-feeder's, and that was hope. Some members of the media even hyped him up as a "savior," while others quickly tabbed him as the "next Michael Jordan."

With that, in an attempt to create the perfect team chemistry, the Wolves weeded out the bad apples and hedged all their bets by rebuilding their team around a kid named Kevin Garnett.

Da Kid

Kevin Garnett was born on May 19, 1976, and grew up in Mauldin, S.C., just outside Greenville, as a die-hard Lakers fan. A four-time all-state player, Kevin was named Mr. Basketball for the state of South Carolina as a junior in 1994. For his senior year, the young phenom moved to Chicago, where at Farragut Academy, he was once again selected as Mr. Basketball, this time for the state of Illinois. As a senior he averaged 25.2 points, 17.9 rebounds, 6.7 assists, and 6.5 blocks per game. For his efforts, he was tabbed the National High School Player of the Year by USA Today and also earned All-America first team honors. He capped off his prep career by being named the MVP of the 1995 McDonald's All-Star Game. It was there where he dominated the country's best college prospects, and gained the reputation of being an NBA "sure thing."

Kevin was wooed by nearly every Division I college in the country. Early reports had him going to either Michigan or North Carolina. But, because he hadn't achieved the necessary college admission test scores and because the big money was there, he bypassed it all and made himself available for the NBA draft.

Drafting a 19-year-old was no easy task. The nay-sayers were out in force, and if the Wolves wanted to keep up any fan base at all, Garnett would have to deliver big-time. The Minnesota fans were skeptical because few had ever seen the lad play, but that added even more to his mystique. Garnett also carried some baggage with him that would raise some questions. The move from South Carolina his senior year to Chicago came in large part as a result of an incident in which he and several friends were charged with assaulting a student. His police record was later cleared, though, because he participated in a pretrial diversion program for first-time offenders.

There were genuine concerns about his maturity, social skills, stamina, sense of responsibility, friends, and even his diet. He was more than a typical NBA "project," and he needed a lot of T.L.C. As one reporter put it, "People in Minnesota hear the word project, and they break out in a Luc Longley-sized rash."

There had only really been four players that had successfully made the transition from high school directly to the NBA — Moses Malone in 1974, Darryl Dawkins and Bill Willoughby in 1975, and Shawn Kemp in 1989 (who played only briefly at the collegiate level). At the same time, Sports Illustrated fed the media frenzy by featuring him on their cover with the headline: "Ready or Not."

Would he dominate and revolutionize the game of pro bas-

Concordia's Aaron Banks wins the Division III Shot Put Indoor Track National Championship	The Augsburg College Wrestling team wins the Division III National Championship	The Bemidji State Hockey team beats Mercyhurst College for the Division III National Championship	St. Cloud State Wrestler Gene Hanemann wins the Division III 158 lb. National Championship	Augsburg Wrestler Jesse Armbruster wins the 126 lb. National Championship	Mankato State runner Jon Keillor wins the Division III 3,000 Meter Steeplechase National Championship	St. Thomas runner Kelly Copps wins the Division III 5,000M and 10,000M National Championships	Gopher diver Pat Bogart wins the NCAA's One Meter Diving National Championship	Twins' outfielder Marty Cordova is named as the American League's Rookie of the Year	Concordia's Renee Erickson wins the Division III Javelin National Championship

ketball? Or would he join a long line of NBA casualties crushed by fame, too much money, and groupies? Sure, there are countless young men who play pro hockey and baseball at even younger ages. But this was different — this was the NBA.

"Is he a franchise player?" retorted former Timberwolves Head Coach Bill Blair at a press conference. "I can't say that but this kid does some things that excite you. From a maturity level? No way he can be ready. He's not ready for the airplanes, the four games in six days, and for the free time he's now possessing. Those things we have to help him with. You just hope he's so interested in basketball, you hope he wants to be the best player in the league."

Reaction around the basketball world was mixed. "He's a genetic freak," said Detroit Coach Doug Collins. "All the great ones are." Said McHale: "Garnett is a basketball junkie. He's the kind of guy we'll have to chase off the court, rather than worry he's not spending enough time on it." University of Minnesota Gopher basketball Coach Clem Haskins added: "You won't find athletes with more raw talent than Garnett. He has great upside with great enthusiasm for the game." Former Seattle General Manager Bob Whitsitt, who drafted Shawn Kemp said: "The team that takes Garnett has to commit its entire organization. Ownership, coaches, other players, everyone has to realize this is a 24-hour-a-day process. You have to be willing to spend the years, not the days, the years, to make this work." Russ Granik, the NBA's deputy commissioner, even put in his two cents worth: "If it were up to us, we'd prefer not to see someone come into the league at that tender age, but the courts say otherwise."

On June 28, 1995, in Toronto's SkyDome, the Wolves, after patiently watching Joe Smith, Jerry Stackhouse, Antonio McDyess, and Rasheed Wallace go in the first four picks, selected Garnett. As McHale presented him with his new No. 21 jersey (ending any speculation that it was going to be retired due to the brilliant performance of its previous owner, Stacey King) Garnett just smiled proudly.

"I'm not gonna rush nothing," said Garnett. "I'm not going to do anything I know I can't do. I can't wait to get in the gym with Mr. McHale, and learn some of those dazzling moves he has."

"The one thing that bothers me is everybody thinking I just got into this without thinking it over," he added. " I thought about it a lot, and I think I'm ready."

Knowing that it was going to be a full-time job, developing and grooming the young player into his new surroundings, the Timberwolves took some steps to protect their investment. General Manager Flip Saunders called the steps "safety nets," and laid out the groundwork to ease his transition. One proposal was to have Garnett live with a family during his rookie season. In addition, his mother was going to move to the Twin Cities to support him for his rookie campaign, but would not live with him.

The Wolves were building for the future and, in 1995, big things were happening at the Target Center. Shortly after the season got underway, Coach Bill Blair was replaced by General Manager Flip Saunders. Later in the season, Christian Laettner was dealt to the Atlanta Hawks. Laettner had complained about the extra treatment the rookie was receiving and, as a result, got shown the door. And, at seasons' end, Rider and all his baggage were sent packing to the Portland Trailblazers. The team finished at a dismal 26-56 that season, good enough for fifth in the Midwest Division. The rookie Garnett did OK though, averaging a modest 10.4 points, 6.3 rebounds and 1.8 assists per game. For his efforts he was named to the NBA all-rookie second team.

There was no question as to whether or not Kevin was going to be a remarkable NBA player. Following his second season, a poll of league coaches and general managers asked who they thought was going to be the star player of the next decade. Garnett was their over-

whelming choice.

Since then KG has emerged as one of the league's elite players. In his seven years in the NBA the perennial All-Star has averaged 19 points per game, 10 rebounds and 4 assists.

From his "poster-dunks" to his animal-like cleansing of the boards, this 6'11" forward (he is actually taller than 7'0" but doesn't want to be known as a seven-footer) is the complete package. The most identifiable traits of the young superstar are his infectious smile and his genuine boyish enthusiasm for the game. Fans seem to live vicariously through

him on the court, and sometimes even his teammates seem to be in awe of him as well. Garnett is, in a word, awesome.

In October of 1997, Kevin signed a six-year contract extension with the Wolves worth an amazing $125 million, or nearly $21 million per season. The Wolves ownership clearly sent a signal to the fans of Minnesota that K.G. was the future, and that they were willing to spend some pretty big bucks to be a contender in the league.

But, while Kevin led the Wolves to the post-season in five straight seasons (1997-2002), the T-Wolves have been bounced out of the first round of the playoffs each time. It has been frustrating for Kevin, his teammates, and for all of Minnesota. He did re-sign a long-term contract with the Timberwolves in 2002-2003, however, ensuring that he will be with the club for a very long time. Untimely injuries, along with the fact that the team was penalized for an illegal contract with Joe Smith which ultimately resulted in the loss of four of the team's first round draft picks, has truly handcuffed this franchise. But, with KG leading the pack, the fans know that the team will only get better. Garnett is that special kind of player who will work tirelessly to get it right, and lead this team to the next level.

Today Kevin Garnett is a franchise all by himself and is a superstar like no other. Full of high octane energy and high flying slam dunks, he has become the prototypical NBA forward. He is seven-feet tall, but plays like a point guard. He is the rarest of big men with an incredible array of skills who just might very well be the most complete all-around player in the league. He is also a fun-loving kid, raw with passion and emotion, and full of charm and wit. A superstar off the court, Kevin also has several major endorsement deals from shoes to video games, and he even his own line of clothing called "OBF," which stands for Original Block Family.

And, technically speaking, Garnett is a freak of nature. He has fabulous running ability, stamina and agility. He can play like a small forward, yet can be just as dominant in the post-up game underneath the basket. He can also handle the ball, pass off the dribble and shoot from the perimeter. Defensively, he is a perfectionist who can rebound like an animal, block shots, and guard much quicker players who are half his size. He is truly the complete package. He is unselfish and exemplifies the term "team player." In just six short seasons this top dog has earned the nicknames of the "Big Ticket," "Da Kid" as well as "The Franchise" — and make no mistake about it, he is the "alpha male" of this pack.

| Stillwater's Tami Oothoudt wins her seventh Twin Cities Marathon - Wheelchair Division | Augsburg Wrestler Tom Layte wins the Division III 150 lb. National Championship | Mankato State Wrestler Tony Kenning wins the Division III 123 lb. National Championship | Gopher center Brian Bonin is named to the All-American hockey team | Gopher defenseman Mike Crowley is named to the All-American hockey team | Gopher catcher Shane Gunderson is named to the All-American baseball team | Gopher Basketball star Voshon Lenard graduates from the U of M as the Gophers' all-time leading scorer, with 2,103 points. The three-time team MVP is the only player in school history ever to surpass the 2,000-point plateau. | Former Gopher quarterback Tony Dungy is named as the head coach of the Tampa Bay Bucs. Dungy was the team MVP in 1975 and 1976 and remains on several all-time offensive categories at the U. He played for the NFL's Steelers and 49ers and was an assistant coach with the Gophers, Vikings, Steelers and Chiefs. The Steelers made him the youngest defensive coordinator in NFL history, at the age of 28. |

TIMELINE

In 1996, while the fans were mourning the retirement of Kirby Puckett, another home-town hero came home — Paul Molitor. A former Cretin High School and Golden Gopher star, Molitor had established himself as one of the game's greatest all-time hitters.

Molly led the Twins that year with an outstanding .341 average and also led the league in hits with 225. Then, on September 16th, in a road game against the Kansas City Royals, with Jose Rosado on the mound, Paul made history. With the entire state waiting in anxious anticipation, Molly became the 21st player in major league history to get 3,000 hits. He did it in style too, becoming the first player ever to reach the milestone with a triple. In an otherwise ho-hum Twins season, Molly had made baseball fun again.

"I definitely tried to put it on the very back burner," said Molitor of the big hit. "You don't go about assuming that you're going to get 211 hits in a year when you're going to turn 40 years old. When that ball got into the gap and I got to third, it finally sunk in. I found out afterwards that no one had ever hit a triple on their 3,000th hit, and that made it kind of special too, because it adds to the uniqueness of joining what is already a pretty small group of people. It's my most memorable game in baseball and just having it happen to me as a member of the Minnesota Twins was amazing."

Incidentally, the Twins, who chased a wild card spot that year, finished with a 78-85 record — good for fourth place in the Central.

Molly

One of eight children, Paul Molitor was born in St. Paul on August 22, 1956. He grew up as a Twins fan, worshipping Harmon Killebrew, and loved to play baseball as a kid. A natural athlete, his talents became apparent as a high schooler for the Cretin Raiders in St. Paul.

"I first thought of Molitor as having the potential to become a professional when he was in the ninth grade," said Bill Peterson, his high school and American Legion team coach. "He was always an exceptional player and had a very strong arm." In his senior year at Cretin High School, Molitor missed the entire regular season with mononucleosis. "He wasn't even supposed to practice," Peterson added, "but he begged and begged to hit. He must have had a month's worth of energy stored up because he put on a hitting exhibition like I've never seen."

Molly rejoined the Raiders for the playoffs and led his team to the Catholic League High School title. So, it was off to the State Tournament, where in the championship game, Paul pounded a 380-foot grand slam, en route to helping Cretin repeat as state champs. Paul would garner All-State honors that year in baseball as well as in basketball.

At this point, Molitor had drawn the interest of both college and major league scouts, who had their eyes on Minnesota . In 1973, when the San Diego Padres drafted fellow St. Paulite Dave Winfield, it had spurned fresh interest in northern baseball. After Winfield, major league baseball scouts paid closer attention to the quality of players who had been developed in the arctic reaches of the U.S., and as a result, Molly got a lot of attention throughout his prep career.

Paul was getting mixed reviews from the major league scouts, particularly those representing the Minnesota Twins. They thought he was too small and would have a difficult time in organized ball. However, the St. Louis Cardinals decided to take a chance on the young shortstop and selected him in the 25th round of the entry draft. The Cards offered him a $4,000 contract, which was just the kick in the rear he needed to opt for a free university education instead.

In 1975, Paul was offered a scholarship by Gopher Baseball Coach Dick Siebert, who had a special eye for talent. Siebert would later say that Paul had the best base-running instincts of any player he ever saw in amateur or professional baseball, and that he was, without a doubt, the best major league prospect he'd ever seen. The Chief apparently had seen something the Twins scouts had overlooked.

"During try-outs Molitor just stood heads above everyone else from the first day he walked on campus," said John Anderson, former Gopher baseball student manager and current U of M head coach.

Molly was a quiet, lead-by-example type of player, who would always play aggressive and go after the ball. As co-captain, he would lead the Gophers to the Big Ten title in 1977.

"Growing up in the St. Paul, as I did, I knew that the Gophers had a tremendous baseball tradition," said Paul of his Gopher career. "I remember in high school, following the Gopher baseball team and, in particular watching Dave Winfield lead the club to the College World Series, before they ended up losing some heart-breakers down in Omaha. When Coach Siebert offered me a scholarship to be a Gopher, I realized how much pride the program had in presenting the state's baseball abilities. Back then, it was a very rare occasion when the Chief would recruit outside the state to bring in players, so almost everyone in uniform was home-grown. I think that when you played for his teams, you realized that it wasn't just the U, but the type of baseball that Minnesota kids played, that was being represented. It carried a lot of significance for me, and it meant a great deal for me to be a Gopher."

As Paul and his teammates prepared for the 1977 College World Series, he heard the substantial news that he had been drafted by the Milwaukee Brewers. He was the third overall player chosen in the draft, after the White Sox took Harold Baines and Expos took Bill Gullickson. The Twins, who had made it clear that they were now interested in drafting him, had missed their chance at the young slugger. "It took me a little while to get down to the ground," said Paul after hearing the news. College baseball's hottest prospect, and newest cheesehead, went ahead and signed with the Brewers for $85,000.

By the time Paul turned pro after his junior season, he had established himself as one of the greatest all-around baseball players in Gopher history. He had become the Gophers' career leader in runs-scored, hits, RBI's, triples, home-runs, total bases, and stolen bases. In his three seasons, he set five single-season records and seven college-career records.

The Gopher shortstop's best year was his sophomore season in which he batted a career-best .376, earning himself first-team All-

TIMELINE

Anoka's Brandon Paulson wins a silver medal on the Olympic wrestling team	Anoka's Briana Scurry wins a gold medal as the goaltender of the U.S. Olympic soccer team	Duluth's Kris Benson wins a bronze medal on the Olympic Baseball team	St. Paul's Thomas Malchow wins a silver medal on the Olympic swimming team in the 200M Butterfly	Minneapolis' William Carlucci wins a bronze medal on the Olympic Lightweight-Four Rowing team	Concordia's Aaron Banks wins the Division III Shot Put Indoor Track National Championship	Gopher diver Pat Bogart wins the NCAA's One Meter Diving National Championship	Concordia's Renee Erickson wins the Division III Javelin National Championship	Mankato State wrestler Tony Kenning wins the Division II 123 lbs. National Championship	Allen Hartley wins the NHRA Champion Auto Nationals at Brainerd International Speedway. The total four-day attendance is over 100,000

122

American honors for the second straight season. He would finish his college baseball with an impressive career batting average of .350.

"I thought he had more ability than any player I have ever coached, and I coached Dave Winfield, so Paul's accomplishment is a pretty tall order," said Coach Siebert of Molitor's Gopher career.

The 20-year-old Molitor was then sent to Milwaukee's Class-A farm team in Iowa, the Burlington Bees. It soon became apparent that Molly was the best player in the Midwest League. He could have gone up to Triple-A after only three weeks with Burlington, but he asked to stay with the Bees to help them win the league championship. He did, leading the Bees to the Midwest League title and, in the process, won the batting crown with a .348 average. From then on, there were no more minor-league stops for Paul. It was off the "show." Winfield had gone directly to the big leagues from the campus of the U of M; it took Molly 64 Midwest League games to get there. Not bad.

Now, Robin Yount was the Brewers everyday shortstop. Even though he was less than a year older than Molitor, he was already a seasoned pro, having gone straight to the majors in 1974. Drafted as the shortstop of the future, Molly was quoted years later on his memories of that first visit to County Stadium: "I remember Sal Bando coming over and throwing Robin an outfielder's glove and saying to him, 'Well, I guess this will be your last year at shortstop, kid...'. "All I wanted was to get out of there!"

Profoundly modest, Molitor doesn't care about personal accolades, rather, he always preferred to be a team player. He was an explosive athlete with an ability to attack with the sudden element of surprise, whether at the plate or on the bases. He was a hitting machine, able to swing so late, stretching time until that optimum instant for contact seems to have passed. His eyes could evaluate a pitch, calculate its curve, its spin, its velocity, and then measure it, to precisely drive the ball exactly where he wanted it to go, all in about the same time it would take the average person to blink. That was his signature, and his knowledge of the physics of the game allowed him to get better with age.

Paul played 15 seasons with the Brewers, making it to the World Series in 1982 before losing to the Cardinals in the so-called "Suds Series." He also gave Joe DiMaggio's consecutive hits record a run for the money in 1987. Molitor left Milwaukee to go north of the border in 1993 where he led the Blue Jays to the World Series championship and was named MVP of the Series. Following this accomplishment, many felt that Paul could have run for the position of Prime Minister in Canada, and they weren't kidding.

On December 5, 1995, Paul Molitor came back to Minnesota. He fulfilled a lifelong, childhood dream by getting the opportunity to play for his hometown Twins. In 1996, he led the Twins with an outstanding .341 average and made major-league history when he got his historic 3,000th hit. And what was the secret of this 40-something's success? Explanations for his longevity included a regiment of common sense, zen, and staying in great shape, combined with a daily focused routine of discipline and thoroughness. Maybe it was just the water? Whatever it was, it worked. He was awesome.

"When the opportunity finally came up where I was available, and they had an interest, I couldn't pass up the opportunity to finally be a Twin in spite of a lot of interest from elsewhere and probably more money from some other teams," said Molly of his move back to Minnesota. "To have a chance to return home and to kind of complete the cycle, so to speak, was something that goes back to that dream as a kid. Now, to have it happen so far down the road was a little bit ironic, but also a real nice way to end my career. I am very content now and am excited about finishing up my career at home."

"I think at least for Dave Winfield, Jack Morris, Terry Steinbach, and I, after growing up and playing high school baseball

here, we had a certain pride about being from Minnesota that maybe people from other parts of the country might not easily understand," he added. "This has to do with the lifestyle and priorities of family — it's a Midwestern thing. I'm not sure if just that on its own would've been enough to entice us back, but when you factored the current status of the team under Manager Tom Kelly, it became even more appealing. Combine that with the chance to return home to friends and family, and then to play for the team we followed as youngsters was just an irresistible package for me."

Paul finally hung up the cleats in 1998. The 21-year veteran played his last game on September 27th at the Dome, where he singled and then scored in his last at-bat. The crowd went nuts. It was an appropriate ending for an amazing ballplayer and person. One thing is for sure. When Paul Molitor comes up for selection into the Hall of Fame in Cooperstown, he will be a first-ballot lock. And when he goes, Minnesota will be right there with him, proud as ever of one of their state's greatest treasures.

Gopher and Twins Tombstone:
"I hope that people will have seen in the way that I played that I had a certain passion and, yet, respect for the game. Whatever I have accomplished, I have tried to do with humility and when I failed, I tried to maintain a certain level of consistency about my demeanor. I think that's important because in a lot of ways sports reflects life. How you handle your ups and downs says a lot about your character. That's what I hope has left an impression, and particularly on young people."

TRIBUTES

"I grew up with Paul in St. Paul," said Jack Morris. "We played Babe Ruth ball, city ball, and American Legion ball against each other. Finally we played with each other in Toronto and won a pennant together. Paul is a great, great player. He is one of the greatest hitters I have ever seen and easily in the top five of all time. I've never seen a guy with better hands than Paul. He is truly a hitting machine."

"He is such a classy and professional individual," said Tom Kelly. "He plays the game at a higher level than anybody that I've ever seen. Paul was on a mission (in 1996) to get that 3,000th hit out of the way, and it was quite an experience that capped off a fabulous season for him."

"I played against Paul in the 'Suds Series' of 1982 and have gotten to know him over the years," said Jim Kaat. "He is a solid individual and one guy that I appreciate very much. He seems to know everyone, calls them by their first names, and has the time for them. He has great respect for the game, and as a result of that, I have great respect for him."

"We always had that local tie together and felt that since we were both Minnesota boys, we should like each other," said Kent Hrbek. "He is a super-nice guy, and I would have to say that if Kirby Puckett is the best right-handed hitter ever, Paul would have to be right behind him."

TIMELINE

Twins radio broadcaster Herb Carneal receives the Ford Frick Award from the Baseball Hall of Fame	Wayzata's Tim "Lumpy" Herron wins the Honda Classic PGA Golf Tournament	Gopher center Brian Bonin is named to the All-American hockey team	The Anoka Spooks win the women's National AA level amateur softball association championship. They are among the winningest teams in the history of the association, the top level of competition	The state's largest white crappie is caught by Maple Lake's Louis Lee on Mary Lake: 2lbs., 14.88 oz.	University of Minnesota, Duluth Football coach Jim Malosky a former Gopher quarterback in the late 1940's, wins number 250. Now in his 40th year behind the bench for the Bulldogs, he ranks in the all-time top-ten for most victories by a coach for all NCAA divisions.

The 1996-97 Gophers came into the season with high expectations of making a serious run at winning the Big Ten title. They had their nucleus back and were the buzz of the Twin Cities. Clem had instilled in the kids that they had been jobbed that last season by not getting an NCAA tourney bid, and the kids responded by working hard that summer during the off-season. They played basketball every day, lifted weights, got into shape, and hung around each other — building the chemistry that would take them farther than any Gopher team in history. Led by Bobby Jackson, the talented transfer from Western Nebraska Community College, Sam Jacobson, Courtney James and John Thomas, who all received honorable mention All-Big Ten honors the year, these Gophers set out to make history.

The team opened its season by winning its first five non-conference games before getting bumped off by a pesky Alabama team, which hit a three-pointer with just seconds remaining to win, 70-67. They rebounded to post an impressive 11-1 non-conference record, even crushing lowly Alabama State, 114-34 (the program's largest all-time margin of victory), along the way.

The Gophers then won their Big Ten opener against Wisconsin, 68-43. From there the Maroon and Gold headed to East Lansing, where they spanked the Spartans thanks to a 53% shooting percentage in a 68-43 victory. The team then beat Indiana and Michigan as Bobby Jackson was named as the Big Ten Player of the Week. After falling to Illinois, the Gophers proceeded to dump Ohio State, 73-67. From there the now 15th-ranked Gophers hosted the 23rd-ranked Iowa Hawkeyes at Williams Arena. There, in front of a national television audience, Sam Jacobson poured in a career-high 29 points to lead Minnesota to a 66-51 victory.

Next, they cruised past Purdue, 91-68, Northwestern, 75-56, and then returned home to beat Penn State, 85-70. They then went back to Purdue to beat the Boilers, 70-67. At Iowa, Eric Harris and John Thomas each hit key free throws down the stretch to lead the team to a 68-66 victory. Then, against Ohio State, back at the Barn, the Gophers held the Buckeyes to just 34% shooting in a 60-48 win. By now the team was on cruise-control and had a chance to clinch at least a share of the Big Ten crown by avenging their earlier loss to the Illini, this time at home. There, behind Thomas' two free throws with just four seconds remaining, the Gophers sealed a 67-66 victory to clinch the title.

Jackson again led all Minnesota scorers, this time with 18 points, in a big 55-54 win over Michigan at Crisler Arena — a building that had not surrendered a victory to the Gophers since 1982. The next game, a 75-72 win over the Indiana Hoosiers, at the Barn, was a classic. Nearly 15,000 Gopher fans showed up to cheer on the Maroon and Gold in this one as Courtney James dished in 14 points, Charles Thomas added 13 and Trevor Winter grabbed a career-high 10 rebounds. The team's home season concluded with an 81-74 victory over Michigan State on Senior Night to round out an amazing 15-0 home record. Before the game, the senior foursome of Bobby Jackson, John Thomas, Trevor Winter and Aaron Stauber, hoisted the 1997 Big Ten championship banner up to the old Barn's rafters for all to see.

They wound up losing their final game of the year in Wisconsin, 66-65, as Sam Jacobson was stripped of the ball while he was attempting a last-second shot which could've won the game. With it, the team's 12-game winning streak was snapped, but they still managed to finish the regular season with the best record in school history at 27-3. And, believe it or not, that was just the beginning of one of the greatest rides in Minnesota sports history — it was a March to Madness...

The Big Ten champion Gophers were then rewarded with a coveted No. 1 seed in the NCAA's Midwest Region, in Kansas City. Thousands of Gopher fans made the trip to KC to watch the Gophers open the 64-team tourney against Southwest Texas State. And, thanks to Charles Thomas' 14 points off the bench, Minnesota cruised to a 78-46 victory. Next up was legendary Coach John Chaney's talented Temple squad, known for its trapping defense. But, thanks to double-figure scoring from Harris, Jacobson, Jackson and Thomas, the Gophers cruised to a 76-57 victory, and a trip back to the "Sweet 16," this time in San Antonio.

Next up for the Gophers was Clemson, a team that would test the very moral fiber of their being. This one came down to a dramatic double-overtime thriller with Minnesota somehow emerging victorious with a 90-84 win. Jacobson and Jackson combined for 65 points, posting career highs of 29 and 36 points, respectively, as the team rallied for its biggest win of the season. With the huge win the team was now headed to the "Elite Eight," to face the mighty UCLA Bruins in the regional final.

With a Final Four berth on the line, Guard Eric Harris, who had gone down with a shoulder injury in the Clemson game, stepped it up and decided to play hurt. The Gophers would need him in this one, the biggest game in the history of the program. The game was a back and forth affair, with Minnesota finding itself down 33-28 at halftime. But, behind a 52-point barrage in the second half, highlighted by Midwest Regional MVP Bobby Jackson's 18 points, the Gophers hung tough and pulled off an amazing 80-72 victory — garnering the school's first-ever Final Four appearance. After the game the players climbed a ladder to proudly cut down the net, a truly amazing site for everyone to see back in Minnesota.

The next stop would be the Final Four at Indianapolis' RCA Dome to take on the defending national champions from Kentucky. No other Gopher hoop squad had ever made it as far in the NCAA tournament, but in reality, there was nothing Cinderella about this team. The Gophers had won the Big Ten outright and had deservedly earned a No. 1 seed in the tournament. No. 1 seeds are given that designation for a reason. What was unexpected was the active support of all the Minnesota fans. When the team came back to Minneapolis, they arrived to a homecoming celebration at the Barn, which was filled well beyond its seating capacity.

Now, there was all kinds of drama leading up the big game against Kentucky, especially with Clem Haskins, who grew up in the

Minneapolis' Dave Peterson, a pioneer of Minnesota hockey and the coach of the 1988 and 1992 Olympic teams, dies	Wayzata's Tim Herron wins the Texas Open PGA Golf Tournament	Twins pitcher Brad Radke sets a team record by winning 12 straight starts	The Timberwolves make their first-ever playoff appearance but are swept by the Houston Rockets	The Minneapolis North boys High School basketball dynasty keeps rolling after winning three state championships	Edina's John Harris wins the U.S. Amateur Golf Championship and is named to yet another U.S. Walker Cup team	Hasting's Larry La Coursiere, a lightweight boxer, loses to reigning champion Julio Ceasar Chavez	Tommy Kendall wins his second Sprint PCS Grand Prix of Minnesota Trans Am race through downtown Minneapolis	Former Augsburg College football and basketball star Lute Olson wins the NCAA Basketball National Championship as head coach of the University of Arizona Wildcats. (He also coached at the University of Iowa.)

Blue Grass State and was a big prep star there. But because of segregation issues back in the early 1960s, Haskins, who wanted to attend the University of Kentucky to play for legendary Coach Adolph Rupp, opted to instead attend Western Kentucky University, where he became the program's first African American player.

Finally, in Indy, as the team made its way to the dome, nearly 10,000 Gopher fans turned out for a rally before the big game to support their team. It was going to be a battle. Things didn't start out so hot for the Gophers though against Kentucky's Wildcats in the opening game of the semifinals. In fact, it would be safe to say that it would be a tale of two halves. In the first 20 minutes, a tense squad in Maroon and Gold turned the ball over 15 times, and the stalwart bench that usually delivered the goods was nowhere to be found. Further, Kentucky's relentless defense was clearly presenting problems for Minnesota.

Then with 14:31 remaining in the second half and Kentucky leading 47-43, James went down the lane and scored on a monster dunk. Everybody in the dome, including droves of North Carolina and Arizona fans, who by now were rooting for the underdog Gophers, went berserk. The deafening roar of the crowd was drowned out, however, by the sound of the referee's whistle, as he negated the basket and called a charging foul on James. Coach Clem was apoplectic and his suit coat went flying. Then, before the Armani jacket could hit the floor, the referee slapped Clem with a "T." It was just one turning point in a game that had many. The resultant six-point swing put the Wildcats up 51-43.

The Gophers came back as they had done all season long though. First, Jacobson floated in mid-air to hit a jumper. Then, Jackson proceeded to hit a leaning double-pump lay-up, and then popped in a three-pointer. The RCA Dome erupted as the Gophers were finally fighting their way back from all the pesky turnovers and fouls that hindered them early on to take a 52-51 lead with 10:45 to play.

Then it got ugly for the Maroon and Gold. With the the game tied at 54, the Wildcats, led by All-American Forward Ron Mercer, reeled off 14 of the next 17 points. The fat lady was, regrettably, warming up her vocal chords. Unable to play at Kentucky's torrid pace, the Gophers ran out of gas down the stretch and lost the game, 78-69. In the end, Minnesota, the escape artists of college hoops, had succumbed to great coaching, a blown charge call, and a terrific Kentucky defense. Throw in the fact that Sam Jacobson, Charles Thomas and Eric Harris were all playing hurt, and it got even worse. The previously mistake-free Gophers had yielded to the relentless Kentucky press that caused them to turn over the ball to the Wildcats a sick 26 times.

The Golden Gophers gave us all some great memories during that magical 1997 season though, and renewed our pride in Minnesota basketball. Jackson, who finished the game with 23 points, had a once-in-a-lifetime season. For his efforts in the tournament, he was named to the All-Final-Four team

"Words can't describe how great that season was for me," said Bobby Jackson. "We worked really hard to get where we went, even when it seemed everybody doubted us. We just wanted to play hard and show everybody what we were about. I had never been in a Final Four situation, and it felt so good to accomplish that much. The Gopher fans played a major part in our success, and I would like to thank them for being there for us."

All in all, it was a storybook season that Gopher fans will never forget. The basketball team finished with an amazing 31-4 record en route to winning its first Big Ten title in 15 years. Led by the NCAA Coach of the Year, Clem Haskins, the Gophers made it all the way to their first-ever Final Four and were ranked as high as No. 2 in the nation for much of the season.

After the season, the awards started to roll in. Bobby Jackson, a consensus second team All-America selection, was named

as both the Big Ten Player of the Year and Big Ten Defensive Player of the Year. Power Forward John Thomas was named as a second team All-Big Ten selection, Eric Harris was third teamer and Courtney James earned honorable mention honors too. Jackson and Thomas were also both chosen in the first round of the NBA draft that June, while several of the other players went on to play pro ball as well.

Action Jackson

Bobby Jackson was born on March 13, 1973, in Salisbury, N.C. He grew up in basketball country, dreaming of playing college hoops. Jackson went on to average 22 points per game over his junior and senior seasons at Salisbury High School, earning all-conference and all-state honors in those same two seasons. From there, the speedy guard went to Western Nebraska Junior College in Scottsbluff, Neb., where he garnered second team All-American honors in 1995.

Jackson then transferred to Minnesota for the 1996 season, and although he was only in Gold Country for two seasons, he made the most of his time here. With his patented long white socks, he finished his illustrious tenure in Gold Country with a career scoring average of 14.4 points, 5.5 rebounds, and 3.5 assists per game. Not only was Jackson named the Big Ten MVP, he was also the conference's Defensive Player of the Year. He even earned second team All-America honors.

"Coming out of junior college, I could've gone to Wake Forest, Cincinnati, or Minnesota," recalled Jackson. "I chose Minnesota because of their team concept. I was looking for an opportunity to come in and help my team out right away and make an impact. I wanted to come in and win a conference championship, and that's exactly what we did during my last year. Being a Gopher really means a lot to me. There are only a certain amount of people that get to wear the Maroon and Gold, and I am just happy that Coach Haskins let me be a part of it all."

After receiving his degree in sports management, Bobby was selected by the Seattle SuperSonics in the first round (23rd pick overall) of the 1997 NBA Draft. Jackson was then immediately traded to the Denver Nuggets, where he emerged as one of the league's top young players. Two years later he was dealt to the Timberwolves, where he rekindled his relationship with Minnesota fans. In 2000 he was sent packing to Sacramento, where, in his fifth year in the league, he has surpassed the coveted 2,000-point plateau.

Bobby Jackson could just flat out play. He was an amazing scorer, who could light it up at any time during the course of a game. He possessed unbelievable speed, quickness, and an explosive first step. With his fantastic court vision and unselfish passing abilities, Bobby has become a tremendous NBA player.

Gopher Tombstone:

"I would hope to be remembered as a guy that went out and played hard every day, and always smiled and had fun every time he stepped on the court."

Gopher swimmer Gretchen Hegener wins the 100-Yard Breaststroke National Championship and sets a new American record	Jim Moynagh, of Hopkins wins Irwin Jacobs' $1 million Forrestwood Open Bass Fishing Tournament on Lake Minnetonka	Ila Borders makes history when she pitches in a game against the Duluth Dukes, thus becoming the first woman ever to play in the Northern League	Former Gopher pitcher Denny Neagle wins 20 games for the Atlanta Braves	The NHRA/NSSR Snowmobile Drag Nationals are held at Brainerd International Raceway. ESPN covers the event live, as more than 110,000 spectators watch the festivities. The NHRA Top Fuel and Funny Car events were supposed to be the main event, but the sleds stole the show.	"Haydays," an annual Summertime snowmobile race extravaganza held in Lino Lakes, draws more than 50,000 spectators	Vikings kicker Eddie Murray sets the NFL's all-time consecutive PAT record with 235 straight extra-points	Gopher defensive tackle Lemanzer Williams is named to the All-American football team

TIMELINE

PAUL KRAUSE

A native of Flint, Mich., Paul Krause went on to star as a defensive back and wide receiver at the University of Iowa. There, in addition to starring as an All-American center fielder on the base-ball team, Krause received All-Conference football honors while playing for future Vikings Coach Jerry Burns, and alongside future Viking teammate, Wally Hilgenberg. (He would've made it as a pro baseball player had he not torn up his shoulder in a football game his senior year.)

In 1964 Krause was selected as a second-round draft choice of the Washington Redskins. The speedy rookie wasted little time making a name for himself in D.C., intercepting two passes in his very first game while going on to lead the NFL with 12 interceptions that year. He soon became known as one of the league's best up-and-coming defenders. Four years and 28 inter-ceptions later, the safety was traded to Minnesota in exchange for Linebacker Marlin McKeever

With the Vikings, Krause became a fixture back in the defensive secondary. He even inter-cepted passes in six consecutive games in his first season in Minnesota. His ball-hawking skills were legendary, making him the Deion Sanders of his day. He even came out as the holder for field goals and conversions, adding another element of danger to opposing teams who now had to watch for fake kicks. Among the many highlights that dotted the canvas of his brilliant career, came on Sept. 30, 1979, when he picked off a pass thrown by Detroit's Jeff Komlo to tie Emlen Tunnell's all-time interception's record. He then became the all-time leader with a pair of inter-ceptions off of both Vince Ferragamo and Bob Lee against the Rams, at the L.A. Coliseum, on Dec. 2, 1979, nabbing Nos. 80 & 81, respectively. It was a huge relief, seeing as he had gone that entire 78' season without inter-cepting a pass — an event that happened just once in his career. Content, he retired from the game just a few weeks later.

He studied his opponents and became a student of the game. Prior to each game he and the other members of the secondary would end with the words "Ban the bomb!" a saying they would live by. He was the leader of a three-deep zone coverage defense that had the linebackers in the short territory while freeing up the defensive backs to contain the deep receivers. The center fielder's nat-ural instincts and reactions really flourished in this system, allowing the crafty veteran to sit back and watch the quarterback's eyes, knowing just when to make his move.

"I would have to say that Paul Krause had the game down to a science," said Bud Grant. "His intuition and instinct for playing the receiver and the football was terrific. His ability to make a big play was almost constant ... he could turn a game around for us."

Krause's total of 81 career interceptions over his illustrious 16-year pro career (53 of which came while wearing the purple), is an all-time NFL record that will probably never be broken. He also ranks third all-time in interception return yardage, with 1,185, and scored three touchdowns as well. In addition, he was named to eight Pro Bowls, was voted All-NFL four times, and started at Safety in four Super Bowls. For his amazing efforts and contributions to the game, he was finally inducted into Pro Football Hall of Fame in the Summer of 1998. His presenter: his old Hawkeye coach, "Burnsie." It was a huge relief for Krause who had been denied a spot in the Hall several times prior because of a bias against the Vikings 0-4 Super Bowl record.

Today, Paul and his wife Pam, the parents of three children, reside in Lakeville, where he has many business interests including owning a golf course, land development, construction and real estate.

BRUCE SMITH

Perhaps famed Minnesota author F. Scott Fitzgerald was thinking of Bruce Smith when he wrote the now famous line: "Show me a hero and I will show you a tragedy."

Bruce Smith grew up in Faribault and like his father, Lucius, went on to stardom as a half-back at the University of Minnesota. The blonde haired, blue-eyed Adonis was the prototypi-cal boyhood idol. He was lightning quick and could run through defenders like a tank. He was a clutch player, who often played hurt and sacrificed his body for the good of the team.

Three times in 1940 alone he scored game-winning touchdowns when his team was behind, including his now infamous 80-yard weak-side reverse through the mud and rain to beat Michigan, 7-6, which made him a virtual household name. Against Iowa in 1941, an injured Smith, after begging to come in late in the game, incredibly, passed or ran for every Minnesota touchdown in a 34-13 win.

The marquis triple-threat tailback of his era, Smith epitomized the single-wing offense and could seemingly do it all. In 1941 the team captain led the Gophers to their second consecutive undefeated, national championship. For his efforts, Smith, on the day after the Japanese had attacked Pearl Harbor, became Minnesota's first, and only, Heisman Trophy winner, beating out Notre Dame Running Back, Angelo Bertelli.

After graduating, the All-American halfback went on to garner MVP honors in the College All-Star game against the Chicago Bears that summer. In 1942, before going off to fight in W.W.II, Smith first went to Hollywood, where he starred in the movie "Smith of Minnesota," about a small-town family whose son becomes an All-American halfback. (A book on his life was also written, appropriately entitled "The Game Breaker.")

Smith went on to become a Navy fighter pilot, where he also played service football for the Great Lakes Navy team. He returned home in 1945, and signed on with the Green Bay Packers and later with the Los Angeles Rams. He played for four years in the NFL, mostly on defense, but injuries prevented him from performing up to his unbelievable collegiate standards.

In 1947 he nearly died when he suffered a ruptured kidney during a game against Chicago. He was even rushed to the hospi-tal and read his last rites by a priest. He survived, but his less than stellar football career didn't. With that, he retired at the young age of 29, and moved back to his native Faribault. There, he and his wife Gloria raised a family and he went on to become a traveling salesman for everything from Hamms Beer, to lawnmowers to formalwear.

Then, in 1964, he moved to Alexandria, to take over a Hamms distributorship. Tragically, that same year he was diagnosed with terminal cancer. Despite his fighting efforts, he soon dwindled from 200 to 90 pounds. On August 26, 1967, at the tender age of 47, Smith finally succumbed to his disease. It was a true tragedy for a real American hero.

He was inducted into the College Football Hall of Fame in 1972, and in 1977, Smith's No. 54 became the first Minnesota foot-ball number to be officially retired from the roster.

LORNE "GUMP" WORSLEY

Asked once in a post-game interview why he refused to wear a facemask, he replied: "What do you mean? I'm wearing one now..." Gump Worsley, then in his 40s, only played for the Minnesota North Stars for four short seasons, but he is arguably the team's most popular goaltender of all time. Here is his wonderful story.

Lorne John Worsley was born May 14, 1929, in Montreal. He grew up in a tough end of town where his neighborhood buddies proclaimed that he looked like then popular roly-poly comic-strip character "Andy Gump," and the nickname stuck with him ever since. As a kid he loved hockey, and tried to emulate his idol, Davey Kerr, hero of the Rangers' 1940 Stanley Cup championship team.

While playing for a commercial league team in a Montreal suburb, Worsley got his first break after winning a tryout with a junior team called the Verdun Cyclones. In 1949, at the age of 20, he caught the eye of a Rangers scout who sent him an invitation to the Rangers training camp. After a few years in the minors, he finally got the call to come to Madison Square Garden and join the Rangers in 1952. Gump would mind the nets in the Big Apple until 1963. The New York fans appreciated the pudgy goaltender's efforts, but his coach, the volatile Phil Watson, rode the Gumper hard about the size of his generous girth, and once accused him of having a "beer belly." To which the portly five-foot-seven, 220 pounder, calmly replied: "As always, Watson doesn't have the faintest idea what he's talking about... I never drink beer, only good Canadian whiskey!"

Working hard and playing hard, night after night Gump was bombarded with 40-50 shot onslaughts from the opposition. One time a reporter asked the goalie which team he thought gave him the most trouble. Worsley, quick to reply, exclaimed, "The Rangers!"

Then, on June 4, 1963, after nine years of live target practice with the Rangers, Gump was traded to the powerful Montreal Canadiens in a multi-player deal involving Goalie Jacques Plante. With a modest 204-271-101 record and a 3.10 goals against average, Worsley spent a total of 10 years on a Rangers team that failed to qualify for the playoffs five times and was eliminated in the opening round the other four. For Gump, who led the NHL in losses four times during his Rangers tenure, the trade was great news.

Though he spent much of the next two seasons up and down with Quebec of the AHL, Worsley got the call of his life on May 1st, 1965, when Habs Coach Toe Blake notified him that he was going to start in Game Seven of the Stanley Cup Finals against the Chicago Blackhawks. For the tubby 36-year-old second-stringer, it was an opportunity of a lifetime. Worsley, who was receiving pain injections for a previously injured thigh, wanted to play his best in front of his hometown fans. Although Montreal's star Center Jean Beliveau scored 14 seconds into the game, it was the Gumper who was the game's real hero, as he went on to blank the Hawks, 4-0.

The following season, both he and Charlie Hodge shared the Vezina Trophy as the league's top keeper, en route to helping the Canadiens win a second straight Stanley Cup. Worsley earned First Team All-Star honors the following 1967-68 season as he and Rogie Vachon shared the Vezina Trophy in the team's third consecutive Stanley Cup-winning season. The Gumper helped his team win a fourth Cup in 1969, but the pressure of playing goal for the mighty Canadiens finally got to him. Disenchanted with his poor treatment from management in Montreal, not to mention the increasing problems brought on by his fear of flying, Gump decided to hang em' up. "I'd had it," he said. "I didn't want to play anymore. I didn't want to fly anymore."

Worsley was a sort of enigma. Here was a man who thought absolutely nothing of standing in front of 100 mph slap-shots without even thinking about wearing a goalie mask, but try and get him in an airplane and he would wimper like a puppy. It would be a mild understatement to say that the Gumper had an abiding distrust of air travel. His horrible fear of flying made him a complete wreck on team flights. The fear apparently dated back to his days with the New York Rovers, when, on a return flight home from Milwaukee, one of the plane's engines caught fire and was forced to make an emergency landing. Although everyone survived unscathed, the Gumper was scarred for life. From that point on, every time he got on a flight he would sit on the aisle, clench the arm rests as tightly as possible, say a prayer, and hang on for dear life. "It's the one time I don't talk," he said, "I'm too scared to say anything!"

Another incident nearly forced him to give up the game for good. While on a Canadiens' team flight, his plane hit some turbulence, causing the players to spill their meals all over themselves. Afterwards the captain calmly emerged from the cockpit and reassured his passengers that the airline was sorry about the incident and that it would pay for the dry-cleaning of their suits. At that point a freaked-out Gump stood up and screamed, "What about our shorts?"

That next year, with the Gump all but washed up, Minnesota GM Wren Blair obtained the rights to negotiate with the 41-year-old goalie and convinced him to make a comeback. For Gump, who had suffered a nervous breakdown after that season, it was another chance to play the game he loved. He agreed. Playing with the enthusiasm of a rookie, Worsley, along with his new partner in crime Cesare Maniago, helped guide the Stars into the playoffs for three straight seasons. "Best move I ever made," said Gump. "We love Minnesota, and we love the team. Jack Gordon is a terrific coach. He tells Cesare and me, 'If you're having problems, don't come to me, go to each other.' So we watch each other for mistakes. We're roommates. We both know that one guy can't play for the bundle. Him and me admit it, just no way, eh?"

The Gumper gave Minnesota four solid seasons in net. And, incredibly, in his fourth and final year of 1974, after nearly a quarter-century of playing with his face as a backstop, he finally decided to break down and put on a mask. But it didn't come easily for the game's last goalie to go maskless. When asked why he would subject himself to constant cuts and stitches, he calmly replied rhetorically: "Would it have been fair not to give the fans the chance to see my beautiful face?" He took his share of licks over the years, too. Hundreds and hundreds of stitches, and dozens of concussions made the Gumper a huge fan favorite. "If Gump got hit in the face by a puck, it could only improve his looks," said the legendary John Mariucci, who scouted for the Stars at that point. "If that's the case," Gump retorted "then you'd have to get hit in the face by a bus!"

Worsley finally played his 862nd NHL regular-season game on April 2, 1974, against Philadelphia. Conveniently, at the age of 45, the Gumper retired just about in time to start receiving his NHL pension checks. Worsley then moved into the Stars' front office, where he became a team scout — a position he retained through the mid 1980s. Playing an amazing 25 professional seasons from 1949 to 1974, Gump finished his career with a 335-353-150 overall record and a 2.90 GA average in 862 games (a number surpassed only by Terry Sawchuk and Jacques Plante). In addition to his 43 regular season shutouts, he also posted five shutouts and a 2.82 GAA in 70 playoff games. Fittingly, he was elected to the Hockey Hall of Fame in 1980.

With his trademark crew-cut, and jovial pot-belly, this happy-go-lucky soul was not only one of the game's greatest and most durable players, he was also one of the its most likable characters. A fun-loving man who claimed that his favorite post game meal was a beer and a cigarette, Gump once said of his profession: "If you want to be a good goaltender, it helps to be a little crazy. Not all goaltenders are nuts, only about 90 percent of them..."

The Vikings made a very bold statement by selecting Marshall University Wide Receiver Randy Moss with their first-round pick of the 1998 NFL draft. The six-foot-five former sprinter would make an instant statement in Minnesota, however, earning Rookie of the Year honors en route to leading his team all the way to the NFC Championship Game. It was one wild ride that year, that was for sure.

Moss wasted little time in letting everyone from Minnesota know that he had officially arrived. He caught his first NFL regular season pass against Tampa Bay on the third play of the game, an 11 yard bullet from Brad Johnson. His next catch, two drives later in the first quarter, went for a 48-yard touchdown. Throughout the game the Buccaneer defensive backs were visibly intimidated by Randy's size and speed. While most rookies got jacked-up off the line of scrimmage, in order to slow them down before they could get open running their routes, Randy was getting a 10-yard cushion. They were giving the rookie the kind of respect usually reserved for All-Pro's. He added another score in the second quarter as well, as the Vikes went on the crush the Bucs by the final score of 31-7.

From there the Vikes just dominated their opposition. In Game Two Randall Cunningham came in for the injured Brad Johnson, and hit Cris Carter for a 19-yard game-winning TD to secure a 38-31 victory. Cunningham and Moss connected immediately, hooking up for a pair of touchdowns in wins over both Detroit and Chicago the next two weeks. Against the Lions Moss caught five balls for 37 yards, including a 5-yard touchdown pass in between double-coverage in the back of the end-zone. Then, against Chicago, Moss somehow leaped and hovered above a trio of Bear defenders only to come down with a miraculous 44-yard come-from-behind game-winning touchdown strike from Cunningham. The kid was legit.

Week Five saw Minnie traveling to rival Green Bay, where Moss put on a show that left the cheese-heads utterly speechless. Moss used the nationally televised Monday Night Football game as his coming out party, en route to torching the defending NFC champions for 190 receiving yards and a pair of touchdowns. (It would've been three had it not been for a 75-yard TD negated by a holding penalty.) Green Bay's sold-out Lambeau Field was as quiet as a Sunday mass after Cunningham threw for a record 442 yards, including a couple of 52 and 44-yard bombs to Moss, as the Vikes rolled to a 37-24 win.

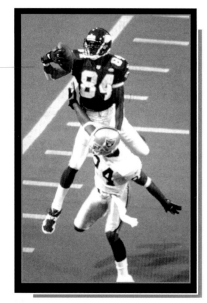

After pummeling the Skins, 41-7, behind Robert Smith and LeRoy Hoard's three scores in Game Six, the Vikings traveled to Detroit for a rematch against the Lions. Minnesota got ahead early and was able to use its running game to tire the Lions defense. Robert Smith rushed for 134 yards in this 34-13 blow-out, while Cornerback Jimmy Hitchcock returned a 79-yard

interception for a touchdown. Oh yeah, Carter and Reed each tallied as well. By now Moss, Carter and Reed were known as "Three Deep."

The undefeated Vikings then hit a bump in the road in Week Eight, getting upset by Tampa Bay, 27-24. After rebounding to win their next two games over both New Orleans and Cincinnati, Minnesota was off to its best start since 1975 and looking good. Moss was playing out of his head, Carter was as steady as ever and Robert Smith was having a career year. The defense was also looking good, having allowed the second fewest points in the NFC (170), and Cunningham, who was named as the NFC's Player of the Month for October, had emerged as the catalyst for this high-octane offense.

No one knew how to handle this potent air attack which was scoring at a record pace, not even Brett Favre and the Green Bay Packers, who got lit up by the Vikings yet again in Week 11 by the final of 28-14. As if to prove that his two touchdowns weren't a fluke back in Week Five, Moss wowed the Metrodome crowd with eight catches for 153 yards that afternoon, including a 49-yard touchdown with 3:17 left on the clock to seal the deal.

Then, on Thanksgiving weekend, Moss gave Minnesotans a whole bunch to be thankful for — a nationally televised 46-36 drubbing of the hated Dallas Cowboys, in Texas. While Randy had performed well all season long in the clutch, this game would stand out as his official "break-out" game. In an offensive explosion, Moss tortured the Cowboys for three 50-plus yard touchdown strikes, not to mention drawing a 50-yard interference penalty that set up another score. While Dallas, which did get three TDs from Emmitt Smith, cried that the loss was simply because their Pro Bowl Cornerback Deion Sanders was out with a sore foot, fans from around the country knew better.

With the division crown now in hand, and the home-dome field playoff advantage secure, the Vikes went out and tried to have fun in their remaining couple of games. With the pressure off, Minnesota routed Chicago 48-22, behind Moss' three touchdowns. From there the Vikes cruised to victories over Baltimore, 38-28, Jacksonville, 50-10, and Tennessee, 26-26, to finish out the franchise's best-ever regular season record at 15-1. For the season, Minnesota's offense had set a new NFL single-season record for total points, with 556 — a statistic that scared the daylights out of any team that would have to face this offensive juggernaut in the playoffs.

After a well deserved playoff bye-week of rest, the Vikes hosted the upstart Arizona Cardinals in the NFC divisional semifinals at the Dome. Feeling the pressure, the Vikes came out and dominated the young Cards. While Quarterback Jake Plummer played heroically for Arizona, his two first-half interceptions, which each led to Vikings scores, rattled his confidence. Minnesota came out and built a 24-7 half-time lead and never looked back. Cunningham threw for 236 yards and tossed three touchdown passes on the day — one to Tight End Andrew Glover, another to LeRoy Hoard and a third to Moss. Robert Smith added 124 yards on the ground, and Kicker Gary Anderson continued his perfect season with a pair field goals and five extra points. Running Back Mario Bates tallied three touchdowns for the Cardinals, but it wasn't nearly enough as the Vikes cruised to a 41-21 blow-out victory. With the win Minnesota had earned themselves a ticket to the final-four of pro football, the NFC Championship Game.

Next up for the Purple were the high flying Atlanta Falcons, who, like Minnesota, were used to playing on artificial turf in a deafening domed stadium. The game got underway in Minneapolis with

Minnesota looking like it was going to blow it wide open. After Atlanta's Pro Bowl Running Back Jamal Anderson scored on a five-yard pass from Chris Chandler to give his club a 7-0 lead, the Vikes rallied. Cunningham was on fire, hitting Moss, Carter and Reed all over the field. Robert Smith and LeRoy Hoard were carrying the load up the middle, and the defense was holding its own. Minnesota made it 20-7 thanks to Cunningham's one-yard TD run, a pair of Anderson field goals, and Moss' 31-yard touchdown strike. But Atlanta battled back behind Wide Receiver Terrence Mathis' 14-yard touchdown pass from Chandler to make it 20-14 at half-time.

After a Morten Andersen 27-yard field goal made it 20-17 in the third, things heated up in the fourth. Cunningham then found Matthew Hatchette on a five-yard slant to give the team some breathing room. After another Morten Andersen field goal, the game then came to a climax late in the game when the Vikings had a chance to ice the Falcons once and for all. All they had to do was kick a 30-yard field goal and put the game out of reach. The good news was that Minnesota Kicker Gary Anderson had set an amazing NFL record that year by not missing a single field goal during the entire season. The bad news was that his luck unfortunately ran out right then and right there in the biggest game of his life. He missed the kick, and Atlanta, behind Chandler's amazing downfield drive in the game's final minutes, rallied back. When he tossed his second TD pass of the day to Terrence Mathis with just 49 seconds left in the game, the score was tied 27-27.

Then Minnesota did something that no one could figure out. Knowing that they had lost a couple of key players to injuries, Green, despite having a time-out left, opted to play it safe by instructing Cunningham to simply take a knee on both third and fourth downs, instead of going for a long bomb to win the game. The crowd boo'd to no avail though and the grudge-match went into overtime. There, after both teams failed to score in their opening drives, Atlanta QB Chris Chandler, hobbling from a leg injury, drove his club deep into Minnesota territory on a quick, tactical drive. As the clock ran down to just a few seconds, they called time-out, brought in Morten Andersen and said a prayer. Andersen, the old veteran war-horse, calmly came in and kicked the 38-yard game-winner with ease. As the ball sailed through the uprights, the Falcons stormed the field. With that, Atlanta had upset the mighty Vikes, 30-27, thus earning themselves a trip to Super Bowl XXXIII in Miami.

The 64,060 Metrodome fans stood in complete disbelief, shock and horror. With the exception of the "Hail Mary" back in 1975, it was probably the worst loss in the history of the franchise. It was also a brutal ending to an otherwise brilliant season. And, while Cunningham stepped it up huge that year, passing for 3,704 yards and 34 touchdowns, the big story was Randy Moss. No. 84, who finished with 69 receptions for 1,313 yards and a league leading 17 touchdowns (10 of which came on plays of over 40 yards), was named as the Rookie of the Year. In addition, he also became the only rookie to be named as a starter, alongside teammate Cris Carter, for the NFC in the Pro Bowl.

Simply Amazing
Born on February 13, 1977, Randy Moss grew up loving sports in the small West Virginia town of Rand. He later attended DuPont High School in the neighboring town of Belle, where he played football, basketball, baseball and ran track as a sprinter. A three-time all-stater and 1994 West Virginia Player of the Year, Moss, who scored 40 touchdowns, led his DuPont Panthers to a pair of state football championships. He also teamed up with Jason Williams (who today stars for the NBA's Memphis Grizzlies), to win a state hoops title. He averaged better than 30 points and 12 rebounds per outing that season, earning a pair of Mr. Basketball Player of the Year awards as well.

After the season the lottery for Randy's athletic services heat-

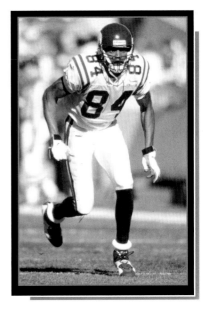

ed up. Randy ended the suspense though when he announced that he had accepted a scholarship to play football at Notre Dame under Coach Lou Holtz. But, a controversial fight during his senior year turned into a criminal charge. And as a result, the Irish said 'no thanks.' Shortly thereafter Florida State Head Football Coach Bobby Bowden called to tell him that there was a scholarship waiting for him at FSU. The only catch would be that he would have to red-shirt his freshman year and keep his nose clean. He agreed, and impressed them all with his blistering speed. That next summer, however, Randy got busted for allegedly smoking pot. This didn't sit too well with ol' Coach Bowden though, and as a result, he was released from his scholarship.

He finally got back on the field that next summer, when nearby Marshall University, a Division I-AA school, said he could play there. He obliged and tore up the gridiron over the next two years, smashing nearly every college receiving record along the way. He led the Thundering Herd to a national championship in 1996 and then, after the program switched to Division I that next year, led them to the inaugural Motor City Bowl in 1997. When the smoke had finally cleared, Moss was being touted as the greatest college football receiver, maybe ever. In just two short college seasons he had amassed 168 receptions, 4,528 all-purpose yards and 53 TD catches. For his efforts, he received the prestigious Biletnikoff Award as the nation's best receiver, was named as a unanimous first team All-American, and also finished fourth in the Heisman Trophy voting.

Despite his amazing talent though, his off-the-field baggage caused his draft stock to plummett. Twenty NFL teams passed on Mr. Moss in that first round before NFL Commissioner Paul Tagliabue announced: "With the 21st pick in the 1998 NFL Draft, the Minnesota Vikings select Randy Moss, Wide Receiver from Marshall University..." Minnesota, which had done a lot of homework on Randy, thought that they had died and gone to heaven when they looked up at the draft board and saw that he was still available so late. Vikings Head Coach Dennis Green felt that he was just a misunderstood kid who had made some bad decisions, and was willing to give him a shot. He felt that the Vikings, with their veteran roster, would be a great place for the youngster to mature and develop into a complete player. Minnesota also acquired Randy's brother, Eric, a Tackle, which they felt would ease his transition.

Today Randy Moss is one of the NFL's biggest superstars. An amazing offensive threat, he is that rare talent who can take a game over almost single-handedly. As of 2002 Moss has caught 350 passes for 5,800 yards and 55 touchdowns. A Pro-Bowl regular, Moss also signed a fat, $75 million contract with the Vikes in 2001, ensuring he will wear the purple for quite some time. And, while Randy does and says things that are sometimes too stupid to comprehend, he is a phenom. From squirting refs with water bottles; to "Randy Ratios;" to leaping, one-handed touchdown grabs in triple coverage; there is never a dull moment with this guy. And, perhaps, that is why we love him. He will no doubt go down as one of the all-time great ones.

The Vikings went into the 1999 season with expectations running high. The team had made big news that off-season by trading Quarterback Brad Johnson to Washington for its No. 1 draft pick. And with it, they surprised everyone by selecting Daunte Culpepper, a six-foot-four, 265-pound gun-slinger from little known Central Florida University. Would he learn under the tutelage of Randall Cunningham, or would Coach Green throw the rookie to the Wolves to fend for himself? It was going to be a wild ride that season in Minnie.

Minnesota opened the season by traveling to Atlanta for the much-anticipated rematch against the same Falcons who had so mercilessly upset them that last January in the NFC title game. With the hype running high, Minnesota hung its pride on the line and rallied to beat the "dirty birds" by the final score of 17-14. It wasn't pretty, but it was a "W," as the Falcons were done in, ironically, by the man who drove the dagger through the hearts of Vikings fans everywhere, Kicker Morten Andersen — who missed two field goals in the game.

While Game Two may have officially been billed as Minnesota vs. Oakland, the media had hyped it up as the Randy Moss vs. Charles Woodson show. The meeting between the two second-year phenoms didn't produce an afternoon of fireworks — rather, just one amazing play. It happened midway through the second quarter when Cunningham dropped back from the Raiders' 34-yard-line and lofted a hanging spiral to Moss on the right sideline. Moss, who was running back towards to ball, leaped over Woodson and somehow made a miraculous one-handed 29-yard grab to give the Vikings a first down at the five yard line. The Vikes fell apart after that big play though, as the Raiders scored on their next four consecutive drives to turn a 10-3 deficit into a 22-17 victory.

The Purple traveled to Green Bay that following week to face the Pack, who incidentally, in an effort to give themselves a fighting chance against Moss that season, selected three tall cornerbacks with their first three picks of the draft. Moss, who capped an 80-yard drive by catching what appeared to be the game-winning touchdown with just under two minutes on the clock, was out-done by Green Bay QB Brett Favre, who completed a miraculous 23-yard game-winning touchdown with 12 seconds left to give his club a dramatic 23-10 victory. Ouch!

With a 1-2 record, and Tampa Bay in town for Week Four, Moss caught a pair of 61 and 27-yard touchdown passes on the Vikings' first two drives of the game, as Minnesota went on to beat the Bucs 21-14. The Vikings went into a slump after that though, losing their next two by just two points each to conference rivals Chicago and Detroit. In the Detroit game, Cunningham just wasn't getting it done. So Denny decided to put in the newly acquired Jeff George at quarterback. While many were rooting for the rookie Culpepper to get the nod, ol' Georgie, baggage and all, would produce. Daunte would have to wait.

That next week George came in and torched the once mighty San Francisco 49ers by the score of 40-16. In Week Eight the Vikes headed west to Denver, to face the two-time defending Super Bowl champion Broncos. This one was a wild one, with the game coming down to a defining moment on a pivotal third-and-10 play late in the game. That's when Moss somehow caught a loose ball that had just been deflected off of both Cris Carter and Denver Cornerback Ray Crockett. The incredible play saved the drive and led to an emotional 23-20 Minnesota victory.

Next up for the Purple was a hyped-up Monday Night Football matchup against the Dallas Cowboys, and the best cover corner in the game, Deion Sanders. Dallas jumped out to a quick 17-0 first-half lead, but when All Pro Running Back Emmitt Smith was forced to leave the game with an injury, the Vikes mounted a comeback. Moss, whose second TD of the day, a spectacular 47-yard bomb from George with 5:10 remaining in the game, helped to rally the team back to an amazing 27-17 victory. But the real excitement came on Cris Carter's game-winning TD grab amidst the back-drop of some premature pyrotechnics. That's right, the dude who shoots the cannon after touchdowns got excited and blew it off as the ball was in mid-air. It was no problem for CC though, who hauled it in like it was nothing.

With the momentum on their side the Vikes went on a roll. Against the Bears Moss was absolutely phenomenal, posting a career-high 12 catches for 204 yards. Carter added nine catches of his own for 141 yards and three touchdowns as well, as the Vikings hung on to win a wild one, 27-24.

After getting a much needed rest over their bye week, the Vikes' high-powered offense revved up and produced a season-high 485 yards in a 35-27 victory over the Chargers. While the offense of old had seemed to be back on track for the Purple, it was the team's shaky defense that was causing the fans to get nervous. The Vikings then hit a couple of road blocks in both Tampa Bay and Kansas City. Down, but not out, Minnesota came back in Week 15 to beat the Packers at the Metrodome, 24-20, thanks to a pair of Moss TDs, including a dramatic 57-yard bomb from George late in the second quarter.

With their playoff lives in jeopardy, the Vikings next traveled to the Big Apple, where they took on the New York Giants. The highlight of the game came late in the third quarter on a razzle-dazzle play called "Z-Pass-Right." George handed the ball off to Moss on a reverse. Moss then faked the run and instead pulled up for a flea-flicker and tossed a perfect strike to a streaking Cris Carter for a 27-yard touchdown. The Purple held on for a 34-17 win, thus guaranteeing them a shot in the post-season.

In the final regular season game of the year, the Vikes went on to beat a very good Detroit team by the final score of 24-17. Minnesota would now host the Cowboys in the first-round of the playoffs.

The Dallas game went back and forth, but behind Robert Smith's team playoff-record 140 yards rushing, and Randy Moss' 127 yards receiving, the Vikings dug out of an early 10-3 hole, scored the game's final 24 points, and advanced to the NFC's final four for the third straight season. With the victory, the Vikings would now face the upstart St. Louis Rams for the right to go to the NFC Championship Game. It would be a tough battle playing in St. Louis' noisy domed stadium, but the Purple embraced the challenge.

TIMELINE

Gopher Coach Doug Woog retires after 14 seasons behind the bench at the University of Minnesota	The WNBA allocates Katie Smith to the Minnesota Lynx	The WNBA's expansion Minnesota Lynx hit the court at the Target Center, and beat Detroit to win their first ever game	Gopher Basketball Coach Clem Haskins' contract is bought out and Gonzaga Head Coach Dan Monson is named as his replacement	Twins Pitcher Eric Milton throws a no-hitter en route to a 7-0 win over the Anaheim Angels at home in the Metrodome	The Timberwolves open their 1999-2000 in Tokyo	The Football Gophers finish with an 8-3 record, their best mark since 1967, and go on to lose to Oregon in the Sun Bowl	Brock "The Rock" Lesnar wins the NCAA Heavyweight National Championship,

130

The Rams, much like the Vikings, were an explosive team with an explosive offense. All predictions were that it was going to be a shoot-out, and that was a huge understatement to say the least. When the smoke had cleared after this one was over, the Rams were declared the victors by the final score of 49-37. The Vikes, despite going into the lockerroom at half-time up 17-14, were completely thrashed in the second half. St. Louis came out of the gates smoking and inflicted a 35-0 second-half run that started with Tony Horne's 95-yard momentum-swinging kickoff return for a touchdown. The Vikes rallied, but it was too little way too late as they came up short. It was yet another ugly season ending loss, as the Vikings found themselves with an early post-season exit for the second frustrating year in a row.

Something drastic needed to be done that next year. It was the beginning of the new millennium, and several of the team's veterans were on their last legs. So, Jeff George hit the road for Washington and Denny made the announcement that his prized pupil, Quarterback Daunte Culpepper, was going to be his guy. He wouldn't disappoint.

Daunte's Inferno

Born on January 28, 1977, Daunte Culpepper grew up in the small northern Florida town of Ocala. His childhood wasn't like most other kids though. You see, Daunte's birth mother was an unmarried prison inmate who was serving time in a Miami jail for armed robbery. In fact, she gave birth to Daunte while behind bars. But fearing that her child would be trapped in the social services system, she decided to give him up for adoption with the hopes that he would get a better life than she could offer at that time. So, she turned to an elderly housemother by the name of Emma Culpepper, who had befriended her a few years earlier when she was in juvenile detention. At 62 years of age, Emma was well-known in those parts as a real-life saint, having already raised 14 children up to that point of her life — with none of them being her own. Little Daunte was going to be her 15th.

Before long Daunte began to thrive in his new environment and sports were his favorite thing to do. By his junior year at Ocala's Vanguard High School college recruiters were all over him. There was one problem though. Daunte had poor grades. So, he sucked it up and decided to go back and re-take several of his freshman classes over again. And, because he couldn't take them during summer school, he had to sit in with the little freshman all year long. Daunte wanted a scholarship and knew that this was the only way. On the gridiron though, Daunte was awesome, passing for 3,074 yards and 31 touchdowns while rushing for 602 yards as well, en route to earning All-American honors and the prestigious title of "Mr. Football Florida."

That next season Daunte set the school record for both career passing yards, with 6,107 and touchdowns, with 57. He also rushed for 927 yards and 26 more touchdowns as well. That winter Daunte also lit up the hardwood by averaging 19.5 points, 11.3 rebounds and 5.1 assists per game on his basketball team. He was even being recruited by several major college basketball powerhouses, including the University of Kentucky. Then, in the spring, he tore up the baseball diamond by hitting nearly .500. So good was he in baseball that he was even selected by the New York Yankees in the 26th round of the Major League Baseball Draft. Daunte had a lot of options at that point, but was set on playing college football.

With that, the school year ended and Daunte's plan had finally worked itself out. His grades were up to an impressive 3.0 that year and just like that, all of those colleges which had ignored him earlier in the year, suddenly started calling again. Nearly every major university in the nation wanted him, but Daunte was particularly grateful to the University of Central Florida, which had stuck with him through his academic troubles, and he wanted to reward them. He did and what a ride it was. When it was all said and done, Daunte ended his amazing

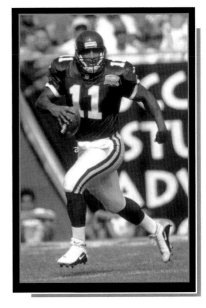

career at UCF with more than 30 school records and garnered All-American honors to boot. He became just the third player in NCAA history to pass for more than 10,000 yards and rush for more than 1,000 yards in a career.

Shortly after the season Daunte began working out diligently to prepare himself for the upcoming NFL draft. The scouting report on him read like that of a superhero, rather than that of a small-town kid from Florida. The critics raved about his poise, his leadership and referred to him as a "strong-armed quarterback who had all the tools to become a star in the NFL." He could run the 40-yard-dash in just 4.42 seconds, he had a 36" vertical leap and could throw the ball an incredible 80 yards. He could also bench-press over 400 pounds while squatting 500 — weights better than some offensive linemen.

The NFL scouts knew he could dominate the college boys, but they weren't totally convinced that he could handle the much bigger and faster professionals. The Minnesota Vikings rolled the dice though and took him with the No. 11 overall pick of the first round of the draft. Daunte then signed a whopping five-year contract which included a $5 million signing bonus. And what do you suppose the first thing he did was? He went out and bought Emma a new home in a very nice neighborhood in Florida.

After learning the ropes in 1999, Daunte came out in 2000 and lit it up. He led the Vikings back to the NFC Championship game that year and wound up being named as the starting quarterback in the Pro Bowl. Not bad! Sure, the team got humiliated by the Giants, 41-0, but they had established themselves as one of the premier teams in the league. Despite the loss, all in all it was an outstanding season for Daunte. He finished the year with a nearly perfect quarterback rating of 98.0 as he threw for 3,937 yards and 33 touchdowns. In addition, he also ran for 470 yards while rushing for seven more touchdowns.

At six-foot-four and 260 pounds, Daunte Culpepper has truly redefined the position of quarterback. He is arguably the game's most versatile and respected offensive threat and, amazingly, is still learning the game. Going into 2002 Daunte's career stats are awesome: He has thrown for more than 8,000 yards and 54 touchdowns, while rushing for more than 1,000 yards and another 16 TDs on the ground. In addition to being a fabulous athlete, Daunte has also become an outstanding role-model and citizen in his community.

"Being a Viking makes me feel very proud," said Daunte. "All of the great players — the Alan Pages, Carl Ellers Jim Marshalls and Ahmad Rashads — to play in the same organization as them means a lot to me. Knowing the history and tradition of the team, it just inspires me to go out and try to be the best player that I can be, and to represent the organization proudly."

"The fans are great up there too," he added. "They are real die-hards and I respect that. They have so much support for the team and that makes us as players try hard to get them victories. They really show me their appreciation and for that I am very grateful. Everyone is so nice and that makes it a very fun place to live and work. I just want to show them my appreciation by being the best I can be."

Gopher First Baseman Robb Quinlan is named as the Big 10 Player of the Year

To the delight of countless of Minnesota hockey fans, the NHL's expansion Wild finally hit the ice in 2000. It was a long and arduous journey that finally came to fruition after several years of very hard work and determination. It had been a long hangover from that cold day back in 1993 when a jerk named Norm hijacked our North Stars to Texas, and Minnesota hockey fans everywhere were eager to get back into the action. On June 25, 1997, the NHL Board of Governors voted unanimously to award an expansion franchise to the state of Minnesota for play to begin in the year 2000. Just hours later a celebration erupted in downtown St. Paul, where a parade of some two dozen Zambonis took to the streets. Team owner Bob Naegele, himself a high school and collegiate goaltender, later unveiled the plans for a new state-of-the-art arena which was to be located on the site of the St. Paul Civic Center.

The team's new $130 million arena, named as the Xcel Energy Center, would be first class. Complete with 74 luxury suites, and all the extras, this 18,600-seat "X" would truly mark the spot.

Shortly thereafter a state-wide name search was conducted with six finalists emerging: Blue Ox, Freeze, Northern Lights, Voyageurs, White Bears and Wild. The latter, of course, was chosen, and was officially unveiled at a naming party in front of a sell-out crowd at historic Aldrich Arena.

By now the team had begun assembling a front-office and hiring key members of its staff. Former NHL star Doug Risebrough was named as the team's first-ever GM and he would later hire the legendary Jacques Lemaire to serve as his head coach. The pieces were starting to come together.

In June the league held an Expansion Draft for the two new kids, the Wild and Columbus Blue Jackets. There, the Wild selected several players who would make the roster, including: Goalie Jamie McLennan; Defensemen Filip Kuba, Curtis Leschyshyn and Sean O'Donnell; and Forwards Jim Dowd, Sergei Krivokrasov, Scott Pellerin, Stacy Roest and Cam Stewart. In addition, a couple of Gophers were added to the mix — Darby Hendrickson and Jeff Nielsen. Shortly thereafter, the 2000 NHL Entry Draft took place with the Wild selecting Winger Marian Gaborik from Slovakia with the No.

3 overall pick. Several other players were selected on that day as well, including Defenseman Nick Schultz, Winger Maxim Sushinsky and Defenseman Lubomir Sekeras, all of whom would pay dividends.

Risebrough wanted to assemble a team that that would not only be a winner, but would also be entertaining and exciting for the fans.

"We are going to build this team through the draft, waivers, free agency, by trades and through our farm system," said Risebrough. "It will be a real fun time, and also a real testing time for these guys who are going to

have to come in here and perform. It is a honeymoon so to speak. History will be made as we go, and that is a very exciting prospect."

In September of 2000 the Xcel Energy Center was completed for the Wild's inaugural NHL season. With the team wrapping up its training camp at Minneapolis' Parade Ice Garden, the opening day roster was starting to take shape. On September 19th the Wild played their first-ever preseason game, tying San Jose, 3-3, at the Rose Garden in Portland, Oregon. That next week the team finally returned home to play their first-ever preseason home game, beating the Mighty Ducks of Anaheim, 3-1.

The club, which was slotted to play in the newly realigned Northwest Division of the Western Conference, along with the Calgary Flames, Colorado Avalanche, Edmonton Oilers and Vancouver Canucks, opened the season on the road in Anaheim. There, Rookie Marian Gaborik scored the first-ever goal in Wild history in the second period, but the team wound up on the short side of a 3-1 game. Finally, on October 11, 2000, the Wild made their home debut vs. the Philadelphia Flyers. Richfield native Darby Hendrickson scored the first Wild goal at Xcel Energy Center and helped guide the team to an impressive 3-3 tie. The crowd went nuts. Hockey was back.

"It was a great pass and I was just in the right place in the right time," said Darby of that first goal. "But that was fun and very memorable. It was a huge thrill. At the time it didn't register. Trust me, at the time I was not thinking about making history and scoring the first ever goal at the X, but it happened and it was very special. We played Philly to a tie that night, which was a real positive, and it was the beginning of a great season that just got better and better. The entire atmosphere in the Twin Cities that night was incredible. Hockey was back and it was great to just be a part of it. It was truly awesome."

From there the team just kept on rolling and the highlights followed. On October 22nd Goalie Jamie McLennan recorded the first shut-out in team history, stopping 24 shots in a scoreless tie at home against Florida. A few weeks later the team notched its first-ever road victory by beating Calgary, 3-2, on Antti Laaksonen's thrilling overtime goal. On November 26th Laaksonen tallied the first-ever hat-trick in franchise history in a 4-2 home win against Vancouver. The team even got hot in January, extending its unbeaten streak to eight games at one point when Filip Kuba scored the team's first home overtime goal to defeat Detroit, 3-2. The sell-out crowds at the X were loving it.

The unequivocal highlight of the year, however, came on December 17th, when the former North Stars, now the Dallas Stars, came to town. The atmosphere in the X was absolutely electric that night and the fans were looped. How would the Wild respond? They shined, spanking the Stars, 6-0, in front of an emotional record sell-out crowd. Minnesota natives Darby Hendrickson and Jeff Nielsen combined for three goals and an assist as the Wild scored a pair in each of the three periods to ice it. The Wild peppered Dallas Goalie Eddie Belfour all night while his former back-up, Manny Fernandez, stopped all 24 shots he faced to earn the amazing shut-out victory.

"That was just unbelievable drama that night," said Darby. "The fans were still chanting 'Norm Sucks!' from the old North Star days and everything. I mean I grew up here and understood the entire saga, but most of the guys on the team had no clue about just how much the North Stars meant to this area. So, when we came out and crushed the Stars that night it was huge. The fans were so into it and I think I was even a fan that night. The atmosphere in there was unbelievable

TIMELINE

The Lady Gophers win their first ever AWCHA Hockey Championship	Gopher Center Joel Przybilla, from Monticello, announces he'll leave school and make himself available for the NBA Draft. He is later drafted in the first round by the Milwaukee Bucks.	Holy Angels' basketball star Susan King surpasses 3,000 points for her prep career	Tartan High School's Jake Sullivan surpasses 3,000 points for his career	Minneapolis' Target Center hosts the NBA Draft	St. Paul's Will Grigsby wins the WBO Flyweight title belt	The Gopher Football team wins at Ohio State for the first time since 1949	The St. Thomas Baseball team becomes one of the first schools in the nation to play a series of games in Cuba

132

and everything just went our way. The fans really deserved that after all they had been through over the years."

Through it all the fans were loving every minute of it. In fact, on March 28th the Wild established an NHL expansion team attendance record with their 39th consecutive sell-out against Phoenix. The team would ultimately finish the season with 41 consecutive regular season sellouts — good for an NHL Expansion Team record of 751,452 fans and an average of 18,329 per game. Throughout the year the fans got to know the players and the

players got to know the fans. One player, however, stood out — rookie Marian Gaborik, who became the first Wild player to be named NHL Player of the Week, after scoring eight points in early March.

Finally, on April 8, 2001, the Wild completed their inaugural season by losing to Colorado, 4-2, at home. In the process, Wes Walz scored his seventh short handed goal and ninth short handed point of the season to set the individual expansion team record. Darby Hendrickson also scored his career-high 18th goal in this one as the Wild finished their inaugural debut with an impressive record of 25-39-13-5, good for 68 points. The leading scorers for the Wild in its inaugural season were Andrew Brunette (69 points), Marian Gaborik (67 points) and Jim Dowd (43 points), while Goalies Dwayne Roloson and Manny Fernandez won 14 and 12 games, respectively, between the pipes as well. Lemaire's infamous "neutral zone trap" had worked its magic and the rest of the league stood up and took notice that these guys were not going to lie down for anybody. They were for real.

By all accounts that first season was a huge success. From top to bottom the organization was just first class. The fans couldn't get enough of their wild and the team even threatened to make the playoffs at one point before slowing down at the end. It was also a rejuvenation of sorts for St. Paul, which embraced the team by redeveloping Kellogg Boulevard and West Seventh Street, complete with new restaurants, bars and even a new children's museum. The fans ate it up.

The Pride of Minnesota

Darby Hendrickson grew up learning to love the game on hockey on the lakes of Minnesota at the age of just three. He went on to become a prep star at Richfield High School, where he led his team to the state tourney in 1991, only to lose to Duluth East in the quarterfinals. Darby won the Mr. Hockey Award that same year as a senior and from there went on to the University of Minnesota. At the U of M Darby lit it up, garnering WCHA Rookie of the Year honors that very next season. He would play just two years in Gold Country, however, scoring 82 points in just 75 collegiate games. After playing on the 1994 U.S. Olympic team in Norway, Darby opted to turn pro and sign an NHL contract. He has been there ever since.

For his career Darby has played in 10 NHL seasons with Toronto, New York (Islanders), Vancouver and Minnesota. He has 62 goals and 56 assists for 118 points in 456 career games. Since coming back to the Wild, however, he has had a rebirth of sorts, establishing career-highs in goals (18) and points (29) in the 2000-2001 season alone. In addition, he was named as the team captain for the second half of that season — an honor befitting of his determined play. The pressure is always on Darby, now being the lone Minnesotan on the club. But he handles it well and truly deserves all the success in the world. A great player and a great guy, Darby is a good friend to Minnesota hockey. Period.

Overall, it was a wild year for Darby, literally. To be thrust into the home-town superstar role on a new expansion team, and then have the pressures of being home with the friends and family was a lot to ask of anyone. He has handled it all in stride though. He did suffer a bad eye injury at the end of the 2001 season and then missed several months of the 2002 season after breaking his wrist early in preseason. But he will be back, this kid is tough – and that is why the fans love him. As for now though, Darby is loving being home with his wife Dana and their son Mason. They have a cabin up on Island Lake near Duluth as well, where they love to get away in the summer to go fishing and golfing. And, while Darby might be the go-to guy on the ice, he doesn't mess with his wife out on the links, she used to play college golf!

On Coming Home

"I knew that the expansion draft was coming up and that I wasn't going to be protected by Vancouver. I was optimistic at that point and hopeful that it was going to happen. Then, when I got the call I was sort of numb. I was so excited about coming back to play for my new home-town team and knew it was going to be a great opportunity for me in my career. Looking back I guess it was just meant-to-be and I am now really grateful that it all worked out the way it did."

On the Team's Success

"I think the success of this team can be traced back to a couple of places. First, the leadership of Jacques LeMaire and his coaching staff has been outstanding. They picked a whole bunch of solid players who were hungry and that was nice to be around. Secondly, the ownership has just done everything right, from the marketing on down. And thirdly, the new building is just first-class and that has made it the place to be in Minnesota sports. We just have great fans here who really understand the game and want to get behind us. That entire situation is a great recipe for success. From there the team kind has formed its own identity. I mean we were all disappointed on not making the playoffs, but we were a part of building something and that was special. Jacque's system is a good system for us and we play well in it. Plus, we have been very competitive and I think the fans really appreciate that. Give us some time, we will be there.

What does it mean for you to be a member of the Wild:

"I grew up wanting to play for the North Stars. I mean Neal Broten was my idol and I followed them so closely. But when they left town, that dream left too. Now, to get the chance to come home and play for Minnesota's newest team is just amazing. It has been more than anything I ever could've asked for. It has been a great ride and everything about it has been so positive. Being home is special, in more ways than one, and I can't thank the fans enough for all their support and encouragement. I really appreciate it."

What did it mean for you to be a Gopher:

"That was a dream-come-true for me. As a kid I dreamt of being a Gopher and to do that was amazing. It just meant everything to me."

Minnesota Hockey Tombstone:

"I just want to be known as a good teammate both on and off the ice and an overall team guy who thought about the team first."

The Football Gophers advance to their second straight bowl game, the Micron PC Bowl, only to lose again to North Carolina State University	The Baseball Gophers, behind Big 10 Coach of the Year, John Anderson, win the conference championship	Roseau native Neal Broten is inducted into the U.S. Hockey Hall of Fame	Eveleth native Doug Palazzari is inducted into the U.S. Hockey Hall of Fame

In 2001 the Golden Gophers won their first ever NCAA Wrestling Championship. It was as good as it gets for longtime head coach J Robinson, who brought home the hardware from arguably the toughest venue in all of team sports, Iowa's Carver-Hawkeye Arena. It was truly a storybook ending to a fairytale season.

The Gophers broke several school and national records along the way to this historic team crown, as all 10 members of the squad made significant contributions along the way. Prior to the national tournament, the Gophers breezed through the 2000-2001 season, going 19-1 in dual meets. The also won team titles at the Midlands Championships, National Duals and Big Ten Championships. Overall, Minnesota outscored its opponents in dual meets on the season by the whopping margin of 573-170.

Along the way the team recorded several lopsided victories, including blow-outs over Northern Iowa (36-3), Hofstra (33-3), Princeton (45-0), Seton Hall (37-2), Nebraska (30-9), Michigan (29-6), Purdue (31-6), Michigan State (32-3), Penn State (37-3) and Wisconsin (33-6). In addition, Minnesota also garnered wins over North Dakota State, Boise State, Indiana and Illinois. They even beat Iowa twice, a feat which a few years ago would have been unheard of. The lone blemish on the team's record was an early-season home dual meet loss to Oklahoma State which saw several of the Gophers' top stars out from injuries. The Gophs rebounded to win 14-straight dual meets to end the regular season though, including a 20-12 revenge victory over those same Oklahoma State Cowboys in the title meet of the National Duals.

All season long different members of the squad stepped up big-time as the team persevered through some tough times. When Owen Elzen went down with a knee injury, true freshman Eli Ross came in and got it done. When Elzen returned, torn ACL and all, he sucked it up and posted a 30-3 overall record, capturing third place at both the Big Tens and NCAAs. It was leadership by example all the way around and a real team effort.

Minnesota then dominated at the conference's dual meet title with an amazing 8-0 campaign in Big Ten competitions. Then, at the Big Ten Championships, sophomore Jared Lawrence (149 lbs.) and redshirt freshman Garrett Lowney (Hwt.) won individual titles to lead Minnesota to a 24-point team victory over both Illinois and Iowa. With all 10 wrestlers placing in the top seven at the conference tourney, Minnesota amazingly advanced its entire lineup to the national tournament in Iowa City.

There, the Gophers played as a team and got the job done. In fact, not one Gopher grappler became a finalist — marking the first time in the 71-year history of the national tournament that the winning team won the team title without one. The U of M got a full-team effort to garner an NCAA-record 10 All-Americans and 138.5 points to capture the school's first ever wrestling crown. (Iowa finished second in the team race with 125.5 points, followed by Oklahoma State with 115.5 points, Oklahoma with 93.5 points and Illinois with 89.0 points.) With the team title, the Gophers unseated the six-time defending champs from Iowa, as well as the perennial powers from Oklahoma State.

All 10 Gophers finished in the top eight, earning All-American status. Three finished in third place (Leroy Vega, Owen Elzen and Garrett Lowney), three in fourth (Luke Becker, Brad Pike and Jacob Volkmann), one in fifth (Damion Hahn), one in sixth (Jared Lawrence) and two in eighth (Brett Lawrence and Chad Erikson).

With the big win the Gophers signified the proverbial "passing of the torch" from Iowa to Minnesota. How sweet it was. The media was all over it and wrestling was finally getting its props.

"I had written down three goals for the 2001 season," said Robinson of that dream season. "The first was to beat Iowa, in Iowa City, one of the toughest venues to compete at in the entire sports world. I mean Iowa had multiple national championships over the years and was like 136-5 or something ridiculous in duals at Carver Hawkeye Arena. So, our chances to win were very remote. But, we went down there and somehow pulled it off. It was amazing. The second was to have 10 All-Americans and the third was to win the Big 10 as well as the national championship. Those were our team goals and I knew that they were going to be tough. I knew we couldn't win with individuals but I knew that collectively, as a team, we could do it. That became our rallying cry for the year and really drove us that season. I remember too that we also spent a ton of time training for the third day of the national tournament, which was notoriously the toughest day. It is the day when guys are just beat up and tired and want to go home. For many, their dreams have been broken and they know they don't have a chance to be an individual champion.

"Then, amazingly, it all came down to that third day. We had six guys in the semifinals that night and incredibly, they all got beat. To top it all off, Garrett Lowney, our heavyweight who was a bronze medalist in the Olympics, wound up losing a coin flip in overtime and lost the match. So, we had no finalists. But we went back and regrouped and came out that third day determined. We had a lot of leadership on that squad with guys like Hartung, Kraft, Eggum and Morgan, and we knew we still had a chance. We calculated the points and figured it out. We were still in it and we knew that this was going to be our day. This is what we had trained for and we were going to do it. I can still remember going to weigh-in with Hartung out in the van with the radio blared to the tune of 'Who Let the Dogs Out?' and that was just a great memory of how that day started. It went back and forth that day and it came down to the finals when Owen Elzen, Damion Hahn and Garrett Lowney all pinned their guys within like three minutes of each other to seal it. When it was over it took us a while to realize what had happened. We won, and it was an amazing experience to see it all come together like that. I will never forget it."

Coach J
Since taking over the program 16 years ago, Head Coach J Robinson has built one of the strongest and most respected wrestling programs in the nation. Originally from California, Robinson grew up loving the sport of wrestling. He went on to wrestle at Oklahoma State University and from there wrestled internationally, competing on two World teams

The University of St. Thomas wins the NCAA Division III National Baseball Championship	The Lady Bulldogs from the University of Minnesota Duluth win their first ever NCAA Hockey championship	Cretin-Derham Hall's Joe Mauer turns down a scholarship to play quarterback at Florida State University and instead signs with the Twins as the No. 1 overall pick of the 2001 amateur draft	St. John's University finishes as the NCAA Division III runner-up in football	Augsburg College wins the NCAA Division III National Championship in Wrestling	The Vikings reach the NFC Championship Game, only to get blanked by the Giants, 41-0, in New York	Long-time Twins Skipper Tom Kelly retires and is replaced by Third Base Coach Ron Gardenhire	The Timberwolves lose to the San Antonio Spurs in the first round of the playoffs

— placing fourth in 1970 and fifth in 1971. Robinson also represented his country in the 1972 Olympic Games as a member of Team U.S.A. In all, Robinson captured four national wrestling titles during his amateur career, two in freestyle and two in Greco-Roman.

After graduating Robinson began his coaching career with the Cowboys as a graduate assistant before moving on to serve as a captain in the U.S. Army from 1969-72. He served a tour with the First Cavalry Division in Vietnam and upon returning home joined Iowa's staff as a graduate assistant. He was later promoted to assistant in 1976. He would serve as an assistant coach at the University of Iowa from 1976-84, helping to lead the Hawks to seven NCAA and eight Big Ten crowns. In addition, he served as an interim head coach during the 1984 Big Ten and NCAA championship season as well. From there Robinson was offered the head coaching position at Minnesota, and he has been in Gold Country ever since.

In his first season, the Gophers finished the year without winning a Big Ten dual match. In 1999 Minnesota went undefeated in conference duals and won the Big Ten title, breaking Iowa's 25-year conference title winning streak. Now, in 2002, Coach Robinson is a two-time defending national champion. He is a phenomenal coach and has built this program from the ground up.

During his tenure at Minnesota, more than three dozen wrestlers have earned more than 60 All-America honors. In addition, he has also coached four NCAA individual titleists as well, with Marty Morgan winning it in 1991, Tim Hartung winning it in 1998 and 1999, Brock Lesnar taking it home in 2000 and Luke Becker doing it in 2002. He has also coached 20 Big Ten Champions and led his teams to top-six conference finishes in 15 of his 16 seasons, including the 1999, 2001 and 2002 titles.

Regarded as one of the top coaches in the nation, Robinson has also coached at the national and international levels as well, serving as an assistant coach on four consecutive U.S. Olympic squads from 1976 to 1988, and then as the head coach for the U.S. at the 1983 Pan American Games. Among his many awards and honors, he was named as the 1998 and 2001 Dan Gable Coach of the Year, and the 2001 National Wrestling Coaches Association Coach of the Year. Robinson is also a four-time Big Ten Coach of the Year as well.

A brilliant tactician and teacher, Robinson's teams are consistently nationally ranked because he knows how to recruit and attract the top talent from around the world to the University of Minnesota. As a result, he has emerged as one of the top college coaches (in any sport) in the nation. With Coach Robinson steering this ship, the sky is the limit for these Gopher grapplers.

What does it mean for you to be a Gopher?

"One of the nicest things about winning a national title is that you can share your achievements with the entire state. The feeling of joy of being No. 1 is a great thing and I am just really happy that I was able to bring that to the people. We did it together and it is all of ours to share. That is a great thing. So being a Gopher is a great, great thing for me. I have a lot of pride in being a part of this program and a part of this university. Being a part of building this tradition has just been a wonderful experience. I also want to add, however, that I am just a part of the process. In fact, when we won that first national championship we had NCAA champion watches made. We then sent one to

TEAM CHAMPIONS

everyone who had coached in the program from years past. We all were a part of that and we wanted to let everyone share in the achievement. A lot of people believed and gave huge parts of themselves to get where we are today. It wasn't just one guy. So, I am just the keeper of the flame for a while until it starts to grow and burn. Then, I will need to pass that torch to the next guys, like Marty Morgan and Mark Schwab, who are ready to make that flame even bigger and brighter. It's a great family and I am honored to be a part of it."

On Making it Back-to-Back Titles in 2002
"It was a little different to win that second one. We came in ranked No. 1 and were in the drivers seat, so everyone wanted to knock us off. But we persevered and made it two in a row and that was special in its own way. We proved to everyone that we belong here and it really validated that we were for real. It was also important for us as a team for everyone to know that we weren't just a one-hit wonder. It was a real statement for our program and it felt really good. It was a different kind of satisfaction, but a tremendous satisfaction nevertheless."

On the Future:
"We have a target on us now and everyone wants to knock us off. That makes us want it even more though. I think our guys know that we aren't here to defend our titles, rather, we know that we have to go out and win it again. We just have to work harder than everybody else and stay on top. We can only take it a year at a time though and keep building on what we are doing. Our goals into the future are to be aggressive, dominate our opponents and have fun. As long as we can control those things, we will be just fine. We also feel like we are carrying the torch for our sport as a whole too. I mean if we can get 20,000 fans into the Xcel Energy Center, then that sends a powerful message across the country that this sport is growing and can be marketed just like the other major sports on campus. We hope to have other programs duplicate our formula for success and grow the sport into the next generation, that is what this is all about."

On Life
"Coming to Minnesota when they weren't very good to begin with and then going through that whole process to get to where we are now, is what it is all about. The journey is what this has all been about and it has been a great ride, that is for sure. I mean you wake up every morning to try and get to the top of the mountain, and for me it was sweet to finally get there on my own."

Gopher Tombstone:
"I am just one of a bunch of guys who came here with a dream and made it happen."

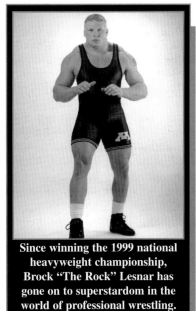

Since winning the 1999 national heavyweight championship, Brock "The Rock" Lesnar has gone on to superstardom in the world of professional wrestling.

Gopher Third Baseman Jack Hannahan is named as the Big 10 Player of the Year	Warroad native Dave Christian is inducted into the U.S. Hockey Hall of Fame	St. Paul native Paul Johnson is inducted into the U.S. Hockey Hall of Fame	Minneapolis native Mike Ramsey is inducted into the U.S. Hockey Hall of Fame

TIMELINE

135

The 2002 Gopher Hockey team was pure magic. And, for the Maroon and Gold faithful who have waited so patiently since Herbie Brooks' boys brought home the hardware all the way back in 1979, it was oh so sweet. The leader of this club was Jordan Leopold, an offensive minded defenseman who patrolled the Mariucci blue lines with authority.

The Gophers opened their season by beating hated North Dakota in the annual Hall of Fame Game at the newly christened Englestad Arena in Grand Forks. There, they quieted the Sioux faithful by beating them 7-5. From there Minnesota went on to sweep upstart Bemidji State, followed by another sweep of Colgate, which resulted in a combined two-game score of 17-0. Goalie Adam Hauser was playing well early on, and Gophers Johnny Pohl, Jordan Leopold, Troy Riddle, Paul Martin and Jeff Taffe were finding the net as well.

Minnesota then went on to rough up Michigan Tech, MSU, Mankato, Minnesota-Duluth, Michigan and Michigan State, sweeping Mankato and Duluth while allowing just one tie each from Tech and Michigan State. They then ran into a road block on November 30th, when St. Cloud upset them, 3-2, at Mariucci Arena for their first loss of the year. They managed a tie that next night in St. Cloud as the Gophs quickly saw who was going to give them trouble that season.

After a tough split with Denver, the Gophers went on to beat Ferris State at the Mariucci Classic, 3-2. From there they crushed Providence, 6-1, only to split a tight one with North Dakota at home. They managed a split with Wisconsin on the road, and then won one and tied on up in Anchorage. Denver was next as they came in and stole one at Mariucci Arena. They split yet another that next weekend up in Duluth but came back to sweep UND in Grand Forks, which was huge. Colorado College managed a split of their own at Mariucci Arena in mid-February, only to see the Gophers rebound and sweep the cheese-heads that next weekend. From there the Gophers rolled, sweeping St. Cloud State in a home-and-home series, which led up to the first round of the WCHA playoffs.

First up for Minnesota was North Dakota, and the Gophers responded by crushing the Sioux, 7-2, in Game One, and 4-3, in overtime, in Game Two. St. Cloud State was next in the semifinals at the Xcel Energy Center, and with a 4-1 win, the Gophs advanced to the Finals. This is where it gets ugly. Denver then came in and knocked off the Gophs to claim the WCHA Final Five crown, winning 5-2.

It wouldn't matter though, as the Gophers had earned a first round NCAA Playoff bye and were set to go that next week in the West Regional Quarterfinals in Ann Arbor, Mich. There, the Gophers wound up beating Colorado College, 4-2, to advance to the Frozen Four. Colorado College got on the board first but just three minutes later the Gophers responded as Johnny Pohl found Grant Potulny in front of the net for a sweet one-timer that beat CC Goalie Jeff Sanger. Minnesota then took the lead in the second on a power-play goal from Nick Angell. Moments

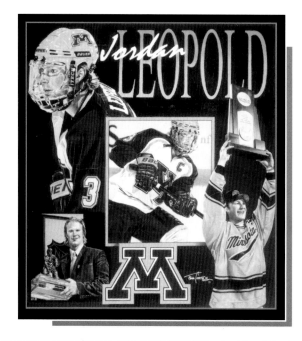

later, Jeff Taffe got in the action as he took a pass from Dan Welch and slid the puck under Sanger's arm to give Minnesota a 3-1 lead. Colorado College pulled to within one late in the second, but Minnesota sealed it in the third on Johnny Pohl's shorthanded breakaway. That 4-2 lead held up as Hauser stopped 33 shots to get the W.

With that, the Gophers were finally back in the final four of college hockey. Sure, they were no strangers to the pinnacle of March Madness, but it had been nearly a quarter century since they had won it all. Things were looking good for the Gophs though. After all, the NCAA's Frozen Four was being held at the posh Xcel Energy Center in St. Paul, right in their very own backyard. West Seventh Street was overflowing with maroon and gold that afternoon as a record crowd of 19,234 showed up at the X to watch the team do battle in the opening semifinal round against Michigan.

The Gophers drew first blood in this one when Jeff Taffe, who was forechecking in to the offensive zone, deflected a clearing attempt towards the net. There, Grant Potulny grabbed the deflection and, while on his knees, flipped it past Michigan Goaltender Josh Blackburn to make it 1-0 midway through the first period.

Minnesota then made it 2-0 at the 4:33 mark of the second period when Potulny netted his second tally of the evening — this one coming on the power play. Potulny redirected a Jordan Leopold slapper from the point to beat Blackburn through the five-hole on this one as Johnny Pohl gathered his second assist of the evening to boot. Hauser played tough through this point and particularly stood on his head with just over 30 seconds to go in the second when he made a leaping glove save across the crease to stop Jed Ortmeyer's scoring bid.

The third period was eerily similar to the previous two in that the Gophers wound up tallying an early goal. This time it was junior Jeff Taffe, scoring his team-best 34th of the season on a thrilling breakaway just over a minute into it. Taffe took a sweet pass from his Hastings High School teammate, Dan Welch, to burn up the ice and deposit the biscuit between Blackburn's legs on a backhander. It was now 3-0 and things were looking promising.

But, as in all good stories, this one too would have its share of drama. The Wolverines were not about to lie down and they roared back midway through the third, finally scoring at the 13:55 mark on a shorthanded goal by J.J. Swistak, which beat Hauser through the five hole. Then, with just under a minute and a half to go in the game, Michigan, playing with six skaters and their goalie pulled, made it 3-2 when Jed Ortmeyer beat Hauser on that very same five-hole on tough angled shot from the goal line.

The drama was thick in the X at this point as the Gophers then hung on for their dear lives to stop the Wolverines in the games' final moments. Hauser, who stopped 25 of 27 shots that night, came up huge in the last minute and when the buzzer finally blew, the Maroon and Gold suddenly

Eagan's Natalie Darwitz wins a silver medal as a member of the 2002 Women's U.S. Olympic Hockey Team	Brooklyn Park's Krissy Wendell wins a silver medal as a member of the 2002 Women's U.S. Olympic Hockey Team	Edina's Jenny Potter wins a silver medal as a member of the 2002 Women's U.S. Olympic Hockey Team	St. Paul's Phil Housley wins a silver medal as a member of the 2002 Men's U.S. Olympic Hockey Team	St. Paul's Herb Brooks wins a silver medal as the coach of the 2002 Men's U.S. Olympic Hockey Team	The Gopher Golf Team, after nearly being eliminated due to budget constraints, goes out and wins its first ever NCAA Championship	The Minnesota Twins win the Central Division and after beating Oakland in the ALDS, lose to the Angels in the American League Championship Series	The University of Minnesota christens its newest facility, the state-of-the-art Ridder Arena, for Women's Hockey and also for Men's and Women's Tennis

found themselves back in their first title game since 1989. (Ironically, that game was also held in St. Paul, at the Civic Center.)

The Finals would go down as one of the greatest ever as Minnesota took the ice that next night against the University of Maine. The Gophers opened the scoring at 7:18 of the first period on the power play. A streaking Keith Ballard slammed home a beautiful one-timer from Troy Riddle that beat Maine Goalie Matt Yeats through the five-hole and lit the lamp.

The Black Bears rallied to tie it up at the 4:47 mark of the second period, however, when Michael Schutte scored on a power play goal that saw Adam Hauser get screened big-time in front. The Gophs jumped back on top less than a minute later though on an awesome wrister by Johnny Pohl which beat Yeats top-shelf glove side. And, with that timely 27th goal of the season, Pohl was able to clinch the national point-scoring race, pulling ahead of New Hampshire's Darren Haydar with 77 points.

Maine tied it up early in the third though as Schutte tallied his second goal of the game, this one coming on a one-timer from the point which beat Hauser low to the glove side. With everything tied up at two apiece, the action was fierce. Things stayed that way for another 14 minutes or so, when Robert Liscak banked a floater off of Hauser's leg pad from behind the net with under five minutes to go to give the Black Bears their first lead of the game. It was a crushing goal.

Minnesota, which had played conservatively throughout the third period, now rallied fiercely in the game's final moments. Maine hung in there though and it appeared to be all but over. Gopher Coach Don Lucia finally pulled Hauser with 58 seconds remaining in the game and put an extra attacker out on the ice. Then, in one of the greatest goals in Gopher history, Matt Koalska tied it up with 54 seconds on the clock to knot the game at three and send the home crowd into hysterics. Johnny Pohl, who won the face-off in the Maine zone, dropped the bouncing puck back to Troy Riddle. Riddle then deflected it over to Koalska in the high slot, where he proceeded to pound home a low liner between Yeats' legs.

So, it was now off to overtime, where the collective breath of every Minnesota hockey fan was held in the balance. The other two times that the Gophers had lost NCAA championship overtime games were back in 1954, when John Mariucci's club was upset by RPI, and then again in 1989, when Wooger's club was beaten by Harvard. This, however, was not going to have the same outcome.

In the extra session the two teams battled mercilessly up and down the ice for nearly 17 agonizing minutes. The fans were beside themselves as the tension mounted with every face-off. Then, at the 16:58 mark of overtime, history was made when North Dakota native Grant Potulny, the Maroon and Gold's lone non-Minnesotan, ended it all. Here's how it went down. Maine, playing on the short side of a controversial power-play for tripping, was trying to ice the puck out of their own end. A face-off in the Black Bear's end wound up going right to Jordan Leopold at the point. Leo then shot the puck into traffic in front of the net with the rebound bouncing to Pohl. Pohl then slid it to Potulny, who slid the puck under Yeats' pads for the thrill of a lifetime. Minnesota had won the game, 4-3.

Absolute bedlam erupted not only at the Xcel Energy Center, but throughout Minnesota as the fans rejoiced. That 23-year-old monkey was now off their backs and the Gophers were NCAA champions for the fourth time in history. The team, coaches and staff stormed the ice and celebrated amidst a sea of sticks, gloves and helmets, which now littered the rink. Minnesota was finally back on top of the hockey world and it felt damn good.

"That was one of the most exciting games I have ever been a part of and it will go down as a classic," said Leopold, who finished with 47 points that season — tops in the nation among defenseman. "It

was just an amazing moment for everybody that has been involved in Gopher Hockey and it is certainly something that I will never forget. All the emotion that came out on the ice following that incredible ending was indescribable. To be out there with my teammates and friends was so special. It was really a day I will always look back on and cherish forever."

The Sign of Leo

Jordan Leopold grew up in Golden Valley and went on to graduate from Armstrong High School, where he earned all-conference honors in both hockey and baseball. After spending his senior prep season with the U.S. National Under-18 Team in Ann Arbor, Mich., he came home to wear the Maroon and Gold sweater that he had once dreamt of.

Jordan went on to become a two-time All-American, earn All-WCHA and WCHA Defensive Player of the Year honors, and to round out a perfect career, was named as the 2002 Hobey Baker Memorial Award Winner — emblematic of the nation's top collegiate player. (Previous U of M Hobey Baker winners included Neal Broten in 1981, Robb Stauber in 1988 and Brian Bonin in 1996.) In 164 career games at Minnesota, Leopold registered 45 goals and 99 assists for 144 points.

Following his graduation that year, Jordan went on join the NHL's Calgary Flames, where he will surely make his mark. In fact, Jordan made his Minnesota debut at that very X in St. Paul when his Flames played the Wild on October 22nd of 2002. His Flames lost in overtime but it was a thrill for Jordan to come home nonetheless.

All in all, Jordan Leopold was one of those special kids who comes along just once in a great while. It was not just his ability to find the back of the net that made him so special though. Jordan led by example, epitomized class and helped to resurrect a program that was recently on the verge of slumping towards mediocrity. He is also as humble as he is talented, a quality that has endeared him to the Golden Gopher faithful. No one has patrolled the blue-line like him before and no one will be able to match his exploits in the future. He is a one of a kind player who has certainly made Minnesota proud.

"It's been so much fun being at the U of M and I have just had a great time here," said the six-foot, 205-pounder. "I grew up watching the Gophers and dreamt of one day playing for them, so it has been a real life dream-come-true for me. Now, to be able to win a national championship was just the perfect ending to a perfect college experience. I will always be grateful to the coaching staff for giving me the chance to play there. Overall, being a Gopher meant everything to me and it always will. I really don't know what my life would be like without it to tell you the truth. The Minnesota fans are so awesome and I have been very lucky to have been able to play here."

Gopher Tombstone:

"I want to be remembered as a champion, period. That was my goal when I first got here and I finally got to experience it four years later. It was an honor to help rebuild that program and I hope that title will be the first of many, many more. My teammates and I went through a lot, but we came together under a new coaching staff and got it done."

TIMELINE

137

TOM LEHMAN

Tom Lehman was born on March 7, 1959, in Austin, Minnesota, but grew up in Alexandria. There, he starred on the high school football and golf teams before going on to become heavily recruited to play college football at his father's alma mater, St. John's University. His father, Jim, who also played for the Baltimore Colts, was a star halfback for the Johnnies in the 50s and led the country in scoring under Head Coach John Gagliardi.

"Tom was a great high school quarterback at Alexandria and was originally supposed to come to St. John's to play football for us," said Gagliardi. "I always kid him and tell him that my great contribution to sports is that I didn't try to rush up there to talk him out of his golf scholarship at the University of Minnesota. I was all set to give him a big speech on 'What the heck kind of future could there be in golf?' I think he went on to an okay career though, what do you think?"

Tom came to Gold Country in 1979 and immediately made an impact. From 1979 to 1981 he was named to the All-Big Ten and All-American teams. In 1981 Tom won the Minnesota Amateur title and soon was considered to be one of the top ten amateurs in the country. He graduated from the University of Minnesota with a B.S. degree in Accounting in 1982 and turned pro that same year. Lehman then spent the next several "nomadic" years struggling on foreign and mini tours. He couldn't seem to catch that big break he needed to make the jump to the PGA Tour. It was a trying period in Lehman's life, but through it all he always maintained his firm belief in God, and believed that he would give him the strength to succeed.

"I've been in every situation imaginable — broke, cardless (PGA Tour Card), even homeless once or twice," said Lehman.

In 1990, Tom came to a crossroads in his career. Looking for more stability in his life, he applied to become the head golf coach at the University of Minnesota. Then, at the last minute he withdrew his name from the running and decided to make one last go of it on the tour. One of the factors in his decision to not pursue the position was that he wasn't too big on a certain aspect of the job description that included having to coordinate cross country ski rentals on the golf course during the off-season. That's when he finally settled down and found his rhythm out on the links. Soon he started to rise in the rankings.

In 1991, ranked 581st on the tour, Tom finished on top of the money list. Two years later he finished third in the Masters and won his first professional victory, the Casio World Open in Japan. Then, in 1994 he finished second in the Masters, while earning his first ever PGA Tour victory at the Memorial. The next year he continued to make huge strides when he won the Colonial, by shooting a tournament record 20-under par, and then finished third in the U.S. Open. For his efforts he was selected as a member of the coveted U.S. Ryder Cup team.

Tom had officially arrived as a bona fide star in the world of golf at this point, and in 1996 he had the season that most tour professionals can only dream about. In that amazing year he captured the prestigious Claret Jug (by winning the British Open at Royal Lytham and St. Anne's) and the Tour Championship. In all he had 13 top-ten finishes — including a tie for second in the US Open. In addition, he won the money title with $1,780,159 in earnings, won the Vardon Trophy with a 69.32 scoring average, and was named the PGA Player of the Year. He also was named as a member of the President's Cup Team.

Then, early in the 1997 season, after finishing fourth in the MCI Classic, he passed Greg Norman to become the world's No. 1 ranked golfer. Norman had held the title for a record 96 weeks until Lehman was able to unseed him. He had jumped an incredible 581 spots to become the world's best golfer! He also won the Loch Lemond that year, was runner-up at the Mercedes Championship and once again finished third in the U.S. Open. Since then, Tom has been steady and continues to play solid golf. He is extremely charitable and always takes time to give back, whether at his annual charity tournament in Minneapolis, or by raising money for his 2002 national champion Gophers — he can always be counted on to be there.

On religion, life, and the tour: Along with Corey Pavin and Steve Jones, Lehman is a proud member of the PGA Tour's "God squad." "Whatever you do, you do the best you can for the glory of God," said Lehman. "He is in control of your best. I would have been a failure if I had God-given talent and didn't work hard at making the most of it. But if I ever lost my card now, I wouldn't consider it a failure. It would just mean that golf is not part of my future any more." He went on to add: "Religion is about who you are. What you believe makes up your character and establishes your integrity, your word. Your word means everything — it's the foundation of every decision you make in life."

Tom is not a bible-thumper. Rather, he is a person who has a strong faith, works hard, is very determined, and believes in family values and success. He is very humble, and when he's at home he just wants to be Tom, the dad and husband. So modest is he that he doesn't even care about displaying his trophies and awards. "I just want to be Tom, not a PGA player, not a British Open champion," he said. "I get so much pleasure coming home and playing $10 Nassau's with my buddies. I'm just one of the guys."

What did it mean for you to be a Gopher? "Choosing the University of Minnesota over Houston or some other southern school was a great decision for me. It allowed me the chance to compete right away against some of the best talent in the country. Contrary to what many people say, you don't have to go to college in the South to be successful in golf; you have to go somewhere where you will get the opportunity to compete all the time against quality opponents. The University of Minnesota program provided a great opportunity for me, and it continues to do so today for many young aspiring golfers."

Golf in Lehman's Terms: "I play golf to be good. Everyone has different motivations for playing — some want to win tournaments, some want to make as much cash as they can. I play because I want to be the best. If you look back at the truly great players, money has never been an object. You play golf and the money will come."

On Pressure: "My swing gets better when the pressure is more intense. I tend to tune in on one shot at a time and rely on my faith in having hit that shot before."

The greatest Minnesota golfer ever? With millions in tour earnings, Tom has etched his name into the sport's record books. He continues to outperform the best pros on the tour and is still playing great golf. He has strategically aligned himself with his brother Jim's company, Signature Sports, in Minneapolis to secure several major marketing ventures, including Levi's Dockers, Northwest Airlines and Taylor Made. His great attitude towards the game have inspired Minnesotans to become one of the top per capita states for total number of golfers — a statistic even more impressive given the fact that we can only play for half the year.

JOHN RANDLE

Born on December 12, 1967, John Randle grew up in the small town of Mumford, located in south central Texas. John and his two brothers grew up pretty fast. They were raised in a small wooden home by a single mother who worked as a maid. "It'd get so windy," he said, "and in the winter the wind would blow through the cracks in the house and under the house, and we'd put eight or nine blankets around us and still be cold." He went on to explain how he and his brothers would hang a bucket of water from a rusty nail on the back wall, from which they would take sponge baths. It was a tough way for a kid to grow up, but he aspired.

John grew up loving sports, and amazingly, he didn't even touch a football until he was a freshman in high school. "Because we lived so far out in the country, and didn't have a car, it was always a big hassle to get a ride into town," he said. "Then, every night after practice I would have to try to get a ride back home — usually around midnight. Dealing with that was really tough." He persevered though, and went on to earn all-district and all-state offensive and defensive lineman honors at Hearne High School, where he also participated in track.

Out of high school, John enrolled at Trinity Valley Community College in Athens, Tex. After two years, the Sociology major moved on to play at Texas A&I, a Division II school, where, in 1990, he earned all-conference as well as Little All-America honors as a senior. After proving he could play big-time football, John wanted to follow his big brother Ervin's footsteps into the promised land of the NFL. (Ervin played linebacker for eight seasons with the Tampa Bay Bucs and Kansas City Chiefs) But, after waiting and watching 331 players get drafted ahead of him, he was devastated.

The six-foot-one, 270-pound pesky pass rusher seemed to be a square peg trying to fit in a round hole. They thought he was too small to be a defensive tackle and wasn't the prototypical defensive end like a Lawrence Taylor or a Bruce Smith. This just made him want to work even harder. After a couple of NFL tryouts, John was invited to the Vikings training camp. He felt that this would be a good match, because Minnesota featured small, quick defensive linemen. He fought and fought, until he had made the team as a free agent.

In 1991 he started eight games — recording nine sacks. He had arrived. But he wasn't just happy to be there. In 1992, John and his bookend tackle counterpart, Henry Thomas, started to redefine the rules of the game. Teams had always built their defensive ideologies upon the premise that the fastest route to the quarterback was by speed-rushing giant defensive ends from the outside. Minnesota's two partners in crime were much smaller, quicker, and had better technique. They figured that the shortest route to point-A was by bull-rushing, and by blowing gaps through guards and centers on the line.

"John is the toughest player I play," said Packers Quarterback Brett Favre. "On artificial turf he's unblockable."

He even started to wear face paint, which soon became the sack-artist's calling card. "The 'war-paint' is about having fun, getting ready, and getting excited about playing the game in a military style," said Randle. "I smear the paint and rub it into different spots and I think it reflects my emotions. It's a combination of "Braveheart," different military movies where guys get ready for combat with war paint, and also from watching Jesse "The Body" Ventura in the movie "Predator." All of those get me fired up to go into battle!" (In 1999, the NFL [or in this case the "**N**o **F**un **L**eague"] banned him from wearing paint, citing it wasn't sportsmanlike.)

When you are double and even triple-teamed the way Randle is, you have to go above and beyond the call of duty. That's why he is a student of the game who works hard and studies his opponents in detail. Why you might ask? Because John is what you might call on the football field, somewhat of a "talker." He feels that by talking to his opponent lined up across from him, he gains a psychological advantage.

"I am one intense guy," he said. "When I'm playing out on the field, I'm giving it my all. I think the best way to describe myself is that I'm like Dr. Jekyll and Mr. Hyde on and off the field. On the playing field I'm going to do whatever I can to help my team win. But, when I come off the field I'm just another quiet, shy guy who tries to stay low-key and out of the spotlight. Out there on the battlefield I need every edge I can get, and if that means getting under my opponents skin, then so be it. I do whatever it takes to out-psyche the guy across from me. I love to talk it up out there! If guys are thinking about me, then they're not thinking about the game that's going on, and that's good for the Vikings!"

One of the preeminent pass rushers in the history of the game, No. 93 is as humble as he is tenacious, and he hasn't forgotten where he came from. Even with his newly found fortune, his modest upbringing hasn't changed him: "I've chopped cotton, picked watermelons, built fences, worked on an assembly line, worked in an oil field, built scaffolding," he said. "You know what? Those jobs are harder than football. So I'll never take it easy in football. I remember how I grew up." Aside from his new truck, he has a very modest $200,000 home in Texas with a swimming pool and a weight room. "I don't need anything more," said John. "I've got a 24-hour grocery store nearby. I've got a Wal-Mart. I've got a Target. I've got a Whataburger. This is all I need."

"To me being a Viking is like being a part of a great legacy," he said, "It's an honor to be a part of what Alan Page, Jim Marshall, Carl Eller, and all of the Purple People Eaters started back in the 1970's. Those guys were great defensive linemen and pass rushers, and it's a privilege to be able to take the reins from those guys who started such a great tradition. With free agency today, there aren't too many guys who are able to stay with one team throughout their entire careers. So, I'm lucky and I feel very honored."

In the decade of the '90s he recorded a league best 107 sacks, garnered more than 500 tackles, forced more than two dozen fumbles and had nearly three dozen stuffs behind enemy lines. Sadly, John Randle became a salary cap victim in 2001 and as a result, went on to sign with the Seattle Seahawks. The fans embraced him while he was here though and rewarded him by making him one of their all-time favorites. John Randle appreciates where he came from and knows that if it wasn't for some hard work and determination back in training camp in 1990, he wouldn't even be in the NFL today.

"I am glad that I can give back to the fans in some way, and for me, playing hard on every play is how I can give back," said Randle. "By encouraging my teammates to do the same so that we can win is my ultimate goal every time I step onto the field. For me it's all about respect, and I want to give the fans as much respect as possible — they deserve it. Because of that, I take every game very personally and that is why I hate to lose — I don't want to let anybody down. At first I wanted to win for me, but now I really want to win for them."

"My whole career has truly been a dream for me," he added. "My personal life, my athletic career, everything — it's been unreal. I never could have imagined so many wonderful things would happen to me and I am very thankful for that. I honestly feel welcome here in Minnesota, and the way I have been treated here has been just amazing."

BRONKO NAGURSKI

The legend of Bronko Nagurski began back in 1926, when then-Gopher Coach Clarence "Doc" Spears was on a recruiting trip up in northern Minnesota. One day, while driving through International Falls, he saw a hulk of a man plowing a field — without a horse. When the curious Spears stopped to ask for directions, instead of using his finger, the kid just lifted the enormous plow and pointed with it! That young man wasn't Paul Bunyan... it was Bronko Nagurski.

Bronislau Nagurski was born Nov. 3, 1908, on the Canadian side of Rainy Lake in Rainy River, Ontario. At the age of four, his family moved to International Falls, just a slap-shot away on the other side of the US border. His nickname supposedly came about when his first-grade teacher, after not being able to understand his mother's thick Ukrainian accent, called the youngster "Bronko," and the name stuck.

He grew up loving all sports, but, amazingly, in his two years of prep football at International Falls High School, his sophomore and junior years, he never played on a team that won a game. In fact, he even transferred to neighboring Bemidji High School for his senior year, because he was upset when his principal canceled the team's trip to a district tournament when a couple of other players required some disciplining. There, the transfer student was ruled ineligible to play football, but he did manage to play basketball and run track however. It was hardly the kind of a prep career that would have attracted college recruiters, even in those days.

Following high school, the "Bronk" headed south, to wear the Maroon and Gold at the University of Minnesota. (In reality, he met Doc Spears while he was up north fishing, and convinced him to come to the University.) Once there, Spears' greatest dilemma quickly became deciding where to play his new star. Then he finally figured it out — he would play him everywhere. And that's exactly what he did. Bronko would go on to play tackle, fullback, defensive end, offensive end, linebacker and he even passed the ball as a quarterback from time to time as well.

He was a massive man for his time, measuring six-feet-two and weighing in at 235 pounds. He had giant hands, donned a size-19 neck and could even run a 10.3 100-yard dash. He literally became the fullback no one could tackle and the tackle no runner could escape. As a sophomore Bronko first got noticed by the national press when he forced and recovered a late-game fumble against a heavily favored Notre Dame team, which led to a game-tying Gopher touchdown. During his junior year, wearing a steel plate to protect a couple of broken vertebrae, he almost single-handedly defeated Wisconsin when, in addition to intercepting three passes and making numerous touchdown-saving tackles, he forced a fumble and ran it in for the game-winning score.

So talented was the powerful Nagurski that he would go on to earn All-America honors at three different positions. Sportswriters decided after his senior season in 1929 that he was the best Fullback and Tackle in the nation, making him the only player in college football history ever to be named a first-team consensus All-American at two different positions in the same season. Incredibly, he was even named as an End on a few other All-America teams! Over his illustrious three year career in Gold Country, the Gophers lost a total of just four games, and none of them by more than two points.

In the fall of 1930, Bronko graduated and became *THE* "Monster of the Midway," literally, when he signed on with the NFL's Chicago Bears for the then-pricey, Depression-era sum of $5,000. The Bronk went on to reach superstar status in the Windy City, where he would lead the team to three NFL championships during his eight-year gridiron tenure.

It was also in Chicago where the bruising fullback's exploits soon took on legendary proportions. Papa Bear Halas, the team's owner, recalled a game against Washington at Wrigley Field, where Nagurski barreled up the middle, sent two linebackers flying in different directions, trampled two defensive backs, ran through the end-zone and bounced off the goal-post, finally bulldozing into the brick wall that bordered the dugout used by the Chicago Cubs — even cracking it. "That last guy hit me awful hard..." the dazed Nagurski would say upon reaching the sidelines.

One tall tale had him falling out of bounds during a game once, and toppling a policeman's horse standing along the sideline. Another had the Bronk missing a wild tackle and shearing the fender off a Model-T Ford that was parked near the sidelines.

As a runner, Nagurski didn't bother with dazzle and finesse, and as a lineman he never bothered to learn great technique. Instead, he simply used his brute strength to overpower his opponents. In other words, he was about as subtle as a Mack Truck. When he ran, he simply tucked the ball under his arm, lowered his giant shoulders, and charged full speed ahead — ramming through anything in his way.

"I was OK, I guess," Bronko said years later. "I wasn't pretty, but I did all right. Our teams won most of the time, so that was good. I know I'd love to do it all over again. I never enjoyed anything as much as I did playing football. I felt like it was something I was born to do."

Bronko wasn't the only star running back on the team though, as future Hall of Famer Red Grange was also in the Bears' backfield as well. In fact, Bronko even took over in that same Bears backfield for another future Hall of Famer, former Duluth Eskimo great, Ernie Nevers.

"Halas stockpiled backs and he believed in spreading it around," Nagurski told Sports Illustrated in 1984. "Plus, he wanted to keep me fresh for defense, where I'd put in a full afternoon."

"I have said it a thousand times, Bronko Nagurski was the greatest player I ever saw, and I saw a lot of them in my lifetime," Red Grange would later say. "Running into him was like getting an electric shock. If you tried to tackle him anywhere above the ankles, you were liable to get killed."

Overall, Nagurski was a clutch player who did whatever it took to get his team a victory. He threw the winning touchdown pass in the 1932 playoff game against the Portsmouth Spartans, and that next season he led the Bears to another NFL championship when he tossed a pair of touchdown passes in Chicago's 23-21 victory over the New York Giants.

"Here's a check for $10,000, Nagurski" said G. A. Richards, owner of the Detroit Lions. "not to play for the Lions, but just to quit and get the hell out of the league. You're ruining my team!"

In 1937, Nagurski, upset about his salary being decreased throughout the 1930s from $5,000 to $4,500 in 1931, and down to $3,700 by 1932, decided to retire, and pursue a career in pro wrestling. The Bronk had gotten into wrestling a few years earlier, but found it tough to juggle both careers. In one three-week stretch that year, he played in five Bears games and wrestled in eight cities: Portland. Vancouver, Seattle, Phoenix, L.A., Oakland, Salt Lake City and Philadelphia. Life in the ring was not as glamorous as he had hoped, but it was a living.

"I wrestled guys like Jim Londos, Strangler Lewis and others," said Bronko. "But they weren't in their prime then. I never liked wrestling. At that time, there wasn't a lot of money in it. And it was a sport where you worked every night and traveled a lot. I had a family at the time and didn't want to be away from home. But we were just getting out of the Depression in those days and we needed the money. The promoters told me I would make a million in no time. But it didn't happen."

Then, in 1943, because of player shortages caused by World War II, the Bears issued an S.O.S. to Nagurski to return for one final season. He agreed, and fittingly, at the age of 35, even scored the game-winning touchdown of the NFL title game against the Washington Redskins. He hung em' up for good after that season though, finishing his amazing NFL career with 242 points scored on 4,301 yards rushing. The six-time All-Pro even averaged nearly five yards per carry, a remarkable feat.

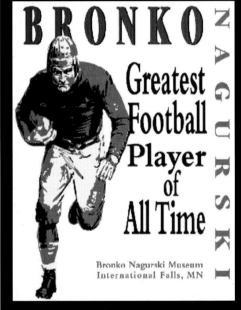

"My greatest thrill in football was the day Bronko announced his retirement," said Green Bay Hall of Fame Fullback Clarke Hinkle. "There's no question he was the most bruising fullback football has ever seen. I know, because I've still got the bruises!"

After wrestling professionally for more than a dozen years — a career he would later call "degrading," Nagurski returned to International Falls with his wife Eileen to raise their six children. (One of his boys, Bronko, Jr., played football at Notre Dame and later in the CFL.) There, quietly and unassumingly, he became the most famous gas station owner in town. He could finally live in peace and privacy, and enjoy the fruits of his labor. He loved the outdoors, and was an avid hunter and fisherman. He even liked the cold weather. "We don't have summer," Bronko once explained of his beloved hometown, "just a season in the middle of the year when the sledding is poor."

He would later do some endorsements, including a couple of $50 deals for promoting Wheaties and Camel Cigarettes — which included a carton of smokes a week. "I bought Kools and gave the Camels away," he later said jokingly.

Tragically, on Jan. 7, 1990, Bronko died at the age of 81. His awards and honors include being named as a charter member of the Pro Football and College Football Halls of Fame, and being elected to the Football Writers Association of America's All-Time team. In 1995 that same group also voted to have his name attached to college football's Defensive Player of the Year award, called the "Nagurski Trophy."

In 1979 his No. 72 was retired by the U of M, and Sports Illustrated later named Bronko as Minnesota's Greatest Athlete of the Century. In addition, in 1992, International Falls honored its most famous son by opening the "Bronko Nagurski Museum," the only museum in America dedicated to a single player. That same year the Gophers' practice facility was renamed as the Gibson-Nagurski Football Complex, after Bronk and his Gopher teammate, 1928 All-American Guard George Gibson. Perhaps the biggest honor came years ago though, when his old high school renamed themselves as the International Falls "Broncos" in his memory.

Legendary Notre Dame Coach Knute Rockne called him "the only football player I ever saw who could have played every position," and George Halas said he was "the greatest fullback who ever lived. He was absolutely unstoppable."

Bronko Nagurski was larger than life, and his size 22 Super Bowl ring, the biggest ever made, was proof! Perhaps no name has become more synonymous in the history of the sport than his. Nothing says leather helmets and high-top cleats louder than Bronko Nagurski. With his barrel chest and tree trunk legs, he became one of America's most colorful all-time characters and greatest sports heroes.

Perhaps Grantland Rice, once the most respected football authority in the nation, summed him up best when he was asked to select an all-time All-Star team. "That's easy. I'd pick 11 Bronko Nagurski's. I honestly don't think it would be a contest. The 11 Nagurski's would be a mop-up. It would be something close to murder and massacre. For the Bronk could star at any position on the field — with 228 pounds of authority to back him up."

He was truly a Bronko that could never be broken...

AFTERWORD BY KENT HRBEK

As a child growing up, literally, in the shadows of Bloomington's Metropolitan Stadium, Kent Hrbek often fell asleep to the sounds of cheering Twins and Vikings fans. It's no wonder then, that he grew up as a die-hard Minnesota sports fan. From his days of rounding the bases on the T-ball field with his big No. 6 jersey (in honor of his hero, Tony Oliva), to "touching em' all" in the Dome years later, Kent Hrbek went on to become one of Minnesota's biggest stars. So, who better to talk about the state-of-the-state of the next century of Minnesota sports, than our favorite home-town hero, Herbie.

"It's kind of weird, but I've come full-circle in my life. I started out as a huge Minnesota sports fan, playing and loving sports, and just wanting to be around the ballpark. Then, I was fortunate to have become an athlete who was considered as an idol to a lot of people and had a successful career in my home town. Now, today, I'm a huge Minnesota sports fan again. It's hard to believe that it's been so long since I hung it up. I guess you don't realize that you're a fan again until you go back to the ballpark and see your mug hanging from a banner out in right field."

"Sports is a really important thing for a lot of people in Minnesota. And, with regard to the fans and athletes of Minnesota, I think we've always been known as a state of underdogs. I don't care if it was the North Stars, the Twins, the Vikings, the Timberwolves, or the Gophers, we've never been favored to win anything. I know that no one expected us to win the World Series in 1987 and 1991, and when we did it, it just made it all that much more special.

"Minnesota fans are great. Not only are they knowledgeable about our local sports teams, but they stick by them. But, that doesn't mean that they're not fickle. They definitely need a winner for them to show up at the ballpark, I found that out first-hand! I think it's hard today for a lot of people to follow a team that's not winning. It's also tough for a fan to go sit in a ballpark during the summer after the hard winters up here. When the sun shines, people want to enjoy the outdoors while they can. They appreciate it and feel that they've earned it. It seems that everyone has a cabin

on a lake somewhere that they can go to, and if they don't, they probably have a relative who does. But when they are in those cabins, hunting and fishing, you can bet that they have their TVs and radios on — and are tuned in to a ballgame.

"I think that a lot of the sentiment against sports that is going on today has to do with money and free-agency. It's a big issue nowadays and it makes it kind of scary to think about what's in store for small markets like us. Back when I was a kid, we followed the Twins and Vikings season after season and got to know them it seemed, as if they were family. Today, with free agency, the fans feel burned when players that they rooted for leave to go somewhere else. And, it's hard for teams to keep a strong nucleus together for any length of time to be successful. So, it's tough for the fans to make an emotional investment in a team and its players when they know that it might change the next year.

"I also think that sports have become a competitive business where people nowadays can follow not only the local players but their heroes from all over the country. When I was a kid, we hardly ever saw Mickey Mantle play on TV. But today, kids can see stars like Ken Griffey Jr. every other night. So, the media has made it easier for people to still be close to their heroes without actually going out to the ballpark. And, I think that has hurt the attendance, which affects the economics of the sport. Because of the big salaries in the game today, professional sports have moved from being a family affair to a corporate one. And that's too bad. The evolution of sports has turned a simple game into more about selling tickets, advertising, naming stadiums, and big corporations. But, if franchises want to survive, that's what has to happen I guess. Everyone seems to be upset at the players and the salaries today, but it's hard to fault them if the owners are willing to give them the money.

"Salaries have gotten out of control too, like Kevin Garnett's contract situation a few years ago. I don't know, is it anyone's business? I mean it never used to be. I never had any idea what the heck Tony Oliva or Rod Carew's salaries were every year. I just loved them for what they did on the field and the joy they brought me when they hit one over the fence. I could give a crap what the heck they did off the field or how much money they made. But, today that's all different. Who knows what's in store for the next 50 years? It will definitely be very interesting. It's scary to think that football and baseball might be a thing of the past here in the near future, and thank goodness we got hockey back. I don't know, it's a tough call. A lot of people would rather see our tax dollars go toward education, which I would have to agree is a very valid argument.

"But I think everything goes hand in hand, and by that I mean that in order to have kids doing well in school, they need positive role models and idols to follow, and who better than sports heroes. As a kid, the only opportunities that I had were all somehow related to sports — little league baseball, football, hockey, soccer, basketball, and what have you. Kids need sports because it's a positive influence in their lives that builds teamwork, a positive attitude, and self esteem. I think it goes right along with education, because they learn a lot of things out there that they wouldn't otherwise learn in the classroom.

"This book is about heroes, and it's too bad that Ross couldn't go into the countless other unsung heroes on all the teams that weren't always in the limelight, because they were just as important. I think too that as a kid grows up and gets older and wiser, they realize that their childhood heroes were just athletes, and it was their moms and dads who were the real heroes — making them the people that they are. I'm optimistic about our future, and am glad that we can celebrate out past. I think that the concept for this book was really neat, and it was an idea that was long overdue. I really enjoyed reading about our rich sports heritage that we have here. It was a fun read and it brought back a lot of great memories of when I was a kid, and I think that's what sports is all about — great memories."

List of Works Cited

1. *Ross Bernstein: Hundreds of personal interviews and also various bits of information from each of his 16 books about sports history.
2. "Hubert H. Humphrey Metrodome Souvenir Book," compiled by Dave Mona. & MSP Publications, Inc.
3. "Rashad," by Ahmad Rashad with Peter Bodo: Viking Press, 1988
4. "Gold Glory": by Richard Rainbolt: Ralph Turtinen Publishing, 1972
5. "Basketball Stars," by Nick Dolin, Chris Dolin & David Check: Black Dog and Leventhal Publishes, 1997
6. "The 100 Greatest Pitchers of All Time": Barnes & Noble Press
7. "The Harmon Killebrew Story": by Hal Butler: Juliann Messner Publishing
8. Star Tribune Article by Curt Brown - March 11, 1993 (An Investment of 26 Years Yields Nothing But Memories)
9. Minnesota Almanacs - various throughout 1970s
10. "The Official National Hockey League 75th Anniversary Commemorative Book": by Dan Diamond, NHL Publications, 1991.
11. "A Thinking Man's Guide to Pro Hockey": by Eskenazi, Gerald, E. P. Dutton, 1972.
12. "The Hockey Encyclopedia": by Fischler, Stan, and Shirley Fischler, Macmillan, 1983.
13. "NHL The World of Professional Hockey": by Jay Greenberg, On Frarik, and Gary Ronberg, Rutledge Press, 1981.
14. "The Pictorial History of Hockey" by Joe Romain and Dan Diamond, Gallery Books, 1987.
15. "The Sporting News Hockey Guide & Register":1984-85, 1986-87, 1989-90.
16. "Season Review": ESPN Sports Almanac by Jerry Trecker, Total Sports Pub., 1983.
17. "NFL Football" by Ron Smith, Collins Publishers, NFL Properties, 1995
18. "Unstoppable": The Story of George Mikan, the First NBA Superstar: by George Mikan and Joseph Oberle, published by Masters Press, Indianapolis, 1997.
19. "The Kid From Cuba" by James Terzian, Doubleday Press
20. "Twenty Five Seasons": The First Quarter Century With the Minnesota Twins by Dave Mona and Dave Jarzyna: Mona Publications
21. "Rod Carew": by Marshall Burchard: Longman Canada, Ltd., 1978
22. "Sid!" The Sports Legends, the Inside Scoops, and the Close Personal Friends: by Sid Hartman and Patrick Reusse - Voyager Press, 1997
23. "Good Timing": The Paul Molitor story, by Stuart Broomer: ECW Press
24. The Winfield Foundation publication
25. Sports Illustrated: article on the Minnesota Twins, May 22, 1997
26. "Kirby Puckett": by Bob Italia: Abdo and Daughters, 1992
27. "Season of Dreams": by Tom Kelly and Ted Robinson: Voyageur Press
28. "Kent Hrbek": by Jerry Carpenter & Steve Dimeglio: Abdo and Daughters, 1988
29. Star Tribune article: Kirby Puckett Weekend, May 23, 1997
30. Star Tribune article: 1987 Twins, Aug. 8, 1997
31. Star Tribune article: "Broten Lived Out a Dream" by Dan Barriero: Oct.16, 1996
32. The U.S. Hockey Hall of Fame Handbook
33. Pioneer Press: Dick Siebert article: "A molder of Champions," by Charley Walters
34. Pioneer Press: Dick Siebert article: "Siebert Built "U" Baseball" by Charley Hallman
35. Sun Times: Kevin McHale article: "He's Just Warming Up," by Phil Hersh
36. University of Minnesota Sports News: Chuck Mencel article: "Making His Mark Through Effort and Intelligence," by Len Levine
37. Press: Dick Siebert article: "From the Majors to Minnesota," by Jim Ramsburg
38. High Minnesota State High School Hockey Tournament Media Guide, 1997
39. "Tony-O," the Trials and Triumphs of Tony Oliva, by Bob Fowler: Hawthorne Books
40. "One Goal - A Chronicle of the 1980 US Olympic Hockey Team": by John Powers and Art Kaminsky: Harper Row, 1984
41. The US Olympic Hockey Guide -1996
42. "Players of Cooperstown": Publishing International
43. "Tarkenton": by Jim Klobuchar and Fran Tarkenton: Harper Publishing, 1976
44. "Winfield" - A Player's Life, by Dave Winfield with Tom Parker: WW Nortan, 1988
45. "Gagliardi of St John's": The Coach, the Man, the Legend: by Don Riley and John Gagliardi: R. Turtinen Publishing
46. Saint John's University Football Media Guide, 1996
47. Star Tribune: North Stars article by Curt Brown - March 11, 1993
48. Star Tribune: "An Investment of 26 Years Yields Nothing But Memories" - 1981
49. "Frank Viola": by Jerry Carpenter And Steve Dimeglio: Abdo and Daughters, 1988
50. Links Magazine - "Heroes of American Golf" March 1995, by Pamela Emory
51. Sports Illustrated: "Ready or Not" artcicle on Kevin Garnett, June 25, 1995
52. Dayton's Challenge Official Souvenir Program, 1997: (Lehman article, by Ken Cohen)
53. North Stars Media Guides (various 1970s - 1990s)
54. "Before the Dome," by David Anderson: Nodin Press, 1993
55. Twins Magazine: "Home for Good" - Terry Steinbach article by Jim Bohem, July 1997
56. Twins Magazine: "Baseball Pioneers" article by Mark Engebretson, July 1997
57. Sports Illustrated Article on Terry Steinbach, "Cold Sweet Home" (1-27-97)
58. Dog World: January 1997, "The Magic And Mystique" - by Roger Pinckney
59. John Beargrease Sled Dog Marathon Race Program - 1996
60. College Hockey Magazine: "Don Roberts Bids Farewell to Gustavus ," by Jim Rueda - Free Lance Writer for the Mankato Free Press
61. Mpls.St. Paul Magazine, Aug. 1997 "North to the Pole" - Ann Bancroft Article
62. "Greg LeMond's Complete Book of Cycling," by Greg LeMond and Kent Gordis: G.P. Putnam Publishing, 1987
63. "On to Nicollet," by Stew Thornley, Nodin Press, 1988
64. "Basketball's Original Dynasty," by Stew Thornley, Nodin Press, 1989
65. "The Christian Story": Christian Brothers, Inc. Press Release Information
66. "Gopher Hockey by the Hockey Gopher," by Ross Bernstein
67. "Minnesota Trivia," by Laurel Winter: Rutledge Hill Press, 1990
68. "Minnesota Awesome Almanac," by Jean Blashfield: B&B Publishing, 1993
69. The University of Minnesota Duluth Hockey Media Guide, 1997
70. "Gopher Sketchbook," by Al Papas, Jr.: Nodin Press, 1990
71. "NCAA Championships": The Official 2001 National Collegiate Championships Records
72. The Phoenix Coyotes Media Guide: 1997
73. "Kirby Puckett, I Love This Game": by Kirby Puckett: Harper Collins, 1993
74. The U.S. Olympic Committee, Olympian Report
75. The In-Fisherman Press Release: 1997
76. Canturbury Park Media Guide: 1997
77. Minnesota Daily: article on Tom Lehman, Jan. 19, 1995
78. Brainerd International Speedway Media Guide: 1997
79. Will Steger internet article: "Solo from the Pole"
80. Ann Bancroft biographical notes, Rhonda Grider Promotions
81. The Star Tribune Minnesota Sports Hall of Fame insert publication
82. Star Tribune: article on Grandma's Marathon: 6/97
83. Star Tribune: article on Kirby Puckett: May 23, 1997
84. Article: "Nicollet Park, Home of the Millers," by Dave Mona
85. "Lexington Park: Campy, The Duke, The Babe, and Oh, That Coliseum!," By Patrick Reusse
86. Babe Winkelman biography information, press release
87. The In Fisherman, press release
88. Star Tribune: articles on Gopher Baseball, June 15-17, 1956
89. Fran Tarkenton press releases: Washington Speakers Bureau
90. "Hockey": The Illustrated History, by Dan Diamond
91. Sports Illustrated: North Stars article, May 25, 1981
92. Sports Illustrated: North Stars article, June 1, 1981
93. "One Hundred Years of Hockey": by Brian McFarlane
94. "The Official NHL Stanley Cup Centennial ," by Dan Diamond
95. Minnesota Twins - 1978 Yearbook
96. "Can You Name That Team?" by David Biesel
97. Tribune: Various articles from Janet Karvonen, March 16-22, 1978
98. Pioneer Press: Various articles from Janet Karvonen, March 16-22, 1978
99. Janet Karvonen Basketball Camp Brochure
100. Tribune: Vikings article, Jan. 13, 1976
101. Sports Illustrated, Fran Tarkenton article, Jan 5, 1976
102. Tribune: Tarkenton article , Dec 29, 1975
103. Star Tribune: Bud Grant article, Jan 7, 1986
104. Star Tribune: Bud Grant article, Jan 28, 1984
105. Tribune: Kevin McHale article, March 20, 1980
106. Tribune: Chuck Mencel article, Feb 21, 1955
107. Star Tribune: Rickey Foggie article, Dec 22, 1985
108. Tribune: Mariucci article, March 13-14, 1984
109. University of Minnesota "Gopher" Year Books: 1954, 1955, 1956
110. Star Tribune: Gopher Hockey article, April 1-2, 1989
111. Links Letter: Patty Berg article, Feb. 1997
112. Country Club Golfer: July 1977, Feb. 1980
113. Golf Course Management: Dec. 1985, March 1986
114. The Senior Golfer: June 1988
115. The Memorial: May 1988
116. Fairway: Patty Berg article and interview 1989
117. Minnesota Golfer: Spring 1993
118. Links: March 1995
119. Duluth News Tribune and Herald: UMD Hockey article, March 25, 1984
120. The Sporting News: UMD Hockey article - April 2, 1984
121. Sports Illustrated: Rod Carew Cover Story article, July 16, 1977
122. "The Autumn Warrior," by Mike Wilkinson, 1992
123. Ivory Tower: "The Coach Behind the Comeback," by Peter Vanderpoel, 1953
124. Ambassador Magazine: "Leveling the Playing Field," by Curt Brown, July, 1996
125. Minnesota Monthly Magazine: "Bent but Not Broken," by Paul Levy, August 1996
126. Star Tribune: article on Alan Page - "Mindworks" by Misti Snow, May 25, 1993
127. Minneapolis Star: "Twice Down for Nine Count - St. John's Rallied" - Dec. 16, 1963
128. St. Cloud Times: John Gagliardi article - Nov. 4, 1963
129. Minneapolis Tribune: Gagliardi article - Nov. 29, 1963
130. "The Vikings: The First Fifteen Years," Minnesota Vikings Publications
131. "Obsession": Bill Musselman's Relentless Quest to Beat the Best "- by Heller: Bonus Books
132. Twins Yearbook: 30th Anniversary Edition - 1991
133. Article: "Year by Year with the Minnesota Twins": by Bill Morlock and Rick Little
134. Article: "How the Vikings Came to Be": by Jim Klobuchar
135. "Hockey Chicago Style:" by Paul Greenland: Sagamore Pub.
136. "No Time for Losing," by Fran Tarkenton: Revell Publishing, 1967
137. "Purple Hearts and Golden Memories," by Jim Klobuchar: Quality Sports Pub, 1995
138. Sports Illustrated Vikings artcicle: "In on a Win and a Prayer," - Jan. 5, 1976
139. Sports Illustrated Twins artcicle: "The Best of the Worst," - Aug. 30, 1982
140. Sports Illustrated: Vikings article: Jan. 13, 1976
141. Minnesota Department of Natural Resources: Fisheries - "Largest fish records"
142. Twin Cities Marathon Race Program, 1997
143. Grandmas Marathon Race Program, 1997
144. Jill Trenary biography press release: IMG
145. "Minnesota Vikings"- Professional Team Histories
146. "Minnesota Timberwolves" - Professional Sports Teams Histories
147. "Minnesota Twins" - Professional Sports Teams Histories
148. "Dallas Stars" - Professional Team Histories
149. The Minnesota Vikings Media Guides (various)
150. The Minnesota Twins Media Guides (various)
151. The Minnesota North Stars Media Guides (various)
152. The Minnesota Timberwolves Media Guides (various)
153. The Minnesota Kicks Media Guides (various)
154. The Minnesota Strikers Media Guides (various)
155. University of Minnesota Men's Athletics Media Guides: Football, Basketball, Hockey, Baseball, Track & Field, Golf, Swimming & Diving, Wrestling, gymnastics and Tennis
156. University of Minnesota Women's Athletics Media Guides: Basketball, Volleyball, Track & Field, Golf, Swimming & Diving, soccer, gymnastics, softball and Tennis
157. Sports Illustrated: "Home at Last," by Peter King: March 2, 1998
158. Star Tribune, "Randle becomes $32.5 million man" - article by Don Banks: Feb. 2, 1998

ABOUT THE AUTHOR

Ross Bernstein is the author of several regionally best-selling coffee-table sports books, including: **"Batter-Up!: Celebrating a Century of Minnesota Baseball," "Hardwood Heroes: Celebrating a Century of Minnesota Basketball," "Pigskin Pride: Celebrating a Century of Minnesota Football,"** & **"Frozen Memories: Celebrating a Century of Minnesota Hockey."**

Bernstein first got into writing through some rather unique circumstances. You see, after a failed attempt to make it as a walk-on to the University of Minnesota's Golden Gopher hockey team, he opted to instead become the team's mascot, "Goldy." His humorous accounts as a mischievous rodent, back at old Mariucci Arena, then inspired the 1992 best-seller: **"Gopher Hockey by the Hockey Gopher."** And the rest, they say... is history!

Bernstein also writes children's and young-reader sports biographies as well. Among these books include bios about such superstars as: Seattle Supersonics All-Star Point Guard **Gary Payton**, Minnesota Vikings All-Pro Wide Receiver **Randy Moss**, Minnesota Timberwolves All-Star Forward **Kevin Garnett**, Minnesota Vikings All-Pro Quarterback **Daunte Culpepper**, and Los Angeles Lakers stars Kobe Bryant and Shaquille O'Neal.

In addition, Bernstein also writes an annual book for the U.S. Hockey Hall of Fame, entitled: **"The Hall: Celebrating the History and Heritage of the U.S. Hockey Hall of Fame."** Proceeds from the sale of the book, which chronicles and updates the history of the Eveleth, Minn., based museum and its more than 100 world-renowned enshrinees, go directly to the Hall of Fame.

Today the Fairmont native works as a full-time sports author for several Midwest and East Coast publishers. He is also the co-founder and Senior Editor of a start-up life-style based hockey magazine entitled: **"Minnesota Hockey Journal."** A sister publication of USA Hockey's **"American Hockey Magazine"** — the nation's largest hockey publication, the **"Journal"** has a regional circulation of nearly 50,000 Minnesota hockey households.

Ross, his wife Sara, their new daughter Campbell, and their sock-snarfing Jack Russell Terrier, "Herbie" (named in honor of local hockey legend Herbie Brooks), presently reside in Eagan. *(Oh yeah, his new coffee-table book celebrating the history and success of Minnesota Coaches will be out in the Fall of 2003. Stay Tuned!)*

To order additional signed and personalized copies of any of these books, please send a check to the following address:

(Ross Bernstein • P.O. Box #22151 • Eagan, MN 55122-0151)

*Prices include tax and bubble-packed Fed-Ex Ground shipping. Thank you!

Ross Bernstein

1.) *"Batter-Up!: Celebrating a Century of Minnesota Baseball"* — $30.00
2.) *"Hardwood Heroes: Celebrating a Century of Minnesota Basketball"* — $30.00
3.) *"Pigskin Pride: Celebrating a Century of Minnesota Football"* — $30.00
4.) *"Frozen Memories: Celebrating a Century of Minnesota Hockey"* — $28.00
5.) *"Fifty Years • Fifty Heroes: A Celebration of Minnesota Sports"* — $25.00
6.) *"55 Years • 55 Heroes: A Celebration of Minnesota Sports"* — $25.00
7.) *"Gopher Hockey by the Hockey Gopher"* — $18.00
8.) *"The Hall: Celebrating the History and Heritage of the U.S. Hockey Hall of Fame"* (Class of 2000) — $18.00
9.) *"The Hall: Celebrating the History and Heritage of the U.S. Hockey Hall of Fame"* (Class of 2001) — $18.00
10.) *"The Hall: Celebrating the History and Heritage of the U.S. Hockey Hall of Fame"* (Class of 2002) — $18.00
11.) *"Gary Payton: Star Guard"* — $25.00
12.) *"Randy Moss: Star Receiver"* — $25.00
13.) *"Kevin Garnett: Star Forward"* — $25.00
14.) *"Daunte Culpepper: Star Quarterback"* (Due out in 2003) — $25.00
15.) *"Kobe Bryant: Star Guard"* (Due out in 2003) — $25.00
16.) *"Shaquille O'Neal"* [Kids Book — 3rd Grade Reading Level] (Due out in 2004) — $25.00

WWW.BERNSTEINBOOKS.COM